PROLOG

PROGRAMMING FOR ARTIFICIAL INTELLIGENCE

SECOND EDITION

INTERNATIONAL COMPUTER SCIENCE SERIES

Consulting editors   **A D McGettrick**   University of Strathclyde

J van Leeuwen   University of Utrecht

PROLOG

PROGRAMMING FOR ARTIFICIAL INTELLIGENCE

SECOND EDITION

IVAN BRATKO

Faculty of Electrical Engineering and Computer Science,
Ljubljana University
and
J. Stefan Institute

ADDISON-WESLEY
PUBLISHING
COMPANY

Wokingham, England · Reading, Massachusetts · Menlo Park, California
New York · Don Mills, Ontario · Amsterdam · Bonn
Sydney · Singapore · Tokyo · Madrid · San Juan

The programs in this book have been included for their instructional value. They have been tested with care but are not guaranteed for any particular purpose. The publisher does not offer any warranties or representations, nor does it accept any liabilities with respect to the programs.

Many of the designations used by the manufacturers and sellers to distinguish their products are claimed as trademarks. Addison-Wesley has made every attempt to supply trademark information about manufacturers and their products mentioned in this book. A list of the trademark designations and their owners appears on p. xxii.

Cover designed by Crayon Design of Henley-on-Thames.
Typeset by CRB Typesetting Services, Ely, Cambs.
Printed in Singapore.

First edition published 1986. Reprinted 1986 (twice), 1987 and 1988.
Second edition printed 1990. Reprinted 1991.

British Library Cataloguing in Publication Data
Bratko, I. (Ivan)
    Prolog programming for artificial intelligence. –
    (International computer science series)
    2nd ed
    1. Artificial intelligence. Applications of computer
    systems
    I. Title   II. Series
    006.302855133

    ISBN 0-201-41606-9

Library of Congress Cataloging in Publication Data
Bratko, Ivan.
    Prolog programming for artificial intelligence / Ivan Bratko. –
    2nd ed.
        p.   cm. – (International computer science series)
        Includes bibliographical references.
        1. Artificial intelligence–Data processing.   2. Prolog (Computer
    language)   I. Title.   II. Series.
    Q336.B74   1990
    006.3′0285′5133–dc20   90–303
    ISBN 0-201-41606-9   CIP

To Branka, Andrej and Tadej

Foreword to the First Edition

In the Middle Ages, knowledge of Latin and Greek was essential for all scholars. The one-language scholar was necessarily a handicapped scholar who lacked the perception that comes from seeing the world from two points of view. Similarly, today's practitioner of Artificial Intelligence is handicapped unless thoroughly familiar with both Lisp and Prolog, for knowledge of the two principal languages of Artificial Intelligence is essential for a broad point of view.

I am dedicated to Lisp, having grown up at MIT where Lisp was invented. Nevertheless, I can never forget my excitement when I saw my first Prolog-style program in action. It was part of Terry Winograd's famous Shrdlu system, whose blocks-world problem solver arranged for a simulated robot arm to move blocks around a screen, solving intricate problems in response to human-specified goals.

Winograd's blocks-world problem solver was written in Microplanner, a language which we now recognize as a sort of Prolog. Nevertheless, in spite of the defects of Microplanner, the blocks-world problem solver was organized explicitly around goals, because a Prolog-style language encourages programmers to think in terms of goals. The goal-oriented procedures for grasping, clearing, getting rid of, moving, and ungrasping made it possible for a clear, transparent, concise program to seem amazingly intelligent.

Winograd's blocks-world problem solver permanently changed the way I think about programs. I even rewrote the blocks-world problem solver in Lisp for my Lisp textbook because that program unalterably impressed me with the power of the goal-oriented philosophy of programming and the fun of writing goal-oriented programs.

But learning about goal-oriented programming through Lisp programs is like reading Shakespeare in a language other than English. Some of the beauty comes through, but not as powerfully as in the original. Similarly, the best way to learn about goal-oriented programming is to read and write goal-oriented programs in Prolog, for goal-oriented programming is what Prolog is all about.

In broader terms, the evolution of computer languages is an evolution away from low-level languages, in which the programmer specifies *how* something is to be done, toward high-level languages, in which the programmer specifies simply *what* is to be done. With the development of Fortran, for example, programmers were no longer forced to speak to the computer in the procrustian low-level language of addresses and registers. Instead, Fortran programmers could speak in their own language, or nearly so, using a notation that made only moderate concessions to the one-dimensional, 80-column world.

Fortran and nearly all other languages are still how-type languages, however. In my view, modern Lisp is the champion of these languages, for Lisp in its Common Lisp form is enormously expressive, but how to do something is still what the Lisp programmer is allowed to be expressive about. Prolog, on the other hand, is a language that clearly breaks away from the how-type languages, encouraging the programmer to describe situations and problems, not the detailed means by which the problems are to be solved.

Consequently, an introduction to Prolog is important for all students of Computer Science, for there is no better way to see what the notion of what-type programming is all about.

In particular, the chapters of this book clearly illustrate the difference between how-type and what-type thinking. In the first chapter, for example, the difference is illustrated through problems dealing with family relations. The Prolog programmer straightforwardly describes the grandfather concept in explicit, natural terms: a grandfather is a father of a parent. Here is the Prolog notation:

grandfather(X, Z) :- father(X, Y), parent(Y, Z).

Once Prolog knows what a grandfather is, it is easy to ask a question: who are Patrick's grandfathers, for example. Here again is the Prolog notation, along with a typical answer:

?- grandfather(X, patrick).

X = james;

X = carl

It is Prolog's job to figure out how to solve the problem by combing through a database of known father and parent relations. The programmer specifies only what is known and what question is to be solved. The programmer is more concerned with knowledge and less concerned with algorithms that exploit the knowledge.

Given that it is important to learn Prolog, the next question is how. I believe that learning a programming language is like learning a natural language in many ways. For example, a reference manual is helpful in learning a programming language, just as a dictionary is helpful in learning a natural language. But no one learns a natural language with only a dictionary, for the words are only part of what must be learned. The student of a natural language must learn the conventions that govern how the words are put legally together, and later, the student should learn the art of those who put the words together with style.

Similarly, no one learns a programming language from only a reference manual, for a reference manual says little or nothing about the way the primitives of the language are put to use by those who use the language well. For this, a textbook is required, and the best textbooks offer copious examples, for good examples are distilled experience, and it is principally through experience that we learn.

In this book, the first example is on the first page, and the remaining pages constitute an example cornucopia, pouring forth Prolog programs written by a passionate Prolog programmer who is dedicated to the Prolog point of view. By carefully studying these examples, the reader acquires not only the mechanics of the language, but also a personal collection of precedents, ready to be taken apart, adapted, and reassembled together into new programs. With this acquisition of precedent knowledge, the transition from novice to skilled programmer is already under way.

Of course, a beneficial side effect of good programming examples is that they expose a bit of interesting science as well as a lot about programming itself. The science behind the examples in this book is Artificial Intelligence. The reader learns about such problem-solving ideas as problem reduction, forward and backward chaining, 'how' and 'why' questioning, and various search techniques.

In fact, one of the great features of Prolog is that it is simple enough for students in introductory Artificial Intelligence subjects to learn to use immediately. I expect that many instructors will use this book as part of their artificial intelligence subjects so that their students can see abstract ideas immediately reduced to concrete, motivating form.

Among Prolog texts, I expect this book to be particularly popular, not only because of its examples, but also because of a number of other features:

- Careful summaries appear throughout.
- Numerous exercises reinforce all concepts.
- Structure selectors introduce the notion of data abstraction.
- Explicit discussions of programming style and technique occupy an entire chapter.
- There is honest attention to the problems to be faced in Prolog programming, as well as the joys.

Features like this make this a well done, enjoyable, and instructive book.

Postscript to the Foreword

I keep the first edition of this textbook in my library on the outstanding-textbooks shelf, programming languages section, for as a textbook it exhibited all the strengths that set the outstanding textbooks apart from the others, including clear and direct writing, copious examples, careful summaries, and numerous exercises. And as a programming language textbook, I especially liked its attention to data abstraction, emphasis on programming style, and honest treatment of Prolog's problems as well as Prolog's advantages.

All of this excellence of the first edition is retained in this second edition, of course, but now Ivan Bratko has added new material on knowledge representation schemes, planning, language parsing, machine learning, Prolog meta-interpreters and object-oriented programming. Thus an outstanding book has become still more persuasive as a testimony to Prolog and even more engaging in its coverage of important Artificial Intelligence ideas.

Patrick H. Winston
Cambridge, Massachusetts
March 1990

Preface

Prolog

Prolog is a programming language centred around a small set of basic mechanisms, including pattern matching, tree-based data structuring and automatic backtracking. This small set constitutes a surprisingly powerful and flexible programming framework. Prolog is especially well suited for problems that involve objects – in particular, structured objects – and relations between them. For example, it is an easy exercise in Prolog to express spatial relationships between objects, such as the blue sphere is behind the green one. It is also easy to state a more general rule: if object X is closer to the observer than object Y, and Y is closer than Z, then X must be closer than Z. Prolog can now reason about the spatial relationships and their consistency with respect to the general rule. Features like this make Prolog a powerful language for Artificial Intelligence (AI) and non-numerical programming in general.

Development of Prolog

Prolog stands for *programming in logic* – an idea that emerged in the early 1970s to use logic as a programming language. The early developers of this idea included Robert Kowalski at Edinburgh (on the theoretical side), Maarten van Emden at Edinburgh (experimental demonstration) and Alain Colmerauer at Marseilles (implementation). The present popularity of Prolog is largely due to David Warren's efficient implementation at Edinburgh in the mid 1970s.

Controversies about Prolog

There are some controversial views that historically accompanied Prolog. Prolog fast gained popularity in Europe as a practical programming tool. In

Japan, Prolog was placed at the centre of the development of the Fifth-Generation computers. On the other hand, in the United States its acceptance began with some delay, due to several historical factors. One of these originated from a previous American experience with the Microplanner language, also akin to the idea of logic programming, but inefficiently implemented. This early experience with Microplanner was unjustifiably generalized to Prolog, but was later convincingly rectified by David Warren's efficient implementation of Prolog. Reservations against Prolog also came in reaction to the 'orthodox school' of logic programming, which insisted on the use of pure logic that should not be marred by adding practical facilities not related to logic. This uncompromising position was modified by Prolog practitioners who adopted a more pragmatic view, benefiting from combining both the new, declarative approach with the traditional, procedural one. A third factor that delayed the acceptance of Prolog was that for a long time Lisp had no serious competition among languages for AI. In research centres with a strong Lisp tradition, there was therefore a natural resistance to Prolog. The dilemma of Prolog vs. Lisp softened over the years and Prolog is now generally accepted as one of the two major languages for AI.

Learning Prolog

Since Prolog has its roots in mathematical logic it is often introduced through logic. However, such a mathematically intensive introduction is not very useful if the aim is to teach Prolog as a practical programming tool. Therefore this book is not concerned with the mathematical aspects, but concentrates on the art of making the few basic mechanisms of Prolog solve interesting problems. Whereas conventional languages are procedurally oriented, Prolog introduces the descriptive, or *declarative*, view. This greatly alters the way of thinking about problems and makes learning to program in Prolog an exciting intellectual challenge.

Contents of the book

Part I of the book introduces the Prolog language and shows how Prolog programs are developed. Techniques to handle important data structures, such as trees and graphs, are also included because of their general importance. These techniques are often used in AI programs and their implementation helps in learning the general skills of Prolog programming.

Part II demonstrates the power of Prolog applied in some central areas of AI, including problem solving and heuristic search, expert systems and knowledge representation, planning, language processing, learning and game playing. The concluding chapter, on meta-programming, shows how Prolog can be used to implement other languages and programming paradigms, including object-oriented programming, pattern-directed programming and writing interpreters for Prolog in Prolog. Fundamental AI techniques are introduced and developed in depth towards their implementation in Prolog, resulting in complete programs. These can be used as building blocks for sophisticated applications. Throughout, the emphasis is on the clarity of programs; efficiency tricks that rely on implementation-dependent features are avoided.

Audience for the book

This book is for students of Prolog and AI. It can be used in a Prolog course or in an AI course in which the principles of AI are brought to life through Prolog. The reader is assumed to have a basic general knowledge of computers, but no knowledge of AI is necessary. No particular programming experience is required; in fact, plentiful experience and devotion to conventional procedural programming – for example, in Pascal – might even be an impediment to the fresh way of thinking Prolog requires.

The book uses Edinburgh syntax

Among several Prolog dialects, the Edinburgh syntax, also known as DEC-10 syntax, is the most widespread, and is therefore also adopted in this book. For compatibility with the various Prolog implementations, this book only uses a relatively small subset of the built-in features that are shared by many Prologs.

How to read the book?

In Part I, the natural reading order corresponds to the order in the book. However, the part of Section 2.4 that describes the procedural meaning of Prolog in a more formalized way can be skipped. Chapter 4 presents programming examples that can be read (or skipped) selectively. Chapter 10 on advanced tree representations can be skipped.

Part II allows more flexible reading strategies as most of the chapters are intended to be mutually independent. However, some topics will still naturally be covered before others, such as basic search strategies (Chapters 11 and 13). The following diagram summarizes the constraints on natural reading sequences:

Part I:

$$1 \to 2 \to 3 \to 4 \text{ (selectively)} \to 5 \to 6 \to 7 \to 8 \to 9 \to 10$$

Part II:

Differences between the first and second edition

The differences between the first and second edition of this book are as follows. Chapters 9 and 10 on data structures have been moved to Part I, so that Part II is now entirely devoted to AI. The most important changes are in Part II where the coverage of AI topics has been greatly increased. Completely new chapters have been included on planning, machine learning and language processing using Prolog grammars. The previous chapter on expert systems has been extended and split into two chapters. The first of these now introduces more generally basic techniques of rule-based expert systems (such as forward and backward chaining) and knowledge representation (semantic nets and frames). The second then develops in full detail a rule-based expert system shell including a query-the-user facility. The previous chapter on pattern-directed programming has been generalized to meta-programming and enhanced by the addition of Prolog meta-interpreters and object-oriented programming in Prolog. The new material in the second edition largely corresponds to the suggestions expressed in a survey among instructors of Prolog and AI using the first edition of this book.

Acknowledgements

Donald Michie was responsible for first inducing my interest in Prolog. I am grateful to Lawrence Byrd, Fernando Pereira and David H.D. Warren, once members of the Prolog development team at Edinburgh, for their programming advice and numerous discussions. The book greatly benefited from comments and suggestions of Andrew McGettrick and Patrick H. Winston.

Other people who read parts of the manuscript and contributed significant comments include: Damjan Bojadziev, Rod Bristow, Peter Clark, David C. Dodson, Matjaz Gams, Peter G. Greenfield, Marko Grobelnik, Chris Hinde, Igor Kononenko, Matevz Kovacic, Peter Tancig, Tanja Urbancic, Igor Mozetic, Timothy B. Niblett, Dusan Peterc, Agata Saje, Simon Weilguny and Franc Zerdin. Several readers helped by pointing out errors in the first edition, most notably G. Oulsnam and Iztok Tvrdy. I would also like to thank Debra Myson-Etherington, and Simon Plumtree, Sheila Chatten and Stephen Bishop of Addison-Wesley for their work in the process of making this book. Most of the artwork was done by Darko Simeršek. Finally, this book would not be possible without the stimulating creativity of the international logic programming community.

The publisher wishes to thank Plenum Publishing Corporation for their permission to reproduce material similar to that in Chapter 10 of *Human and Machine Problem Solving*, (1989), K. Gilhooly (ed.).

Ivan Bratko
January 1990

Contents

Part I

The Prolog Language

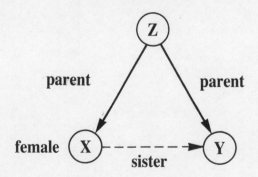

1 An Overview of Prolog

This chapter reviews basic mechanisms of Prolog through an example program. Although the treatment is largely informal many important concepts are introduced such as: Prolog clauses, facts, rules and procedures. Prolog's built-in backtracking mechanism and the distinction between declarative and procedural meanings of a program are discussed.

1.1 An example program: defining family relations

Prolog is a programming language for symbolic, non-numeric computation. It is specially well suited for solving problems that involve objects and relations between objects. Figure 1.1 shows an example: a family relation. The fact that Tom is a parent of Bob can be written in Prolog as:

    parent(tom, bob).

Here we choose **parent** as the name of a relation; **tom** and **bob** are its arguments. For reasons that will become clear later we write names like **tom** with an initial lower-case letter. The whole family tree of Figure 1.1 is defined by the following Prolog program:

    parent(pam, bob).
    parent(tom, bob).
    parent(tom, liz).
    parent(bob, ann).
    parent(bob, pat).
    parent(pat, jim).

This program consists of six *clauses*. Each of these clauses declares one fact about the **parent** relation. For example, **parent(tom, bob)** is a particular *instance* of the **parent** relation. Such an instance is also called a *relationship*. In general, a relation is defined as the set of all its instances.

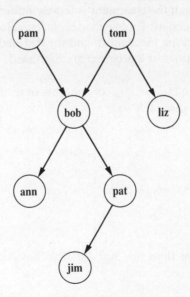

Figure 1.1   A family tree.

When this program has been communicated to the Prolog system, Prolog can be posed some questions about the **parent** relation. For example: Is Bob a parent of Pat? This question can be communicated to the Prolog system by typing into the terminal:

?- parent(bob, pat).

Having found this as an asserted fact in the program, Prolog will answer:

yes

A further query can be:

?- parent(liz, pat).

Prolog answers

no

because the program does not mention anything about Liz being a parent of Pat. It also answers 'no' to the question

?- parent(tom, ben).

because the program has not even heard of the name Ben.

More interesting questions can also be asked. For example: Who is Liz's parent?

?- parent(X, liz).

Prolog's answer will not be just 'yes' or 'no' this time. Prolog will tell us what is the (yet unknown) value of X such that the above statement is true. So the answer is:

X = tom

The question Who are Bob's children? can be communicated to Prolog as:

?- parent(bob, X).

This time there is more than just one possible answer. Prolog first answers with one solution:

X = ann

We may now request another solution (in many Prolog implementations by typing a semicolon), and Prolog will find:

X = pat

If we request more solutions again, Prolog will answer 'no' because all the solutions have been exhausted.

Our program can be asked an even broader question: Who is a parent of whom? Another formulation of this question is:

Find X and Y such that X is a parent of Y.

This is expressed in Prolog by:

?- parent(X, Y).

Prolog now finds all the parent-child pairs one after another. The solutions will be displayed one at a time as long as we tell Prolog we want more solutions, until all the solutions have been found. The answers are output as:

X = pam
Y = bob;

X = tom
Y = bob;

X = tom
Y = liz;

...

We can stop the stream of solutions by typing, for example, a period instead of a semicolon (this depends on the implementation of Prolog).

Our example program can be asked still more complicated questions like: Who is a grandparent of Jim? As our program does not directly know the **grandparent** relation this query has to be broken down into two steps, as illustrated by Figure 1.2.

(1)   Who is a parent of Jim? Assume that this is some Y.
(2)   Who is a parent of Y? Assume that this is some X.

Such a composed query is written in Prolog as a sequence of two simple ones:

?- parent(Y, jim), parent(X, Y).

The answer will be:

X = bob
Y = pat

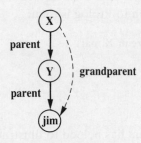

Figure 1.2 The **grandparent** relation expressed as a composition of two **parent** relations.

Our composed query can be read: Find such X and Y that satisfy the following two requirements:

   parent(Y, jim)   and   **parent(X, Y)**

If we change the order of the two requirements the logical meaning remains the same:

   parent(X, Y)   and   **parent(Y, jim)**

We can indeed do this in our Prolog program and the query

   ?- parent(X, Y), parent(Y, jim).

will produce the same result.
      In a similar way we can ask: Who are Tom's grandchildren?

   ?- parent(tom, X), parent(X, Y).

Prolog's answers are:

   X = bob
   Y = ann;

   X = bob
   Y = pat

Yet another question could be: Do Ann and Pat have a common parent? This can be expressed again in two steps:

(1)   Who is a parent, X, of Ann?
(2)   Is (this same) X a parent of Pat?

The corresponding question to Prolog is then:

?- parent(X, ann), parent(X, pat).

The answer is:

X = bob

Our example program has helped to illustrate some important points:

- It is easy in Prolog to define a relation, such as the **parent** relation, by stating the n-tuples of objects that satisfy the relation.
- The user can easily query the Prolog system about relations defined in the program.
- A Prolog program consists of *clauses*. Each clause terminates with a full stop.
- The arguments of relations can (among other things) be: concrete objects, or constants (such as **tom** and **ann**), or general objects such as X and Y. Objects of the first kind in our program are called *atoms*. Objects of the second kind are called *variables*.
- Questions to the system consist of one or more *goals*. A sequence of goals, such as

    parent(X, ann), parent(X, pat)

means the conjunction of the goals:

    X is a parent of Ann, and
    X is a parent of Pat.

The word 'goals' is used because Prolog accepts questions as goals that are to be satisfied.

- An answer to a question can be either positive or negative, depending on whether the corresponding goal can be satisfied or not. In the case of a positive answer we say that the corresponding goal was *satisfiable* and that the goal *succeeded*. Otherwise the goal was *unsatisfiable* and it *failed*.
- If several answers satisfy the question then Prolog will find as many of them as desired by the user.

EXERCISES

1.1   Assuming the **parent** relation as defined in this section (see Figure 1.1), what will be Prolog's answers to the following questions?

(a)   ?- parent(jim, X).

(b)   ?- parent(X, jim).

(c)   ?- parent(pam, X), parent(X, pat).

(d)   ?- parent(pam, X), parent(X, Y), parent(Y, jim).

1.2   Formulate in Prolog the following questions about the **parent** relation:

(a)   Who is Pat's parent?

(b)   Does Liz have a child?

(c)   Who is Pat's grandparent?

1.2   Extending the example program by rules

Our example program can be easily extended in many interesting ways. Let us first add the information on the sex of the people that occur in the **parent** relation. This can be done by simply adding the following facts to our program:

```
female( pam).
male( tom).
male( bob).
female( liz).
female( pat).
female( ann).
male( jim).
```

The relations introduced here are **male** and **female**. These relations are unary (or one-place) relations. A binary relation like **parent** defines a relation between *pairs* of objects; on the other hand, unary relations can be used to declare simple yes/no properties of objects. The first unary clause above can be read: Pam is a female. We could convey the same information declared in the two unary relations with one binary relation, sex, instead. An alternative piece of program would then be:

```
sex( pam, feminine).
sex( tom, masculine).
sex( bob, masculine).
...
```

As our next extension to the program let us introduce the **offspring** relation as the inverse of the **parent** relation. We could define **offspring** in a similar way as the **parent** relation; that is, by simply providing a list of simple facts about the **offspring** relation, each fact mentioning one pair of people such that one is an offspring of the other. For example:

> **offspring(liz, tom).**

However, the offspring relation can be defined much more elegantly by making use of the fact that it is the inverse of **parent**, and that **parent** has already been defined. This alternative way can be based on the following logical statement:

> For all X and Y,
>   Y is an offspring of X if
>   X is a parent of Y.

This formulation is already close to the formalism of Prolog. The corresponding Prolog clause which has the same meaning is:

> **offspring(Y, X) :- parent(X, Y).**

This clause can also be read as:

> For all X and Y,
>   if X is a parent of Y then
>   Y is an offspring of X.

> Prolog clauses such as

> **offspring(Y, X) :- parent(X, Y).**

are called *rules*. There is an important difference between facts and rules. A fact like

> **parent(tom, liz).**

is something that is always, unconditionally, true. On the other hand, rules specify things that are true if some condition is satisfied. Therefore we say that rules have:

- a condition part (the right-hand side of the rule) and
- a conclusion part (the left-hand side of the rule).

The conclusion part is also called the *head* of a clause and the condition part the *body* of a clause. For example:

offspring(Y, X) :- parent(X, Y).
      head   body

If the condition parent(X, Y) is true then a logical consequence of this is offspring(Y, X).

How rules are actually used by Prolog is illustrated by the following example. Let us ask our program whether Liz is an offspring of Tom:

?- offspring(liz, tom).

There is no fact about offsprings in the program, therefore the only way to consider this question is to apply the rule about offsprings. The rule is general in the sense that it is applicable to any objects X and Y; therefore it can also be applied to such particular objects as liz and tom. To apply the rule to liz and tom, Y has to be substituted with liz, and X with tom. We say that the variables X and Y become instantiated to:

X = tom   and   Y = liz

After the instantiation we have obtained a special case of our general rule. The special case is:

offspring(liz, tom) :- parent(tom, liz).

The condition part has become:

parent(tom, liz)

Now Prolog tries to find out whether the condition part is true. So the initial goal

offspring(liz, tom)

has been replaced with the subgoal:

parent(tom, liz)

This (new) goal happens to be trivial as it can be found as a fact in our program. This means that the conclusion part of the rule is also true, and Prolog will answer the question with yes.

Let us now add more family relations to our example program. The specification of the mother relation can be based on the following logical statement:

> For all X and Y,
>   X is the mother of Y if
>   X is a parent of Y and
>   X is a female.

This is translated into Prolog as the following rule:

mother(X, Y) :- parent(X, Y), female(X).

A comma between two conditions indicates the conjunction of the conditions, meaning that *both* conditions have to be true.

Relations such as **parent, offspring** and **mother** can be illustrated by diagrams such as those in Figure 1.3. These diagrams conform to the following conventions. Nodes in the graphs correspond to objects – that is, arguments of relations. Arcs between nodes correspond to binary (or two-place) relations. The arcs are oriented so as to point from the first argument of the relation to the second argument. Unary relations are indicated in the diagrams by simply marking the corresponding objects with the name of the relation. The relations that are being defined are represented by dashed arcs. So each diagram should be understood as follows: if relations shown by solid arcs hold, then the relation shown by a dashed arc also holds. The **grandparent** relation can be, according to Figure 1.3, immediately written in Prolog as:

grandparent(X, Z) :- parent(X, Y), parent(Y, Z).

At this point it will be useful to make a comment on the layout of our programs. Prolog gives us almost full freedom in choosing the layout of the program. So we can insert spaces and new lines as it best suits our taste. In general we want to make our programs look nice and tidy, and, above all, easy to read. To this end we will often choose to write the head of a clause and

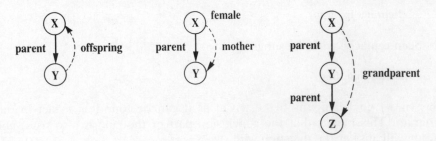

Figure 1.3 Definition graphs for the relations **offspring**, **mother** and **grandparent** in terms of other relations.

each goal of the body on a separate line. When doing this, we will indent goals
in order to make the difference between the head and the goals more visible.
For example, the **grandparent** rule would be, according to this convention,
written as follows:

```
grandparent( X, Z) :-
   parent( X, Y),
   parent( Y, Z).
```

Figure 1.4 illustrates the **sister** relation:

For any X and Y,
   X is a sister of Y if
   (1) both X and Y have the same parent, and
   (2) X is a female.

The graph in Figure 1.4 can be translated into Prolog as:

```
sister( X, Y) :-
   parent( Z, X),
   parent( Z, Y),
   female( X).
```

Notice the way in which the requirement 'both X and Y have the same parent'
has been expressed. The following logical formulation was used: some Z must
be a parent of X, and this *same* Z must be a parent of Y. An alternative, but
less elegant way would be to say: Z1 is a parent of X, and Z2 is a parent of Y,
and Z1 is equal to Z2.
   We can now ask:

```
?- sister( ann, pat).
```

The answer will be 'yes', as expected (see Figure 1.1). Therefore we might
conclude that the **sister** relation, as defined, works correctly. There is,

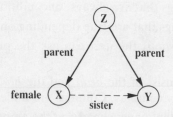

Figure 1.4 Defining the **sister** relation.

however, a rather subtle flaw in our program which is revealed if we ask the question Who is Pat's sister?:

> ?- sister(X, pat).

Prolog will find two answers, one of which may come as a surprise:

> X = ann;
>
> X = pat

So, Pat is a sister to herself?! This is probably not what we had in mind when defining the sister relation. However, according to our rule about sisters Prolog's answer is perfectly logical. Our rule about sisters does not mention that X and Y must not be the same if X is to be a sister of Y. As this is not required Prolog (rightfully) assumes that X and Y can be the same, and will as a consequence find that any female who has a parent is a sister of herself.

To correct our rule about sisters we have to add that X and Y must be different. We will see in later chapters how this can be done in several ways, but for the moment we will assume that a relation different is already known to Prolog, and that

> different(X, Y)

is satisfied if and only if X and Y are not equal. An improved rule for the sister relation can then be:

> sister(X, Y) :-
>   parent(Z, X),
>   parent(Z, Y),
>   female(X),
>   different(X, Y).

Some important points of this section are:

- Prolog programs can be extended by simply adding new clauses.
- Prolog clauses are of three types: *facts*, *rules* and *questions*.
- *Facts* declare things that are always, unconditionally true.
- *Rules* declare things that are true depending on a given condition.
- By means of *questions* the user can ask the program what things are true.
- Prolog clauses consist of the *head* and the *body*. The body is a list of *goals* separated by commas. Commas are understood as conjunctions.
- Facts are clauses that have a head and the empty body. Questions only have the body. Rules have the head and the (non-empty) body.

- In the course of computation, a variable can be substituted by another object. We say that a variable becomes *instantiated*.

- Variables are assumed to be universally quantified and are read as 'for all'. Alternative readings are, however, possible for variables that appear only in the body. For example

  hasachild(X) :- parent(X, Y).

can be read in two ways:

(a) *For all* X and Y,
     if X is a parent of Y then
     X has a child.
(b) *For all* X,
     X has a child if
     there is *some* Y such that X is a parent of Y.

EXERCISES

1.3 Translate the following statements into Prolog rules:

(a) Everybody who has a child is happy (introduce a one-argument relation **happy**).

(b) For all X, if X has a child who has a sister then X has two children (introduce new relation **hastwochildren**).

1.4 Define the relation **grandchild** using the **parent** relation. Hint: It will be similar to the **grandparent** relation (see Figure 1.3).

1.5 Define the relation **aunt(X, Y)** in terms of the relations **parent** and **sister**. As an aid you can first draw a diagram in the style of Figure 1.3 for the **aunt** relation.

1.3 A recursive rule definition

Let us add one more relation to our family program, the **predecessor** relation. This relation will be defined in terms of the **parent** relation. The whole definition can be expressed with two rules. The first rule will define the direct (immediate) predecessors and the second rule the indirect predecessors. We say that some X is an indirect predecessor of some Z if there is a parentship chain of people between X and Z, as illustrated in Figure 1.5. In our example of Figure 1.1, Tom is a direct predecessor of Liz and an indirect predecessor of Pat.

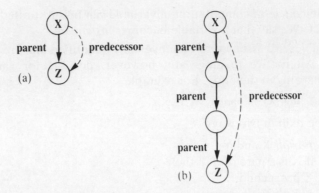

Figure 1.5 Examples of the **predecessor** relation: (a) X is a *direct* predecessor of Z; (b) X is an *indirect* predecessor of Z.

The first rule is simple and can be formulated as:

For all X and Z,
   X is a predecessor of Z if
   X is a parent of Z.

This is straightforwardly translated into Prolog as:

```
predecessor( X, Z) :-
    parent( X, Z).
```

The second rule, on the other hand, is more complicated because the chain of parents may present some problems. One attempt to define indirect predecessors could be as shown in Figure 1.6. According to this, the **predecessor**

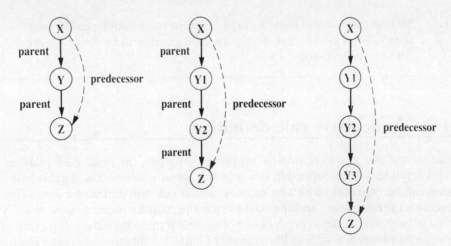

Figure 1.6 Predecessor-successor pairs at various distances.

relation would be defined by a set of clauses as follows:

```
predecessor( X, Z) :-
  parent( X, Z).

predecessor( X, Z) :-
  parent( X, Y),
  parent( Y, Z).

predecessor( X, Z) :-
  parent( X, Y1),
  parent( Y1, Y2),
  parent( Y2, Z).

predecessor( X, Z) :-
  parent( X, Y1),
  parent( Y1, Y2),
  parent( Y2, Y3),
  parent( Y3, Z).

...
```

This program is lengthy and, more importantly, it only works to some extent. It would only discover predecessors to a certain depth in a family tree because the length of the chain of people between the predecessor and the successor would be limited according to the length of our predecessor clauses.

There is, however, an elegant and correct formulation of the **predecessor** relation: it will be correct in the sense that it will work for predecessors at any depth. The key idea is to define the **predecessor** relation in terms of itself. Figure 1.7 illustrates the idea:

For all X and Z,
    X is a predecessor of Z if
    there is a Y such that
    (1) X is a parent of Y and
    (2) Y is a predecessor of Z.

A Prolog clause with the above meaning is:

```
predecessor( X, Z) :-
  parent( X, Y),
  predecessor( Y, Z).
```

We have thus constructed a complete program for the **predecessor** relation, which consists of two rules: one for direct predecessors and one for indirect predecessors. Both rules are rewritten together here:

```
predecessor( X, Z) :-
  parent( X, Z).
```

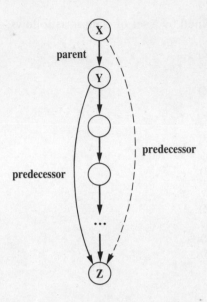

Figure 1.7   Recursive formulation of the **predecessor** relation.

```
predecessor( X, Z)  :-
  parent( X, Y),
  predecessor( Y, Z).
```

The key to this formulation was the use of **predecessor** itself in its definition. Such a definition may look surprising in view of the question: When defining something, can we use this same thing that has not yet been completely defined? Such definitions are, in general, called *recursive* definitions. Logically, they are perfectly correct and understandable, which is also intuitively obvious if we look at Figure 1.7. But will the Prolog system be able to use recursive rules? It turns out that Prolog can indeed very easily use recursive definitions. Recursive programming is, in fact, one of the fundamental principles of programming in Prolog. It is not possible to solve tasks of any significant complexity in Prolog without the use of recursion.

Going back to our program, we can ask Prolog: Who are Pam's successors? That is: Who is a person that Pam is his or her predecessor?

```
?-  predecessor( pam, X).
```

X = bob;

X = ann;

X = pat;

X = jim

Prolog's answers are of course correct and they logically follow from our definition of the **predecessor** and the **parent** relation. There is, however, a rather important question: *How* did Prolog actually use the program to find these answers?

An informal explanation of how Prolog does this is given in the next section. But first let us put together all the pieces of our family program, which was extended gradually by adding new facts and rules. The final form of the program is shown in Figure 1.8. Looking at Figure 1.8, two further

```
parent( pam, bob).                  % Pam is a parent of Bob
parent( tom, bob).
parent( tom, liz).
parent( bob, ann).
parent( bob, pat).
parent( pat, jim).

female( pam).                       % Pam is female
male( tom).                         % Tom is male
male( bob).
female( liz).
female( ann).
female( pat).
male( jim).

offspring( Y, X) :-                 % Y is an offspring of X if
    parent( X, Y).                  % X is a parent of Y

mother( X, Y) :-                    % X is the mother of Y if
    parent( X, Y),                  % X is a parent of Y and
    female( X).                     % X is female

grandparent( X, Z) :-              % X is a grandparent of Z if
    parent( X, Y),                  % X is a parent of Y and
    parent( Y, Z).                  % Y is a parent of Z

sister( X, Y) :-                    % X is a sister of Y if
    parent( Z, X),
    parent( Z, Y),                  % X and Y have the same parent and
    female( X),                     % X is female and
    different( X, Y).               % X and Y are different

predecessor( X, Z) :-              % Rule pr1: X is a predecessor of Z
    parent( X, Z).

predecessor( X, Z) :-              % Rule pr2: X is a predecessor of Z
    parent( X, Y),
    predecessor( Y, Z).
```

Figure 1.8 The family program.

points are in order here: the first will introduce the term 'procedure', the second will be about comments in programs.

The program in Figure 1.8 defines several relations – **parent**, **male**, **female**, **predecessor**, etc. The **predecessor** relation, for example, is defined by two clauses. We say that these two clauses are *about* the **predecessor** relation. Sometimes it is convenient to consider the whole set of clauses about the same relation. Such a set of clauses is called a *procedure*.

In Figure 1.8, the two rules about the **predecessor** relation have been distinguished by the names 'pr1' and 'pr2', added as *comments* to the program. These names will be used later as references to these rules. Comments are, in general, ignored by the Prolog system. They only serve as a further clarification to the person who reads the program. Comments are distinguished in Prolog from the rest of the program by being enclosed in special brackets '/*' and '*/'. Thus comments in Prolog look like this:

    /* This is a comment */

Another method, more practical for short comments, uses the percent character '%'. Everything between '%' and the end of the line is interpreted as a comment:

    % This is also a comment

EXERCISE

1.6 Consider the following alternative definition of the **predecessor** relation:

    predecessor(X, Z) :-
        parent(X, Z).

    predecessor(X, Z) :-
        parent(Y, Z),
        predecessor(X, Y).

Does this also seem to be a proper definition of predecessors? Can you modify the diagram of Figure 1.7 so that it would correspond to this new definition?

1.4 How Prolog answers questions

This section gives an informal explanation of *how* Prolog answers questions. A question to Prolog is always a sequence of one or more goals. To answer a question, Prolog tries to satisfy all the goals. What does it mean to *satisfy* a goal? To satisfy a goal means to demonstrate that the goal is true, assuming that the relations in the program are true. In other words, to satisfy a goal means to demonstrate that the goal *logically follows* from the facts and rules in the program. If the question contains variables, Prolog also has to find what are the particular objects (in place of variables) for which the goals are satisfied. The particular instantiation of variables to these objects is displayed to the user. If Prolog cannot demonstrate for some instantiation of variables that the goals logically follow from the program, then Prolog's answer to the question will be 'no'.

An appropriate view of the interpretation of a Prolog program in mathematical terms is then as follows: Prolog accepts facts and rules as a set of axioms, and the user's question as a *conjectured theorem*; then it tries to prove this theorem – that is, to demonstrate that it can be logically derived from the axioms.

We will illustrate this view by a classical example. Let the axioms be:

All men are fallible.
Socrates is a man.

A theorem that logically follows from these two axioms is:

Socrates is fallible.

The first axiom above can be rewritten as:

For all X, if X is a man then X is fallible.

Accordingly, the example can be translated into Prolog as follows:

```
fallible( X) :- man( X).       % All men are fallible
man( socrates).                % Socrates is a man
?- fallible( socrates).        % Socrates is fallible?
yes
```

A more complicated example from the family program of Figure 1.8 is:

```
?- predecessor( tom, pat).
```

We know that **parent(bob, pat)** is a fact. Using this fact and rule *pr1* we can conclude **predecessor(bob, pat)**. This is a *derived* fact: it cannot be found explicitly in our program, but it can be derived from facts and rules in the program. An inference step, such as this, can be written in a more compact form as:

```
parent( bob, pat)  ⟹  predecessor( bob, pat)
```

This can be read: from parent(bob, pat) it follows predecessor(bob, pat), by rule *pr1*. Further, we know that parent(tom, bob) is a fact. Using this fact and the derived fact predecessor(bob, pat) we can conclude predecessor(tom, pat), by rule *pr2*. We have thus shown that our goal statement predecessor(tom, pat) is true. This whole inference process of two steps can be written as:

parent(bob, pat) $\Longrightarrow$ predecessor(bob, pat)

parent(tom, bob) *and* predecessor(bob, pat) $\Longrightarrow$ predecessor(tom, pat)

We have thus shown *what* can be a sequence of steps that satisfy a goal – that is, make it clear that the goal is true. Let us call this a proof sequence. We have not, however, shown *how* the Prolog system actually finds such a proof sequence.

Prolog finds the proof sequence in the inverse order to that which we have just used. Instead of starting with simple facts given in the program, Prolog starts with the goals and, using rules, substitutes the current goals with new goals, until new goals happen to be simple facts. Given the question

?- predecessor(tom, pat).

Prolog will try to satisfy this goal. In order to do so it will try to find a clause in the program from which the above goal could immediately follow. Obviously, the only clauses relevant to this end are *pr1* and *pr2*. These are the rules about the predecessor relation. We say that the heads of these rules *match* the goal.

The two clauses, *pr1* and *pr2*, represent two alternative ways for Prolog to proceed. Prolog first tries that clause which appears first in the program:

predecessor(X, Z) :- parent(X, Z).

Since the goal is predecessor(tom, pat), the variables in the rule must be instantiated as follows:

X = tom, Z = pat

The original goal predecessor(tom, pat) is then replaced by a new goal:

parent(tom, pat)

This step of using a rule to transform a goal into another goal, as above, is graphically illustrated in Figure 1.9. There is no clause in the program whose head matches the goal parent(tom, pat), therefore this goal fails. Now Prolog *backtracks* to the original goal in order to try an alternative way to derive the top goal predecessor(tom, pat). The rule *pr2* is thus tried:

predecessor(X, Z) :-
    parent(X, Y),
    predecessor(Y, Z).

Figure 1.9   The first step of the execution. The top goal is true if the bottom goal is true.

As before, the variables X and Z become instantiated as:

X = tom, Z = pat

But Y is not instantiated yet. The top goal **predecessor(tom, pat)** is replaced by two goals:

parent(tom, Y),
predecessor(Y, pat)

This executional step is shown in Figure 1.10, which is an extension to the situation we had in Figure 1.9.

Being now faced with *two* goals, Prolog tries to satisfy them in the order that they are written. The first one is easy as it matches one of the facts in the program. The matching forces Y to become instantiated to bob. Thus the first goal has been satisfied, and the remaining goal has become:

predecessor(bob, pat)

To satisfy this goal the rule *pr1* is used again. Note that this (second) application of the same rule has nothing to do with its previous application. Therefore, Prolog uses a new set of variables in the rule each time the rule is

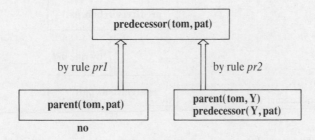

Figure 1.10   Execution trace continued from Figure 1.9.

applied. To indicate this we shall rename the variables in rule *pr1* for this application as follows:

> predecessor(X', Z') :-
>   parent(X', Z').

The head has to match our current goal **predecessor(bob, pat)**. Therefore:

> X' = bob, Z' = pat

The current goal is replaced by:

> parent(bob, pat)

This goal is immediately satisfied because it appears in the program as a fact. This completes the execution trace which is graphically shown in Figure 1.11.

   The graphical illustration of the execution trace in Figure 1.11 has the form of a tree. The nodes of the tree correspond to goals, or to lists of goals that are to be satisfied. The arcs between the nodes correspond to the application of (alternative) program clauses that transform the goals at one node into the goals at another node. The top goal is satisfied when a path is found from the root node (top goal) to a leaf node labelled 'yes'. A leaf is labelled 'yes' if it is a simple fact. The execution of Prolog programs is the

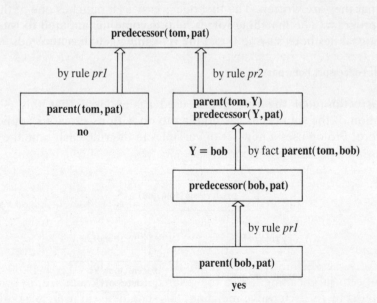

Figure 1.11   The complete execution trace to satisfy the goal **predecessor(tom, pat)**. The right-hand branch proves the goal is satisfiable.

searching for such paths. During the search Prolog may enter an unsuccessful branch. When Prolog discovers that a branch fails it automatically *backtracks* to the previous node and tries to apply an alternative clause at that node.

EXERCISE

1.7   Try to understand how Prolog derives answers to the following questions, using the program of Figure 1.8. Try to draw the corresponding derivation diagrams in the style of Figures 1.9 to 1.11. Will any backtracking occur at particular questions?

(a)   ?- parent(pam, bob).

(b)   ?- mother(pam, bob).

(c)   ?- grandparent(pam, ann).

(d)   ?- grandparent(bob, jim).

1.5   Declarative and procedural meaning of programs

In our examples so far it has always been possible to understand the results of the program without exactly knowing *how* the system actually found the results. It therefore makes sense to distinguish between two levels of meaning of Prolog programs; namely,

- the *declarative meaning* and
- the *procedural meaning*.

The declarative meaning is concerned only with the *relations* defined by the program. The declarative meaning thus determines *what* will be the output of the program. On the other hand, the procedural meaning also determines *how* this output is obtained; that is, how are the relations actually evaluated by the Prolog system.

The ability of Prolog to work out many procedural details on its own is considered to be one of its specific advantages. It encourages the programmer to consider the declarative meaning of programs relatively independently of their procedural meaning. Since the results of the program are, in principle, determined by its declarative meaning, this should be (in principle) sufficient for writing programs. This is of practical importance because the declarative aspects of programs are usually easier to understand than the procedural details. To take full advantage of this, the programmer should concentrate mainly on the declarative meaning and, whenever possible, avoid being distracted by the executional details. These should be left to the greatest possible extent to the Prolog system itself.

This declarative approach indeed often makes programming in Prolog easier than in typical procedurally oriented programming languages such as Pascal. Unfortunately, however, the declarative approach is not always sufficient. It will later become clear that, especially in large programs, the procedural aspects cannot be completely ignored by the programmer for practical reasons of executional efficiency. Nevertheless, the declarative style of thinking about Prolog programs should be encouraged and the procedural aspects ignored to the extent that is permitted by practical constraints.

SUMMARY

- Prolog programming consists of defining relations and querying about relations.

- A program consists of *clauses*. These are of three types: *facts*, *rules* and *questions*.

- A relation can be specified by *facts*, simply stating the n-tuples of objects that satisfy the relation, or by stating *rules* about the relation.

- A *procedure* is a set of clauses about the same relation.

- Querying about relations, by means of *questions*, resembles querying a database. Prolog's answer to a question consists of a set of objects that satisfy the question.

- In Prolog, to establish whether an object satisfies a query is often a complicated process that involves logical inference, exploring among alternatives and possibly *backtracking*. All this is done automatically by the Prolog system and is, in principle, hidden from the user.

- Two types of meaning of Prolog programs are distinguished: declarative and procedural. The declarative view is advantageous from the programming point of view. Nevertheless, the procedural details often have to be considered by the programmer as well.

- The following concepts have been introduced in this chapter:

  clause, fact, rule, question
  the head of a clause, the body of a clause
  recursive rule, recursive definition
  procedure
  atom, variable
  instantiation of a variable
  goal

goal is satisfiable, goal succeeds
goal is unsatisfiable, goal fails
backtracking
declarative meaning, procedural meaning

References

Various implementations of Prolog use different syntactic conventions. In this book we use the so-called Edinburgh syntax (also called DEC-10 syntax, established by the influential implementation of Prolog for the DEC-10 computer; Pereira *et al*. 1978; Bowen 1981) which has been adopted by many popular Prologs such as: AAIS Prolog, ALS Prolog, Arity/Prolog, BIM Prolog, C-Prolog, IF/Prolog, LPA Prolog, MacProlog, MProlog, Poplog Prolog, Prolog-2, Quintus Prolog, SD-Prolog, Xilog and many others.

Bowen, D.L. (1981) *DECsystem-10 Prolog User's Manual*. University of Edinburgh: Department of Artificial Intelligence.

Pereira, L.M., Pereira, F. and Warren, D.H.D. (1978) *User's Guide to DECsystem-10 Prolog*. University of Edinburgh: Department of Artificial Intelligence.

2 Syntax and Meaning of Prolog Programs

This chapter gives a systematic treatment of the syntax and semantics of basic concepts of Prolog, and introduces structured data objects. The topics included are:

- simple data objects (atoms, numbers, variables)
- structured objects
- matching as the fundamental operation on objects
- declarative (or non-procedural) meaning of a program
- procedural meaning of a program
- relation between the declarative and procedural meanings of a program, and
- altering the procedural meaning by reordering clauses and goals.

Most of these topics have already been reviewed in Chapter 1. Here the treatment will become more formal and detailed.

2.1   Data objects

Figure 2.1 shows a classification of data objects in Prolog. The Prolog system recognizes the type of an object in the program by its syntactic form. This is possible because the syntax of Prolog specifies different forms for each type of data objects. We have already seen a method for distinguishing between atoms and variables in Chapter 1: variables start with upper-case letters whereas atoms start with lower-case letters. No additional information (such as data-type declaration) has to be communicated to Prolog in order to recognize the type of an object.

2.1.1   Atoms and numbers

In Chapter 1 we have seen some simple examples of atoms and variables. In general, however, they can take more complicated forms – that is, strings of the following characters:

- upper-case letters A, B, ..., Z
- lower-case letters a, b, ..., z
- digits 0, 1, 2, ..., 9
- special characters such as $+ - * / < > = : . \& \_ \sim$

Atoms can be constructed in three ways:

(1)   Strings of letters, digits and the underscore character, '_', starting with a lower-case letter:

      anna
      nil
      x25
      x_25
      x_25AB
      x_
      x___y
      alpha_beta_procedure
      miss_Jones
      sarah_jones

(2)   Strings of special characters:

      <--->
      ======>
      ...
      .:.

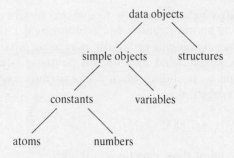

Figure 2.1   Data objects in Prolog.

When using atoms of this form, some care is necessary because some strings of special characters already have a predefined meaning; an example is ':-'.

(3)   Strings of characters enclosed in single quotes. This is useful if we want, for example, to have an atom that starts with a capital letter. By enclosing it in quotes we make it distinguishable from variables:

   'Tom'
   'South_America'
   'Sarah Jones'

Numbers used in Prolog include integer numbers and real numbers. The syntax of integers is simple, as illustrated by the following examples:

   1   1313   0   −97

Not all integer numbers can be represented in a computer, therefore the range of integers is limited to an interval between some smallest and some largest number permitted by a particular Prolog implementation. Normally the range allowed by an implementation is at least between −16383 and 16383, and often it is considerably wider.

   The treatment of real numbers depends on the implementation of Prolog. We will assume the simple syntax of numbers, as shown by the following examples:

   3.14   −0.0035   100.2

Real numbers are not used very much in typical Prolog programming. The reason for this is that Prolog is primarily a language for symbolic, non-numeric computation, as opposed to number crunching oriented languages such as Fortran. In symbolic computation, integers are often used, for example, to count the number of items in a list; but there is little need for real numbers.

Apart from this lack of necessity to use real numbers in typical Prolog applications, there is another reason for avoiding real numbers. In general, we want to keep the meaning of programs as neat as possible. The introduction of real numbers somewhat impairs this neatness because of numerical errors that arise due to rounding when doing arithmetic. For example, the evaluation of the expression

$$10000 + 0.0001 - 10000$$

may result in 0 instead of the correct result 0.0001.

2.1.2   Variables

Variables are strings of letters, digits and underscore characters. They start with an upper-case letter or an underscore character:

```
X
Result
Object2
Participant_list
ShoppingList
_x23
_23
```

When a variable appears in a clause once only, we do not have to invent a name for it. We can use the so-called 'anonymous' variable, which is written as a single underscore character. For example, let us consider the following rule:

```
hasachild( X) :- parent( X, Y).
```

This rule says: for all X, X has a child if X is a parent of some Y. We are defining the property **hasachild** which, as it is meant here, does not depend on the name of the child. Thus, this is a proper place in which to use an anonymous variable. The clause above can thus be rewritten:

```
hasachild( X) :- parent( X, _).
```

Each time a single underscore character occurs in a clause it represents a new anonymous variable. For example, we can say that there is somebody who has a child if there are two objects such that one is a parent of the other:

```
somebody_has_child :- parent( _, _).
```

This is equivalent to:

```
somebody_has_child :- parent( X, Y).
```

But this is, of course, quite different from:

> somebody_has_child :- parent(X, X).

If the anonymous variable appears in a question clause then its value is not output when Prolog answers the question. If we are interested in people who have children, but not in the names of the children, then we can simply ask:

> ?- parent(X, _).

The *lexical scope* of variable names is one clause. This means that, for example, if the name X15 occurs in two clauses, then it signifies two different variables. But each occurrence of X15 within the same clause means the same variable. The situation is different for constants: the same atom always means the same object in any clause – that is, throughout the whole program.

2.1.3 Structures

Structured objects (or simply *structures*) are objects that have several components. The components themselves can, in turn, be structures. For example, the date can be viewed as a structure with three components: day, month, year. Although composed of several components, structures are treated in the program as single objects. In order to combine the components into a single object we have to choose a *functor*. A suitable functor for our example is **date**. Then the date 1st May 1983 can be written as:

> date(1, may, 1983)

(see Figure 2.2).

All the components in this example are constants (two integers and one atom). Components can also be variables or other structures. Any day in May

(a)   (b)

Figure 2.2 Date is an example of a structured object: (a) as it is represented as a tree; (b) as it is written in Prolog.

can be represented by the structure:

      date(Day, may, 1983)

Note that **Day** is a variable and can be instantiated to any object at some later point in the execution.

This method for data structuring is simple and powerful. It is one of the reasons why Prolog is so naturally applied to problems that involve symbolic manipulation.

Syntactically, all data objects in Prolog are *terms*. For example,

      may

and

      date(1, may, 1983)

are terms.

All structured objects can be pictured as trees (see Figure 2.2 for an example). The root of the tree is the functor, and the offsprings of the root are the components. If a component is also a structure then it is a subtree of the tree that corresponds to the whole structured object.

Our next example will show how structures can be used to represent some simple geometric objects (see Figure 2.3). A point in two-dimensional space is defined by its two coordinates; a line segment is defined by two points; and a triangle can be defined by three points. Let us choose the following functors:

      point   for points,
      seg   for line segments, and
      triangle for triangles.

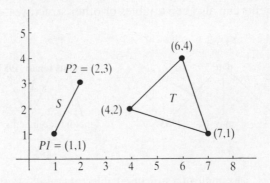

Figure 2.3 Some simple geometric objects.

Then the objects in Figure 2.3 can be represented as follows:

P1 = point(1,1)
P2 = point(2,3)
S = seg(P1, P2) = seg(point(1,1), point(2,3))
T = triangle(point(4,2), point(6,4), point(7,1))

The corresponding tree representation of these objects is shown in Figure 2.4. In general, the functor at the root of the tree is called the *principal functor* of the term.

If in the same program we also had points in three-dimensional space then we could use another functor, **point3**, say, for their representation:

point3(X, Y, Z)

We can, however, use the same name, **point**, for points in both two and three dimensions, and write for example:

point(X1, Y1)   and   point(X, Y, Z)

If the same name appears in the program in two different roles, as is the case for point above, the Prolog system will recognize the difference by the number of arguments, and will interpret this name as two functors: one of them with two arguments and the other one with three arguments. This is so

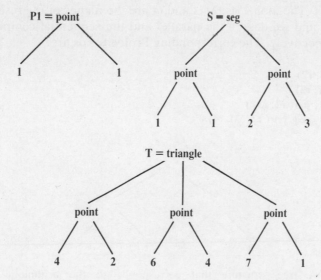

Figure 2.4   Tree representation of the objects in Figure 2.3.

because each functor is defined by two things:

(1)   the name, whose syntax is that of atoms;
(2)   the *arity* – that is, the number of arguments.

As already explained, all structured objects in Prolog are trees, represented in the program by terms. We will study two more examples to illustrate how naturally complicated data objects can be represented by Prolog terms. Figure 2.5 shows the tree structure that corresponds to the arithmetic expression:

$$(a + b) * (c - 5)$$

According to the syntax of terms introduced so far this can be written, using the symbols '*', '+' and '−' as functors, as follows:

$$*(+(a, b), -(c, 5))$$

This is of course a legal Prolog term; but this is not the form that we would normally like to have. We would normally prefer the usual, infix notation as used in mathematics. In fact, Prolog also allows us to use the infix notation so that the symbols '*', '+' and '−' are written as infix operators. Details of how the programmer can define his or her own operators will be discussed in Chapter 3.

As the last example we consider some simple electric circuits shown in Figure 2.6. The right-hand side of the figure shows the tree representation of these circuits. The atoms **r1**, **r2**, **r3** and **r4** are the names of the resistors. The functors **par** and **seq** denote the parallel and the sequential compositions of resistors respectively. The corresponding Prolog terms are:

```
seq( r1, r2)
par( r1, r2)
par( r1, par( r2, r3) )
par( r1, seq( par( r2, r3), r4) )
```

Figure 2.5 A tree structure that corresponds to the arithmetic expression $(a + b) * (c - 5)$.

Figure 2.6 Some simple electric circuits and their tree representations: (a) sequential composition of resistors r1 and r2; (b) parallel composition of two resistors; (c) parallel composition of three resistors; (d) parallel composition of r1 and another circuit.

EXERCISES

2.1 Which of the following are syntactically correct Prolog objects? What kinds of object are they (atom, number, variable, structure)?

   (a) **Diana**

   (b) **diana**

       (c)   'Diana'

       (d)   _diana

       (e)   'Diana goes south'

       (f)   goes(diana, south)

       (g)   45

       (h)   5(X, Y)

       (i)   +(north, west)

       (j)   three(Black(Cats))

2.2   Suggest a representation for rectangles, squares and circles as structured Prolog objects. Use an approach similar to that in Figure 2.4. For example, a rectangle can be represented by four points (or maybe three points only). Write some example terms that represent some concrete objects of these types using the suggested representation.

2.2 Matching

In the previous section we have seen how terms can be used to represent complex data objects. The most important operation on terms is *matching*. Matching alone can produce some interesting computation.

    Given two terms, we say that they *match* if:

(1)   they are identical, or

(2)   the variables in both terms can be instantiated to objects in such a way that after the substitution of variables by these objects the terms become identical.

For example, the terms date(D, M, 1983) and date(D1, may, Y1) match. One instantiation that makes both terms identical is:

- D is instantiated to D1
- M is instantiated to may
- Y1 is instantiated to 1983

This instantiation is more compactly written in the familiar form in which

Prolog outputs results:

>   D = D1
>   M = may
>   Y1 = 1983

On the other hand, the terms date(D, M, 1983) and date(D1, M1, 1444) do not match, nor do the terms date(X, Y, Z) and point(X, Y, Z).

Matching is a process that takes as input two terms and checks whether they match. If the terms do not match we say that this process *fails*. If they do match then the process *succeeds* and it also instantiates the variables in both terms to such values that the terms become identical.

Let us consider again the matching of the two dates. The request for this operation can be communicated to the Prolog system by the following question, using the operator ' = ':

>   ?- date(D, M, 1983) = date(D1, may, Y1).

We have already mentioned the instantiation D = D1, M = may, Y1 = 1983, which achieves the match. There are, however, other instantiations that also make both terms identical. Two of them are as follows:

>   D = 1
>   D1 = 1
>   M = may
>   Y1 = 1983
>
>   D = third
>   D1 = third
>   M = may
>   Y1 = 1983

These two instantiations are said to be *less general* than the first one because they constrain the values of the variables D and D1 stronger than necessary. For making both terms in our example identical, it is only important that D and D1 have the same value, although this value can be anything. Matching in Prolog always results in the *most general* instantiation. This is the instantiation that commits the variables to the least possible extent, thus leaving the greatest possible freedom for further instantiations if further matching is required. As an example consider the following question:

>   ?- date(D, M, 1983) = date(D1, may, Y1),
>   date(D, M, 1983) = date(15, M, Y).

To satisfy the first goal, Prolog instantiates the variables as follows:

>   D = D1
>   M = may
>   Y1 = 1983

After having satisfied the second goal, the instantiation becomes more specific as follows:

D = 15
D1 = 15
M = may
Y1 = 1983
Y = 1983

This example also illustrates that variables, during the execution of consecutive goals, typically become instantiated to increasingly more specific values.

The general rules to decide whether two terms, S and T, match are as follows:

> (1) If S and T are constants then S and T match only if they are the same object.
>
> (2) If S is a variable and T is anything, then they match, and S is instantiated to T. Conversely, if T is a variable then T is instantiated to S.
>
> (3) If S and T are structures then they match only if
>
> (a) S and T have the same principal functor, and
> (b) all their corresponding components match.
>
> The resulting instantiation is determined by the matching of the components.

The last of these rules can be visualized by considering the tree representation of terms, as in the example of Figure 2.7. The matching process starts at the root (the principal functors). As both functors match, the process proceeds to the arguments where matching of the pairs of corresponding arguments occurs. So the whole matching process can be thought of as consisting of the following sequence of (simpler) matching operations:

triangle = triangle,
point(1,1) = X,
A = point(4,Y),
point(2,3) = point(2,Z).

The whole matching process succeeds because all the matchings in the sequence succeed. The resulting instantiation is:

X = point(1,1)
A = point(4,Y)
Z = 3

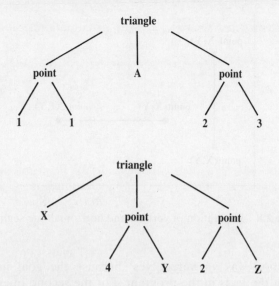

Figure 2.7   Matching **triangle(point(1,1), A, point (2,3))** = **triangle(X, point(4,Y), point(2,Z))**.

The following example will illustrate how matching alone can be used for interesting computation. Let us return to the simple geometric objects of Figure 2.4, and define a piece of program for recognizing horizontal and vertical line segments. 'Vertical' is a property of segments, so it can be formalized in Prolog as a unary relation. Figure 2.8 helps to formulate this relation. A segment is vertical if the *x*-coordinates of its end-points are equal, otherwise there is no other restriction on the segment. The property 'horizontal' is similarly formulated, with only *x* and *y* interchanged. The following program, consisting of two facts, does the job:

vertical(seg(point(X,Y), point(X,Y1))).

horizontal(seg(point(X,Y), point(X1,Y))).

The following conversation is possible with this program:

?- vertical(seg(point(1,1), point(1,2))).

yes

?- vertical(seg(point(1,1), point(2,Y))).

no

?- horizontal(seg(point(1,1), point(2,Y))).

Y = 1

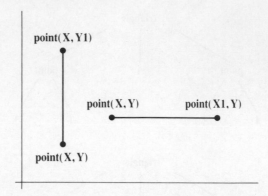

Figure 2.8   Illustration of vertical and horizontal line segments.

The first question was answered 'yes' because the goal in the question matched one of the facts in the program. For the second question no match was possible. In the third question, Y was forced to become 1 by matching the fact about horizontal segments.

A more general question to the program is: Are there any vertical segments that start at the point (2,3)?

> ?- vertical(seg(point(2,3), P)).
>
> P = point(2,Y)

This answer means: Yes, any segment that ends at any point (2,Y), which means anywhere on the vertical line $x = 2$. It should be noted that Prolog's actual answer would probably not look as neat as above, but (depending on the Prolog implementation used) something like this:

> P = point(2,_136)

This is, however, only a cosmetic difference. Here _136 is a variable that has not been instantiated. _136 is, of course, a legal variable name that the system has constructed during the execution. The system has to generate new names in order to rename the user's variables in the program. This is necessary for two reasons: first, because the same name in different clauses signifies different variables, and second, in successive applications of the same clause, its 'copy' with a new set of variables is used each time.

Another interesting question to our program is: Is there a segment that is both vertical and horizontal?

> ?- vertical(S), horizontal(S).
>
> S = seg(point(X,Y), point(X,Y))

This answer by Prolog says: Yes, any segment that is degenerated to a point has the property of being vertical and horizontal at the same time. The answer was, again, derived simply by matching. As before, some internally generated names may appear in the answer, instead of the variable names X and Y.

EXERCISES

2.3 Will the following matching operations succeed or fail? If they succeed, what are the resulting instantiations of variables?

(a)   point(A, B) = point(1, 2)

(b)   point(A, B) = point(X, Y, Z)

(c)   plus(2, 2) = 4

(d)   +(2, D) = +(E, 2)

(e)   triangle(point(−1,0), P2, P3) = triangle(P1, point(1,0), point(0,Y))

  The resulting instantiation defines a family of triangles. How would you describe this family?

2.4 Using the representation for line segments as described in this section, write a term that represents any vertical line segment at $x = 5$.

2.5 Assume that a rectangle is represented by the term
rectangle(P1, P2, P3, P4) where the P's are the vertices of the rectangle positively ordered. Define the relation

  regular(R)

which is true if R is a rectangle whose sides are vertical and horizontal.

2.3   Declarative meaning of Prolog programs

We have already seen in Chapter 1 that Prolog programs can be understood in two ways: declaratively and procedurally. In this and the next section we will consider a more formal definition of the declarative and procedural meanings of programs in basic Prolog. But first let us look at the difference between these two meanings again.

  Consider a clause

  P :- Q, R.

where P, Q and R have the syntax of terms. Some alternative declarative readings of this clause are:

> P is true if Q and R are true.
>
> From Q and R follows P.

Two alternative procedural readings of this clause are:

> To solve problem P, *first* solve the subproblem Q and *then* the subproblem R.
>
> To satisfy P, *first* satisfy Q and *then* R.

Thus the difference between the declarative readings and the procedural ones is that the latter do not only define the logical relations between the head of the clause and the goals in the body, but also the *order* in which the goals are processed.

Let us now formalize the declarative meaning.

The declarative meaning of programs determines whether a given goal is true, and if so, for what values of variables it is true. To precisely define the declarative meaning we need to introduce the concept of *instance* of a clause. An instance of a clause C is the clause C with each of its variables substituted by some term. A *variant* of a clause C is such an instance of the clause C where each variable is substituted by another variable. For example, consider the clause:

> hasachild(X) :- parent(X, Y).

Two variants of this clause are:

> hasachild(A) :- parent(A, B).
> hasachild(X1) :- parent(X1, X2).

Instances of this clause are:

> hasachild(peter) :- parent(peter, Z).
> hasachild(barry) :- parent(barry, small(caroline)).

Given a program and a goal G, the declarative meaning says:

> A goal G is true (that is, satisfiable, or logically follows from the program) if and only if
>
> (1)   there is a clause C in the program such that
> (2)   there is a clause instance I of C such that
>
> > (a)   the head of I is identical to G, and
> > (b)   all the goals in the body of I are true.

This definition extends to Prolog questions as follows. In general, a question to the Prolog system is a *list* of goals separated by commas. A list of goals is true if *all* the goals in the list are true for the *same* instantiation of variables. The values of the variables result from the most general instantiation.

A comma between goals thus denotes the *conjunction* of goals: they *all* have to be true. But Prolog also accepts the *disjunction* of goals: *any one* of the goals in a disjunction has to be true. Disjunction is indicated by a semicolon. For example,

P :- Q; R.

is read: P is true if Q is true *or* R is true. The meaning of this clause is thus the same as the meaning of the following two clauses together:

P :- Q.
P :- R.

The comma binds stronger than the semicolon. So the clause

P :- Q, R; S, T, U.

is understood as

P :- (Q, R); (S, T, U).

and means the same as the clauses:

P :- Q, R.
P :- S, T, U.

EXERCISES

2.6 Consider the following program:

```
f( 1, one).
f( s(1), two).
f( s(s(1)), three).
f( s(s(s(X))), N) :-
    f( X, N).
```

How will Prolog answer the following questions? Whenever several answers are possible, give at least two.

(a) ?- f(s(1), A).

(b) ?- f(s(s(1)), two).

(c) ?- f(s(s(s(s(s(s(1)))))), C).

(d) ?- f(D, three).

2.7 The following program says that two people are relatives if

(a) one is a predecessor of the other, or

(b) they have a common predecessor, or

(c) they have a common successor:

```
relatives( X, Y) :-
    predecessor( X, Y).

relatives( X, Y) :-
    predecessor( Y, X).

relatives( X, Y) :-          % X and Y have a common predecessor
    predecessor( Z, X),
    predecessor( Z, Y).

relatives( X, Y) :-          % X and Y have a common successor
    predecessor( X, Z),
    predecessor( Y, Z).
```

Can you shorten this program by using the semicolon notation?

2.8 Rewrite the following program without using the semicolon notation.

```
translate( Number, Word) :-
    Number = 1, Word = one;
    Number = 2, Word = two;
    Number = 3, Word = three.
```

2.4 Procedural meaning

The procedural meaning specifies *how* Prolog answers questions. To answer a question means to try to satisfy a list of goals. They can be satisfied if the variables that occur in the goals can be instantiated in such a way that the goals logically follow from the program. Thus the procedural meaning of Prolog is a procedure for executing a list of goals with respect to a given program. To 'execute goals' means: try to satisfy them.

Figure 2.9 Input/output view of the procedure that executes a list of goals.

Let us call this procedure **execute**. As shown in Figure 2.9, the inputs to and the outputs from this procedure are:

input: a program and a goal list

output: a success/failure indicator and an instantiation of variables

The meaning of the two output results is as follows:

(1) The success/failure indicator is 'yes' if the goals are satisfiable and 'no' otherwise. We say that 'yes' signals a *successful* termination and 'no' a *failure*.

(2) An instantiation of variables is only produced in the case of a successful termination; in the case of failure there is no instantiation.

In Chapter 1, we have in effect already discussed informally what procedure **execute** does, under the heading 'How Prolog answers questions?'. What follows in the rest of this section is just a more formal and systematic description of this process, and can be skipped without seriously affecting the understanding of the rest of the book.

Particular operations in the goal execution process are illustrated by the example in Figure 2.10. It may be helpful to study Figure 2.10 before reading the following general description.

Figure 2.10 An example to illustrate the procedural meaning of Prolog: a sample trace of the procedure **execute**.

PROGRAM

big(bear).	% Clause 1
big(elephant).	% Clause 2
small(cat).	% Clause 3
brown(bear).	% Clause 4
black(cat).	% Clause 5
gray(elephant).	% Clause 6

(continues)

Figure 2.10 (cont.)

dark(Z) :-   % Clause 7: Anything black is dark
   black(Z).

dark(Z) :-   % Clause 8: Anything brown is dark
   brown(Z).

QUESTION

?- dark(X), big(X).   % Who is dark and big?

EXECUTION TRACE

(1)   Initial goal list: **dark(X), big(X).**

(2)   Scan the program from top to bottom looking for a clause whose head matches the first goal
      dark(X). Clause 7 found:

      dark(Z) :- black(Z).

      Replace the first goal by the instantiated body of clause 7, giving a new goal list.

      black(X), big(X)

(3)   Scan the program to find a match with **black(X).** Clause 5 found: **black(cat).** This clause has
      no body, so the goal list, properly instantiated, shrinks to:

      big(cat)

(4)   Scan the program for the goal **big(cat).** No clause found. Therefore backtrack to step (3) and
      undo the instantiation X = **cat**. Now the goal list is again:

      black(X), big(X)

      Continue scanning the program below clause 5. No clause found. Therefore backtrack to step
      (2) and continue scanning below clause 7. Clause 8 is found:

      dark(Z) :- brown(Z).

      Replace the first goal in the goal list by **brown(X),** giving:

      brown(X), big(X)

(5)   Scan the program to match **brown(X),** finding **brown(bear).** This clause has no body, so the
      goal list shrinks to:

      big(bear)

(6)   Scan the program and find clause **big(bear).** It has no body so the goal list shrinks to empty.
      This indicates successful termination, and the corresponding variable instantiation is:

      X = **bear**

To execute a list of goals

G1, G2, ..., Gm

the procedure **execute** does the following:

- If the goal list is empty then terminate with *success*.
- If the goal list is not empty then continue with (the following) operation called 'SCANNING'.
- *SCANNING*: Scan through the clauses in the program from top to bottom until the first clause, C, is found such that the head of C matches the first goal G1. If there is no such clause then terminate with *failure*.

  If there is such a clause C of the form

  H :- B1, ..., Bn.

  then rename the variables in C to obtain a variant C' of C, such that C' and the list G1, ..., Gm have no common variables. Let C' be

  H' :- B1', ..., Bn'.

  Match G1 and H'; let the resulting instantiation of variables be S.

  In the goal list G1, G2, ..., Gm, replace G1 with the list B1', ..., Bn', obtaining a new goal list

  B1', ..., Bn', G2, ..., Gm

  (Note that if C is a fact then $n = 0$ and the new goal list is shorter than the original one; such shrinking of the goal list may eventually lead to the empty list and thereby a successful termination.)

  Substitute the variables in this new goal list with new values as specified in the instantiation S, obtaining another goal list

  B1", ..., Bn", G2', ..., Gm'

- Execute (recursively with this same procedure) this new goal list. If the execution of this new goal list terminates with success then terminate the execution of the original goal list also with success. If the execution of the new goal list is not successful then abandon this new goal list and go back to SCANNING through the program. Continue the scanning with the clause that immediately follows the clause C (C is the clause that was last used) and try to find a successful termination using some other clause.

This procedure is more compactly written in a Pascal-like notation in Figure 2.11.

Several additional remarks are in order here regarding the procedure execute as presented. First, it was not explicitly described how the final resulting instantiation of variables is produced. It is the instantiation S which led to a successful termination, and was possibly further refined by additional instantiations that were done in the nested recursive calls to execute.

Whenever a recursive call to execute fails, the execution returns to SCANNING, continuing at the program clause C that had been last used before. As the application of the clause C did not lead to a successful termination Prolog has to try an alternative clause to proceed. What effectively happens is that Prolog abandons this whole part of the unsuccessful execution and backtracks to the point (clause C) where this failed branch of the execution was started. When the procedure backtracks to a certain point, all the variable instantiations that were done after that point are undone. This ensures that Prolog systematically examines all the possible alternative paths of execution until one is found that eventually succeeds, or until all of them have been shown to fail.

We have already seen that even after a successful termination the user can force the system to backtrack to search for more solutions. In our description of execute this detail was left out.

Of course, in actual implementations of Prolog, several other refinements have to be added to execute. One of them is to reduce the amount of scanning through the program clauses to improve efficiency. So a practical Prolog implementation will not scan through all the clauses of the program, but will only consider the clauses about the relation in the current goal.

EXERCISE

2.9   Consider the program in Figure 2.10 and simulate, in the style of Figure 2.10, Prolog's execution of the question:

   ?- big(X), dark(X).

Compare your execution trace with that of Figure 2.10 when the question was essentially the same, but with the goals in the order:

   ?- dark(X), big(X).

In which of the two cases does Prolog have to do more work before the answer is found?

---

procedure *execute* (*Program, GoalList, Success*);

Input arguments:
   Program: list of clauses
   GoalList: list of goals
Output argument:
   Success: truth value; *Success* will become true if
      GoalList is true with respect to *Program*
Local variables:
   Goal: goal
   OtherGoals: list of goals
   Satisfied: truth value
   MatchOK: truth value
   Instant: instantiation of variables
   H, H', B1, B1', . . . , Bn, Bn': goals
Auxiliary functions:
   empty(L): returns true if L is the empty list
   head(L): returns the first element of list L
   tail(L): returns the rest of L
   append(L1,L2): appends list L2 at the end of list L1
   match(T1,T2,MatchOK,Instant): tries to match terms T1 and T2; if
      succeeds then *MatchOK* is true and *Instant* is the corresponding
      instantiation of variables
   substitute(Instant,Goals): substitutes variables in *Goals* according
      to instantiation *Instant*

```
begin
    if empty(GoalList) then Success := true
    else
        begin
            Goal := head(GoalList);
            OtherGoals := tail(GoalList);
            Satisfied := false;
            while not Satisfied and "more clauses in program" do
                begin
                    Let next clause in Program be
                        H :- B1, . . . , Bn.
                    Construct a variant of this clause
                        H' :- B1', . . . , Bn'.
                    match(Goal,H',MatchOK,Instant);
                    if MatchOK then
                        begin
                            NewGoals := append([B1',...,Bn'],OtherGoals);
                            NewGoals := substitute(Instant,NewGoals);
                            execute(Program,NewGoals,Satisfied)
                        end
                end;
            Success := Satisfied
        end
end;
```

Figure 2.11 Executing Prolog goals.

2.5 Example: monkey and banana

The monkey and banana problem is often used as a simple example of problem solving. Our Prolog program for this problem will show how the mechanisms of matching and backtracking can be used in such exercises. We will develop the program in the non-procedural way, and then study its procedural behaviour in detail. The program will be compact and illustrative.

We will use the following variation of the problem. There is a monkey at the door into a room. In the middle of the room a banana is hanging from the ceiling. The monkey is hungry and wants to get the banana, but he cannot stretch high enough from the floor. At the window of the room there is a box the monkey may use. The monkey can perform the following actions: walk on the floor, climb the box, push the box around (if it is already at the box) and grasp the banana if standing on the box directly under the banana. Can the monkey get the banana?

One important task in programming is that of finding a representation of the problem in terms of the programming language used. In our case we can think of the 'monkey world' as always being in some *state* that can change in time. The current state is determined by the positions of the objects. For example, the initial state of the world is determined by:

(1) Monkey is at door.
(2) Monkey is on floor.
(3) Box is at window.
(4) Monkey does not have banana.

It is convenient to combine all of these four pieces of information into one structured object. Let us choose the word 'state' as the functor to hold the four components together. Figure 2.12 shows the initial state represented as a structured object.

Our problem can be viewed as a one-person game. Let us now formalize the rules of the game. First, the goal of the game is a situation in which the monkey has the banana; that is, any state in which the last component is 'has':

state(_, _, _, has)

Second, what are the allowed moves that change the world from one state to another? There are four types of moves:

(1) grasp banana,
(2) climb box,
(3) push box,
(4) walk around.

Figure 2.12   The initial state of the monkey world represented as a structured object. The four components are: horizontal position of monkey, vertical position of monkey, position of box, monkey has or has not banana.

Not all moves are possible in every possible state of the world. For example, the move 'grasp' is only possible if the monkey is standing on the box directly under the banana (which is in the middle of the room) and does not have the banana yet. Such rules can be formalized in Prolog as a three-place relation named **move**:

> move(State1, Move, State2)

The three arguments of the relation specify a move thus:

> State1 --------> State2
>   Move

State1 is the state before the move, **Move** is the move executed and State2 is the state after the move.

The move 'grasp', with its necessary precondition on the state before the move, can be defined by the clause:

```
move( state( middle, onbox, middle, hasnot),    % Before move
      grasp,                                     % Move
      state( middle, onbox, middle, has) ).      % After move
```

This fact says that after the move the monkey has the banana, and he has remained on the box in the middle of the room.

In a similar way we can express the fact that the monkey on the floor can walk from any horizontal position Pos1 to any position Pos2. The monkey can do this regardless of the position of the box and whether it has the banana or not. All this can be defined by the following Prolog fact:

```
move( state( Pos1, onfloor, Box, Has),
      walk( Pos1, Pos2),                          % Walk from Pos1 to Pos2
      state( Pos2, onfloor, Box, Has) ).
```

Note that this clause says many things, including, for example:

- the move executed was 'walk from some position Pos1 to some position Pos2';

- the monkey is on the floor before and after the move;
- the box is at some point **Box** which remained the same after the move;
- the 'has banana' status **Has** remains the same after the move.

The clause actually specifies a whole set of possible moves because it is applicable to any situation that matches the specified state before the move. Such a specification is therefore sometimes also called a move *schema*. Due to the concept of Prolog variables such schemas can be easily programmed in Prolog.

The other two types of moves, 'push' and 'climb', can be similarly specified.

The main kind of question that our program will have to answer is: Can the monkey in some initial state **State** get the banana? This can be formulated as a predicate

    canget(State)

where the argument **State** is a state of the monkey world. The program for **canget** can be based on two observations:

(1)   For any state in which the monkey already has the banana, the predicate **canget** must certainly be true; no move is needed in this case. This corresponds to the Prolog fact:

        canget(state(_, _, _, has)).

(2)   In other cases one or more moves are necessary. The monkey can get the banana in any state **State1** if there is some move **Move** from **State1** to some state **State2**, such that the monkey can then get the banana in state **State2** (in zero or more moves). This principle is illustrated in Figure 2.13. A Prolog clause that corresponds to this rule is:

        canget(State1) :-
          move(State1, Move, State2),
          canget(State2).

This completes our program which is shown in Figure 2.14.

The formulation of **canget** is recursive and is similar to that of the **predecessor** relation of Chapter 1 (compare Figures 2.13 and 1.7). This principle is used in Prolog again and again.

Figure 2.13 Recursive formulation of **canget**.

```
% move( State1, Move, State2): making Move in State1 results in State2;
%    a state is represented by a term:
%    state( MonkeyHorizontal, MonkeyVertical, BoxPosition, HasBanana)
```

```
move( state( middle, onbox, middle, hasnot),        % Before move
      grasp,                                          % Grasp banana
      state( middle, onbox, middle, has) ).           % After move

move( state( P, onfloor, P, H),
      climb,                                          % Climb box
      state( P, onbox, P, H) ).

move( state( P1, onfloor, P1, H),
      push( P1, P2),                                  % Push box from P1 to P2
      state( P2, onfloor, P2, H) ).

move( state( P1, onfloor, B, H),
      walk( P1, P2),                                  % Walk from P1 to P2
      state( P2, onfloor, B, H) ).
```

```
% canget( State): monkey can get banana in State
```

```
canget( state( _, _, _, has) ).                       % can 1: Monkey already has it

canget( State1)                                       % can 2: Do some work to get it
      move( State1, Move, State2),                     % Do something
      canget( State2).                                 % Get it now
```

Figure 2.14   A program for the monkey and banana problem.

We have developed our monkey and banana program in the non-procedural way. Let us now study its *procedural* behaviour by considering the following question to the program:

?- canget(state(atdoor, onfloor, atwindow, hasnot)).

Prolog's answer is 'yes'. The process carried out by Prolog to reach this answer proceeds, according to the procedural semantics of Prolog, through a sequence of goal lists. It involves some search for right moves among the possible alternative moves. At some point this search will take a wrong move leading to a dead branch. At this stage, backtracking will help it to recover. Figure 2.15 illustrates this search process.

To answer the question Prolog had to backtrack once only. A right sequence of moves was found almost straight away. The reason for this efficiency of the program was the order in which the clauses about the move relation occurred in the program. The order in our case (luckily) turned out to be quite suitable. However, less lucky orderings are possible. According to the rules of the game, the monkey could just as easily try to walk here or there

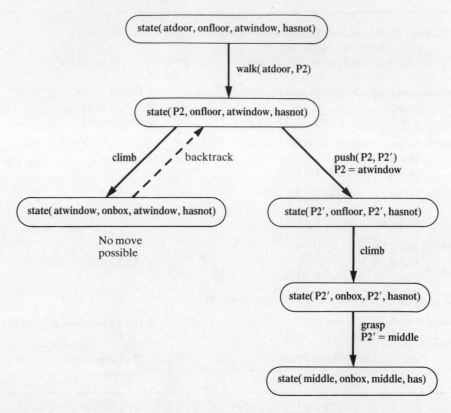

Figure 2.15 The monkey's search for the banana. The search starts at the top node and proceeds downwards, as indicated. Alternative moves are tried in the left-to-right order. Backtracking occurred once only.

without ever touching the box, or aimlessly push the box around. A more thorough investigation will reveal, as shown in the following section, that the ordering of clauses is, in the case of our program, in fact critical.

2.6 Order of clauses and goals

2.6.1 Danger of indefinite looping

Consider the following clause:

    p :- p.

This says that 'p is true if p is true'. This is declaratively perfectly correct, but procedurally is quite useless. In fact, such a clause can cause problems to Prolog. Consider the question:

?- p.

Using the clause above, the goal p is replaced by the same goal p; this will be in turn replaced by p, etc. In such a case Prolog will enter an infinite loop not noticing that no progress is being made.

This example is a simple way of getting Prolog to loop indefinitely. However, similar looping could have occurred in some of our previous example programs if we changed the order of clauses, or the order of goals in the clauses. It will be instructive to consider some examples.

In the monkey and banana program, the clauses about the **move** relation were ordered thus: grasp, climb, push, walk (perhaps 'unclimb' should be added for completeness). These clauses say that grasping is possible, climbing is possible, etc. According to the procedural semantics of Prolog, the order of clauses indicates that the monkey prefers grasping to climbing, climbing to pushing, etc. This order of preferences in fact helps the monkey to solve the problem. But what could happen if the order was different? Let us assume that the 'walk' clause appears first. The execution of our original goal of the previous section

?- canget(state(atdoor, onfloor, atwindow, hasnot)).

would this time produce the following trace. The first four goal lists (with variables appropriately renamed) are the same as before:

(1)   canget(state(atdoor, onfloor, atwindow, hasnot))

The second clause of **canget** ('can2') is applied, producing:

(2)   move(state(atdoor, onfloor, atwindow, hasnot), M', S2'),
        canget(S2')

By the move walk(atdoor, P2') we get:

(3)   canget(state(P2', onfloor, atwindow, hasnot))

Using the clause 'can2' again the goal list becomes:

(4)   move(state(P2', onfloor, atwindow, hasnot), M'', S2''),
        canget(S2'')

Now the difference occurs. The first clause whose head matches the first goal above is now 'walk' (and not 'climb' as before). The instantiation is

S2″ = state(P2″, onfloor, atwindow, hasnot). Therefore the goal list becomes:

(5)   canget(state(P2″, onfloor, atwindow, hasnot))

Applying the clause 'can2' we obtain:

(6)   move(state(P2″, onfloor, atwindow, hasnot), M‴, S2‴),
       canget(S2‴)

Again, 'walk' is now tried first, producing:

(7)   canget(state(P2‴, onfloor, atwindow, hasnot))

Let us now compare the goals (3), (5) and (7). They are the same apart from one variable; this variable is, in turn, P′, P″ and P‴. As we know, the success of a goal does not depend on particular names of variables in the goal. This means that from goal list (3) the execution trace shows no progress. We can see, in fact, that the same two clauses, 'can2' and 'walk', are used repetitively. The monkey walks around without ever trying to use the box. As there is no progress made this will (theoretically) go on for ever: Prolog will not realize that there is no point in continuing along this line.

This example shows Prolog trying to solve a problem in such a way that a solution is never reached, although a solution exists. Such situations are not unusual in Prolog programming. Infinite loops are, also, not unusual in other programming languages. What *is* unusual in comparison with other languages is that a Prolog program may be declaratively correct, but at the same time be procedurally incorrect in that it is not able to produce an answer to a question. In such cases Prolog may not be able to satisfy a goal because it tries to reach an answer by choosing a wrong path.

A natural question to ask at this point is: Can we not make some more substantial change to our program so as to drastically prevent any danger of looping? Or shall we always have to rely just on a suitable ordering of clauses and goals? As it turns out programs, especially large ones, would be too fragile if they just had to rely on some suitable ordering. There are several other methods that preclude infinite loops, and these are much more general and robust than the ordering method itself. These techniques will be used regularly later in the book, especially in those chapters that deal with path finding, problem solving and search.

2.6.2 Program variations through reordering of clauses and goals

Already in the example programs of Chapter 1 there was a latent danger of producing a cycling behaviour. Our program to specify the **predecessor** relation in Chapter 1 was:

```
predecessor( Parent, Child) :-
    parent( Parent, Child).

predecessor( Predecessor, Successor) :-
    parent( Predecessor, Child),
    predecessor( Child, Successor).
```

Let us analyze some variations of this program. All the variations will clearly have the same declarative meaning, but not the same procedural meaning. According to the declarative semantics of Prolog we can, without affecting the declarative meaning, change

(1)   the order of clauses in the program, and

(2)   the order of goals in the bodies of clauses.

The **predecessor** procedure consists of two clauses, and one of them has two goals in the body. There are, therefore, four variations of this program, all with the same declarative meaning. The four variations are obtained by

(1)   swapping both clauses, and

(2)   swapping the goals for each order of clauses.

The corresponding four procedures, called **pred1**, **pred2**, **pred3** and **pred4**, are shown in Figure 2.16.

There are important differences in the behaviour of these four declaratively equivalent procedures. To demonstrate these, consider the parent relation as shown in Figure 1.1 of Chapter 1. Now, what happens if we ask whether Tom is a predecessor of Pat using the four variations of the **predecessor** relation:

```
?- pred1( tom, pat).

yes

?- pred2( tom, pat).

yes

?- pred3( tom, pat).

yes

?- pred4( tom, pat).
```

In the last case Prolog cannot find the answer. This is manifested on the terminal by a Prolog message such as 'More core needed'.

Figure 1.11 in Chapter 1 showed the trace of **pred1** (in Chapter 1 called **predecessor**) produced for the above question. Figure 2.17 shows the

% Four versions of the predecessor program

% The original version

```
pred1( X, Z) :-
  parent( X, Z).

pred1( X, Z) :-
  parent( X, Y),
  pred1( Y, Z).
```

% Variation a: swap clauses of the original version

```
pred2( X, Z) :-
  parent( X, Y),
  pred2( Y, Z).

pred2( X, Z) :-
  parent( X, Z).
```

% Variation b: swap goals in second clause of the original version

```
pred3( X, Z) :-
  parent( X, Z).

pred3( X, Z) :-
  pred3( X, Y),
  parent( Y, Z).
```

% Variation c: swap goals and clauses of the original version

```
pred4( X, Z) :-
  pred4( X, Y),
  parent( Y, Z).

pred4( X, Z) :-
  parent( X, Z).
```

Figure 2.16   Four versions of the **predecessor** program.

corresponding traces for **pred2**, **pred3** and **pred4**. Figure 2.17(c) clearly shows that **pred4** is hopeless, and Figure 2.17(a) indicates that **pred2** is rather inefficient compared to **pred1**: **pred2** does much more searching and backtracking in the family tree.

This comparison should remind us of a general practical heuristic in problem solving: it is often useful to try the simplest idea first. In our case, all the versions of the **predecessor** relation are based on two ideas:

- the simpler idea is to check whether the two arguments of the **predecessor** relation satisfy the **parent** relation;

- the more complicated idea is to find somebody 'between' both people (somebody who is related to them by the **parent** and **predecessor** relations).

Of the four variations of the **predecessor** relation, **pred1** does simplest things first. On the contrary, **pred4** always tries complicated things first. **pred2** and **pred3** are in between the two extremes. Even without a detailed study of the execution traces, **pred1** should be clearly preferred merely on the grounds of the rule 'try simple things first'. This rule will be in general a useful guide in programming.

pred2(X,Z) :-
    parent(X,Y),
    pred2(Y,Z).

pred2(X,Z) :-
    parent(X,Z).

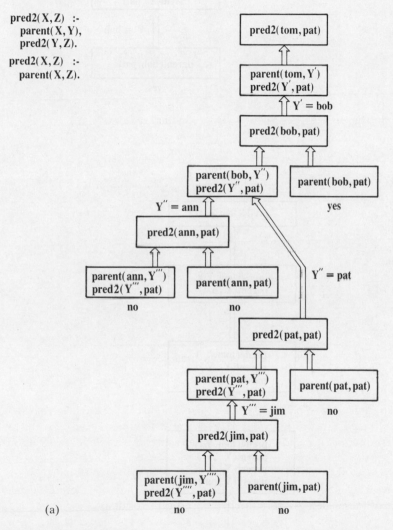

Figure 2.17 The behaviour of three formulations of the **predecessor** relation on the question: Is Tom a predecessor of Pat? *(continues)*

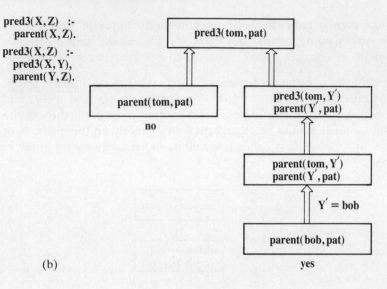

$$\text{pred3}(X, Z) :- \\ \quad \text{parent}(X, Z).$$

$$\text{pred3}(X, Z) :- \\ \quad \text{pred3}(X, Y), \\ \quad \text{parent}(Y, Z).$$

(b)

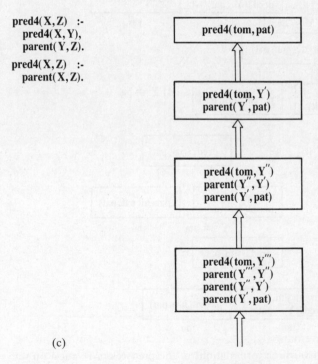

$$\text{pred4}(X, Z) :- \\ \quad \text{pred4}(X, Y), \\ \quad \text{parent}(Y, Z).$$

$$\text{pred4}(X, Z) :- \\ \quad \text{parent}(X, Z).$$

(c)

Figure 2.17 (cont.)

Our four variations of the **predecessor** procedure can be further compared by considering the question: What types of questions can particular variations answer, and what types can they not answer? It turns out that **pred1** and **pred2** are both able to reach an answer for any type of question about predecessors; **pred4** can never reach an answer; and **pred3** sometimes can and sometimes cannot. One example in which **pred3** fails is:

> ?- pred3(liz, jim).

This question again brings the system into an infinite sequence of recursive calls. Thus **pred3** also cannot be considered procedurally correct.

2.6.3   Combining declarative and procedural views

The foregoing section has shown that the order of goals and clauses does matter. Furthermore, there are programs that are declaratively correct, but do not work in practice. Such discrepancies between the declarative and procedural meaning may appear annoying. One may argue: Why not simply forget about the declarative meaning. This argument can be brought to an extreme with a clause such as

> predecessor(X, Z) :- predecessor(X, Z).

which is declaratively correct, but is completely useless as a working program.

The reason why we should not forget about the declarative meaning is that progress in programming technology is achieved by moving away from procedural details toward declarative aspects, which are normally easier to formulate and understand. The system itself, not the programmer, should carry the burden of filling in the procedural details. Prolog does help toward this end, although, as we have seen in this section, it only helps partially; it sometimes does work out the procedural details itself properly, and sometimes it does not. The philosophy adopted by many is that it is better to have at least *some* declarative meaning rather than *none* ('none' is the case in most other programming languages). The practical aspect of this view is that it is often rather easy to get a working program once we have a program that is declaratively correct. Consequently, a useful practical approach that often works is to concentrate on the declarative aspects of the problem, then test the resulting program on the computer, and if it fails procedurally try to rearrange the clauses and goals into a suitable order.

2.7   The relation between Prolog and logic

Prolog is related to mathematical logic, so its syntax and meaning can be specified most concisely with references to logic. Prolog is indeed often defined that way. However, such an introduction to Prolog assumes that the reader is familiar with certain concepts of mathematical logic. These concepts are, on the other hand, certainly not necessary for understanding and using Prolog as a programming tool, which is the aim of this book. For the reader who is especially interested in the relation between Prolog and logic, the following are some basic links to mathematical logic, together with some appropriate references.

Prolog's syntax is that of the *first-order predicate logic* formulas written in the so-called *clause form* (a conjunctive normal form in which quantifiers are not explicitly written), and further restricted to Horn clauses only (clauses that have at most one positive literal). Clocksin and Mellish (1981) give a Prolog program that transforms a first-order predicate calculus formula into the clause form. The procedural meaning of Prolog is based on the *resolution principle* for mechanical theorem proving introduced by Robinson in his classical paper (1965). Prolog uses a special strategy for resolution theorem proving called SLD. An introduction to the first-order predicate calculus and resolution-based theorem proving can be found in Nilsson 1981. Mathematical questions regarding the properties of Prolog's procedural meaning with respect to logic are analyzed by Lloyd (1984).

Matching in Prolog corresponds to what is called *unification* in logic. However, we avoid the word unification because matching, for efficiency reasons in most Prolog systems, is implemented in a way that does not exactly correspond to unification (see Exercise 2.10). But from the practical point of view this approximation to unification is quite adequate.

EXERCISE

2.10 What happens if we ask Prolog:

   ?-   X = f(X).

Should this request for matching succeed or fail? According to the definition of unification in logic this should fail, but what happens according to our definition of matching in Section 2.2? Try to explain why many Prolog implementations answer the question above with:

   X = f(f(f(f(f(f(f(f(f(f(f(f(f(...

SUMMARY

So far we have covered a kind of basic Prolog, also called 'pure Prolog'. It is 'pure' because it corresponds closely to formal logic. Extensions whose aim is to tailor the language toward some practical needs will be covered later in the book (Chapters 3, 5, 6, 7). Important points of this chapter are:

- Simple objects in Prolog are *atoms*, *variables* and *numbers*. Structured objects, or *structures*, are used to represent objects that have several components.

- Structures are constructed by means of *functors*. Each functor is defined by its name and arity.

- The type of object is recognized entirely by its syntactic form.

- The *lexical* scope of variables is one clause. Thus the same variable name in two clauses means two different variables.

- Structures can be naturally pictured as trees. Prolog can be viewed as a language for processing trees.

- The *matching* operation takes two terms and tries to make them identical by instantiating the variables in both terms.

- Matching, if it succeeds, results in the *most general* instantiation of variables.

- The *declarative semantics* of Prolog defines whether a goal is true with respect to a given program, and if it is true, for what instantiation of variables it is truc.

- A comma between goals means the conjunction of goals. A semicolon between goals means the disjunction of goals.

- The *procedural semantics* of Prolog is a procedure for satisfying a list of goals in the context of a given program. The procedure outputs the truth or falsity of the goal list and the corresponding instantiations of variables. The procedure automatically backtracks to examine alternatives.

- The declarative meaning of programs in 'pure Prolog' does not depend on the order of clauses and the order of goals in clauses.

- The procedural meaning does depend on the order of goals and clauses. Thus the order can affect the efficiency of the program; an unsuitable order may even lead to infinite recursive calls.

- Given a declaratively correct program, changing the order of clauses and goals can improve the program's efficiency while retaining its declarative correctness. Reordering is one method of preventing indefinite looping.

- There are other more general techniques, apart from reordering, to prevent indefinite looping and thereby make programs procedurally robust.

- Concepts discussed in this chapter are:

    data objects: atom, number, variable, structure
    term
    functor, arity of a functor
    principal functor of a term
    matching of terms
    most general instantiation
    declarative semantics
    instance of a clause, variant of a clause
    procedural semantics
    executing goals

References

Clocksin, W.F. and Mellish, C.S. (1981) *Programming in Prolog*. Springer-Verlag.

Lloyd, J.W. (1984) *Foundations of Logic Programming*. Springer-Verlag.

Nilsson, N.J. (1981) *Principles of Artificial Intelligence*. Tioga; also Springer-Verlag.

Robinson, A.J. (1965) A machine-oriented logic based on the resolution principle. *JACM* **12**: 23–41.

3 Lists, Operators, Arithmetic

3.1 Representation of lists
3.2 Some operations on lists
3.3 Operator notation
3.4 Arithmetic

In this chapter we will study a special notation for lists, one of the simplest and most useful structures, and some programs for typical operations on lists. We will also look at simple arithmetic and the operator notation which often improves the readability of programs. Basic Prolog of Chapter 2, extended with these three additions, becomes a convenient framework for writing interesting programs.

3.1   Representation of lists

The *list* is a simple data structure widely used in non-numeric programming. A list is a sequence of any number of items, such as **ann, tennis, tom, skiing**. Such a list can be written in Prolog as:

> [ann, tennis, tom, skiing]

This is, however, only the external appearance of lists. As we have already seen in Chapter 2, all structured objects in Prolog are trees. Lists are no exception to this.

How can a list be represented as a standard Prolog object? We have to consider two cases: the list is either empty or non-empty. In the first case, the list is simply written as a Prolog atom, [ ]. In the second case, the list can be viewed as consisting of two things:

(1)   the first item, called the *head* of the list;
(2)   the remaining part of the list, called the *tail*.

For our example list

> [ann, tennis, tom, skiing]

the head is **ann** and the tail is the list:

> [tennis, tom, skiing]

In general, the head can be anything (any Prolog object, for example, a tree or a variable); the tail has to be a list. The head and the tail are then combined into a structure by a special functor. The choice of this functor depends on the Prolog implementation; we will assume here that it is the dot:

> .(Head, Tail)

Since **Tail** is in turn a list, it is either empty or it has its own head and tail. Therefore, to represent lists of any length no additional principle is needed. Our example list is then represented as the term:

> .(ann, .(tennis, .(tom, .(skiing, [ ]))))

Figure 3.1 shows the corresponding tree structure. Note that the empty list appears in our term. This is because the one but last tail is a single item list:

> [skiing]

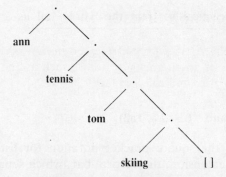

Figure 3.1   Tree representation of the list [ann, tennis, tom, skiing].

This list has the empty list as its tail:

[skiing] = .(skiing, [ ])

This example shows how the general principle for structuring data objects in Prolog also applies to lists of any length. As our example also shows, the straightforward notation with dots and possibly deep nesting of subterms in the tail part can produce rather confusing expressions. This is the reason why Prolog provides the neater notation for lists, so that they can be written as sequences of items enclosed in square brackets. A programmer can use both notations, but the square bracket notation is, of course, normally preferred. We will be aware, however, that this is only a cosmetic improvement and that our lists will be internally represented as binary trees. When such terms are output they will be automatically converted into their neater form. Thus the following conversation with Prolog is possible:

```
?- List1 = [a,b,c],
   List2 = .( a, .( b, .( c, [ ] ) ) ).

List1 = [a,b,c]
List2 = [a,b,c]

?- Hobbies1 = .( tennis, .( music, [ ] ) ),
   Hobbies2 = [ skiing, food],
   L = [ ann, Hobbies1, tom, Hobbies2].

Hobbies1 = [ tennis, music]
Hobbies2 = [ skiing, food]
L = [ ann, [tennis,music], tom, [skiing,food] ]
```

This example also reminds us that the elements of a list can be objects of any kind, in particular they can also be lists.

It is often practical to treat the whole tail as a single object. For example, let:

L = [a,b,c]

Then we could write:

Tail = [b,c]   and   L = .(a, Tail)

To express this in the square bracket notation for lists, Prolog provides another notational extension, the vertical bar, which separates the head and the tail:

L = [a | Tail]

The vertical bar notation is in fact more general: we can list any number of elements followed by '|' and the list of remaining items. Thus alternative ways of writing the above list are:

[a,b,c] = [a | [b,c]] = [a,b | [c]] = [a,b,c | [ ]]

To summarize:

- A list is a data structure that is either empty or consists of two parts: a *head* and a *tail*. The tail itself has to be a list.
- Lists are handled in Prolog as a special case of binary trees. For improved readability Prolog provides a special notation for lists, thus accepting lists written as:

    [Item1, Item2, ...]

or

    [Head | Tail]

or

    [Item1, Item2, ... | Others]

3.2 Some operations on lists

Lists can be used to represent sets although there is a difference: the order of elements in a set does not matter while the order of items in a list does; also, the same object can occur repeatedly in a list. Still, the most common operations on lists are similar to those on sets. Among them are:

- checking whether some object is an element of a list, which corresponds to checking for the set membership;

- concatenation of two lists, obtaining a third list, which may correspond to the union of sets;
- adding a new object to a list, or deleting some object from it.

In the remainder of this section we give programs for these and some other operations on lists.

3.2.1 Membership

Let us implement the membership relation as

    member(X, L)

where X is an object and L is a list. The goal member(X, L) is true if X occurs in L. For example,

    member(b, [a,b,c])

is true,

    member(b, [a,[b,c]])

is not true, but

    member([b,c], [a,[b,c]])

is true. The program for the membership relation can be based on the following observation:

    X is a member of L if either
    (1)   X is the head of L, or
    (2)   X is a member of the tail of L.

This can be written in two clauses, the first is a simple fact and the second is a rule:

    member(X, [X | Tail]).

    member(X, [Head | Tail]) :-
      member(X, Tail).

3.2.2 Concatenation

For concatenating lists we will define the relation:

    conc(L1, L2, L3)

Here L1 and L2 are two lists, and L3 is their concatenation. For example

conc([a,b], [c,d], [a,b,c,d])

is true, but

conc([a,b], [c,d], [a,b,a,c,d])

is false. In the definition of conc we will have again two cases, depending on the first argument, L1:

(1) If the first argument is the empty list then the second and the third arguments must be the same list (call it L); this is expressed by the following Prolog fact:

conc([ ], L, L).

(2) If the first argument of conc is a non-empty list then it has a head and a tail and must look like this:

[X | L1]

Figure 3.2 illustrates the concatenation of [X | L1] and some list L2. The result of the concatenation is the list [X | L3] where L3 is the concatenation of L1 and L2. In Prolog this is written as:

conc([X | L1], L2, [X | L3]) :-
conc(L1, L2, L3).

This program can now be used for concatenating given lists, for example:

?- conc([a,b,c], [1,2,3], L).

L = [a,b,c,1,2,3]

?- conc([a,[b,c],d], [a,[ ],b], L).

L = [a, [b,c], d, a, [ ], b]

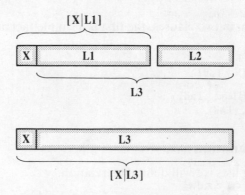

Figure 3.2 Concatenation of lists.

Although the conc program looks rather simple it can be used flexibly in many other ways. For example, we can use conc in the inverse direction for *decomposing* a given list into two lists, as follows:

```
?- conc( L1, L2, [a,b,c] ).
```

L1 = [ ]
L2 = [a,b,c];

L1 = [a]
L2 = [b,c];

L1 = [a,b]
L2 = [c];

L1 = [a,b,c]
L2 = [ ];

no

It is possible to decompose the list [a,b,c] in four ways, all of which were found by our program through backtracking.

We can also use our program to look for a certain pattern in a list. For example, we can find the months that precede and the months that follow a given month, as in the following goal: conc([], L, L).
conc([X|L1], L2, [X|L3]) :- conc(L1, L2, L3)

```
?- conc( Before, [may | After],
         [jan,feb,mar,apr,may,jun,jul,aug,sep,oct,nov,dec] ).
```

Before = [jan,feb,mar,apr]
After = [jun,jul,aug,sep,oct,nov,dec].

Further we can find the immediate predecessor and the immediate successor of May by asking:

```
?- conc( _, [Month1,may,Month2 | _],
         [jan,feb,mar,apr,may,jun,jul,aug,sep,oct,nov,dec] ).
```

Month1 = apr
Month2 = jun

Further still, we can, for example, delete from some list, L1, everything that follows three successive occurrences of z in L1 together with the three z's. For example:

```
?- L1 = [a,b,z,z,c,z,z,z,d,e],
   conc( L2, [z,z,z | _], L1).
```

L1 = [a,b,z,z,c,z,z,z,d,e]
L2 = [a,b,z,z,c]

We have already programmed the membership relation. Using conc, however, the membership relation could be elegantly programmed by the clause:

    member1(X, L) :-
        conc(L1, [X | L2], L).

This clause says: X is a member of list L if L can be decomposed into two lists so that the second one has X as its head. Of course, member1 defines the same relation as member. We have just used a different name to distinguish between the two implementations. Note that the above clause can be written using anonymous variables as:

    member1(X, L) :-
        conc(_, [X | _], L).

It is interesting to compare both implementations of the membership relation, member and member1. member has a rather straightforward procedural meaning, which is as follows:

> To check whether some X is a member of some list L:
> (1)   first check whether the head of L is equal to X, and then
> (2)   check whether X is a member of the tail of L.

On the other hand, the declarative reading of member1 is straightforward, but its procedural meaning is not so obvious. An interesting exercise is to find how member1 actually computes something. An example execution trace will give some idea: let us consider the question:

    ?- member1(b, [a,b,c]).

Figure 3.3 shows the execution trace. From the trace we can infer that member1 behaves similarly to member. It scans the list, element by element, until the item in question is found or the list is exhausted.

EXERCISES

3.1   (a)   Write a goal, using conc, to delete the last three elements from a list L producing another list L1. Hint: L is the concatenation of L1 and a three-element list.

   (b)   Write a sequence of goals to delete the first three elements and the last three elements from a list L producing list L2.

member1(x,L) :-
   conc(L1, [x|L2], L).

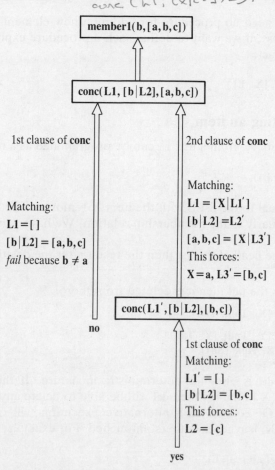

Figure 3.3 Procedure **member1** finds an item in a given list by sequentially searching the list.

3.2   Define the relation

last(Item, List)

so that Item is the last element of a list List. Write two versions:
(a) using the **conc** relation, (b) without **conc**.

3.2.3   Adding an item

To add an item to a list, it is easiest to put the new item in front of the list so that it becomes the new head. If X is the new item and the list to which X is added is L then the resulting list is simply:

[X | L]

So we actually need no procedure for adding a new element in front of the list. Nevertheless, if we want to define such a procedure explicitly, it can be written as the fact:

add(X, L, [X | L]).

3.2.4 Deleting an item

Deleting an item, X, from a list, L, can be programmed as a relation

del(X, L, L1)

where L1 is equal to the list L with the item X removed. The **del** relation can be defined similarly to the membership relation. We have, again, two cases:

(1)   If X is the head of the list then the result after the deletion is the tail of the list.

(2)   If X is in the tail then it is deleted from there.

del(X, [X | Tail], Tail).

del(X, [Y | Tail], [Y | Tail1]) :-
    del(X, Tail, Tail1).

Like **member**, **del** is also non-deterministic in nature. If there are several occurrences of X in the list then **del** will be able to delete anyone of them by backtracking. Of course, each alternative execution will only delete one occurrence of X, leaving the others untouched. For example:

?- del(a, [a,b,a,a], L).

L = [b,a,a];

L = [a,b,a];

L = [a,b,a];

no

del will fail if the list does not contain the item to be deleted.

del can also be used in the inverse direction, to add an item to a list by inserting the new item anywhere in the list. For example, if we want to insert a at any place in the list [1,2,3] then we can do this by asking the question: What is L such that after deleting a from L we obtain [1,2,3]?

?- del(a, L, [1,2,3]).

L = [a,1,2,3];

.   L = [1,a,2,3];

L = [1,2,a,3];

L = [1,2,3,a];

no

In general, the operation of inserting X at any place in some list **List** giving
BiggerList can be defined by the clause:

    insert(X, List, BiggerList) :-
        del(X, BiggerList, List).

In **member1** we elegantly implemented the membership relation by
using **conc**. We can also use **del** to test for membership. The idea is simple:
some X is a member of **List** if X can be deleted from **List**:

    member2(X, List) :-
        del(X, List, _).

3.2.5   Sublist

Let us now consider the **sublist** relation. This relation has two arguments, a list
L and a list S such that S occurs within L as its sublist. So

    sublist([c,d,e], [a,b,c,d,e,f])

is true, but

    sublist([c,e], [a,b,c,d,e,f])

is not. The Prolog program for **sublist** can be based on the same idea as
member1, only this time the relation is more general (see Figure 3.4).

Figure 3.4   The **member** and **sublist** relations.

Accordingly, the relation can be formulated as:

S is a sublist of L if

(1)   L can be decomposed into two lists, L1 and L2, and

(2)   L2 can be decomposed into two lists, S and some L3.

As we have seen before, the **conc** relation can be used for decomposing lists. So the above formulation can be expressed in Prolog as:

```
sublist( S, L) :-
    conc( L1, L2, L),
    conc( S, L3, L2).
```

Of course, the **sublist** procedure can be used flexibly in several ways. Although it was designed to check if some list occurs as a sublist within another list it can also be used, for example, to find all sublists of a given list:

```
?- sublist( S, [a,b,c] ).

S = [ ];

S = [a];

S = [a,b];

S = [a,b,c];

S = [b];

...
```

3.2.6   Permutations

Sometimes it is useful to generate permutations of a given list. To this end, we will define the **permutation** relation with two arguments. The arguments are two lists such that one is a permutation of the other. The intention is to generate permutations of a list through backtracking using the **permutation** procedure, as in the following example:

```
?- permutation( [a,b,c], P).

P = [a,b,c];

P = [a,c,b];

P = [b,a,c];

...
```

insert **X** obtaining a permutation of [**X**|**L**]

Figure 3.5   One way of constructing a permutation of the list [X | L].

The program for **permutation** can be, again, based on the consideration of two cases, depending on the first list:

(1)   If the first list is empty then the second list must also be empty.

(2)   If the first list is not empty then it has the form [X | L], and a permutation of such a list can be constructed as shown in Figure 3.5: first permute L obtaining L1 and then insert X at any position into L1.

Two Prolog clauses that correspond to these two cases are:

```
permutation( [ ], [ ] ).

permutation( [X | L], P) :-
   permutation( L, L1),
   insert( X, L1, P).
```

One alternative to this program would be to delete an element, X, from the first list, permute the rest of it obtaining a list P, and then add X in front of P. The corresponding program is:

```
permutation2( [ ], [ ] ).

permutation2( L, [X | P] ) :-
   del( X, L, L1),
   permutation2( L1, P).
```

It is instructive to do some experiments with our permutation programs. Its normal use would be something like this:

```
?- permutation( [red,blue,green], P).
```

This would result in all six permutations, as intended:

P = [red, blue, green];

P = [red, green, blue];

P = [blue, red, green];

P = [blue, green, red];

P = [green, red, blue];

P = [green, blue, red];

no

Another attempt to use **permutation** is:

?- permutation(L, [a,b,c]).

Our first version, **permutation**, will now instantiate L successfully to all six permutations. If the user then requests more solutions, the program would never answer 'no' because it would get into an infinite loop trying to find another permutation when there is none. Our second version, **permutation2**, will in this case find only the first (identical) permutation and then immediately get into an infinite loop. Thus, some care is necessary when using these **permutation** relations.

EXERCISES

3.3   Define two predicates

evenlength(List)   and   **oddlength(List)**

so that they are true if their argument is a list of even or odd length respectively. For example, the list [a,b,c,d] is 'evenlength' and [a,b,c] is 'oddlength'.

3.4   Define the relation

reverse(List, ReversedList)

that reverses lists. For example, **reverse([a,b,c,d], [d,c,b,a])**.

3.5   Define the predicate **palindrome(List)**. A list is a palindrome if it reads the same in the forward and in the backward direction. For example, [m,a,d,a,m].

3.6   Define the relation

shift(List1, List2)

so that List2 is List1 'shifted rotationally' by one element to the left. For example,

```
?- shift( [1,2,3,4,5], L1),
   shift( L1, L2).
```

produces:

```
L1 = [2,3,4,5,1]
L2 = [3,4,5,1,2]
```

3.7   Define the relation

> translate(List1, List2)

to translate a list of numbers between 0 and 9 to a list of the corresponding words. For example:

> translate([3,5,1,3], [three,five,one,three])

Use the following as an auxiliary relation:

> means(0, zero). means(1, one). means(2, two). . . .

3.8   Define the relation

> subset(Set, Subset)

where Set and Subset are two lists representing two sets. We would like to be able to use this relation not only to check for the subset relation, but also to generate all possible subsets of a given set. For example:

> ?- subset([a,b,c], S).
>
> S = [a,b,c];
>
> S = [b,c];
>
> S = [c];
>
> S = [ ];
>
> S = [a,c];
>
> S = [a];
>
> . . .

3.9   Define the relation

> dividelist(List, List1, List2)

so that the elements of List are partitioned between List1 and List2, and List1 and List2 are of approximately the same length. For example, dividelist([a,b,c,d,e], [a,c,e], [b,d]).

3.10 Rewrite the monkey and banana program of Chapter 2 as the relation

canget(State, Actions)

to answer not just 'yes' or 'no', but to produce a sequence of monkey's actions represented as a list of moves. For example:

Actions = [walk(door,window), push(window,middle), climb, grasp]

3.11 Define the relation

flatten(List, FlatList)

where List can be a list of lists, and FlatList is List 'flattened' so that the elements of List's sublists (or sub-sublists) are reorganized as one plain list. For example:

?- flatten([a,b,[c,d],[ ],[[[e]]],f], L).

L = [a,b,c,d,e,f]

3.3 Operator notation

In mathematics we are used to writing expressions like

$2*a + b*c$

where + and * are operators, and 2, a, b, c are arguments. In particular, + and * are said to be *infix* operators because they appear *between* the two arguments. Such expressions can be represented as trees, as in Figure 3.6, and can be written as Prolog terms with + and * as functors:

+(*(2,a), *(b,c))

Since we would normally prefer to have such expressions written in the usual, infix style with operators, Prolog caters for this notational convenience. Prolog will therefore accept our expression written simply as:

2*a + b*c

This will be, however, only the external representation of this object, which will be automatically converted into the usual form of Prolog terms. Such a term will be output for the user, again, in its external, infix form.

Thus operators in Prolog are merely a notational extension. If we write a + b, Prolog will handle it exactly as if it had been written +(a,b). In order that Prolog properly understands expressions such as a + b*c, Prolog has to know that * binds stronger than +. We say that + has higher precedence than *. So the precedence of operators decides what is the correct interpretation of

Figure 3.6   Tree representation of the expression 2*a + b*c.

expressions. For example, the expression a + b*c can be, in principle, understood either as

> +(a, *(b,c))

or as

> *(+(a,b), c)

The general rule is that the operator with the highest precedence is the
principal functor of the term. If expressions containing + and * are to be
understood according to our normal conventions, then + has to have a higher
precedence than *. Then the expression a + b*c means the same as a + (b*c). If
another interpretation is intended, then it has to be explicitly indicated by
parentheses – for example, (a + b)*c.

   A programmer can define his or her own operators. So, for example,
we can define the atoms **has** and **supports** as infix operators and then write in
the program facts like:

> **peter has information,**
> **floor supports table.**

These facts are exactly equivalent to:

> **has(peter, information).**
> **supports(floor, table).**

   A programmer can define new operators by inserting into the program
special kinds of clauses, sometimes called *directives*, which act as operator
definitions. An operator definition must appear in the program before any
expression containing that operator. For our example, the operator **has** can be
properly defined by the directive:

> **:- op(600, xfx, has).**

This tells Prolog that we want to use 'has' as an operator, whose precedence is
600 and its type is 'xfx', which is a kind of infix operator. The form of the

specifier 'xfx' suggests that the operator, denoted by 'f', is between the two arguments denoted by 'x'.

Notice that operator definitions do not specify any operation or action. In principle, *no operation on data is associated with an operator* (except in very special cases). Operators are normally used, as functors, only to combine objects into structures and not to invoke actions on data, although the word 'operator' appears to suggest an action.

Operator names are atoms, and their precedence must be in some range which depends on the implementation. We will assume that the range is between 1 and 1200.

There are three groups of operator types which are indicated by type specifiers such as **xfx**. The three groups are:

(1)   infix operators of three types:

     xfx   xfy   yfx

(2)   prefix operators of two types:

     fx   fy

(3)   postfix operators of two types:

     xf   yf

The specifiers are chosen so as to reflect the structure of the expression where 'f' represents the operator and 'x' and 'y' represent arguments. An 'f' appearing between the arguments indicates that the operator is infix. The prefix and postfix specifiers have only one argument, which follows or precedes the operator respectively.

There is a difference between 'x' and 'y'. To explain this we need to introduce the notion of the *precedence of argument*. If an argument is enclosed in parentheses or it is an unstructured object then its precedence is 0; if an argument is a structure then its precedence is equal to the precedence of its principal functor. 'x' represents an argument whose precedence must be strictly lower than that of the operator. 'y' represents an argument whose precedence is lower or equal to that of the operator.

These rules help to disambiguate expressions with several operators of the same precedence. For example, the expression

    a − b − c

is normally understood as **(a − b) − c**, and not as **a − (b − c)**. To achieve the normal interpretation the operator ' − ' has to be defined as **yfx**. Figure 3.7 shows why the second interpretation is then ruled out.

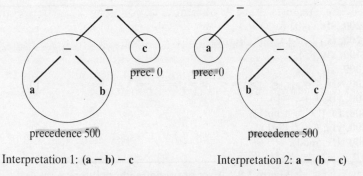

Interpretation 1: **(a − b) − c**   Interpretation 2: **a − (b − c)**

Figure 3.7 Two interpretations of the expression **a − b − c** assuming that '−' has precedence 500. If '−' is of type **yfx**, then interpretation 2 is invalid because the precedence of **b − c** is not less than the precedence of '−'.

As another example consider the prefix operator **not**. If **not** is defined as **fy** then the expression

not not p

is legal; but if **not** is defined as **fx** then this expression is illegal because the argument to the first **not** is **not p**, which has the same precedence as **not** itself. In this case the expression has to be written with parentheses:

not(not p)

For convenience, some operators are predefined in the Prolog system so that they can be readily used and no definition is needed for them. What these operators are and what their precedences are depends on the implementation of Prolog. We will assume that this set of 'standard' operators is as if defined by the clauses in Figure 3.8. As Figure 3.8 also shows, several operators can be declared by one clause if they all have the same precedence and if they are all of the same type. In this case the operators' names are written as a list.

The use of operators can greatly improve the readability of programs. As an example let us assume that we are writing a program for manipulating Boolean expressions. In such a program we may want to state, for example, one of de Morgan's equivalence theorems, which can in mathematics be written as:

~(A & B) <==>   ~A v ~B

One way to state this in Prolog is by the clause:

equivalence(not(and(A, B)), or(not(A), not(B))).

```
:- op( 1200, xfx, ':-').
:- op( 1200, fx [ :-, ?-] ).
:- op( 1100, xfy, ';').
:- op( 1000, xfy, ',').
:- op( 700, xfx, [ =, is, < , > , =< , >= , == , = \ =, \ ==, =:=] ).
:- op( 500, yfx, [ + , −] ).
:- op( 500, fx, [ + , −, not] ).
:- op( 400, yfx, [ *, /, div] ).
:- op( 300, xfx, mod).
```

Figure 3.8 A set of predefined operators.

However, it is in general a good programming practice to try to retain as much resemblance as possible between the original problem notation and the notation used in the program. In our example, this can be achieved almost completely by using operators. A suitable set of operators for our purpose can be defined as:

```
:- op( 800, xfx, <===>).
:- op( 700, xfy, v).
:- op( 600, xfy, &).
:- op( 500, fy, ~).
```

Now the de Morgan's theorem can be written as the fact:

~(A & B) <===> ~A v ~B.

According to our specification of operators above, this term is understood as shown in Figure 3.9.

To summarize:

- The readability of programs can be often improved by using the operator notation. Operators can be infix, prefix or postfix.

- In principle, no operation on data is associated with an operator except in special cases. Operator definitions do not define any action, they only introduce new notation. Operators, as functors, only hold together components of structures.

- A programmer can define his or her own operators. Each operator is defined by its name, precedence and type.

- The precedence is an integer within some range, say between 1 and 1200. The operator with the highest precedence in the expression is the principal functor of the expression. Operators with lowest precedence bind strongest.

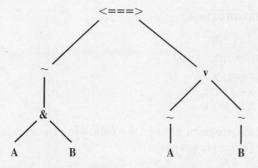

Figure 3.9 Interpretation of the term ~(A & B) <===> ~A v ~B.

● The type of the operator depends on two things: (1) the position of the operator with respect to the arguments, and (2) the precedence of the arguments compared to the precedence of the operator itself. In a specifier like xfy, x indicates an argument whose precedence is strictly lower than that of the operator; y indicates an argument whose precedence is less or equal to that of the operator.

EXERCISES

3.12 Assuming the operator definitions

        :- op(300, xfx, plays).
        :- op(200, xfy, and).

then the following two terms are syntactically legal objects:

        Term1 = jimmy plays football and squash
        Term2 = susan plays tennis and basketball and volleyball

How are these terms understood by Prolog? What are their principal functors and what is their structure?

3.13 Suggest an appropriate definition of operators ('was', 'of', 'the') to be able to write clauses like

        diana was the secretary of the department.

and then ask Prolog:

        ?- Who was the secretary of the department.
        Who = diana

        ?- diana was What.
        What = the secretary of the department

3.14   Consider the program:

```
t( 0+1, 1+0).
t( X+0+1, X+1+0).
t( X+1+1, Z) :-
    t( X+1, X1),
    t( X1+1, Z).
```

How will this program answer the following questions if '+' is an infix operator of type **yfx** (as usual):

(a)   ?- t(0+1, A).

(b)   ?- t(0+1+1, B).

(c)   ?- t(1+0+1+1+1, C).

(d)   ?- t(D, 1+1+1+0).

3.15   In the previous section, relations involving lists were written as:

```
member( Element, List),
conc( List1, List2, List3),
del( Element, List, NewList), ...
```

Suppose that we would prefer to write these relations as:

```
Element in List,
concatenating List1 and List2 gives List3,
deleting Element from List gives NewList, ...
```

Define 'in', 'concatenating', 'and', etc. as operators to make this possible. Also, redefine the corresponding procedures.

3.4   Arithmetic

Prolog is mainly a language for symbolic computation where the need for numerical calculation is comparatively modest. Accordingly, the means for numerical computing in Prolog are also rather simple. Some of the predefined operators can be used for basic arithmetic operations. These are:

+	addition
−	subtraction
*	multiplication
/	division
mod	modulo, the remainder of integer division

Notice that this is an exceptional case in which an operator may in fact invoke an operation. But even in such cases an additional indication to perform the action will be necessary. Prolog knows how to carry out the calculation denoted by these operators, but this is not entirely sufficient for direct use. The following question is a naive attempt to request arithmetic computation:

> ?- X = 1 + 2.

Prolog will 'quietly' answer

> X = 1 + 2

and not X = 3 as we might possibly expect. The reason is simple: the expression 1 + 2 merely denotes a Prolog term where + is the functor and 1 and 2 are its arguments. There is nothing in the above goal to force Prolog to actually activate the addition operation. A special predefined operator, is, is provided to circumvent this problem. The is operator will force evaluation. So the right way to invoke arithmetic is:

> ?- X is 1 + 2.

Now the answer will be:

> X = 3

The addition here was carried out by a special procedure that is associated with the operator is. We call such procedures *built-in procedures*.

There is no generally agreed notational convention for arithmetic in Prolog, so different implementations of Prolog may use somewhat different notations. For example, the '/' operator may denote integer division or real division, depending on the implementation. In this book, we will assume that '/' denotes real division, and that the div operator denotes integer division. Accordingly, the question

> ?- X is 3/2,
>   Y is 3 div 2.

is answered by:

> X = 1.5
> Y = 1

The left argument of the is operator is a simple object. The right argument is an arithmetic expression composed of arithmetic operators, numbers and variables. Since the is operator will force the evaluation, all the variables in the expression must already be instantiated to numbers at the time of execution of this goal. The precedence of the predefined arithmetic operators (see Figure 3.8) is such that the associativity of arguments with operators is the same as normally in mathematics. Parentheses can be used to indicate different associations. Note that +, −, *, / and **div** are defined as **yfx**, which means that evaluation is carried out from left to right. For example,

> X is 5 − 2 − 1

is interpreted as:

> X is (5 − 2) − 1

Arithmetic is also involved when *comparing* numerical values. We can, for example, test whether the product of 277 and 37 is greater than 10000 by the goal:

> ?- 277 * 37 > 10000.
>
> yes

Note that, similarly to **is**, the '>' operator also forces the evaluation.

Suppose that we have in the program a relation **born** that relates the names of people with their birth years. Then we can retrieve the names of people born between 1950 and 1960 inclusive with the following question:

> ?- born(Name, Year),
>   Year >= 1950,
>   Year =< 1960.

The comparison operators are as follows:

X	> Y	X is greater than Y
X	< Y	X is less than Y
X	>= Y	X is greater than or equal to Y
X	=< Y	X is less than or equal to Y
X	=:= Y	the values of X and Y are equal
X	= \ = Y	the values of X and Y are not equal

Notice the difference between the matching operator '=' and '=:='; for example, in the goals X = Y and X =:= Y. The first goal will cause the matching of the objects X and Y, and will, if X and Y match, possibly instantiate some variables in X and Y. There will be no evaluation. On the other hand, X =:= Y causes the arithmetic evaluation and cannot cause any instantiation of variables. These differences are illustrated by the following examples:

```
?- 1 + 2 = := 2 + 1.

yes

?- 1 + 2 = 2 + 1.

no

?- 1 + A = B + 2.

A = 2
B = 1
```

Let us further illustrate the use of arithmetic operations by two simple examples. The first is computing the greatest common divisor; the second, counting the items in a list.

Given two positive integers, X and Y, their greatest common divisor, D, can be found according to three cases:

(1)   If X and Y are equal then D is equal to X.

(2)   If $X < Y$ then D is equal to the greatest common divisor of X and the difference $Y - X$.

(3)   If $Y < X$ then do the same as in case (2) with X and Y interchanged.

It can be easily shown by an example that these three rules actually work. Choosing, for example, $X = 20$ and $Y = 25$, the above rules would give $D = 5$ after a sequence of subtractions.

These rules can be formulated into a Prolog program by defining a three-argument relation, say:

```
gcd( X, Y, D)
```

The three rules are then expressed as three clauses, as follows:

```
gcd( X, X, X).

gcd( X, Y, D) :-
    X < Y,
    Y1 is Y - X,
    gcd( X, Y1, D).

gcd( X, Y, D) :-
    Y < X,
    gcd( Y, X, D).
```

Of course, the last goal in the third clause could be equivalently replaced by the two goals:

X1 is X − Y,
gcd(X1, Y, D)

Our next example involves counting, which usually requires some arithmetic. An example of such a task is to establish the length of a list; that is, we have to count the items in the list. Let us define the procedure

length(List, N)

which will count the elements in a list **List** and instantiate N to their number. As was the case with our previous relations involving lists, it is useful to consider two cases:

(1)   If the list is empty then its length is 0.
(2)   If the list is not empty then **List** = [Head | Tail]; then its length is equal to 1 plus the length of the tail **Tail**.

These two cases correspond to the following program:

length([ ], 0).

length([_ | Tail], N) :-
  length(Tail, N1),
  N is 1 + N1.

An application of **length** can be:

?- length([a,b,[c,d],e], N).

N = 4

Note that in the second clause of **length**, the two goals of the body cannot be swapped. The reason for this is that N1 has to be instantiated before the goal

N is 1 + N1

can be processed. With the built-in procedure **is**, a relation has been introduced that is sensitive to the order of processing and therefore the procedural considerations have become vital.

It is interesting to see what happens if we try to program the **length** relation without the use of **is**. Such an attempt can be:

length1([ ], 0).

```
length1( [_ | Tail], N)  :-
   length1( Tail, N1),
   N = 1 + N1.
```

Now the goal

```
?- length1( [a,b,[c,d],e], N).
```

will produce the answer:

```
N = 1+(1+(1+(1+0))).
```

The addition was never explicitly forced and was therefore not carried out at all. But in length1 we can, unlike in length, swap the goals in the second clause:

```
length1( [_ | Tail], N)  :-
   N = 1 + N1,
   length1( Tail, N1).
```

This version of length1 will produce the same result as the original version. It can also be written shorter, as follows,

```
length1( [_ | Tail], 1 + N)  :-
   length1( Tail, N).
```

still producing the same result. We can, however, use length1 to find the number of elements in a list as follows:

```
?- length1( [a,b,c], N), Length is N.

N = 1+(1+(1+0))
Length = 3
```

To summarize:

- Built-in procedures can be used for doing arithmetic.

- Arithmetic operations have to be explicitly requested by the built-in procedure **is**. There are built-in procedures associated with the pre-defined operators +, −, ∗, /, **div** and **mod**.

- At the time that evaluation is carried out, all arguments must be already instantiated to numbers.

- The values of arithmetic expressions can be compared by operators such as <, =<, etc. These operators force the evaluation of their arguments.

EXERCISES

3.16 Define the relation

max(X, Y, Max)

so that **Max** is the greater of two numbers X and Y.

3.17 Define the predicate

maxlist(List, Max)

so that **Max** is the greatest number in the list of numbers **List**.

3.18 Define the predicate

sumlist(List, Sum)

so that **Sum** is the sum of a given list of numbers **List**.

3.19 Define the predicate

ordered(List)

which is true if **List** is an ordered list of numbers. For example,
ordered([1,5,6,6,9,12]).

3.20 Define the predicate

subsum(Set, Sum, SubSet)

so that **Set** is a list of numbers, **SubSet** is a subset of these numbers,
and the sum of the numbers in **SubSet** is **Sum**. For example:

?- subsum([1,2,5,3,2], 5, Sub).

Sub = [1,2,2];
Sub = [2,3];
Sub = [5];
. . .

3.21 Define the procedure

between(N1, N2, X)

which, for two given integers N1 and N2, generates through
backtracking all the integers X that satisfy the constraint
$N1 \leq X \leq N2$.

3.22 Define the operators 'if', 'then', 'else' and ':=' so that the following becomes a legal term:

> if X > Y then Z := X else Z := Y

Choose the precedences so that 'if' will be the principal functor. Then define the relation 'if' as a small interpreter for a kind of 'if-then-else' statement of the form

> if Val1 > Val2 then Var := Val3 else Var := Val4

where **Val1**, **Val2**, **Val3** and **Val4** are numbers (or variables instantiated to numbers) and **Var** is a variable. The meaning of the 'if' relation should be: if the value of **Val1** is greater than the value of **Val2** then **Var** is instantiated to **Val3**, otherwise to **Val4**. Here is an example of the use of this interpreter:

> ?- X = 2, Y = 3,
>   Val2 is 2*X,
>   Val4 is 4*X,
>   if Y > Val2 then Z := Y else Z := Val4,
>   if Z > 5 then W := 1 else W := 0.
>
> X = 2
> Y = 3
> Z = 8
> W = 1
> Val2 = 4
> Val4 = 8

SUMMARY

- The list is a frequently used structure. It is either empty or consists of a *head* and a *tail* which is a list as well. Prolog provides a special notation for lists.

- Common operations on lists, programmed in this chapter, are: list membership, concatenation, adding an item, deleting an item, sublist.

- The *operator notation* allows the programmer to tailor the syntax of programs toward particular needs. Using operators the readability of programs can be greatly improved.

- New operators are defined by the directive op, stating the name of an operator, its type and precedence.

- In principle, there is no operation associated with an operator; operators are merely a syntactic device providing an alternative syntax for terms.

- Arithmetic is done by built-in procedures. Evaluation of an arithmetic expression is forced by the procedure is and by the comparison predicates <, =<, etc.

- Concepts introduced in this chapter are:

  list, head of list, tail of list
  list notation
  operators, operator notation
  infix, prefix and suffix operators
  precedence of an operator
  arithmetic built-in procedures

4 Using Structures: Example Programs

4.1 Retrieving structured information from a database
4.2 Doing data abstraction
4.3 Simulating a non-deterministic automaton
4.4 Travel planning
4.5 The eight queens problem

Data structures, with matching, backtracking and arithmetic, are a powerful programming tool. In this chapter we will develop the skill of using this tool through programming examples: retrieving structured information from a database, simulating a non-deterministic automaton, travel planning and eight queens on the chessboard. We will also see how the principle of data abstraction can be carried out in Prolog.

4.1 Retrieving structured information from a database

This exercise develops the skill of representing and manipulating structured data objects. It also illustrates Prolog as a natural database query language.

A database can be naturally represented in Prolog as a set of facts. For example, a database about families can be represented so that each family is described by one clause. Figure 4.1 shows how the information about each family can be structured. Each family has three components: husband, wife and children. As the number of children varies from family to family the children are represented by a list that is capable of accommodating any number of items. Each person is, in turn, represented by a structure of four components: name, surname, date of birth, job. The job information is 'unemployed', or it specifies the working organization and salary. The family of Figure 4.1 can be stored in the database by the clause:

```
family(
    person( tom, fox, date(7,may,1950), works(bbc,15200) ),
    person( ann, fox, date(9,may,1951), unemployed),
    [ person( pat, fox, date(5,may,1973), unemployed),
      person( jim, fox, date(5,may,1973), unemployed) ] ).
```

Our database would then be comprised of a sequence of facts like this describing all families that are of interest to our program.

Prolog is, in fact, a very suitable language for retrieving the desired information from such a database. One nice thing about Prolog is that we can refer to objects without actually specifying all the components of these objects. We can merely indicate the *structure* of objects that we are interested in, and leave the particular components in the structures unspecified or only partially specified. Figure 4.2 shows some examples. So we can refer to all

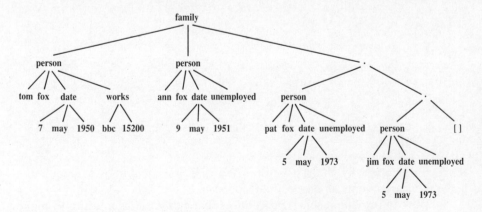

Figure 4.1 Structuring information about the family.

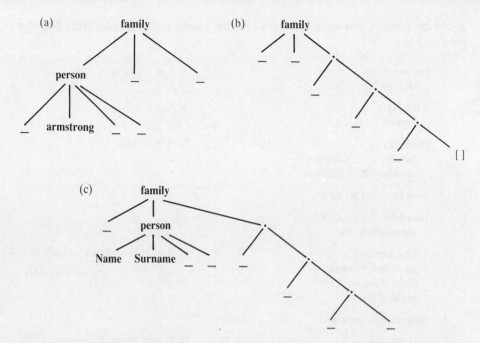

Figure 4.2   Specifying objects by their structural properties: (a) any Armstrong family; (b) any family with exactly three children; (c) any family with at least three children. Structure (c) makes provision for retrieving the wife's name through the instantiation of the variables **Name** and **Surname**.

Armstrong families by:

> family(person(_, armstrong, _, _), _, _)

The underscore characters denote different anonymous variables; we do not care about their values. Further, we can refer to all families with three children by the term:

> family(_, _, [_, _, _])

To find all married women that have at least three children we can pose the question:

> ?- family(_, person(Name, Surname, _, _), [_, _, _ | _]).

The point of these examples is that we can specify objects of interest not by their content, but by their structure. We only indicate their structure and leave their arguments as unspecified slots.

   We can provide a set of procedures that can serve as a utility to make the interaction with the database more comfortable. Such utility procedures could be part of the user interface. Some useful utility procedures for our database are:

```
husband( X) :-                          % X is a husband
   family( X, _, _).

wife( X) :-                             % X is a wife
   family( _, X, _).

child( X) :-                            % X is a child
   family( _, _, Children),
   member( X, Children).

member( X, [X | L] ).

member( X, [Y | L] ) :-
   member( X, L).

exists( Person) :-                      % Any person in the database
   husband( Person);
   wife( Person);
   child( Person).

dateofbirth( person( _, _, Date, _), Date).

salary( person( _, _, _, works( _, S) ), S).    % Salary of working person

salary( person( _, _, _, unemployed), 0).       % Salary of unemployed
```

We can use these utilities, for example, in the following queries to the database:

- Find the names of all the people in the database:

  ```
  ?- exists( person( Name, Surname, _, _) ).
  ```

- Find all children born in 1981:

  ```
  ?- child( X),
     dateofbirth( X, date( _, _, 1981) ).
  ```

- Find all employed wives:

  ```
  ?- wife( person( Name, Surname, _, works( _, _) ) ).
  ```

- Find the names of unemployed people who were born before 1963:

  ```
  ?- exists( person( Name, Surname, date( _, _, Year), unemployed) ),
     Year < 1963.
  ```

- Find people born before 1950 whose salary is less than 8000:

  ```
  ?- exists( Person),
     dateofbirth( Person, date( _, _, Year) ),
     Year < 1950,
     salary( Person, Salary),
     Salary < 8000.
  ```

- Find the names of families with at least three children:

    ?- family(person(_, Name, _, _), _, [_, _, _ | _]).

To calculate the total income of a family it is useful to define the sum of salaries of a list of people as a two-argument relation:

total(List_of_people, Sum_of_their_salaries)

This relation can be programmed as:

total([ ], 0).	% Empty list of people
total([Person | List], Sum) :-	
salary(Person, S),	% S: salary of first person
total(List, Rest),	% Rest: sum of salaries of others
Sum is S + Rest.	

The total income of families can then be found by the question:

    ?- family(Husband, Wife, Children),
       total([Husband, Wife | Children], Income).

Let the **length** relation count the number of elements of a list, as defined in Section 3.4. Then we can specify all families that have an income per family member of less than 2000 by:

    ?- family(Husband, Wife, Children),
       total([Husband, Wife | Children], Income),
       length([Husband, Wife | Children], N),   % N: size of family
       Income/N < 2000.

EXERCISES

4.1   Write queries to find the following from the family database:

   (a)   names of families without children;

   (b)   all employed children;

   (c)   names of families with employed wives and unemployed husbands;

   (d)   all the children whose parents differ in age by at least 15 years.

4.2 Define the relation

twins(Child1, Child2)

to find twins in the family database.

4.2 Doing data abstraction

Data abstraction can be viewed as a process of organizing various pieces of information into natural units (possibly hierarchically), thus structuring the information into some conceptually meaningful form. Each such unit of information should be easily accessible in the program. Ideally, all the details of implementing such a structure should be invisible to the user of the structure – the programmer can then just concentrate on objects and relations between them. The point of the process is to make the use of information possible without the programmer having to think about the details of how the information is actually represented.

Let us discuss one way of carrying out this principle in Prolog. Consider our family example of the previous section again. Each family is a collection of pieces of information. These pieces are all clustered into natural units such as a person or a family, so they can be treated as single objects. Assume again that the family information is structured as in Figure 4.1. In the previous section, each family was represented by a Prolog clause. Here, a family will be represented as a structured object, for example:

FoxFamily = family(person(tom, fox, _, _), _, _)

Let us now define some relations through which the user can access particular components of a family without knowing the details of Figure 4.1. Such relations can be called *selectors* as they select particular components. The name of such a selector relation will be the name of the component to be selected. The relation will have two arguments: first, the object that contains the component, and second, the component itself:

selector_relation(Object, Component_selected)

Here are some selectors for the family structure:

husband(family(Husband, _, _), Husband).

wife(family(_, Wife, _), Wife).

children(family(_, _, ChildList), ChildList).

We can also define selectors for particular children:

>   firstchild(Family, First) :-
>   children(Family, [First | _]).
>
>   secondchild(Family, Second) :-
>   children(Family, [_, Second | _]).
>
>   ...

We can generalize this to selecting the Nth child:

>   nthchild(N, Family, Child) :-
>   children(Family, ChildList),
>   nth_member(N, ChildList, Child).   % Nth element of a list

Another interesting object is a person. Some related selectors according to Figure 4.1 are:

>   firstname(person(Name, _, _, _), Name).
>
>   surname(person(_, Surname, _, _), Surname).
>
>   born(person(_, _, Date, _), Date).

How can we benefit from selector relations? Having defined them, we can now forget about the particular way that structured information is represented. To create and manipulate this information, we just have to know the names of the selector relations and use these in the rest of the program. In the case of complicated representations, this is easier than always referring to the representation explicitly. In our family example in particular, the user does not have to know that the children are represented as a list. For example, assume that we want to say that Tom Fox and Jim Fox belong to the same family and that Jim is the second child of Tom. Using the selector relations above, we can define two persons, call them **Person1** and **Person2**, and the family. The following list of goals does this:

>   firstname(Person1, tom), surname(Person1, fox),   % Person1 is Tom Fox
>   firstname(Person2, jim), surname(Person2, fox),   % Person2 is Jim Fox
>   husband(Family, Person1),
>   secondchild(Family, Person2)

As a result, the variables **Person1**, **Person2** and **Family** are instantiated as:

>   Person1 = person(tom, fox, _, _)
>   Person2 = person(jim, fox, _, _)
>   Family = family(person(tom, fox, _, _), _, [_, person(jim, fox) | _])

The use of selector relations also makes programs easier to modify. Imagine that we would like to improve the efficiency of a program by changing the representation of data. All we have to do is to change the definitions of the selector relations, and the rest of the program will work unchanged with the new representation.

EXERCISE

4.3 Complete the definition of **nthchild** by defining the relation

nth_member(N, List, X)

which is true if X is the Nth member of **List**.

4.3   Simulating a non-deterministic automaton

This exercise shows how an abstract mathematical construct can be translated into Prolog. In addition, our resulting program will be much more flexible than initially intended.

A *non-deterministic finite automaton* is an abstract machine that reads as input a string of symbols and decides whether to *accept* or to *reject* the input string. An automaton has a number of *states* and it is always in one of the states. It can change its state by moving from the current state to another state. The internal structure of the automaton can be represented by a transition graph such as that in Figure 4.3. In this example, s_1, s_2, s_3 and s_4 are the *states* of the automaton. Starting from the initial state (s_1 in our example), the automaton moves from state to state while reading the input string. Transitions depend on the current input symbol, as indicated by the arc labels in the transition graph.

A transition occurs each time an input symbol is read. Note that transitions can be non-deterministic. In Figure 4.3, if the automaton is in state s_1 and the current input symbol is *a* then it can transit into s_1 or s_2. Some arcs are labelled *null* denoting the 'null symbol'. These arcs correspond to 'silent moves' of the automaton. Such a move is said to be *silent* because it occurs without any reading of input, and the observer, viewing the automaton as a black box, will not be able to notice that any transition has occurred.

The state s_3 is double circled, which indicates that it is a *final state*. The automaton is said to *accept* the input string if there is a transition path in the

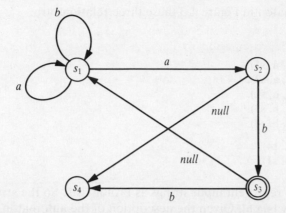

Figure 4.3 An example of a non-deterministic finite automaton.

graph such that

(1) it starts with the initial state,

(2) it ends with a final state, and

(3) the arc labels along the path correspond to the complete input string.

It is entirely up to the automaton to decide which of the possible moves to execute at any time. In particular, the automaton may choose to make or not to make a silent move, if it is available in the current state. But abstract non-deterministic machines of this kind have a magic property: if there is a choice then they always choose a 'right' move; that is, a move that leads to the acceptance of the input string, if such a move exists. The automaton in Figure 4.3 will, for example, accept the strings *ab* and *aabaab*, but it will reject the strings *abb* and *abba*. It is easy to see that this automaton accepts any string that terminates with *ab*, and rejects all others.

In Prolog, an automaton can be specified by three relations:

(1) A unary relation **final** which defines the final states of the automaton;

(2) A three-argument relation **trans** which defines the state transitions so that

> **trans(S1, X, S2)**

means that a transition from a state S1 to S2 is possible when the current input symbol X is read.

(3) A binary relation

> **silent(S1, S2)**

meaning that a silent move is possible from S1 to S2.

For the automaton in Figure 4.3 these three relations are:

    final(s3).

    trans(s1, a, s1).
    trans(s1, a, s2).
    trans(s1, b, s1).
    trans(s2, b, s3).
    trans(s3, b, s4).

    silent(s2, s4).
    silent(s3, s1).

We will represent input strings as Prolog lists. So the string *aab* will be represented by [a,a,b]. Given the description of the automaton, the simulator will process a given input string and decide whether the string is accepted or rejected. By definition, the non-deterministic automaton accepts a given string if (starting from an initial state), after having read the whole input string, the automaton can (possibly) be in its final state. The simulator is programmed as a binary relation, **accepts**, which defines the acceptance of a string from a given state. So

    accepts(State, String)

is true if the automaton, starting from the state **State** as initial state, accepts the string **String**. The **accepts** relation can be defined by three clauses. They correspond to the following three cases:

(1)   The empty string, [ ], is accepted from a state **State** if **State** is a final state.

(2)   A non-empty string is accepted from **State** if reading the first symbol in the string can bring the automaton into some state **State1**, and the rest of the string is accepted from **State1**. Figure 4.4(a) illustrates.

(3)   A string is accepted from **State** if the automaton can make a silent move from **State** to **State1** and then accept the (whole) input string from **State1**. Figure 4.4(b) illustrates.

These rules can be translated into Prolog as:

    accepts(State, [ ]) :-   % Accept empty string
      final(State).

    accepts(State, [X | Rest]) :-   % Accept by reading first symbol
      trans(State, X, State1),
      accepts(State1, Rest).

    accepts(State, String) :-   % Accept by making silent move
      silent(State, State1),
      accepts(State1, String).

Figure 4.4   Accepting a string: (a) by reading its first symbol X; (b) by making a silent move.

The program can be asked, for example, about the acceptance of the string *aaab* by:

    ?- accepts(s1, [a,a,a,b]).

    yes

As we have already seen, Prolog programs are often able to solve more general problems than problems for which they were originally developed. In our case, we can also ask the simulator which state our automaton can be in initially so that it will accept the string *ab*:

    ?- accepts(S, [a,b]).

    S = s1;

    S = s3

Amusingly, we can also ask: What are all the strings of length 3 that are accepted from state s_1?

    ?- accepts(s1, [X1,X2,X3]).

    X1 = a
    X2 = a
    X3 = b;

    X1 = b
    X2 = a
    X3 = b;

    no

If we prefer the acceptable input strings to be typed out as lists then we can formulate the question as:

?- String = [_, _, _], accepts(s1, String).

String = [a,a,b];

String = [b,a,b];

no

We can make further experiments asking even more general questions, such as: From what states will the automaton accept input strings of length 7?

Further experimentation could involve modifications in the structure of the automaton by changing the relations **final**, **trans** and **silent**. The automaton in Figure 4.3 does not contain any cyclic 'silent path' (a path that consists only of silent moves). If in Figure 4.3 a new transition

silent(s1, s3)

is added then a 'silent cycle' is created. But our simulator may now get into trouble. For example, the question

?- accepts(s1, [a]).

would induce the simulator to cycle in state s_1 indefinitely, all the time hoping to find some way to the final state.

EXERCISES

4.4 Why could cycling not occur in the simulation of the original automaton in Figure 4.3, when there was no 'silent cycle' in the transition graph?

4.5 Cycling in the execution of **accepts** can be prevented, for example, by counting the number of moves made so far. The simulator would then be requested to search only for paths of some limited length. Modify the **accepts** relation this way. Hint: Add a third argument: the maximum number of moves allowed:

accepts(State, String, MaxMoves)

4.4   Travel planning

In this section we will construct a program that gives advice on planning air travel. The program will be a rather simple advisor, yet it will be able to answer some useful questions, such as:

- What days of the week is there a direct flight from London to Ljubljana?
- How can I get from Ljubljana to Edinburgh on Thursday?
- I have to visit Milan, Ljubljana and Zurich, starting from London on Tuesday and returning to London on Friday. In what sequence should I visit these cities so that I have no more than one flight each day of the tour?

The program will be centred around a database holding the flight information. This will be represented as a three-argument relation

   timetable(Place1, Place2, List_of_flights)

where List_of_flights is a list of structured items of the form:

   Departure_time / Arrival_time / Flight_number / List_of_days

List_of_days is either a list of weekdays or the atom 'alldays'. One clause of the timetable relation can be, for example:

   timetable(london, edinburgh,
         [9:40 / 10:50 / ba4733 / alldays,
            19:40 / 20:50 / ba4833 / [mo,tu,we,th,fr,su]]).

The times are represented as structured objects with two components, hours and minutes, combined by the operator ':'.
   The main problem is to find exact routes between two given cities on a given day of the week. This will be programmed as a four-argument relation:

   route(Place1, Place2, Day, Route)

Here Route is a sequence of flights that satisfies the following criteria:

(1)   the start point of the route is Place1;
(2)   the end point is Place2;
(3)   all the flights are on the same day of the week, Day;
(4)   all the flights in Route are in the timetable relation;
(5)   there is enough time for transfer between flights.

The route is represented as a list of structured objects of the form:

> From - To : Flight_number : Departure_time

We will also use the following auxiliary predicates:

(1)   flight(Place1, Place2, Day, Flight_num, Dep_time, Arr_time)

This says that there is a flight, Flight_num, between Place1 and Place2 on the day of the week Day with the specified departure and arrival times.

(2)   deptime(Route, Time)

Departure time of Route is Time.

(3)   transfer(Time1, Time2)

There is at least 40 minutes between Time1 and Time2, which should be sufficient for transfer between two flights.

The problem of finding a route is reminiscent of the simulation of the non-deterministic automaton of the previous section. The similarities of both problems are as follows:

- The states of the automaton correspond to the cities.
- A transition between two states corresponds to a flight between two cities.
- The transition relation of the automaton corresponds to the timetable relation.
- The automaton simulator finds a path in the transition graph between the initial state and a final state; the travel planner finds a route between the start city and the end city of the tour.

Not surprisingly, therefore, the route relation can be defined similarly to the accepts relation, with the exception that here we have no 'silent moves'. We have two cases:

(1)   Direct flight connection: if there is a direct flight between places Place1 and Place2 then the route consists of this flight only:

> route(Place1, Place2, Day, [Place1-Place2 : Fnum : Dep]) :-
>   flight(Place1, Place2, Day, Fnum, Dep, Arr).

(2)   Indirect flight connection: the route between places P1 and P2 consists of the first flight, from P1 to some intermediate place P3, followed by a route between P3 to P2. In addition, there must be enough time between the arrival of the first flight and the departure of the second flight for transfer.

```
        route( P1, P2, Day, [P1-P3 : Fnum1 : Dep1 | Route] )  :-
            route( P3, P2, Day, Route),
            flight( P1, P3, Day, Fnum1, Dep1, Arr1),
            deptime( Route, Dep2),
            transfer( Arr1, Dep2).
```

The auxiliary relations **flight**, **transfer** and **deptime** are easily programmed and are included in the complete travel planning program in Figure 4.5. Also included is an example timetable database.

Our route planner is extremely simple and may examine paths that obviously lead nowhere. Yet it will suffice if the flight database is not large.

Figure 4.5   A flight route planner and an example flight timetable.

```
% A FLIGHT ROUTE PLANNER

:-  op( 50, xfy, :).

% route( Place1, Place2, Day, Route):
%     Route is a sequence of flights on Day, starting at Place1, ending at Place2

route( P1, P2, Day, [P1-P2 : Fnum : Deptime] )  :-          % Direct flight
    flight( P1, P2, Day, Fnum, Deptime, _).

route( P1, P2, Day, [P1-P3 : Fnum1 : Dep1 | Route] )  :-    % Indirect connection
    route( P3, P2, Day, Route),
    flight( P1, P3, Day, Fnum1, Dep1, Arr1),
    deptime( Route, Dep2),                                  % Departure time of Route
    transfer( Arr1, Dep2).                                  % Enough time for transfer

flight( Place1, Place2, Day, Fnum, Deptime, Arrtime)  :-
    timetable( Place1, Place2, Flightlist),
    member( Deptime / Arrtime / Fnum / Daylist , Flightlist),
    flyday( Day, Daylist).

flyday( Day, Daylist)  :-
    member( Day, Daylist).

flyday( Day, alldays)  :-
    member( Day, [mo,tu,we,th,fr,sa,su] ).

deptime( [P1-P2 : Fnum : Dep | _], Dep).

transfer( Hours1:Mins1, Hours2:Mins2)  :-
    60 * (Hours2 - Hours1) + Mins2 - Mins1 >= 40.

member( X, [X | L] ).

member( X, [Y | L] )  :-
    member( X, L).
```

(continues)

Figure 4.5 (cont.)

% A FLIGHT DATABASE

timetable(edinburgh, london,
        [9:40 / 10:50 / ba4733 / alldays,
          13:40 / 14:50 / ba4773 / alldays,
          19:40 / 20:50 / ba4833 / [mo,tu,we,th,fr,su]]).

timetable(london, edinburgh,
        [9:40 / 10:50 / ba4732 / alldays,
          11:40 / 12:50 / ba4752 / alldays,
          18:40 / 19:50 / ba4822 / [mo,tu,we,th,fr]]).

timetable(london, ljubljana,
        [13:20 / 16:20 / ju201 / [fr],
          13:20 / 16:20 / ju213 / [su]]).

timetable(london, zurich,
        [9:10 / 11:45 / ba614 / alldays,
          14:45 / 17:20 / sr805 / alldays]).

timetable(london, milan,
        [8:30 / 11:20 / ba510 / alldays,
          11:00 / 13:50 / az459 / alldays]).

timetable(ljubljana, zurich,
        [11:30 / 12:40 / ju322 / [tu,th]]).

timetable(ljubljana, london,
        [11:10 / 12:20 / yu200 / [fr],
          11:25 / 12:20 / yu212 / [su]]).

timetable(milan, london,
        [9:10 / 10:00 / az458 / alldays,
          12:20 / 13:10 / ba511 / alldays]).

timetable(milan, zurich,
        [9:25 / 10:15 / sr621 / alldays,
          12:45 / 13:35 / sr623 / alldays]).

timetable(zurich, ljubljana,
        [13:30 / 14:40 / yu323 / [tu,th]]).

timetable(zurich, london,
        [9:00 / 9:40 / ba613 / [mo,tu,we,th,fr,sa],
          16:10 / 16:55 / sr806 / [mo,tu,we,th,fr,su]]).

timetable(zurich, milan,
        [7:55 / 8:45 / sr620 / alldays]).

A really large database would require more intelligent planning to cope with the large number of potential candidate paths.

Some example questions to the program are as follows:

- What days of the week is there a direct flight from London to Ljubljana?

  ?- flight(london, ljubljana, Day, _, _, _).

  Day = fr;

  Day = su;

  no

- How can I get from Ljubljana to Edinburgh on Thursday?

  ?- route(ljubljana, edinburgh, th, R).

  R = [ljubljana-zurich:yu322:11:30, zurich-london:sr806:16:10,
      london-edinburgh:ba4822:18:40]

- How can I visit Milan, Ljubljana and Zurich, starting from London on Tuesday and returning to London on Friday, with no more than one flight each day of the tour? This question is somewhat trickier. It can be formulated by using the **permutation** relation, programmed in Chapter 3. We are asking for a permutation of the cities Milan, Ljubljana and Zurich such that the corresponding flights are possible on successive days:

  ?- permutation([milan, ljubljana, zurich], [City1, City2, City3]),
      flight(london, City1, tu, FN1, Dep1, Arr1),
      flight(City1, City2, we, FN2, Dep2, Arr2),
      flight(City2, City3, th, FN3, Dep3, Arr3),
      flight(City3, london, fr, FN4, Dep4, Arr4).

  City1 = milan
  City2 = zurich
  City3 = ljubljana
  FN1 = ba510
  Dep1 = 8:30
  Arr1 = 11:20
  FN2 = sr621
  Dep2 = 9:25
  Arr2 = 10:15
  FN3 = yu323
  Dep3 = 13:30
  Arr3 = 14:40
  FN4 = yu200
  Dep4 = 11:10
  Arr4 = 12:20

4.5   The eight queens problem

The problem here is to place eight queens on the empty chessboard in such a way that no queen attacks any other queen. The solution will be programmed as a unary predicate

solution(Pos)

which is true if and only if Pos represents a position with eight queens that do not attack each other. It will be interesting to compare various ideas for programming this problem. Therefore we will present three programs based on somewhat different representations of the problem.

4.5.1   Program 1

First we have to choose a representation of the board position. One natural choice is to represent the position by a list of eight items, each of them corresponding to one queen. Each item in the list will specify a square of the board on which the corresponding queen is sitting. Further, each square can be specified by a pair of coordinates (X and Y) on the board, where each coordinate is an integer between 1 and 8. In the program we can write such a pair as

X/Y

where, of course, the '/' operator is not meant to indicate division, but simply combines both coordinates together into a square. Figure 4.6 shows one solution of the eight queens problem and its list representation.

Having chosen this representation, the problem is to find such a list of the form

[X1/Y1, X2/Y2, X3/Y3, . . . , X8/Y8]

which satisfies the no-attack requirement. Our procedure solution will have to search for a proper instantiation of the variables X1, Y1, X2, Y2, . . . , X8, Y8. As we know that all the queens will have to be in different columns to prevent vertical attacks, we can immediately constrain the choice and so make the search task easier. We can thus fix the X-coordinates so that the solution list will fit the following, more specific template:

[1/Y1, 2/Y2, 3/Y3, . . . , 8/Y8]

We are interested in the solution on a board of size 8 by 8. However, in programming, in general, the key to the solution is often in considering a more general problem. Paradoxically, it is often the case that the solution for

Figure 4.6   A solution to the eight queens problem. This position can be specified by the list [1/4, 2/2, 3/7, 4/3, 5/6, 6/8, 7/5, 8/1].

the more general problem is easier to formulate than that for the more specific, original problem; then the original problem is simply solved as a special case of the more general problem.

The creative part of the problem is to find the correct generalization of the original problem. In our case, a good idea is to generalize the number of queens (the number of columns in the list) from 8 to any number, including zero. The **solution** relation can then be formulated by considering two cases:

Case 1   The list of queens is empty: the empty list is certainly a solution because there is no attack.

Case 2   The list of queens is non-empty: then it looks like this:

[X/Y | Others]

In case 2, the first queen is at some square X/Y and the other queens are at squares specified by the list Others. If this is to be a solution then the following conditions must hold:

(1)   There must be no attack between the queens in the list Others; that is, Others itself must also be a solution.

(2)   X and Y must be integers between 1 and 8.

(3)   A queen at square X/Y must not attack any of the queens in the list Others.

To program the first condition we can simply use the **solution** relation itself. The second condition can be specified as follows: Y will have to be a member of the list of integers between 1 and 8 – that is, [1,2,3,4,5,6,7,8]. On the other hand, we do not have to worry about X since the solution list will have to match the template in which the X-coordinates are already specified. So X will be guaranteed to have a proper value between 1 and 8. We can implement the third condition as another relation, **noattack**. All this can then be written in Prolog as follows:

```
solution( [X/Y | Others] ) :-
    solution( Others),
    member( Y, [1,2,3,4,5,6,7,8] ),
    noattack( X/Y, Others).
```

It now remains to define the **noattack** relation:

```
noattack( Q, Qlist)
```

Again, this can be broken down into two cases:

(1)   If the list **Qlist** is empty then the relation is certainly true because there is no queen to be attacked.

(2)   If **Qlist** is not empty then it has the form [**Q1** | **Qlist1**] and two conditions must be satisfied:

(a)   the queen at Q must not attack the queen at Q1, and
(b)   the queen at Q must not attack any of the queens in **Qlist1**.

To specify that a queen at some square does not attack another square is easy: the two squares must not be in the same row, the same column or the same diagonal. Our solution template guarantees that all the queens are in different columns, so it only remains to specify explicitly that:

●   the Y-coordinates of the queens are different, and
●   they are not in the same diagonal, either upward or downward; that is, the distance between the squares in the X-direction must not be equal to that in the Y-direction.

Figure 4.7 shows the complete program. To alleviate its use a template list has been added. This list can be retrieved in a question for generating solutions. So we can now ask

```
?- template( S), solution( S).
```

and the program will generate solutions as follows:

```
S = [ 1/4, 2/2, 3/7, 4/3, 5/6, 6/8, 7/5, 8/1];
S = [ 1/5, 2/2, 3/4, 4/7, 5/3, 6/8, 7/6, 8/1];
S = [ 1/3, 2/5, 3/2, 4/8, 5/6, 6/4, 7/7, 8/1];
...
```

% solution(BoardPosition) if BoardPosition is a list of non-attacking queens

solution([ ]).

solution([X/Y | Others]) :-   % First queen at X/Y, other queens at Others
   solution(Others),
   member(Y, [1,2,3,4,5,6,7,8]),
   noattack(X/Y, Others).   % First queen does not attack others

noattack(_, [ ]).   % Nothing to attack

noattack(X/Y, [X1/Y1 | Others]) :-
   Y = \ = Y1,   % Different Y-coordinates
   Y1-Y = \ = X1-X,   % Different diagonals
   Y1-Y = \ = X-X1,
   noattack(X/Y, Others).

member(Item, [Item | Rest]).

member(Item, [First | Rest]) :-
   member(Item, Rest).

% A solution template

template([1/Y1,2/Y2,3/Y3,4/Y4,5/Y5,6/Y6,7/Y7,8/Y8]).

Figure 4.7   Program 1 for the eight queens problem.

EXERCISE

4.6   When searching for a solution, the program of Figure 4.7 explores alternative values for the Y-coordinates of the queens. At which place in the program is the order of alternatives defined? How can we easily modify the program to change the order? Experiment with different orders with the view of studying the executional efficiency of the program.

4.5.2   Program 2

In the board representation of program 1, each solution had the form

   [1/Y1, 2/Y2, 3/Y3, ..., 8/Y8]

because the queens were simply placed in consecutive columns. No information is lost if the X-coordinates were omitted. So a more economical representation of the board position can be used, retaining only the Y-coordinates of the queens:

   [Y1, Y2, Y3, ..., Y8]

To prevent the horizontal attacks, no two queens can be in the same row. This imposes a constraint on the Y-coordinates. The queens have to occupy all the rows 1, 2, ..., 8. The choice that remains is the *order* of these eight numbers. Each solution is therefore represented by a permutation of the list

```
[1,2,3,4,5,6,7,8]
```

Such a permutation, S, is a solution if all the queens are safe. So we can write:

```
solution( S) :-
    permutation( [1,2,3,4,5,6,7,8], S),
    safe( S).
```

We have already programmed the **permutation** relation in Chapter 3, but the **safe** relation remains to be specified. We can split its definition into two cases:

(1)   S is the empty list: this is certainly safe as there is nothing to be attacked.

(2)   S is a non-empty list of the form [Queen | Others]. This is safe if the list **Others** is safe, and **Queen** does not attack any queen in the list **Others**.

In Prolog, this is:

```
safe( [ ] ).

safe( [Queen | Others] ) :-
    safe( Others),
    noattack( Queen, Others).
```

The **noattack** relation here is slightly trickier. The difficulty is that the queens' positions are only defined by their Y-coordinates, and the X-coordinates are not explicitly present. This problem can be circumvented by a small generalization of the **noattack** relation, as illustrated in Figure 4.8. The goal

noattack(Queen,Others)

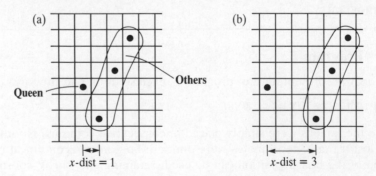

Figure 4.8 (a) X-distance between **Queen** and **Others** is 1. (b) X-distance between **Queen** and **Others** is 3.

is meant to ensure that Queen does not attack Others when the X-distance between Queen and Others is equal to 1. What is needed is the generalization of the X-distance between Queen and Others. So we add this distance as the third argument of the noattack relation:

> noattack(Queen, Others, Xdist)

Accordingly, the noattack goal in the safe relation has to be modified to

> noattack(Queen, Others, 1)

The noattack relation can now be formulated according to two cases, depending on the list Others: if Others is empty then there is no target and certainly no attack; if Others is non-empty then Queen must not attack the first queen in Others (which is Xdist columns from Queen) and also the tail of Others at Xdist + 1. This leads to the program shown in Figure 4.9.

```
% solution( Queens) if Queens is a list of Y-coordinates of eight non-attacking queens

solution( Queens) :-
   permutation( [1,2,3,4,5,6,7,8], Queens),
   safe( Queens).

permutation( [ ], [ ] ).

permutation( [Head | Tail], PermList) :-
   permutation( Tail, PermTail),
   del( Head, PermList, PermTail).          % Insert Head in permuted Tail

% del( Item, List, NewList): deleting Item from List gives NewList

del( Item, [Item | List], List).

del( Item, [First | List], [First | List1] ) :-
   del( Item, List, List1).

% safe( Queens) if Queens is a list of Y-coordinates of non-attacking queens

safe( [ ] ).

safe( [Queen | Others] ) :-
   safe( Others),
   noattack( Queen, Others, 1).

noattack( _, [ ], _).

noattack( Y, [Y1 | Ylist], Xdist) :-
   Y1-Y =\= Xdist,
   Y-Y1 =\= Xdist,
   Dist1 is Xdist + 1,
   noattack( Y, Ylist, Dist1).
```

Figure 4.9   Program 2 for the eight queens problem.

4.5.3   Program 3

Our third program for the eight queens problem will be based on the following reasoning. Each queen has to be placed on some square; that is, into some column, some row, some upward diagonal and some downward diagonal. To make sure that all the queens are safe, each queen must be placed in a different column, a different row, a different upward and a different downward diagonal. It is thus natural to consider a richer representation system with four coordinates:

    x columns
    y rows
    u upward diagonals
    v downward diagonals

The coordinates are not independent: given x and y, u and v are determined (Figure 4.10 illustrates). For example, as:

$$u = x - y$$

$$v = x + y$$

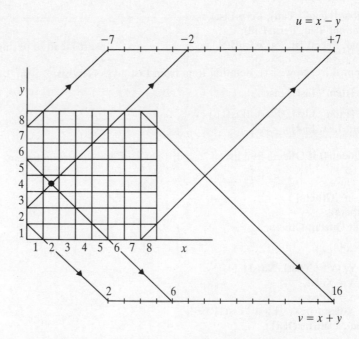

Figure 4.10   The relation between columns, rows, upward and downward diagonals. The indicated square has coordinates: $x = 2$, $y = 4$, $u = 2 - 4 = -2$, $v = 2 + 4 = 6$.

The domains for all four dimensions are:

Dx = [1,2,3,4,5,6,7,8]

Dy = [1,2,3,4,5,6,7,8]

Du = [−7,−6,−5,−4,−3,−2,−1,0,1,2,3,4,5,6,7]

Dv = [2,3,4,5,6,7,8,9,10,11,12,13,14,15,16]

The eight queens problem can now be stated as follows: select eight 4-tuples (X,Y,U,V) from the domains (X from Dx, Y from Dy, etc.), never using the same element twice from any of the domains. Of course, once X and Y are chosen, U and V are determined. The solution can then be, roughly speaking, as follows: given all four domains, select the position of the first queen, delete the corresponding items from the four domains, and then use the rest of the domains for placing the rest of the queens. A program based on this idea is shown in Figure 4.11. The board position is, again, represented by a list of Y-coordinates. The key relation in this program is

  sol(Ylist, Dx, Dy, Du, Dv)

which instantiates the Y-coordinates (in **Ylist**) of the queens, assuming that they are placed in consecutive columns taken from Dx. All Y-coordinates and

---

% solution(Ylist) if Ylist is a list of Y-coordinates of eight non-attacking queens

```
solution( Ylist) :-
  sol( Ylist,                                   % Y-coordinates of queens
      [1,2,3,4,5,6,7,8],                        % Domain for Y-coordinates
      [1,2,3,4,5,6,7,8],                        % Domain for X-coordinates
      [−7,−6,−5,−4,−3,−2,−1,0,1,2,3,4,5,6,7],   % Upward diagonals
      [2,3,4,5,6,7,8,9,10,11,12,13,14,15,16] ). % Downward diagonals

sol( [ ], [ ], Dy, Du, Dv).

sol( [Y | Ylist], [X | Dx1], Dy, Du, Dv) :-
  del( Y, Dy, Dy1),                             % Choose a Y-coordinate
  U is X−Y,                                      % Corresponding upward diagonal
  del( U, Du, Du1),                             % Remove it
  V is X+Y,                                      % Corresponding downward diagonal
  del( V, Dv, Dv1),                             % Remove it
  sol( Ylist, Dx1, Dy1, Du1, Dv1).              % Use remaining values

del( Item, [Item | List], List).

del( Item, [First | List], [First | List1] ) :-
  del( Item, List, List1).
```

Figure 4.11   Program 3 for the eight queens problem.

the corresponding U and V-coordinates are taken from the lists Dy, Du and Dv. The top procedure, solution, can be invoked by the question:

>   ?- solution(S).

This will cause the invocation of sol with the complete domains that correspond to the problem space of eight queens.

The sol procedure is general in the sense that it can be used for solving the N-queens problem (on a chessboard of size N by N). It is only necessary to properly set up the domains Dx, Dy, etc.

It is practical to mechanize the generation of the domains. For that we need a procedure

>   gen(N1, N2, List)

which will, for two given integers N1 and N2, produce the list:

>   List = [N1, N1 + 1, N1 + 2, ..., N2 − 1, N2]

Such a procedure is:

```
gen( N, N, [N] ).

gen( N1, N2, [N1 | List] ) :-
    N1 < N2,
    M is N1 + 1,
    gen( M, N2, List).
```

The top level relation, solution, has to be accordingly generalized to

>   solution(N, S)

where N is the size of the board and S is a solution represented as a list of Y-coordinates of N queens. The generalized solution relation is:

```
solution( N, S) :-
    gen( 1, N, Dxy),                    % Dxy – domain for X and Y
    Nu1 is 1 − N, Nu2 is N − 1,
    gen( Nu1, Nu2, Du),
    Nv2 is N + N,
    gen( 2, Nv2, Dv),
    sol( S, Dxy, Dxy, Du, Dv).
```

For example, a solution to the 12-queens problem would be generated by:

>   ?- solution(12, S).
>
>   S = [1,3,5,8,10,12,6,11,2,7,9,4]

4.5.4 Concluding remarks

The three solutions to the eight queens problem show how the same problem can be approached in different ways. We also varied the representation of data. Sometimes the representation was more economical, sometimes it was more explicit and partially redundant. The drawback of the more economical representation is that some information always has to be recomputed when it is required.

At several points, the key step toward the solution was to generalize the problem. Paradoxically, by considering a more general problem, the solution became easier to formulate. This generalization principle is a kind of standard technique that can often be applied.

Of the three programs, the third one illustrates best how to approach general problems of constructing under constraints a structure from a given set of elements.

A natural question is: Which of the three programs is most efficient? In this respect, program 2 is far inferior while the other two programs are similar. The reason is that permutation-based program 2 constructs complete permutations while the other two programs are able to recognize and reject unsafe permutations when they are only partially constructed. Program 3 is the most efficient. It avoids some of the arithmetic computation that is essentially captured in the redundant board representation this program uses.

EXERCISE

4.7   Let the squares of the chessboard be represented by pairs of their coordinates of the form **X/Y**, where both X and Y are between 1 and 8.

(a)   Define the relation **jump(Square1, Square2)** according to the knight jump on the chessboard. Assume that **Square1** is always instantiated to a square while **Square2** can be uninstantiated. For example:

   ?- jump(1/1, S).

   S = 3/2;

   S = 2/3;

   no

(b)   Define the relation **knightpath(Path)** where **Path** is a list of squares that represent a legal path of a knight on the empty chessboard.

(c)   Using this **knightpath** relation, write a question to find any knight's path of length 4 moves from square 2/1 to the opposite edge of the board (Y = 8) that goes through square 5/4 after the second move.

SUMMARY

The examples of this chapter illustrate some strong points and characteristic features of Prolog programming:

- A database can be naturally represented as a set of Prolog facts.
- Prolog's mechanisms of querying and matching can be flexibly used for retrieving structured information from a database. In addition, utility procedures can be easily defined to further alleviate the interaction with a particular database.
- *Data abstraction* can be viewed as a programming technique that makes the use of complex data structures easier, and contributes to the clarity of programs. It is easy in Prolog to carry out the essential principles of data abstraction.
- Abstract mathematical constructs, such as automata, can often be readily translated into executable Prolog definitions.
- As in the case of eight queens, the same problem can be approached in different ways by varying the representation of the problem. Often, introducing redundancy into the representation saves computation. This entails trading space for time.
- Often, the key step toward a solution is to generalize the problem. Paradoxically, by considering a more general problem the solution may become easier to formulate.

5 Controlling Backtracking

5.1 Preventing backtracking
5.2 Examples using cut
5.3 Negation as failure
5.4 Problems with cut and negation

We have already seen that a programmer can control the execution of a program through the ordering of clauses and goals. In this chapter we will look at another control facility, called 'cut', for preventing backtracking. The cut also extends the expressive power of Prolog and enables the definition of a kind of negation, called 'negation as failure' and associated with the 'closed world assumption'.

5.1 Preventing backtracking

Prolog will automatically backtrack if this is necessary for satisfying a goal. Automatic backtracking is a useful programming concept because it relieves the programmer of the burden of programming backtracking explicitly. On the other hand, uncontrolled backtracking may cause inefficiency in a program. Therefore we sometimes want to control, or to prevent, backtracking. We can do this in Prolog by using the 'cut' facility.

Let us first study the behaviour of a simple example program whose execution involves some unnecessary backtracking. We will identify those points at which the backtracking is useless and leads to inefficiency.

Consider the double-step function shown in Figure 5.1. The relation between X and Y can be specified by three rules:

Rule 1:   if $X < 3$ then $Y = 0$
Rule 2:   if $3 \leq X$ and $X < 6$ then $Y = 2$
Rule 3:   if $6 \leq X$ then $Y = 4$

This can be written in Prolog as a binary relation

    f(X, Y)

as follows:

```
f( X, 0) :- X < 3.            % Rule 1
f( X, 2) :- 3 =< X, X < 6.    % Rule 2
f( X, 4) :- 6 =< X.           % Rule 3
```

This program, of course, assumes that before f(X, Y) is executed X is already instantiated to a number, as this is required by the comparison operators.

We will make two experiments with this program. Each experiment will reveal some source of inefficiency in the program, and we will remove each source in turn by using the cut mechanism.

Figure 5.1   A double-step function.

5.1.1 Experiment 1

Let us analyze what happens when the following question is posed:

?- f(1, Y), 2 < Y.

When executing the first goal, f(1, Y), Y becomes instantiated to 0. So the second goal becomes

2 < 0

which fails, and so does the whole goal list. This is straightforward, but before admitting that the goal list is not satisfiable, Prolog tries, through backtracking, two useless alternatives. The detailed trace is shown in Figure 5.2.

The three rules about the f relation are mutually exclusive so that one of them at most will succeed. Therefore we, not Prolog, know that as soon as one rule succeeds there is no point in trying to use the others, as they are bound to fail. In the example of Figure 5.2, rule 1 has become known to succeed at the point indicated by 'CUT'. In order to prevent futile backtracking at this point we have to tell Prolog explicitly *not* to backtrack. We can do this by using the cut mechanism. The 'cut' is written as ! and is inserted between goals as a kind of pseudo-goal. Our program, rewritten with cuts, is:

f(X, 0) :- X < 3, !.

f(X, 2) :- 3 =< X, X < 6, !.

f(X, 4) :- 6 =< X.

The ! symbol will now prevent backtracking at the points that it appears in the program. If we now ask

?- f(1, Y), 2 < Y.

Prolog will produce the same left-hand branch as in Figure 5.2. This branch will fail at the goal 2 < 0. Now Prolog will try to backtrack, but not beyond the point marked ! in the program. The alternative branches that correspond to 'rule 2' and 'rule 3' will not be generated.

The new program, equipped with cuts, is in general more efficient than the original version without cuts. When the execution fails, the new program will in general recognize this sooner than the original program.

To conclude, we have improved the efficiency by adding cuts. If the cuts are now removed in this example, the program will still produce the same result; it will perhaps only spend more time. It can be said that, in our case, by introducing the cut we only changed the procedural meaning of the program; that is, the declarative meaning was not affected. We will see later that using a cut may affect the declarative meaning as well.

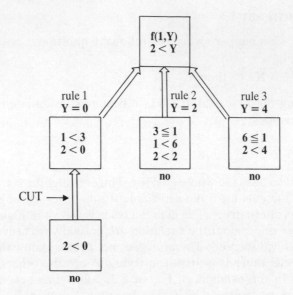

Figure 5.2 At the point marked 'CUT' we already know that the rules 2 and 3 are bound to fail.

5.1.2 Experiment 2

Let us now perform a second experiment with the second version of our program. Suppose we ask:

> ?- f(7, Y).
>
> Y = 4

Let us analyze what has happened. All three rules were tried before the answer was obtained. This produced the following sequence of goals:

Try rule 1: 7 < 3 fails, backtrack and try rule 2 (cut was not reached)

Try rule 2: 3 ≤ 7 succeeds, but then 7 < 6 fails, backtrack and try rule 3 (cut was not reached)

Try rule 3: 6 ≤ 7 succeeds

This trace reveals another source of inefficiency. First it is established that X < 3 is not true (7 < 3 fails). The next goal is 3 =< X (3 ≤7 succeeds). But we know that once the first test has failed the second test is bound to succeed as it is the negation of the first. Therefore the second test is redundant and the corresponding goal can be omitted. The same is true about the goal 6 =< X in rule 3. This leads to the following, more economical formulation of the three rules:

>   if X < 3 then Y = 0,
>   otherwise if X < 6 then Y = 2,
>   otherwise Y = 4.

We can now omit the conditions in the program that are guaranteed to be true whenever they are executed. This leads to the third version of the program:

>   **f(X, 0) :- X < 3, !.**
>
>   **f(X, 2) :- X < 6, !.**
>
>   **f(X, 4).**

This program produces the same results as our original version, but is more efficient than both previous versions. But what happens if we *now* remove the cuts? The program becomes:

>   **f(X, 0) :- X < 3.**
>
>   **f(X, 2) :- X < 6.**
>
>   **f(X, 4).**

This may produce multiple solutions some of which are not correct. For example:

>   **?- f(1, Y).**
>
>   **Y = 0;**
>
>   **Y = 2;**
>
>   **Y = 4;**
>
>   **no**

It is important to notice that, in contrast to the second version of the program, this time the cuts do not only affect the procedural behaviour, but also change the declarative meaning of the program.

A more precise meaning of the cut mechanism is as follows:

> Let us call the 'parent goal' the goal that matched the head of the clause containing the cut. When the cut is encountered as a goal it succeeds immediately, but it commits the system to all choices made between the time the 'parent goal' was invoked and the time the cut was encountered. All the remaining alternatives between the parent goal and the cut are discarded.

To clarify this definition consider a clause of the form:

> H :- B1, B2, ..., Bm, !, ..., Bn.

Let us assume that this clause was invoked by a goal G that matched H. Then G is the parent goal. At the moment that the cut is encountered, the system has already found some solution of the goals B1, ..., Bm. When the cut is executed, this (current) solution of B1, ..., Bm becomes frozen and all possible remaining alternatives are discarded. Also, the goal G now becomes committed to this clause: any attempt to match G with the head of some other clause is precluded.

Let us apply these rules to the following example:

> C :- P, Q, R, !, S, T, U.
>
> C :- V.
>
> A :- B, C, D.
>
> ?- A.

Here A, B, C, D, P, etc. have the syntax of terms. The cut will affect the execution of the goal C in the following way. Backtracking will be possible within the goal list P, Q, R; however, as soon as the cut is reached, all alternative solutions of the goal list P, Q, R are suppressed. The alternative clause about C,

> C :- V.

will also be discarded. However, backtracking will still be possible within the goal list S, T, U. The 'parent goal' of the clause containing the cut is the goal C in the clause:

> A :- B, C, D.

Therefore the cut will only affect the execution of the goal C. On the other hand, it will be 'invisible' from goal A. So automatic backtracking within the goal list B, C, D will remain active regardless of the cut within the clause used for satisfying C.

5.2 Examples using cut

5.2.1 Computing maximum

The procedure for finding the larger of two numbers can be programmed as a relation

> max(X, Y, Max)

where Max = X if X is greater than or equal to Y, and Max is Y if X is less than Y. This corresponds to the following two clauses:

max(X, Y, X) :- X >= Y.
max(X, Y, Y) :- X < Y.

These two rules are mutually exclusive. If the first one succeeds then the second one will fail. If the first one fails then the second must succeed. Therefore a more economical formulation, with 'otherwise', is possible:

If X $\geq$ Y then Max = X,
otherwise Max = Y.

This is written in Prolog using a cut as:

max(X, Y, X) :- X >= Y, !.
max(X, Y, Y).

5.2.2 Single-solution membership

We have been using the relation

member(X, L)

for establishing whether X is in list L. The program was:

member(X, [X | L]).
member(X, [Y | L]) :- member(X, L).

This is 'non-deterministic': if X occurs several times then any occurrence can be found. Let us now change **member** into a deterministic procedure which will find only the first occurrence. The change is simple: we only have to prevent backtracking as soon as X is found, which happens when the first clause succeeds. The modified program is:

member(X, [X | L]) :- !.
member(X, [Y | L]) :- member(X, L).

This program will generate just one solution. For example:

?- member(X, [a,b,c]).

X = a;

no

5.2.3 Adding an element to a list without duplication

Often we want to add an item X to a list L so that X is added only if X is not yet in L. If X is already in L then L remains the same because we do not want to have redundant duplicates in L. The **add** relation has three arguments

    add(X, L, L1)

where X is the item to be added, L is the list to which X is to be added and L1 is the resulting new list. Our rule for adding can be formulated as:

> If X is a member of list L then L1 = L,
> otherwise L1 is equal to L with X inserted.

It is easiest to insert X in front of L so that X becomes the head of L1. This is then programmed as follows:

    add(X, L, L) :- member(X, L), !.
    add(X, L, [X | L]).

The behaviour of this procedure is illustrated by the following example:

    ?- add(a, [b,c], L).
    L = [a,b,c]

    ?- add(X, [b,c], L).
    L = [b,c]
    X = b

    ?- add(a, [b,c,X], L).
    L = [b,c,a]
    X = a

This example is instructive because we cannot easily program the 'non-duplicate adding' without the use of cut or another construct derived from the cut. If we omit the cut in the foregoing program then the **add** relation will also add duplicate items. For example:

    ?- add(a, [a,b,c], L).
    L = [a,b,c];
    L = [a,a,b,c]

So the cut is necessary here to specify the intended relation, and not only to improve efficiency. The next example also illustrates this point.

5.2.4   Classification into categories

Assume we have a database of results of tennis games played by members of a club. The pairings were not arranged in any systematic way, so each player just played some other players. The results are in the program represented as facts like:

```
beat( tom, jim).
beat( ann, tom).
beat( pat, jim).
```

We want to define a relation

```
class( Player, Category)
```

that ranks the players into categories. We have just three categories:

winner: every player who won all his or her games is a winner

fighter: any player that won some games and lost some

sportsman: any player who lost all his or her games

For example, if all the results available are just those above then Ann and Pat are winners, Tom is a fighter and Jim is a sportsman.

It is easy to specify the rule for a fighter:

X is a fighter if
 there is some Y such that X beat Y and
 there is some Z such that Z beat X.

Now a rule for a winner:

X is a winner if
 X beat some Y and
 X was not beaten by anybody.

This formulation contains 'not' which cannot be directly expressed with our present Prolog facilities. So the formulation of **winner** appears trickier. The same problem occurs with **sportsman**. The problem can be circumvented by combining the definition of **winner** with that of **fighter**, and using the 'otherwise' connective. Such a formulation is:

If X beat somebody and X was beaten by somebody
 then X is a fighter.
 otherwise if X beat somebody
  then X is a winner.
  otherwise if X got beaten by somebody
   then X is a sportsman.

This formulation can be readily translated into Prolog. The mutual exclusion of the three alternative categories is indicated by the cuts:

```
class( X, fighter) :-
   beat( X, _ ),
   beat( _, X), !.

class( X, winner) :-
   beat( X, _), !.

class( X, sportsman) :-
   beat( _, X).
```

Notice that the cut in the clause for **winner** is not necessary. Care is needed when using such procedures containing cuts. Here is what can happen:

```
?- class( tom, C).
C = fighter;                        % As intended
no
?- class( tom, sportsman).
yes                                 % Not as intended
```

EXERCISES

5.1   Let a program be:

```
p( 1).
p( 2) :- !.
p( 3).
```

Write all Prolog's answers to the following questions:

(a)   ?- p(X).

(b)   ?- p(X), p(Y).

(c)   ?- p(X), !, p(Y).

5.2   The following relation classifies numbers into three classes: positive, zero and negative:

```
class( Number, positive) :-  Number > 0.
class( 0, zero).
class( Number, negative) :-  Number < 0.
```

Define this procedure in a more efficient way using cuts.

5.3   Define the procedure

> split(Numbers, Positives, Negatives)

which splits a list of numbers into two lists: positive ones (including zero) and negative ones. For example:

> split([3,−1,0,5,−2], [3,0,5], [−1,−2])

Propose two versions: one with a cut and one without.

5.3   Negation as failure

'Mary likes all animals but snakes'. How can we say this in Prolog? It is easy to express one part of this statement: Mary likes any X if X is an animal. This is in Prolog:

```
likes( mary, X) :- animal( X).
```

But we have to exclude snakes. This can be done by using a different formulation:

> If X is a snake then 'Mary likes X' is not true,
> otherwise if X is an animal then Mary likes X.

That something is not true can be said in Prolog by using a special goal, **fail**, which always fails, thus forcing the parent goal to fail. The above formulation is translated into Prolog, using **fail**, as follows:

```
likes( mary, X) :-
    snake( X), !, fail.
likes( mary, X) :-
    animal( X).
```

The first rule here will take care of snakes: if X is a snake then the cut will prevent backtracking (thus excluding the second rule) and **fail** will cause the failure. These two clauses can be written more compactly as one clause:

```
likes( mary, X) :-
    snake( X), !, fail
    ;
    animal( X).
```

We can use the same idea to define the relation

> different(X, Y)

which is true if X and Y are different. We have to be more precise, however, because 'different' can be understood in several ways:

- X and Y are not literally the same;
- X and Y do not match;
- the values of arithmetic expressions X and Y are not equal.

Let us choose here that X and Y are different if they do not match. The key to saying this in Prolog is:

> If X and Y match then different(X, Y) fails,
> otherwise different(X, Y) succeeds.

We again use the cut and **fail** combination:

> different(X, X) :- !, fail.
>
> different(X, Y).

This can also be written as one clause:

> different(X, Y) :-
>   X = Y, !, fail
>   ;
>   true.

true is a goal that always succeeds.

These examples indicate that it would be useful to have a unary predicate 'not' such that

> not(Goal)

is true if **Goal** is not true. We will now define the **not** relation as follows:

> If **Goal** succeeds then not(Goal) fails,
> otherwise not(Goal) succeeds.

This definition can be written in Prolog as:

> not(P) :-
>   P, !, fail
>   ;
>   true.

Henceforth, we will assume that **not** is a built-in Prolog procedure that behaves as defined here. We will also assume that **not** is defined as a prefix operator, so that we can also write the goal

    not(snake(X))

as:

    not snake(X)

Many Prolog implementations do in fact support this notation. If not, then we can always define **not** ourselves.

It should be noted that **not** defined as failure, as here, does not exactly correspond to negation in mathematical logic. This difference can cause unexpected behaviour if **not** is used without care. This will be discussed later in the chapter.

Nevertheless, **not** is a useful facility and can often be used advantageously in place of cut. Our two examples can be rewritten with **not** as:

    likes(mary, X) :-
       animal(X),
       not snake(X).

    different(X, Y) :-
       not(X = Y).

This certainly looks better than our original formulations. It is more natural and is easier to read.

Our tennis classification program of the previous section can also be rewritten, using **not**, in a way that is closer to the initial definition of the three categories:

    class(X, fighter) :-
       beat(X, _),
       beat(_, X).

    class(X, winner) :-
       beat(X, _),
       not beat(_, X).

    class(X, sportsman) :-
       beat(_, X),
       not beat(X, _).

As another example of the use of **not** let us reconsider program 1 for the eight queens problem of the previous chapter (Figure 4.7). We specified the no_attack relation between a queen and other queens. This relation can be formulated also as the negation of the **attack** relation. Figure 5.3 shows a program modified accordingly.

```
solution( [ ] ).

solution( [X/Y | Others] ) :-
   solution( Others),
   member( Y, [1,2,3,4,5,6,7,8] ),
   not attacks( X/Y, Others).

attacks( X/Y, Others) :-
   member( X1/Y1, Others),
   ( Y1 = Y;
     Y1 is Y + X1 - X;
     Y1 is Y - X1 + X ).

member( A, [A | L] ).

member( A, [B | L] ) :-
   member( A, L).

% Solution template

template( [1/Y1,2/Y2,3/Y3,4/Y4,5/Y5,6/Y6,7/Y7,8/Y8] ).
```

Figure 5.3   Another eight queens program.

EXERCISES

5.4   Given two lists, **Candidates** and **RuledOut**, write a sequence of goals (using **member** and **not**) that will through backtracking find all the items in **Candidates** that are not in **RuledOut**.

5.5   Define the set subtraction relation

   difference(Set1, Set2, SetDifference)

where all the three sets are represented as lists. For example:

   difference([a,b,c,d], [b,d,e,f], [a,c])

5.6   Define the predicate

   unifiable(List1, Term, List2)

where **List2** is the list of all the members of **List1** that match **Term**, but are not instantiated by this matching. For example:

   ?- **unifiable([X, b, t(Y)], t(a), List).**

   List = [X, t(Y)]

Note that X and Y have to remain uninstantiated although the matching with t(a) does cause their instantiation. Hint: Use **not(Term1 = Term2)**. If **Term1 = Term2** succeeds then **not(Term1 = Term2)** fails and the resulting instantiation is undone!

5.4   Problems with cut and negation

Using the cut facility we get something, but not for nothing. The advantages and disadvantages of using cut were illustrated by examples in the previous sections. Let us summarize, first the advantages:

(1)   With cut we can often improve the efficiency of the program. The idea is to explicitly tell Prolog: do not try other alternatives because they are bound to fail.

(2)   Using cut we can specify mutually exclusive rules; so we can express rules of the form:

> *if* condition P *then* conclusion Q,
> *otherwise* conclusion R

In this way, cut enhances the expressive power of the language.

The reservations against the use of cut stem from the fact that we can lose the valuable correspondence between the declarative and procedural meaning of programs. If there is no cut in the program we can change the order of clauses and goals, and this will only affect the efficiency or termination of the program, not the declarative meaning. On the other hand, in programs with cuts, a change in the order of clauses may affect the declarative meaning. This means that we can get different results. The following example illustrates:

```
p :- a, b.

p :- c.
```

The declarative meaning of this program is: p is true if and only if a and b are both true or c is true. This can be written as a logic formula:

$$p \iff (a \,\&\, b) \vee c$$

We can change the order of the two clauses and the declarative meaning remains the same. Let us now insert a cut:

```
p :- a, !, b.

p :- c.
```

The declarative meaning is now:

$$p \iff (a \,\&\, b) \vee (\sim a \,\&\, c)$$

If we swap the clauses,

```
p :- c.
p :- a, !, b.
```

then the meaning becomes:

$$p \iff c \lor (a \& b)$$

The important point is that when we use the cut facility we have to pay more attention to the procedural aspects. Unfortunately, this additional difficulty increases the probability of a programming error.

In our examples in the previous sections we have seen that sometimes the removal of a cut from the program can change the declarative meaning of the program. But there were also cases in which the cut had no effect on the declarative meaning. The use of cuts of the latter type is less delicate, and therefore cuts of this kind are sometimes called 'green cuts'. From the point of view of readability of programs, green cuts are 'innocent' and their use is quite acceptable. When reading a program, green cuts can simply be ignored.

On the contrary, cuts that do affect the declarative meaning are called 'red cuts'. Red cuts are the ones that make programs hard to understand, and they should be used with special care.

Cut is often used in combination with a special goal, **fail**. In particular, we defined the negation of a goal (**not**) as the failure of the goal. The negation, so defined, is just a special (more restricted) way of using cut. For reasons of clarity we will prefer to use **not** instead of the *cut–fail* combination (whenever possible), because the negation is a higher level concept and is intuitively clearer than the *cut–fail* combination.

It should be noted that **not** may also cause problems, and so should also be used with care. The problem is that **not**, as defined here, does not correspond exactly to negation in mathematics. If we ask Prolog

```
?- not human( mary).
```

Prolog will probably answer 'yes'. But this should not be understood as Prolog saying 'Mary is not human'. What Prolog really means to say is: 'There is not enough information in the program to prove that Mary is human'. This arises because when processing a **not** goal, Prolog does not try to prove this goal directly. Instead, it tries to prove the opposite, and if the opposite cannot be proved then Prolog assumes that the **not** goal succeeds. Such reasoning is based on the so-called *closed world assumption*. According to this assumption *the world is closed* in the sense that everything that exists is in the program or can be derived from the program. Accordingly then, if something is not in the program (or cannot be derived from it) then it is not true and consequently its negation is true. This deserves special care because we do not normally assume that 'the world is closed': with not explicitly entering the clause

> human(mary).

into our program, we do not normally mean to imply that Mary is not human. We will, by example, further study the special care that **not** requires:

> good_standard(jeanluis).
> expensive(jeanluis).
> good_standard(francesco).
> reasonable(Restaurant) :-
>   not expensive(Restaurant).

If we now ask

> ?- good_standard(X), reasonable(X).

then Prolog will answer:

> X = francesco

If we ask apparently the same question

> ?- reasonable(X), good_standard(X).

then Prolog will answer:

> no

The reader is invited to trace the program to understand why we get different answers. The key difference between both questions is that the variable X is, in the first case, already instantiated when **reasonable(X)** is executed, whereas at that point X is not yet instantiated in the second case.

We have discussed problems with cut, which also indirectly occur in **not**, in detail. The intention has been to warn users about the necessary care, not to definitely discourage the use of cut. Cut is useful and often necessary. And after all, the kind of complications that are incurred by cut in Prolog commonly occur when programming in other languages as well.

SUMMARY

- The cut facility prevents backtracking. It is used both to improve the efficiency of programs and to enhance the expressive power of the language.

- Efficiency is improved by explicitly telling Prolog (with cut) not to explore alternatives that we know are bound to fail.

- Cut makes it possible to formulate mutually exclusive conclusions through rules of the form:

  if Condition *then* Conclusion1 *otherwise* Conclusion2

- Cut makes it possible to introduce *negation as failure*: not Goal is defined through the failure of Goal.

- Two special goals are sometimes useful: true always succeeds, fail always fails.

- There are also some reservations against cut: inserting a cut may destroy the correspondence between the declarative and procedural meaning of a program. Therefore, it is part of good programming style to use cut with care and not to use it without reason.

- not defined through failure does not exactly correspond to negation in mathematical logic. Therefore, the use of not also requires special care.

Reference

The distinction between 'green cuts' and 'red cuts' was proposed by van Emden (1982).

van Emden, M. (1982) Red and green cuts. *Logic Programming Newsletter*: **2**.

6 Input and Output

6.1 Communication with files
6.2 Processing files of terms
6.3 Manipulating characters
6.4 Constructing and decomposing atoms
6.5 Reading programs: *consult, reconsult*

In this chapter we will investigate some built-in facilities for reading data from computer files and for outputting data to files. These procedures can also be used for formatting data objects in the program to achieve a desired external representation of these objects. We will also look at facilities for reading programs and for constructing and decomposing atoms.

6.1 Communication with files

The method of communication between the user and the program that we have been using up to now consists of user questions to the program and program answers in terms of instantiations of variables. This method of communication is simple and practical and, in spite of its simplicity, suffices to get the information in and out. However, it is often not quite sufficient because it is too rigid. Extensions to this basic communication method are needed in the following areas:

- input of data in forms other than questions – for example, in the form of English sentences
- output of information in any format desired, and
- input from and output to any computer file or device and not just the user terminal.

Built-in predicates aimed at these extensions depend on the implementation of Prolog. We will study here a simple and handy repertoire of such predicates, which is part of many Prolog implementations. However, the implementation manual should be consulted for details and specificities. Many Prolog implementations provide various additional facilities not covered here. Such extra facilities handle windows, provide graphics primitives for drawing on the screen, input information from the mouse, and so on.

We will first consider the question of directing input and output to files, and then how data can be input and output in different forms.

Figure 6.1 shows a general situation in which a Prolog program communicates with several files. The program can, in principle, read data from several input files, also called *input streams*, and output data to several output files, also called *output streams*. Data coming from the user's terminal is treated as just another input stream. Data output to the terminal is, analogously, treated as another output stream. Both of these 'pseudo-files' are referred to by the name **user**. The names of other files can be chosen by the programmer according to the rules for naming files in the computer system used.

At any time during the execution of a Prolog program, only two files are 'active': one for input and one for output. These two files are called the *current input stream* and the *current output stream* respectively. At the beginning of execution these two streams correspond to the user's terminal. The current input stream can be changed to another file, **Filename**, by the goal:

    see(Filename)

Such a goal succeeds (unless there is something wrong with **Filename**) and causes, as a side effect, that input to be switched from the previous input stream to **Filename**. So a typical example of using the **see** predicate is the

Figure 6.1 Communication between a Prolog program and several files.

following sequence of goals, which reads something from **file1** and then switches back to the terminal:

```
...
see( file1),
read_from_file( Information),
see( user),
...
```

The current output stream can be changed by a goal of the form:

```
tell( Filename)
```

A sequence of goals to output some information to **file3**, and then redirect succeeding output back to the terminal, is:

```
...
tell( file3),
write_on_file( Information),
tell( user),
...
```

The goal

```
seen
```

closes the current input file. The goal

```
told
```

closes the current output file.

We will assume here that files can only be processed sequentially although many Prolog implementations also handle files with random access. Sequential files behave in the same way as the terminal. Each request to read something from an input file will cause reading at the current position in the current input stream. After the reading, the current position will be, of course, moved to the next unread item. So the next request for reading will start reading at this new current position. If a request for reading is made at the end of a file, then the information returned by such a request is the atom end_of_file. Once some information has been read, it is not possible to reread it again.

Writing is similar; each request to output information will append this information at the end of the current output stream. It is not possible to move backward and to overwrite part of the file.

All files are 'text-files' – that is, files of characters. Characters are letters, digits and special characters. Some of them are said to be non-printable because when they are output on the terminal they do not appear on the screen. They may, however, have other effects, such as spacing between columns and lines.

There are two main ways in which files can be viewed in Prolog, depending on the form of information. One way is to consider the character as the basic element of the file. Accordingly, one input or output request will cause a single character to be read or written. The built-in predicates for this are **get**, **get0** and **put**.

The other way of viewing a file is to consider bigger units of information as basic building blocks of the file. Such a natural bigger unit is the Prolog term. So each input/output request of this type would transfer a whole term from the current input stream or to the current output stream respectively. Predicates for transfer of terms are **read** and **write**. Of course, in this case, the information in the file has to be in a form that is consistent with the syntax of terms.

What kind of file organization is chosen will, of course, depend on the problem. Whenever the problem specification will allow the information to be naturally squeezed into the syntax of terms, we will prefer to use a file of terms. It will then be possible to transfer a whole meaningful piece of information with a single request. On the other hand, there are problems whose nature dictates some other organization of files. An example is the processing of natural language sentences, say, to generate a dialogue in English between the system and the user. In such cases, files will have to be viewed as sequences of characters that cannot be parsed into terms.

6.2 Processing files of terms

6.2.1 *read* and *write*

The built-in predicate **read** is used for reading terms from the current input stream. The goal

read(X)

will cause the next term, T, to be read, and this term will be matched with X. If X is a variable then, as a result, X will become instantiated to T. If matching does not succeed then the goal **read(X)** fails. The predicate **read** is deterministic, so in the case of failure there will be no backtracking to input another term. Each term in the input file must be followed by a full stop and a space or carriage-return.

If **read(X)** is executed when the end of the current input file has been reached then X will become instantiated to the atom **end_of_file**.

The built-in predicate **write** outputs a term. So the goal

    write(X)

will output the term X on the current output file. X will be output in the same standard syntactic form in which Prolog normally displays values of variables. A useful feature of Prolog is that the **write** procedure 'knows' to display any term no matter how complicated it may be.

There are additional built-in predicates for formatting the output. They insert spaces and new lines into the output stream. The goal

    tab(N)

causes N spaces to be output. The predicate **nl** (which has no arguments) causes the start of a new line at output.

The following examples will illustrate the use of these procedures.

Let us assume that we have a procedure that computes the cube of a number:

    cube(N, C) :-
      C is N * N * N.

Suppose we want to use this for calculating the cubes of a sequence of numbers. We could do this by a sequence of questions:

    ?- cube(2, X).

    X = 8

    ?- cube(5, Y).

    Y = 125

    ?- cube(12, Z).

    Z = 1728

For each number, we had to type in the corresponding goal. Let us now modify this program so that the **cube** procedure will read the data itself. Now the program will keep reading data and outputting their cubes until the atom stop is read:

```
cube :-
   read( X),
   process( X).

process( stop) :- !.

process( N) :-
   C is N * N * N,
   write( C),
   cube.
```

This is an example of a program whose declarative meaning is awkward to formulate. However, its procedural meaning is straightforward: to execute **cube**, first read X and then process it; if X = **stop** then everything has been done, otherwise write the cube of X and recursively call the **cube** procedure to process further data. A table of the cubes of numbers can be produced using this new procedure as follows:

```
?- cube.
2.
8
5.
125
12.
1728
stop.
yes
```

The numbers 2, 5 and 12 were typed in by the user on the terminal; the other numbers were output by the program. Note that each number entered by the user had to be followed by a full stop, which signals the end of a term.

It may appear that the above **cube** procedure could be simplified. However, the following attempt to simplify is not correct:

```
cube :-
   read( stop), !.

cube :-
   read( N),
   C is N * N * N,
   write( C),
   cube.
```

The reason why this is wrong can be seen easily if we trace the program with input data 5, say. The goal **read(stop)** will fail when the number is read, and this number will be lost for ever. The next **read** goal will input the next term.

On the other hand, it could happen that the stop signal is read by the goal read(N), which would then cause a request to multiply non-numeric data.

The cube procedure conducts interaction between the user and the program. In such cases it is usually desirable that the program, before reading new data from the terminal, signals to the user that it is ready to accept the information, and perhaps also says what kind of information it is expecting. This is usually done by sending a 'prompt' signal to the user before reading. Our cube procedure would be accordingly modified, for example, as follows:

```
cube :-
   write( 'Next item, please: '),
   read( X),
   process( X).

process( stop) :- !.

process( N) :-
   C is N * N * N,
   write( 'Cube of '), write( N), write( ' is '),
   write( C), nl,
   cube.
```

A conversation with this new version of cube would then be, for example, as follows:

```
?- cube.
Next item, please: 5.
Cube of 5 is 125
Next item, please: 12.
Cube of 12 is 1728
Next item, please: stop.
yes
```

Depending on the implementation, an extra request (like ttyflush, say) after writing the prompt might be necessary in order to force the prompt to actually appear on the screen before reading.

In the following sections we will look at some typical examples of operations that involve reading and writing.

6.2.2 Displaying lists

Besides the standard Prolog format for lists, there are several other natural forms for displaying lists which have advantages in some situations. The following procedure

```
writelist( L)
```

outputs a list L so that each element of L is written on a separate line:

```
writelist( [ ] ).

writelist( [X | L] ) :-
    write( X), nl,
    writelist( L).
```

If we have a list of lists, one natural output form is to write the elements of each list in one line. To this end, we will define the procedure writelist2. An example of its use is:

```
?- writelist2( [ [a,b,c], [d,e,f], [g,h,i] ] ).

a b c
d e f
g h i
```

A procedure that accomplishes this is:

```
writelist2( [ ] ).

writelist2( [L | LL] ) :-
    doline( L), nl,
    writelist2( LL).

doline( [ ] ).

doline( [X | L] ) :-
    write( X), tab( 1),
    doline( L).
```

A list of integer numbers can be sometimes conveniently shown as a bar graph. The following procedure, bars, will display a list in this form, assuming that the numbers in the list are between 0 and 80. An example of using bars is:

```
?- bars( [3,4,6,5] ).
***
****
******
*****
```

The bars procedure can be defined as follows:

```
bars( [ ] ).

bars( [N | L] ) :-
    stars( N), nl,
    bars( L).
```

```
stars( N) :-
   N > 0,
   write( *),
   N1 is N − 1,
   stars( N1).
stars( N) :-
   N =< 0.
```

6.2.3   Formatting terms

Let us suppose that our program deals with families that are represented as terms, as in Chapter 4 (Figure 4.1). Then, for example, if F is instantiated to the term shown in Figure 4.1, the goal

write(F)

will cause this term to be output in the standard form, something like this:

family(person(tom,fox,date(7,may,1950),works(bbc,15200)),
person(ann,fox,date(9,may,1951),unemployed),[person(pat,
fox,date(5,may,1973),unemployed),person(jim,fox,date(5,
may,1973),unemployed)])

This contains all the information, but the form is rather confusing as it is hard to follow what parts of information form semantic units. We would therefore normally prefer to have this displayed in a formatted manner; for example, as shown in Figure 6.2. The procedure, shown in Figure 6.3,

writefamily(F)

achieves this format.

---

parents

   tom fox, born 7 may 1950, works bbc, salary 15200
   ann fox, born 9 may 1951, unemployed

children

   pat fox, born 5 may 1973, unemployed
   jim fox, born 5 may 1973, unemployed

Figure 6.2   Improved format for family terms.

```
writefamily( family( Husband, Wife, Children) ) :-
   nl, write( parents), nl, nl,
   writeperson( Husband), nl,
   writeperson( Wife), nl, nl,
   write( children), nl, nl,
   writepersonlist( Children).

writeperson( person( Firstname, Secname, date(D,M,Y), Work) ) :-
   tab( 4), write( Firstname),
   tab( 1), write( Secname),
   write( ', born '),
   write( D), tab( 1),
   write( M), tab( 1),
   write( Y), write( ', '),
   writework( Work).

writepersonlist( [ ] ).

writepersonlist( [P | L] ) :-
   writeperson( P), nl,
   writepersonlist( L).

writework( unemployed) :-
   write( unemployed).

writework( works( Comp, Sal) ) :-
   write( 'works '), write( Comp),
   write( ', salary '), write( Sal).
```

Figure 6.3   A program to produce the format of Figure 6.2.

6.2.4   Processing a file of terms

A typical sequence of goals to process a whole file, F, would look something like this:

   ..., see(F), processfile, see(user), ...

Here processfile is a procedure to read and process each term in F, one after another, until the end of the file is encountered. A typical schema for processfile is:

```
processfile :-
   read( Term),              % Assuming Term not a variable
   process( Term).

process( end_of_file) :- !.   % All done

process( Term) :-
   treat( Term),             % Process current item
   processfile.              % Process rest of file
```

Here treat(Term) represents whatever is to be done with each term. An example would be a procedure to display on the terminal each term together with its consecutive number. Let us call this procedure showfile. It has to have an additional argument to count the terms read:

```
showfile( N) :-
  read( Term),
  show( Term, N).

show( end_of_file, _) :- !.

show( Term, N) :-
  write( N), tab( 2), write( Term), nl,
  N1 is N + 1,
  showfile( N1).
```

Another example of using this schema for processing a file is as follows. We have a file, named file1, of terms of the form:

item(ItemNumber, Description, Price, SupplierName)

Each term describes an entry in a catalogue of items. We want to produce another file that contains only items supplied by a specified supplier. As the supplier, in this new file, will always be the same, his or her name need only be written at the beginning of the file, and omitted from other terms. The procedure will be:

makefile(Supplier)

For example, if the original catalogue is stored in file1, and we want to produce the special catalogue on file2 of everything that Harrison supplies, then we would use the makefile procedure as follows:

?- see(file1), tell(file2), makefile(harrison), see(user), tell(user).

The procedure makefile can be defined as follows:

```
makefile( Supplier) :-
  write( Supplier), write( '.' ), nl,
  makerest( Supplier).

makerest( Supplier) :-
  read( Item),
  process( Item, Supplier).

process( end_of_file, _) :- !.

process( item( Num, Desc, Price, Supplier), Supplier) :- !,
  write( item( Num, Desc, Price) ),
  write( '.' ), nl,
  makerest( Supplier).
```

```
process( _, Supplier) :-
    makerest( Supplier).
```

Notice that **process** writes full stops between terms to make future reading of the file possible by the **read** procedure.

EXERCISES

6.1   Let f be a file of terms. Define a procedure

>   **findterm(Term)**

that displays on the terminal the first term in f that matches **Term**.

6.2   Let f be a file of terms. Write a procedure

>   **findallterms(Term)**

that displays on the terminal all the terms in f that match **Term**. Make sure that **Term** is not instantiated in the process (which could prevent its match with terms that occur later in the file).

6.3   Manipulating characters

A character is written on the current output stream with the goal

>   put(C)

where C is the ASCII code (a number between 0 and 127) of the character to be output. For example, the question

>   ?- put(65), put(66), put(67).

would cause the following output:

>   ABC

65 is the ASCII code of 'A', 66 of 'B', 67 of 'C'.

A single character can be read from the current input stream by the goal

>   get0(C)

This causes the current character to be read from the input stream, and the variable C becomes instantiated to the ASCII code of this character. A variation of the predicate get0 is get, which is used for reading non-blank characters. So the goal

get(C)

will cause the skipping over of all non-printable characters (blanks in particular) from the current input position in the input stream up to the first printable character. This character is then also read and C is instantiated to its ASCII code.

As an example of using predicates that transfer single characters let us define a procedure, squeeze, to do the following: read a sentence from the current input stream, and output the same sentence reformatted so that multiple blanks between words are replaced by single blanks. For simplicity we will assume that any input sentence processed by squeeze ends with a full stop and that words are separated simply by one or more blanks, but no other character. An acceptable input is then:

The   robot tried   to pour wine out   of the   bottle.

The goal squeeze would output this in the form:

The robot tried to pour wine out of the bottle.

The squeeze procedure will have a similar structure to the procedures for processing files in the previous section. First it will read the first character, output this character, and then complete the processing depending on this character. There are three alternatives that correspond to the following cases: the character is either a full stop, a blank or a letter. The mutual exclusion of the three alternatives is achieved in the program by cuts:

```
squeeze :-
  get0( C),
  put( C),
  dorest( C).

dorest( 46) :- !.            % 46 is ASCII for full stop, all done

dorest( 32) :- !,            % 32 is ASCII for blank
  get( C),                   % Skip other blanks
  put( C),
  dorest( C).

dorest( Letter) :-
  squeeze.
```

EXERCISE

6.3   Generalize the **squeeze** procedure to handle commas as well. All blanks
immediately preceding a comma are to be removed, and we want to
have one blank after each comma.

6.4   Constructing and decomposing atoms

It is often desirable to have information, read as a sequence of characters,
represented in the program as an atom. There is a built-in predicate, **name**,
which can be used to this end. **name** relates atoms and their ASCII encodings.
Thus

> **name(A, L)**

is true if L is the list of ASCII codes of the characters in A. For example

> **name(zx232, [122,120,50,51,50])**

is true. There are two typical uses of **name**:

(1)   given an atom, break it down into single characters;
(2)   given a list of characters, combine them into an atom.

An example of the first kind of application would be a program that
deals with orders, taxies and drivers. These would be, in the program,
represented by atoms such as:

> **order1, order2, driver1, driver2, taxia1, taxilux**

The following predicate

> **taxi(X)**

tests whether an atom X represents a taxi:

```
taxi( X) :-
   name( X, Xlist),
   name( taxi, Tlist),
   conc( Tlist, _, Xlist).          % Is word 'taxi' prefix of X?

conc( [ ], L, L).

conc( [A | L1], L2, [A | L3] ) :-
   conc( L1, L2, L3).
```

Predicates **order** and **driver** can be defined analogously.

The next example illustrates the use of combining characters into atoms. We will define a predicate

getsentence(Wordlist)

that reads a free-form natural language sentence and instantiates **Wordlist** to some internal representation of the sentence. A natural choice for the internal representation, which would enable further processing of the sentence, is this: each word of the input sentence is represented as a Prolog atom; the whole sentence is represented as a list of atoms. For example, if the current input stream is

Mary was pleased to see the robot fail.

then the goal **getsentence(Sentence)** will cause the instantiation:

Sentence = ['Mary', was, pleased, to, see, the, robot, fail]

For simplicity, we will assume that each sentence terminates with a full stop and that there are no punctuation symbols within the sentence.

The program is shown in Figure 6.4. The procedure **getsentence** first reads the current input character, **Char**, and then supplies this character to the procedure **getrest** to complete the job. **getrest** has to react properly according to three cases:

(1)   **Char** is the full stop: then everything has been read.
(2)   **Char** is the blank: ignore it, **getsentence** from rest of input.
(3)   **Char** is a letter: first read the word, **Word**, which begins with **Char**, and then use **getsentence** to read the rest of the sentence, producing **Wordlist**. The cumulative result is the list [**Word** | **Wordlist**].

The procedure that reads the characters of one word is:

getletters(Letter, Letters, Nextchar)

The three arguments are:

(1)   **Letter** is the current letter (already read) of the word being read.
(2)   **Letters** is the list of letters (starting with **Letter**) up to the end of the word.
(3)   **Nextchar** is the input character that immediately follows the word read. **Nextchar** must be a non-letter character.

```
/*
```

Procedure getsentence reads in a sentence and combines the words into a list of atoms. For example

    getsentence(Wordlist)

produces

    Wordlist = ['Mary', was, pleased, to, see, the, robot, fail]

if the input sentence is:

    Mary was pleased to see the robot fail.

```
*/
```

```
getsentence( Wordlist) :-
    get0( Char),
    getrest( Char, Wordlist).
```

```
getrest( 46, [ ] ) :- !.                              % End of sentence: 46 = ASCII for '.'

getrest( 32, Wordlist) :- !,                          % 32 = ASCII for blank
    getsentence( Wordlist).                           % Skip the blank

getrest( Letter, [Word | Wordlist] ) :-
    getletters( Letter, Letters, Nextchar),           % Read letters of current word
    name( Word, Letters),
getrest( Nextchar, Wordlist).

getletters( 46, [ ], 46) :- !.                        % End of word: 46 = full stop

getletters( 32, [ ], 32) :- !.                        % End of word: 32 = blank

getletters( Let, [Let | Letters], Nextchar) :-
    get0( Char),
    getletters( Char, Letters, Nextchar).
```

Figure 6.4   A procedure to transform a sentence into a list of atoms.

We conclude this example with a comment on the possible use of the **getsentence** procedure. It can be used in a program to process text in natural language. Sentences represented as lists of words are in a form that is suitable for further processing in Prolog. A simple example is to look for certain keywords in input sentences. A much more difficult task would be to understand the sentence; that is, to extract from the sentence its meaning, represented in some chosen formalism. This is an important research area of Artificial Intelligence, and is introduced in Chapter 17.

EXERCISES

6.4 Define the relation

  starts(Atom, Character)

to check whether **Atom** starts with **Character**.

6.5 Define the procedure **plural** that will convert nouns into their plural form. For example:

  ?- **plural(table, X).**

  X = tables

6.6 Write the procedure

  search(KeyWord, Sentence)

that will, each time it is called, find a sentence in the current input file that contains the given **KeyWord**. **Sentence** should be in its original form, represented as a sequence of characters or as an atom (procedure **getsentence** of this section can be accordingly modified).

6.5 Reading programs: *consult, reconsult*

We can communicate our programs to the Prolog system by means of two built-in predicates: **consult** and **reconsult**. We tell Prolog to read a program from a file F with the goal:

  ?- **consult(F).**

The effect will be that all clauses in F are read and will be used by Prolog when answering further questions from the user. If another file is 'consulted' at some later time during the same session, clauses from this new file are simply added at the end of the current set of clauses.

The built-in predicate **reconsult** is similar to **consult**. A goal

  ?- **reconsult(F).**

will have the same effect as **consult(F)** with one exception. If there are clauses in F about a relation that has been previously defined, the old definition will be superseded by the new clauses about this relation in F. The difference between **consult** and **reconsult** is that **consult** always *adds* new clauses while **reconsult** *redefines* previously defined relations. **reconsult(F)** will, however, not affect any relation about which there is no clause in F.

It should be noted, again, that the details of 'consulting' files depend on the implementation of Prolog, as is the case with most other built-in procedures. Many Prolog implementations also allow the user to enter and edit the program interactively.

SUMMARY

- Input and output (other than that associated with querying the program) is done using built-in procedures. This chapter introduced a simple and practical repertoire of such procedures that can be found in many Prolog implementations.

- This repertoire assumes that files are sequential. There is the *current input stream* and the *current output stream*. The user terminal is treated as a file called user.

- Switching between streams is done by:

see(File)	File becomes the current input stream
tell(File)	File becomes the current output stream
seen	close the current input stream
told	close the current output stream

- Files are read and written in two ways:

  as sequences of characters
  as sequences of terms

  Built-in procedures for reading and writing characters and terms are:

read(Term)	input next term
write(Term)	output Term
put(CharCode)	output character with the given ASCII code
get0(CharCode)	input next character
get(CharCode)	input next 'printable' character

- Two procedures help formatting:

  | nl | output new line |
  | tab(N) | output N blanks |

- The procedure name(Atom, CodeList) decomposes and constructs atoms. CodeList is the list of ASCII codes of the characters in Atom.

- Many Prolog implementations provide additional facilities to handle nonsequential files, windows, provide graphics primitives, input information from the mouse, etc.

7 More Built-in Procedures

In this chapter we will examine some more built-in procedures for advanced Prolog programming. These features enable the programming of operations that are not possible using only the features introduced so far. One set of such procedures manipulates terms: testing whether some variable has been instantiated to an integer, taking terms apart, constructing new terms, etc. Another useful set of procedures manipulates the 'database': they add new relations to the program or remove existing ones.

The built-in procedures largely depend on the implementation of Prolog. However, the procedures discussed in this chapter are provided by many Prolog implementations. Various implementations may provide additional features.

7.1   Testing the type of terms

7.1.1   Predicates *var*, *nonvar*, *atom*, *integer*, *real*, *atomic*

Terms may be of different types: variable, integer, atom, etc. If a term is a variable then it can be, at some point during the execution of the program, instantiated or uninstantiated. Further, if it is instantiated, its value can be an atom, a structure, etc. It is sometimes useful to know what is the type of this value. For example, we may want to add the values of two variables, X and Y, by

   Z is X + Y

Before this goal is executed, X and Y have to be instantiated to integers. If we are not sure that X and Y will indeed be instantiated to integers then we should check this in the program before arithmetic is done.

   To this end we can use the built-in predicate **integer**. **integer**(X) is true if X is an integer or if it is a variable whose value is an integer. We say that X must 'currently stand for' an integer. The goal of adding X and Y can then be protected by the following test on X and Y:

   ..., integer(X), integer(Y), Z is X + Y, ...

If X and Y are not both integers then no arithmetic will be attempted. So the **integer** goals 'guard' the goal **Z is X + Y** before meaningless execution.

   Built-in predicates of this sort are: **var**, **nonvar**, **atom**, **integer**, **real**, **atomic**. Their meaning is as follows:

   var(X)

This goal succeeds if X is currently an uninstantiated variable.

   nonvar(X)

This goal succeeds if X is a term other than a variable, or X is an already instantiated variable.

   atom(X)

This is true if X currently stands for an atom.

   integer(X)

This goal is true if X currently stands for an integer.

   real(X)

This is true if X currently stands for a real number.

atomic(X)

This goal is true if X currently stands for an integer or an atom.

The following example questions to Prolog illustrate the use of these built-in predicates:

?- var(Z), Z = 2.

Z = 2

?- Z = 2, var(Z).

no

?- integer(Z), Z = 2.

no

?- Z = 2, integer(Z), nonvar(Z).

Z = 2

?- atom(22).

no

?- atomic(22).

yes

?- atom(==>).

yes

?- atom(p(1)).

no

We will illustrate the need for **atom** by an example. We would like to count how many times a given atom occurs in a given list of objects. To this purpose we will define a procedure

count(A, L, N)

where A is the atom, L is the list and N is the number of occurrences. The first attempt to define **count** could be:

```
count( _, [], 0).
count( A, [A | L], N) :- !,
   count( A, L, N1),            % N1 = number of occurrences in tail
   N is N1 + 1.
count( A, [_ | L], N) :-
   count( A, L, N).
```

Now let us try to use this procedure on some examples:

```
?- count( a, [a,b,a,a], N).
N = 3

?- count( a, [a,b,X,Y], Na).
Na = 3
...

?- count( b, [a,b,X,Y], Nb).
Nb = 3
...

?- L = [a, b, X, Y], count( a, L, Na), count( b, L, Nb).
Na = 3
Nb = 1
X = a
Y = a
...
```

In the last example, X and Y both became instantiated to a and therefore we only got Nb = 1; but this is not what we had in mind. We are interested in the number of real occurrences of the given *atom*, and not in the number of terms that *match* this atom. According to this more precise definition of the count relation we have to check whether the head of the list is an atom. The modified program is as follows:

```
count( _, [], 0).
count( A, [B | L], N) :-
    atom( B), A = B, !,      % B is atom A?
    count( A, L, N1),        % Count in tail
    N is N1 + 1
    ;
    count( A, L, N).         % Otherwise just count the tail
```

The following, more complex programming exercise in solving crypt-arithmetic puzzles makes use of the **nonvar** predicate.

7.1.2   A cryptarithmetic puzzle using *nonvar*

A popular example of a cryptarithmetic puzzle is

```
    DONALD
  + GERALD
    ROBERT
```

The problem here is to assign decimal digits to the letters D, O, N, etc., so that the above sum is valid. All letters have to be assigned different digits, otherwise trivial solutions are possible – for example, all letters equal zero.

We will define a relation

sum(N1, N2, N)

where N1, N2 and N represent the three numbers of a given cryptarithmetic puzzle. The goal sum(N1, N2, N) is true if there is an assignment of digits to letters such that N1 + N2 = N.

The first step toward finding a solution is to decide how to represent the numbers N1, N2 and N in the program. One way of doing this is to represent each number as a list of decimal digits. For example, the number 225 would be represented by the list [2,2,5]. As these digits are not known in advance, an uninstantiated variable will stand for each digit. Using this representation, the problem can be depicted as:

```
  [D,O,N,A,L,D]
+ [G,E,R,A,L,D]
= [R,O,B,E,R,T]
```

The task is to find such an instantiation of the variables D, O, N, etc., for which the sum is valid. When the sum relation has been programmed, the puzzle can be stated to Prolog by the question:

?- sum([D,O,N,A,L,D], [G,E,R,A,L,D], [R,O,B,E,R,T]).

To define the sum relation on lists of digits, we have to implement the actual rules for doing summation in the decimal number system. The summation is done digit by digit, starting with the right-most digits, continuing toward the left, always taking into account the carry digit from the right. It is also necessary to maintain a set of available digits; that is, digits that have not yet been used for instantiating variables already encountered. So, in general, besides the three numbers N1, N2 and N, some additional information is involved, as illustrated in Figure 7.1:

- carry digit before the summation of the numbers
- carry digit after the summation
- set of digits available before the summation
- remaining digits, not used in the summation

To formulate the sum relation we will use, once again, the principle of generalization of the problem: we will introduce an auxiliary, more general relation, sum1. sum1 has some extra arguments, which correspond to the

Figure 7.1 Digit by digit summation. The relations at the indicated ith digit position are: $D_{3i} = (C1 + D_{1i} + D_{2i})$ mod 10; $C = (C1 + D_{1i} + D_{2i})$ div 10.

foregoing additional information:

    sum1(N1, N2, N, C1, C, Digits1, Digits)

N1, N2 and N are our three numbers, as in the **sum** relation, C1 is carry from the right (before summation of N1 and N2), and C is carry to the left (after the summation). The following example illustrates:

    ?- sum1([H,E], [6,E], [U,S], 1, 1, [1,3,4,7,8,9], Digits).

    H = 8
    E = 3
    S = 7
    U = 4
    Digits = [1,9]

As Figure 7.1 shows, C1 and C have to be 0 if N1, N2 and N are to satisfy the **sum** relation. **Digits1** is the list of available digits for instantiating the variables in N1, N2 and N; **Digits** is the list of digits that were not used in the instantiation of these variables. Since we allow the use of any decimal digit in satisfying the **sum** relation, the definition of **sum** in terms of **sum1** is as follows:

    sum(N1, N2, N) :-
        sum1(N1, N2, N, 0, 0, [0,1,2,3,4,5,6,7,8,9], _).

The burden of the problem has now shifted to the **sum1** relation. This relation is, however, general enough so that it can be defined recursively. We will assume, without loss of generality, that the three lists representing the three numbers are of equal length. Our example problem, of course, satisfies this constraint; if not a 'shorter' number can be prefixed by zeros.

The definition of **sum1** can be divided into two cases:

(1) The three numbers are represented by empty lists. Then:

    sum1([ ], [ ], [ ], 0, 0, Digs, Digs).

(2) All three numbers have some left-most digit and the remaining digits on their right. So they are of the form:

    [D1 | N1],   [D2 | N2],   [D | N]

In this case two conditions must be satisfied:

(a) The remaining digits themselves, viewed as three numbers N1, N2 and N, have to satisfy the **sum1** relation, giving some carry digit, C2, to the left, and leaving some unused subset of decimal digits, **Digs2**.

(b) The left-most digits D1, D2 and D, and the carry digit C2 have to satisfy the relation indicated in Figure 7.1: C2, D1 and D2 are added giving D and a carry to the left. This condition will be formulated in our program as a relation **digitsum**.

Translating this case into Prolog we have:

    sum1([D1 | N1], [D2 | N2], [D | N], C1, C, Digs1, Digs) :-
    sum1(N1, N2, N, C1, C2, Digs1, Digs2),
    digitsum(D1, D2, C2, D, C, Digs2, Digs).

It only remains to define the **digitsum** relation in Prolog. There is one subtle detail that involves the use of the metalogical predicate **nonvar**. D1, D2 and D have to be decimal digits. If any of them is not yet instantiated then it has to become instantiated to one of the digits in the list **Digs2**. Once it is instantiated to one of the digits, this digit has to be deleted from the set of available digits. If D1, D2 or D is already instantiated then, of course, none of the available digits will be spent. This is realized in the program as a non-deterministic deletion of an item from a list. If this item is non-variable then nothing is deleted (no instantiation occurs). This is programmed as:

```
del( Item, List, List) :-
     nonvar( Item), !.            % Item already instantiated

del( Item, [Item | List], List).  % Delete the head

del( Item, [A | List], [A | List1] ) :-
     del( Item, List, List1).      % Delete Item from tail
```

A complete program for cryptarithmetic puzzles is shown in Figure 7.2. The program also includes the definition of two puzzles. The question to Prolog about DONALD, GERALD and ROBERT, using this program, would be:

    ?- puzzle1(N1, N2, N), sum(N1, N2, N).

% Solving cryptarithmetic puzzles

```
sum( N1, N2, N) :-                          % Numbers represented as lists of digits
  sum1( N1, N2, N,
      0, 0,                                 % Carries from right and to left both 0
      [0,1,2,3,4,5,6,7,8,9], _).            % All digits available

sum1( [ ], [ ], [ ], 0, 0, Digits, Digits).

sum1( [D1 | N1], [D2 | N2], [D | N], C1, C, Digs1, Digs) :-
  sum1( N1, N2, N, C1, C2, Digs1, Digs2),
  digitsum( D1, D2, C2, D, C, Digs2, Digs).

digitsum( D1, D2, C1, D, C, Digs1, Digs) :-
  del( D1, Digs1, Digs2),                   % Select an available digit for D1
  del( D2, Digs2, Digs3),                   % Select an available digit for D2
  del( D, Digs3, Digs),                     % Select an available digit for D
  S is D1 + D2 + C1,
  D is S mod 10,
  C is S div 10.

del( A, L, L) :-
  nonvar( A), !.                            % A already instantiated

del( A, [A | L], L).                        % Delete the head

del( A, [B | L], [B | L1] ) :-
  del( A, L, L1).                           % Delete from tail
```

% Some puzzles

```
puzzle1( [D,O,N,A,L,D],
         [G,E,R,A,L,D],
         [R,O,B,E,R,T] ).

puzzle2( [0,S,E,N,D],
         [0,M,O,R,E],
         [M,O,N,E,Y] ).
```

Figure 7.2   A program for cryptarithmetic puzzles.

Sometimes this puzzle is made easier by providing part of the solution as an additional constraint that D be equal 5. The puzzle in this form could be communicated to Prolog using **sum1**:

```
?- sum1( [5,O,N,A,L,5],
         [G,E,R,A,L,5],
         [R,O,B,E,R,T],
         0, 0, [0,1,2,3,4,6,7,8,9], _).
```

It is interesting that in both cases there is only one solution. That is, there is only one way of assigning digits to letters.

EXERCISES

7.1   Write a procedure **simplify** to symbolically simplify summation
expressions with numbers and symbols (lower-case letters). Let the
procedure rearrange the expressions so that all the symbols precede
numbers. These are examples of its use:

>   ?- **simplify(1 + 1 + a, E).**

>   E = a + 2

>   ?- **simplify(1 + a + 4 + 2 + b + c, E).**

>   E = a + b + c + 7

>   ?- **simplify(3 + x + x, E).**

>   E = 2∗x + 3

7.2   Define the procedure

>   **add(Item, List)**

to store a new element into a list. Assume that all of the elements that
can be stored are atoms. **List** contains all the stored elements followed
by a tail that is not instantiated and can thus accommodate new
elements. For example, let the existing elements stored be **a**, **b** and **c**.
Then

>   **List = [a, b, c | Tail]**

where **Tail** is a variable. The goal

>   **add(d, List)**

will cause the instantiation

>   **Tail = [d | NewTail]   and   List = [a, b, c, d | NewTail]**

Thus the structure can, in effect, grow by accepting new items. Define
also the corresponding membership relation.

7.2   Constructing and decomposing terms:
=.., *functor*, *arg*, *name*

There are three built-in predicates for decomposing terms and constructing
new terms: **functor**, **arg** and =... We will first look at =.., which is written as
an infix operator. The goal

>   **Term =.. L**

is true if L is a list that contains the principal functor of **Term**, followed by its arguments. The following examples illustrate:

```
?- f( a, b) =.. L.
L = [f, a, b]
?- T =.. [rectangle, 3, 5].
T = rectangle( 3, 5)
?- Z =.. [p, X, f(X,Y)].
Z = p( X, f(X,Y) )
```

Why would we want to decompose a term into its components – its functor and its arguments? Why construct a new term from a given functor and arguments? The following example illustrates the need for this.

Let us consider a program that manipulates geometric figures. Figures are squares, rectangles, triangles, circles, etc. They can, in the program, be represented as terms such that the functor indicates the type of figure, and the arguments specify the size of the figure, as follows:

```
square( Side)
triangle( Side1, Side2, Side3)
circle( R)
```

One operation on such figures can be enlargement. We can implement this as a three-argument relation

```
enlarge( Fig, Factor, Fig1)
```

where **Fig** and **Fig1** are geometric figures of the same type (same functor), and the parameters of **Fig1** are those of **Fig** multiplicatively enlarged by **Factor**. For simplicity, we will assume that all the parameters of **Fig** are already known; that is, instantiated to numbers, and so is **Factor**. One way of programming the enlarge relation is:

```
enlarge( square(A), F, square(A1) )  :-
    A1 is F*A.
enlarge( circle(R), F, circle(R1) )  :-
    R1 is F*R1.
enlarge( rectangle(A,B), F, rectangle(A1,B1) )  :-
    A1 is F*A, B1 is F*B.
...
```

This works, but it is awkward when there are many different figure types. We have to foresee all types that may possibly occur. Thus, we need an extra clause for each type although each clause says essentially the same thing: take the parameters of the original figure, multiply all the parameters by the factor, and make a figure of the same type with new parameters.

One (unsuccessful) attempt to handle, at least, all one-parameter figures with one clause could be:

> enlarge(Type(Par), F, Type(Par1)) :-
>   Par1 is F*Par.

However, this is normally not allowed in Prolog because the functor has to be an atom; so the variable **Type** would not be accepted syntactically as a functor. The correct method is to use the predicate '=..'. Then the **enlarge** procedure can be stated completely generally, for any type of object, as follows:

> enlarge(Fig, F, Fig1) :-
>   Fig =.. [Type | Parameters],
>   multiplylist(Parameters, F, Parameters1),
>   Fig1 =.. [Type | Parameters1].
>
> multiplylist([ ], _, [ ]).
>
> multiplylist([X | L], F, [X1 | L1]) :-
>   X1 is F*X, multiplylist(L, F, L1).

Our next example of using the '=..' predicate comes from symbolic manipulation of formulas where a frequent operation is to substitute some subexpression by another expression. We will define the relation

> substitute(Subterm, Term, Subterm1, Term1)

as follows: if all occurrences of **Subterm** in **Term** are substituted by **Subterm1** then we get **Term1**. For example:

> ?- substitute(sin(x), 2*sin(x)*f(sin(x)), t, F).
>
> F = 2*t*f(t)

By 'occurrence' of **Subterm** in **Term** we will mean something in **Term** that *matches* **Subterm**. We will look for occurrences from top to bottom. So the goal

> ?- substitute(a+b, f(a, A+B), v, F).

will produce

F = f(a, v)		F = f(a, v+v)
A = a	and not	A = a+b
B = b		B = a+b

In defining the **substitute** relation we have to consider the following decisions depending on the case:

If **Subterm** = **Term** then **Term1** = **Subterm1**;
otherwise if **Term** is 'atomic' (not a structure)
then **Term1** = **Term** (nothing to be substituted),
otherwise the substitution is to be carried out on the arguments of **Term**.

These rules can be converted into a Prolog program, shown in Figure 7.3.

Terms that are constructed by the '=..' predicate can be, of course, also used as goals. The advantage of this is that the program itself can, during execution, generate and execute goals of forms that were not necessarily foreseen at the time of writing the program. A sequence of goals illustrating this effect would be something like the following:

obtain(Functor),
compute(Arglist),
Goal =.. [Functor | Arglist],
Goal

% substitute(Subterm, Term, Subterm1, Term1):
%   if all occurrences of Subterm in Term are substituted with Subterm1 then we get Term1.

% Case 1: Substitute whole term

substitute(Term, Term, Term1, Term1) :- !.

% Case 2: Nothing to substitute if Term atomic

substitute(_, Term, _, Term) :-
  atomic(Term), !.

% Case 3: Do substitution on arguments

substitute(Sub, Term, Sub1, Term1) :-
  Term =.. [F | Args],   % Get arguments
  substlist(Sub, Args, Sub1, Args1),   % Perform substitution on them
  Term1 =.. [F | Args1].

substlist(_, [], _, []).

substlist(Sub, [Term | Terms], Sub1, [Term1 | Terms1]) :-
  substitute(Sub, Term, Sub1, Term1),
  substlist(Sub, Terms, Sub1, Terms1).

Figure 7.3 A procedure for substituting a subterm of a term by another subterm.

Here, **obtain** and **compute** are some user-defined procedures for getting the components of the goal to be constructed. The goal is then constructed by '=..', and invoked for execution by simply stating its name, **Goal**.

Some implementations of Prolog may require that all the goals, as they appear in the program, are *syntactically* either atoms or structures with an atom as the principal functor. Thus a variable, regardless of its eventual instantiation, in such a case may not be syntactically acceptable as a goal. This problem is circumvented by another built-in predicate, **call**, whose argument is the goal to be executed. Accordingly, the above example would be rewritten as:

```
...
Goal =.. [Functor | Arglist],
call( Goal)
```

Sometimes we may want to extract from a term just its principal functor or one of its arguments. In such a case we can, of course, use the '=..' relation. But it can be neater and more practical, and also more efficient, to use one of the other two built-in procedures for manipulating terms: **functor** and **arg**. Their meaning is as follows: a goal

```
functor( Term, F, N)
```

is true if F is the principal functor of **Term** and N is the arity of F. A goal

```
arg( N, Term, A)
```

is true if A is the Nth argument in **Term**, assuming that arguments are numbered from left to right starting with 1. The following examples illustrate:

```
?- functor( t( f(X), X, t), Fun, Arity).

Fun = t
Arity = 3

?- arg( 2, f( X, t(a), t(b)), Y).

Y = t(a)

?- functor( D, date, 3),
     arg( 1, D, 29),
     arg( 2, D, june),
     arg( 3, D, 1982).

D = date( 29, june, 1982)
```

The last example shows a special application of the **functor** predicate. The goal functor(D, date, 3) generates a 'general' term whose principal functor is **date** with three arguments. The term is general in that the three arguments are uninstantiated variables whose names are generated by Prolog. For example:

$$D = date(\_5, \_6, \_7)$$

These three variables are then instantiated in the example above by the three **arg** goals.

Related to this set of built-in predicates is the predicate **name** for constructing/decomposing atoms, introduced in Chapter 6. We will repeat its meaning here for completeness.

name(A, L)

is true if L is the list of ASCII codes of the characters in atom A.

EXERCISES

7.3 Define the predicate **ground(Term)** so that it is true if **Term** does not contain any uninstantiated variables.

7.4 The **substitute** procedure of this section only produces the 'outer-most' substitution when there are alternatives. Modify the procedure so that all possible alternative substitutions are produced through backtracking. For example:

?- substitute(a+b, f(A+B), new, NewTerm).

A = a
B = b
NewTerm = f(new);

A = a+b
B = a+b
NewTerm = f(new+new)

Our original version only finds the first answer.

7.5 Define the relation

subsumes(Term1, Term2)

so that **Term1** is more general than **Term2**. For example:

?- subsumes(X, c).

yes

```
?- subsumes( g(X), g(t(Y)) ).

yes

?- subsumes( f(X,X), f(a,b) ).

no
```

7.3 Various kinds of equality

When do we consider two terms to be equal? Until now we have introduced three kinds of equality in Prolog. The first was based on matching, written as:

X = Y

This is true if X and Y match. Another type of equality was written as:

X is E

This is true if X matches the value of the arithmetic expression E. We also had:

E1 = : = E2

This is true if the values of the arithmetic expressions E1 and E2 are equal. In contrast, when the values of two arithmetic expressions are not equal, we write:

E1 = \ = E2

Sometimes we are interested in a stricter kind of equality: the *literal equality* of two terms. This kind of equality is implemented as another built-in predicate written as an infix operator '= =':

T1 = = T2

This is true if terms T1 and T2 are identical; that is, they have exactly the same structure and all the corresponding components are the same. In particular, the names of the variables also have to be the same. The complementary relation is 'not identical', written as:

T1 \ = = T2

Here are some examples:

?- f(a, b) = = f(a, b).

yes

?- f(a, b) = = f(a, X).

no

?- f(a, X) = = f(a, Y).

no

?- X \ = = Y.

yes

?- t(X, f(a,Y)) = = t(X, f(a,Y)).

yes

As an example, let us redefine the relation

count(Term, List, N)

from Section 7.1. This time let N be the number of literal occurrences of the term **Term** in a list **List**:

```
count( _, [ ], 0).
count( Term, [Head | Tail ], N) :-
   Term = = Head, !,
   count( Term, L, N1),
   N is N1 + 1
   ;
   count( Term, L, N).
```

7.4   Database manipulation

According to the relational model of databases, a database is a specification of a set of relations. A Prolog program can be viewed as such a database: the specification of relations is partly explicit (facts) and partly implicit (rules). Furthermore, built-in predicates make it possible to update this database during the execution of the program. This is done by adding (during execution) new clauses to the program or by deleting existing clauses. Predicates that serve these purposes are **assert**, **asserta**, **assertz** and **retract**.

A goal

assert(C)

always succeeds and, as its side effect, causes a clause C to be 'asserted' – that is, added to the database. A goal

> **retract(C)**

does the opposite: it deletes a clause that matches C. The following conversation with Prolog illustrates:

> **?- crisis.**
>
> **no**
>
> **?- assert(crisis).**
>
> **yes**
>
> **?- crisis.**
>
> **yes**
>
> **?- retract(crisis).**
>
> **yes**
>
> **?- crisis.**
>
> **no**

Clauses thus asserted act exactly as part of the 'original' program. The following example shows the use of **assert** and **retract** as one method of handling changing situations. Let us assume that we have the following program about weather:

> **nice :-**
>   **sunshine, not raining.**
>
> **funny :-**
>   **sunshine, raining.**
>
> **disgusting :-**
>   **raining, fog.**
>
> **raining.**
>
> **fog.**

The following conversation with this program will gradually update the database:

> **?- nice.**
>
> **no**
>
> **?- disgusting.**
>
> **yes**

?- retract(fog).

yes

?- disgusting.

no

?- assert(sunshine).

yes

?- funny.

yes

?- retract(raining).

yes

?- nice.

yes

Clauses of any form can be asserted or retracted. The next example illustrates that **retract** is also non-deterministic: a whole set of clauses can, through backtracking, be removed by a single **retract** goal. Let us assume that we have the following facts in the 'consulted' program:

```
fast( ann).
slow( tom).
slow( pat).
```

We can add a rule to this program, as follows:

```
?- assert(
        ( faster(X,Y) :-
            fast(X), slow(Y) ) ).
```

yes

?- faster(A, B).

A = ann
B = tom

?- retract(slow(X)).

X = tom;
X = pat;
no

?- faster(ann, _).

no

Notice that when a rule is asserted, the syntax requires that the rule (as an argument to **assert**) be enclosed in parentheses.

When asserting a clause, we may want to specify the position at which the new clause is inserted to the database. The predicates **asserta** and **assertz** enable us to control the position of insertion. The goal

    asserta(C)

adds C at the beginning of the database. The goal

    assertz(C)

adds C at the end of the database. The following example illustrates these effects:

    ?- assert(p(a)), assertz(p(b)), asserta(p(c)).

    yes

    ?- p(X).

    X = c;

    X = a;

    X = b

There is a relation between **consult** and **assertz**. Consulting a file can be defined in terms of **assertz** as follows: to consult a file, read each term (clause) in the file and assert it at the end of the database.

One useful application of **asserta** is to store already computed answers to questions. For example, let there be a predicate

    solve(Problem, Solution)

defined in the program. We may now ask some question and request that the answer be remembered for future questions.

    ?- solve(problem1, Solution),
       asserta(solve(problem1, Solution)).

If the first goal above succeeds then the answer (**Solution**) is stored and used, as any other clause, in answering further questions. The advantage of such a 'memoization' of answers is that a further question that matches the asserted fact will normally be answered much quicker than the first one. The result now will be simply retrieved as a fact, and not computed through a possibly time-consuming process. This technique of storing derived solutions is also called 'caching'.

An extension of this idea is to use asserting for generating all solutions in the form of a table of facts. For example, we can generate a table of products of all pairs of integers between 0 and 9 as follows: generate a pair of integers X and Y, compute Z is X*Y, assert the three numbers as one line of the product table, and then force the failure. The failure will cause, through backtracking, another pair of integers to be found and so another line tabulated, etc. The following procedure **maketable** implements this idea:

```
maketable :-
    L = [0,1,2,3,4,5,6,7,8,9],
    member( X, L),              % Choose first factor
    member( Y, L),              % Choose second factor
    Z is X*Y,
    assert( product(X,Y,Z) ),
    fail.
```

Only within the same clause [handwritten margin note]

The question

```
?- maketable.
```

will, of course, not succeed, but it will, as a side effect, add the whole product table to the database. After that, we can ask for example, what pairs give the product 8:

```
?- product( A, B, 8).

A = 1
B = 8;

A = 2
B = 4;

...
```

A remark on the style of programming should be made at this stage. The foregoing examples illustrate some obviously useful applications of **assert** and **retract**. However, their use requires special care. Excessive and careless use of these facilities cannot be recommended as good programming style. By asserting and retracting we, in fact, modify the program. Therefore relations that hold at some point will not be true at some other time. At different times the same questions receive different answers. A lot of asserting and retracting may thus obscure the meaning of the program and it may become hard to imagine what is true and what is not. The resulting behaviour of the program may become difficult to understand, difficult to explain and to trust.

EXERCISES

7.6 (a) Write a Prolog question to remove the whole **product** table from the database.

(b) Modify the question so that it only removes those entries where the product is 0.

7.7 Define the relation

    copy(Term, Copy)

which will produce a copy of **Term** so that **Copy** is **Term** with all its variables renamed. This can be easily programmed by using **assert** and **retract**.

7.5 Control facilities

So far we have covered most of the extra control facilities except **repeat**. For completeness the complete set is presented here.

- *cut*, written as '!', prevents backtracking. It was introduced in Chapter 5.
- **fail** is a goal that always fails.
- **true** is a goal that always succeeds.
- **not(P)** is a type of negation that behaves exactly as if defined as:

    not(P) :- P, !, fail; true.

Some problems with **cut** and **not** were discussed in detail in Chapter 5.

- **call(P)** invokes a goal P. It succeeds if P succeeds.
- **repeat** is a goal that always succeeds. Its special property is that it is non-deterministic; therefore, each time it is reached by backtracking it generates another alternative execution branch. **repeat** behaves as if defined by:

    repeat.
    repeat :- repeat.

A typical way of using **repeat** is illustrated by the following procedure **dosquares** which reads a sequence of numbers and outputs their squares. The sequence is concluded with the atom stop which serves as a signal for the procedure to terminate.

```
dosquares :-
  repeat,
  read( X),
  ( X = stop, !
  ;
    Y is X*X, write(Y),
    fail
  ).
```

7.6 *bagof, setof* and *findall*

We can generate, by backtracking, all the objects, one by one, that satisfy some goal. Each time a new solution is generated, the previous one disappears and is not accessible any more. However, sometimes we would prefer to have all the generated objects available together – for example, collected into a list. The built-in predicates **bagof** and **setof** serve this purpose; the predicate **findall** is sometimes provided instead.

The goal

    bagof(X, P, L)

will produce the list L of all the objects X such that a goal P is satisfied. Of course, this usually makes sense only if X and P have some common variables. For example, let us have these facts in the program:

```
age( peter, 7).
age( ann, 5).
age( pat, 8).
age( tom, 5).
```

Then we can obtain the list of all the children of age 5 by the goal:

    ?- bagof(Child, age(Child, 5), List).

    List = [ann, tom]

If, in the above goal, we leave the age unspecified, then we get, through backtracking, three lists of children, corresponding to the three age values:

    ?- bagof(Child, age(Child, Age), List).

    Age = 7
    List = [peter];

    Age = 5
    List = [ann, tom];

```
Age = 8
List = [ pat];
```

no

We may prefer to have all of the children in one list regardless of their age. This can be achieved by explicitly stating in the call of **bagof** that we do not care about the value of **Age** as long as such a value exists. This is stated as:

?- **bagof(Child, Age ^ age(Child, Age), List).**

List = [peter, ann, pat, tom]

Syntactically, '^' is a predefined infix operator.

If there is no solution for P in the goal **bagof(X, P, L)**, then the **bagof** goal simply fails. If the same object X is found repeatedly, then all of its occurrences will appear in L, which leads to duplicate items in L.

The predicate **setof** is similar to **bagof**. The goal

setof(X, P, L)

will again produce a list L of objects X that satisfy P. Only this time the list L will be ordered and duplicate items, if there are any, will be eliminated. The ordering of the objects is according to the alphabetical order or to the relation '<', if objects in the list are numbers. If the objects are structures, then the principal functors are compared for the ordering. If these are equal, then the left-most, top-most functors that are not equal in the terms compared decide. For example:

?- **setof(Child, Age ^ age(Child, Age), ChildList),**
   setof(Age, Child ^ age(Child, Age), AgeList).

ChildList = [ann, pat, peter, tom]
AgeList = [5, 7, 8]

There is no restriction on the kind of objects that are collected. So we can, for example, construct the list of children ordered by their age, by collecting pairs of the form **Age/Child**:

?- **setof(Age/Child, age(Child, Age), List).**

List = [5/ann, 5/tom, 7/peter, 8/pat]

Another predicate of this family, similar to **bagof**, is **findall**.

findall(X, P, L)

produces, again, a list of objects that satisfy P. The difference with respect to **bagof** is that *all* of the objects X are collected regardless of (possibly) different solutions for variables in P that are not shared with X. This difference is shown in the following example:

> ?- findall(Child, age(Child, Age), List).
>
> List = [peter, ann, pat, tom]

If there is no object X that satisfies P then **findall** will succeed with L = [ ].

If **findall** is not available as a built-in predicate in the implementation used then it can be easily programmed as follows. All solutions for P are generated by forced backtracking. Each solution is, when generated, immediately asserted into the database so that it is not lost when the next solution is found. After all the solutions have been generated and asserted, they have to be collected into a list and retracted from the database. This whole process can be imagined as all the solutions generated forming a queue. Each newly generated solution is, by assertion, added to the end of this queue. When the solutions are collected the queue dissolves. Note, in addition, that the end of this queue has to be marked, for example, by the atom 'bottom' (which, of course, should be different from any solution that is possibly expected). An implementation of **findall** along these lines is shown as Figure 7.4.

```
findall( X, Goal, Xlist) :-
    call( Goal),                        % Find a solution
    assertz( queue(X) ),                % Assert it
    fail;                               % Try to find more solutions
    assertz( queue(bottom) ),           % Mark end of solutions
    collect( Xlist).                    % Collect the solutions

collect( L) :-
    retract( queue(X) ), !,             % Retract next solution
    ( X == bottom, !, L = []            % End of solutions?
    ;
    L = [X | Rest], collect( Rest) ).   % Otherwise collect the rest
```

Figure 7.4 An implementation of the **findall** relation.

EXERCISES

7.8 Use **bagof** to define the relation **powerset(Set, Subsets)** to compute the set of all subsets of a given set (all sets represented as lists).

7.9 Use bagof to define the relation

copy(Term, Copy)

such that Copy is Term with all its variables renamed.

SUMMARY

- A Prolog implementation normally provides a set of built-in procedures to accomplish several useful operations that are not possible in pure Prolog. In this chapter, such a set of predicates, available in many Prolog implementations, was introduced.

- The type of a term can be tested by the following predicates:

var(X)	X is a (non-instantiated) variable
nonvar(X)	X is not a variable
atom(X)	X is an atom
integer(X)	X is an integer
real(X)	X is a real number
atomic(X)	X is either an atom or an integer

- Terms can be constructed or decomposed:

  Term =.. [Functor | ArgumentList]
  functor(Term, Functor, Arity)
  arg(N, Term, Argument)
  name(Atom, CharacterCodes)

- A Prolog program can be viewed as a relational database that can be updated by the following procedures:

assert(Clause)	add Clause to the program
asserta(Clause)	add at the beginning
assertz(Clause)	add at the end
retract(Clause)	remove a clause that matches Clause

- All the objects that satisfy a given condition can be collected into a list by the predicates:

bagof(X, P, L)	L is the list of all X that satisfy condition P
setof(X, P, L)	L is the sorted list of all X that satisfy condition P
findall(X, P, L)	similar to bagof

- repeat is a control facility that generates an unlimited number of alternatives for backtracking

8 Programming Style and Technique

In this chapter we will review some general principles of good programming and discuss the following questions in particular: How to think about Prolog programs? What are elements of good programming style in Prolog? How to debug Prolog programs? How to make Prolog programs more efficient?

8.1 General principles of good programming

A fundamental question, related to good programming, is: What is a good program? Answering this question is not trivial as there are several criteria for judging how good a program is. Generally accepted criteria include the following:

- *Correctness* Above all, a good program should be correct. That is, it should do what it is supposed to do. This may seem a trivial, self-explanatory requirement. However, in the case of complex programs, correctness is often not attained. A common mistake when writing programs is to neglect this obvious criterion and pay more attention to other criteria, such as efficiency.

- *Efficiency* A good program should not needlessly waste computer time and memory space.

- *Transparency, readability* A good program should be easy to read and easy to understand. It should not be more complicated than necessary. Clever programming tricks that obscure the meaning of the program should be avoided. The general organization of the program and its layout help its readability.

- *Modifiability* A good program should be easy to modify and to extend. Transparency and modular organization of the program help modifiability.

- *Robustness* A good program should be robust. It should not crash immediately when the user enters some incorrect or unexpected data. The program should, in the case of such errors, stay 'alive' and behave reasonably (should report errors).

- *Documentation* A good program should be properly documented. The minimal documentation is the program's listing including sufficient program comments.

The importance of particular criteria depends on the problem and on the circumstances in which the program is written, and on the environment in which it is used. There is no doubt that correctness has the highest priority. The issues of transparency, modifiability, robustness and documentation are usually given, at least, as much priority as the issue of efficiency.

There are some general guidelines for practically achieving the above criteria. One important rule is to first *think* about the problem to be solved, and only then to start writing the actual code in the programming language used. Once we have developed a good understanding of the problem and the whole solution is well thought through, the actual coding will be fast and easy, and there is a good chance that we will soon get a correct program.

A common mistake is to start writing the code even before the full definition of the problem has been understood. A fundamental reason why early coding is bad practice is that the thinking about the problem and the ideas for a solution should be done in terms that are most relevant to the problem. These terms are usually far from the syntax of the programming language used, and they may include natural language statements and pictorial representation of ideas.

Such a formulation of the solution will have to be transformed into the programming language, but this transformation process may not be easy. A good approach is to use the principle of *stepwise refinement*. The initial formulation of the solution is referred to as the 'top-level solution', and the final program as the 'bottom-level solution'.

According to the principle of stepwise refinement, the final program is developed through a sequence of transformations, or 'refinements', of the solution. We start with the first, top-level solution and then proceed through a sequence of solutions; these are all equivalent, but each solution in the sequence is expressed in more detail. In each refinement step, concepts used in previous formulations are elaborated to greater detail and their representation gets closer to the programming language. It should be realized that refinement applies both to procedure definitions and to data structures. In the initial stages we normally work with more abstract, bulky units of information whose structure is refined later.

Such a strategy of top-down stepwise refinement has the following advantages:

- it allows for formulation of rough solutions in terms that are most relevant to the problem;
- in terms of such powerful concepts, the solution should be succint and simple, and therefore likely to be correct;
- each refinement step should be small enough so that it is intellectually manageable; if so, the transformation of a solution into a new, more detailed representation is likely to be correct, and so is the resulting solution at the next level of detail.

In the case of Prolog we may talk about the stepwise refinement of *relations*. If the nature of the problem suggests thinking in algorithmic terms, then we can also talk about refinement of *algorithms*, adopting the procedural point of view on Prolog.

In order to properly refine a solution at some level of detail, and to introduce useful concepts at the next lower level, we need ideas. Therefore programming is creative, especially so for beginners. With experience, programming gradually becomes less of an art and more of a craft. But, nevertheless, a major question is: How do we get ideas? Most ideas come from experience, from similar problems whose solutions we know. If we do not know a direct programming solution, another similar problem could be helpful. Another source of ideas is everyday life. For example, if the problem is to write a program to sort a list of items we may get an idea from considering the question: How would I myself sort a set of exam papers according to the alphabetical order of students?

General principles of good programming outlined in this section are also known as the ingredients of 'structured programming', and they basically apply to Prolog as well. We will discuss some details with particular reference to Prolog in the following sections.

8.2 How to think about Prolog programs

One characteristic feature of Prolog is that it allows for both the procedural and declarative way of thinking about programs. The two approaches have been discussed in detail in Chapter 2, and illustrated by examples throughout the text. Which approach will be more efficient and practical depends on the problem. Declarative solutions are usually easier to develop, but may lead to an inefficient program.

During the process of developing a solution we have to find ideas for reducing problems to one or more easier subproblems. An important question is: How do we find proper subproblems? There are several general principles that often work in Prolog programming. These will be discussed in the following sections.

8.2.1 Use of recursion

The principle here is to split the problem into cases belonging to two groups:

(1)   trivial, or 'boundary' cases;
(2)   'general' cases where the solution is constructed from solutions of (simpler) versions of the original problem itself.

In Prolog we use this technique all the time. Let us look at one more example: processing a list of items so that each item is transformed by the same transformation rule. Let this procedure be

maplist(List, F, NewList)

where List is an original list, F is a transformation rule (a binary relation) and NewList is the list of all transformed items. The problem of transforming List can be split into two cases:

(1)   Boundary case: List = [ ]

if List = [ ] then NewList = [ ], regardless of F

(2)   General case: **List = [X | Tail]**

>   To transform a list of the form **[X | Tail]**, do:
>   transform the item X by rule F obtaining **NewX**, and
>   transform the list **Tail** obtaining **NewTail**;
>   the whole transformed list is **[NewX | NewTail]**.

In Prolog:

```
maplist( [ ], _, [ ] ).

maplist( [X | Taii], F, [NewX | NewTail] ) :-
   G =.. [F, X, NewX],
   call( G),
   maplist( Tail, F, NewTail).
```

One reason why recursion so naturally applies to defining relations in Prolog is that data objects themselves often have recursive structure. Lists and trees are such objects. A list is either empty (boundary case) or has a head and a tail that is itself a list (general case). A binary tree is either empty (boundary case) or it has a root and two subtrees that are themselves binary trees (general case). Therefore, to process a whole non-empty tree, we must do something with the root, and process the subtrees.

8.2.2   Generalization

It is often a good idea to generalize the original problem, so that the solution to the generalized problem can be formulated recursively. The original problem is then solved as a special case of its more general version. Generalization of a relation typically involves the introduction of one or more extra arguments. A major problem, which may require deeper insight into the problem, is how to find the right generalization.

As an example let us revisit the eight queens problem. The original problem was to place eight queens on the chessboard so that they do not attack each other. Let us call the corresponding relation:

```
eightqueens( Pos)
```

This is true if **Pos** is some representation of a position with eight non-attacking queens. A good idea in this case is to generalize the number of queens from eight to N. The number of queens now becomes the additional argument:

```
nqueens( Pos, N)
```

The advantage of this generalization is that there is an immediate recursive formulation of the **nqueens** relation:

(1)   Boundary case: N = 0

To safely place zero queens is trivial.

(2)   General case: N > 0

To safely place N queens on the board, satisfy the following:

- achieve a safe configuration of (N − 1) queens; and
- add the remaining queen so that she does not attack any other queen.

Once the generalized problem has been solved, the original problem is easy:

    eightqueens(Pos) :- nqueens(Pos, 8).

8.2.3   Using pictures

When searching for ideas about a problem, it is often useful to introduce some graphical representation of the problem. A picture may help us to perceive some essential relations in the problem. Then we just have to describe what we *see* in the picture in the programming language.

The use of pictorial representations is often useful in problem solving in general; it seems, however, that it works with Prolog particularly well. The following arguments explain why:

(1)   Prolog is particularly suitable for problems that involve objects and relations between objects. Often, such problems can be naturally illustrated by graphs in which nodes correspond to objects and arcs correspond to relations.

(2)   Structured data objects in Prolog are naturally pictured as trees.

(3)   The declarative meaning of Prolog facilitates the translation of pictorial representations into Prolog because, in principle, the order in which the picture is described does not matter. We just put what we see into the program in any order. (For practical reasons of the program's efficiency this order will possibly have to be polished later.)

8.3   Programming style

The purpose of conforming to some stylistic conventions is:

- to reduce the danger of programming errors; and
- to produce programs that are readable and easy to understand, easy to debug and to modify.

We will review here some ingredients of good programming style in Prolog: some general rules of good style, tabular organization of long procedures and commenting.

8.3.1   Some rules of good style

- Program clauses should be short. Their body should typically contain no more than a few goals.

- Procedures should be short because long procedures are hard to understand. However, long procedures are acceptable if they have some uniform structure (this will be discussed later in this section).

- Mnemonic names for procedures and variables should be used. Names should indicate the meaning of relations and the role of data objects.

- The layout of programs is important. Spacing, blank lines and indentation should be consistently used for the sake of readability. Clauses about the same procedure should be clustered together; there should be blank lines between clauses (unless, perhaps, there are numerous facts about the same relation); each goal can be placed on a separate line. Prolog programs sometimes resemble poems for the aesthetic appeal of ideas and form.

- Stylistic conventions of this kind may vary from program to program as they depend on the problem and personal taste. It is important, however, that the same conventions are used consistently throughout the whole program.

- The cut operator should be used with care. Cut should not be used if it can be easily avoided. It is better to use, where possible, 'green cuts' rather than 'red cuts'. As discussed in Chapter 5, a cut is called 'green' if it can be removed without altering the declarative meaning of the clause. The use of 'red cuts' should be restricted to clearly defined constructs such as not or the selection between alternatives. An example of the latter construct is:

    if Condition *then* Goal1 *else* Goal2

    This translates into Prolog, using cut, as:

    ```
    Condition, !,      % Condition true?
    Goal1              % If yes then Goal1
    ;
    Goal2              % Otherwise Goal2
    ```

- The not procedure can also lead to surprising behaviour, as it is related to cut. We have to be well aware of how not is defined in Prolog. However, if there is a dilemma between not and cut, the former is perhaps better than some obscure construct with cut.

- Program modification by **assert** and **retract** can grossly degrade the transparency of the program's behaviour. In particular, the same program will answer the same question differently at different times. In such cases, if we want to reproduce the same behaviour we have to make sure that the whole previous state, which was modified by assertions and retractions, is completely restored.

- The use of a semicolon may obscure the meaning of a clause. The readability can sometimes be improved by splitting the clause containing the semicolon into more clauses; but this will, possibly, be at the expense of the length of the program and its efficiency.

To illustrate some points of this section consider the relation

```
merge( List1, List2, List3)
```

where List1 and List2 are ordered lists that merge into List3. For example:

```
merge( [2,4,7], [1,3,4,8], [1,2,3,4,4,7,8] )
```

The following is an implementation of merge in bad style:

```
merge( List1, List2, List3) :-
    List1 = [ ], !, List3 = List2;       % First list empty
    List2 = [ ], !, List3 = List1;       % Second list empty
    List1 = [X | Rest1],
    List2 = [Y | Rest2],
    ( X < Y, !,
      Z = X,                             % Z is head of List3
      merge( Rest1, List2, Rest3);
      Z = Y,
      merge( List1, Rest2, Rest3) ),
    List3 = [Z | Rest3].
```

Here is a better version which avoids semicolons:

```
merge( [ ], List, List) :-
    !.                                   % Prevent redundant solutions

merge( List, [ ], List).

merge( [X | Rest1], [Y | Rest2], [X | Rest3] ) :-
    X < Y, !,
    merge( Rest1, [Y | Rest2], Rest3).

merge( List1, [Y | Rest2], [Y | Rest3] ) :-
    merge( List1, Rest2, Rest3).
```

8.3.2   Tabular organization of long procedures

Long procedures are acceptable if they have some uniform structure. Typically, such a form is a set of facts when a relation is effectively defined in the tabular form. Advantages of such an organization of a long procedure are:

- Its structure is easily understood.
- Incrementability: it can be refined by simply adding new facts.
- It is easy to check and correct or modify (by simply replacing some fact independently of other facts).

8.3.3   Commenting

Program comments should explain in the first place what the program is about and how to use it, and only then the details of the solution method used and other programming details. The main purpose of comments is to enable the user to use the program, to understand it and to possibly modify it. Comments should describe, in the shortest form possible, everything that is essential to these ends. Undercommenting is a usual fault, but a program can also be overcommented. Explanation of details that are obvious from the program code itself is only a needless burden to the program.

Long passages of comments should precede the code they refer to, while short comments should be interspersed with the code itself. Information that should, in general, be included in comments comprises the following:

- What the program does, how it is used (for example, what goal is to be invoked and what are the expected results), examples of using the program.
- What are top-level predicates?
- How are main concepts (objects) represented?
- Execution time and memory requirements of the program.
- What are the program's limitations?
- Are there any special system-dependent features used?
- What is the meaning of the predicates in the program? What are their arguments? Which arguments are 'input' and which are 'output', if known? (Input arguments have fully specified values, without uninstantiated variables, when the predicate is called.)
- Algorithmic and implementation details.

8.4   Debugging

When a program does not do what it is expected to do the main problem is to locate the error(s). It is easier to locate an error in a part of the program (or a module) than in the program as a whole. Therefore, a good principle of debugging is to start by testing smaller units of the program, and when these can be trusted, to start testing bigger modules or the whole program.

Debugging in Prolog is facilitated by two things: first, Prolog is an interactive language so any part of the program can be directly invoked by a proper question to the Prolog system; second, Prolog implementations usually provide special debugging aids. As a result of these two features, debugging of Prolog programs can, in general, be done far more efficiently than in most other programming languages.

The basis for debugging aids is *tracing*. 'Tracing a goal' means that the information regarding the goal's satisfaction is displayed during execution. This information includes:

- Entry information: the predicate name and the values of arguments when the goal is invoked.
- Exit information: in the case of success, the values of arguments that satisfy the goal; otherwise an indication of failure.
- Re-entry information: invocation of the same goal caused by backtracking.

Between entry and exit, the trace information for all the subgoals of this goal can be obtained. So we can trace the execution of our question all the way down to the lowest level goals until facts are encountered. Such detailed tracing may turn out to be impractical due to the excessive amount of tracing information; therefore, the user can specify selective tracing. There are two selection mechanisms: first, suppress tracing information beyond a certain level; second, trace only some specified subset of predicates, and not all of them.

Such debugging aids are activated by system-dependent built-in predicates. A typical subset of such predicates is as follows:

trace

triggers exhaustive tracing of goals that follow.

notrace

stops further tracing.

spy(P)

specifies that a predicate P be traced. This is used when we are particularly interested in the named predicate and want to avoid tracing information from other goals (either above or below the level of a call of P). Several predicates can be simultaneously active for 'spying'.

nospy(P)

stops 'spying' P.

Tracing beyond a certain depth can be suppressed by special commands during execution. There may be several other debugging commands available, such as returning to a previous point of execution. After such a return we can, for example, repeat the execution at a greater detail of tracing.

8.5 Efficiency

There are several aspects of efficiency, including the most common ones, execution time and space requirements of a program. Another aspect is the time needed by the programmer to develop the program.

The traditional computer architecture is not particularly suitable for the Prolog style of program execution – that is, satisfying a list of goals. Therefore, the limitations of time and space may be experienced earlier in Prolog than in many other programming languages. Whether this will cause difficulties in a practical application depends on the problem. The issue of time efficiency is practically meaningless if a Prolog program that is run a few times per day takes 1 second of CPU time and a corresponding program in some other language, say Fortran, takes 0.1 seconds. The difference in efficiency will perhaps matter if the two programs take 50 minutes and 5 minutes respectively.

On the other hand, in many areas of application Prolog will greatly reduce the program development time. Prolog programs will, in general, be easier to write, to understand and to debug than in traditional languages. Problems that gravitate toward the 'Prolog domain' involve symbolic, non-numeric processing, structured data objects and relations between them. In particular, Prolog has been successfully applied in areas, such as symbolic solving of equations, planning, databases, general problem solving, prototyping, implementation of programming languages, discrete and qualitative simulation, architectural design, machine learning, natural language understanding, expert systems, and other areas of artificial intelligence. On the other hand, numerical mathematics is an area for which Prolog is not a natural candidate.

With respect to the execution efficiency, executing a *compiled* program is generally more efficient than *interpreting* the program. Therefore, if the Prolog system contains both an interpreter and a compiler, then the compiler should be used if efficiency is critical.

If a program suffers from inefficiency then it can often be radically improved by improving the algorithm itself. However, to do this, the procedural aspects of the program have to be studied. A simple way of improving the executional efficiency is to find a better ordering of clauses of procedures, and of goals in the bodies of procedures. Another relatively simple method is to provide guidance to the Prolog system by means of cuts.

Ideas for improving the efficiency of a program usually come from a deeper understanding of the problem. A more efficient algorithm can, in general, result from improvements of two kinds:

- Improving search efficiency by avoiding unnecessary backtracking and stopping the execution of useless alternatives as soon as possible.
- Using more suitable data structures to represent objects in the program, so that operations on objects can be implemented more efficiently.

We will study both kinds of improvements by looking at examples. Yet another technique of improving efficiency will be illustrated by an example. This technique, called caching, is based on asserting into the database intermediate results that are likely to be needed again in the future computation. Instead of repeating the computation, such results are simply retrieved as already known facts.

8.5.1   Improving the efficiency of an eight queens program

As a simple example of improving the search efficiency let us revisit the eight queens problem (see Figure 4.7). In this program, the Y-coordinates of the queens are found by successively trying, for each queen, the integers between 1 and 8. This was programmed as the goal:

```
member( Y, [1,2,3,4,5,6,7,8] )
```

The way that **member** works is that $Y = 1$ is tried first, and then $Y = 2$, $Y = 3$, etc. As the queens are placed one after another in adjacent columns on the board, it is obvious that this order of trials is not the most appropriate. The reason for this is that the queens in adjacent columns will attack each other if they are not placed at least two squares apart in the vertical direction. According to this observation, a simple attempt to improve the efficiency is to rearrange the candidate coordinate values. For example:

```
member( Y, [1,5,2,6,3,7,4,8] )
```

This minor change will reduce the time needed to find the first solution by a factor of 3 or 4.

In the next example, a similarly simple idea of reordering will convert a practically unacceptable time complexity into a trivial one.

8.5.2   Improving the efficiency in a map colouring program

The map colouring problem is to assign each country in a given map one of four given colours in such a way that no two neighbouring countries are painted with the same colour. There is a theorem which guarantees that this is always possible.

Let us assume that a map is specified by the neighbour relation

ngb(Country, Neighbours)

where Neighbours is the list of countries bordering on Country. So the map of Europe, with 20 countries, would be specified (in alphabetical order) as:

```
ngb( albania, [greece, yugoslavia] ).
ngb( andorra, [france, spain] ).
ngb( austria, [czechoslovakia, hungary, italy, liechtenstein,
            switzerland, westgermany, yugoslavia] ).
```

. . .

Let a solution be represented as a list of pairs of the form

Country/Colour

which specifies a colour for each country in a given map. For the given map, the names of countries are fixed in advance, and the problem is to find the values for the colours. Thus, for Europe, the problem is to find a proper instantiation of variables C1, C2, C3, etc. in the list:

[albania/C1, andorra/C2, austria/C3, ...]

Now let us define the predicate

colours(Country_colour_list)

which is true if the Country_colour_list satisfies the map colouring constraint with respect to a given ngb relation. Let the four colours be yellow, blue, red and green. The condition that no two neighbouring countries are of the same colour can be formulated in Prolog as follows:

```
colours( [ ] ).

colours( [Country/Colour | Rest] )  :-
    colours( Rest),
    member( Colour, [yellow, blue, red, green] ),
    not( member( Country1/Colour, Rest), neighbour( Country, Country1) ).

neighbour( Country, Country1) :-
    ngb( Country, Neighbours),
    member( Country1, Neighbours).
```

Here, member(X,L) is, as usual, the list membership relation. This will work well for simple maps, with a small number of countries. Europe might be problematic, however. Assuming that the built-in predicate setof is available, one attempt to colour Europe could be as follows. First, let us define an auxiliary relation:

    country(C) :- ngb(C, _).

Then the question for colouring Europe can be formulated as:

    ?- setof(Cntry/Colour, country(Cntry), CountryColourList),
       colours(CountryColourList).

The **setof** goal will construct a template country/colour list for Europe in which uninstantiated variables stand for colours. Then the **colours** goal is supposed to instantiate the colours. However, this attempt will probably fail because of inefficiency.

A detailed study of the way Prolog tries to satisfy the **colours** goal reveals the source of inefficiency. Countries in the country/colour list are arranged in alphabetical order, and this has nothing to do with their geographical arrangement. The order in which the countries are assigned colours corresponds to the order in the list (starting at the end), which is in our case independent of the **ngb** relation. So the colouring process starts at some end of the map, continues at some other end, etc., moving around more or less randomly. This may easily lead to a situation in which a country that is to be coloured is surrounded by many other countries, already painted with all four available colours. Then backtracking is necessary which leads to inefficiency.

It is clear, then, that the efficiency depends on the order in which the countries are coloured. Intuition suggests a simple colouring strategy that should be better than random: start with some country that has many neighbours, and then proceed to the neighbours, then to the neighbours of neighbours, etc. For Europe, then, West Germany (having most neighbours, 9) is a good candidate to start with. Of course, when the template country/colour list is constructed, West Germany has to be put at the end of the list and other countries have to be added at the front of the list. In this way the colouring algorithm, which starts at the rear end, will commence with West Germany and proceed from there from neighbour to neighbour.

Such a country/colour template dramatically improves the efficiency with respect to the original, alphabetical order, and possible colourings for the map of Europe will be now produced without difficulty.

We can construct a properly ordered list of countries manually, but we do not have to. The following procedure, **makelist**, does it. It starts the construction with some specified country (West Germany in our case) and collects the countries into a list called **Closed**. Each country is first put into another list, called **Open**, before it is transferred to **Closed**. Each time that a country is transferred from **Open** to **Closed**, its neighbours are added to **Open**.

    makelist(List) :-
        collect([westgermany], [ ], List).

    collect([ ], Closed, Closed).   % No more candidates for Closed

```
collect( [X | Open], Closed, List)  :-
    member( X, Closed), !,                  % X has already been collected?
    collect( Open, Closed, List).           % Discard X

collect( [X | Open], Closed, List)  :-
    ngb( X, Ngbs),                          % Find X's neighbours
    conc( Ngbs, Open, Open1),               % Put them to Open1
    collect( Open1, [X | Closed], List).    % Collect the Rest
```

The conc relation is, as usual, the list concatenation relation.

8.5.3 Improving the efficiency of a list concatenation by a better data structure

In our programs so far, the concatenation of lists has been programmed as:

```
conc( [ ], L, L).

conc( [X | L1], L2, [X | L3] )  :-
    conc( L1, L2, L3).
```

This is inefficient when the first list is long. The following example explains why:

```
?- conc( [a,b,c], [d,e], L).
```

This produces the following sequence of goals:

```
conc( [a,b,c], [d,e], L)
    conc( [b,c], [d,e], L')       where L = [a | L']
        conc( [c], [d,e], L'')     where L' = [b | L'']
            conc( [ ], [d,e], L''')    where L'' = [c | L''']
                true                     where L''' = [d,e]
```

From this it is clear that the program in effect scans all of the first list, until the empty list is encountered.

But could we not simply skip the whole of the first list in a single step and append the second list, instead of gradually working down the first list? To do this, we need to know where the end of a list is; that is, we need another representation of lists. One solution is to represent a list by a pair of lists. For example, the list

```
[a,b,c]
```

can be represented by the two lists:

```
L1 = [a,b,c,d,e]
L2 = [d,e]
```

Such a pair of lists, which we will for brevity choose to write as **L1-L2**, represents the 'difference' between L1 and L2. This of course only works under the condition that L2 is a suffix of L1. Note that the same list can be represented by several 'difference pairs'. So the list **[a,b,c]** can be represented by

> **[a,b,c] - [ ]**

or

> **[a,b,c,d,e] - [d,e]**

or

> **[a,b,c,d,e | T] - [d,e | T]**

or

> **[a,b,c | T] - T**

where T is any list, etc. The empty list is represented by any pair **L-L**.

As the second member of the pair indicates the end of the list, the end is directly accessible. This can be used for an efficient implementation of concatenation. The method is illustrated in Figure 8.1. The corresponding concatenation relation translates into Prolog as the fact:

> **concat(A1 - Z1, Z1 - Z2, A1 - Z2).**

Let us use **concat** to concatenate the lists **[a,b,c]**, represented by the pair **[a,b,c | T1]-T1**, and the list **[d,e]**, represented by **[d,e | T2]-T2**:

> **?- concat([a,b,c | T1] - T1, [d,e | T2] - T2, L).**

The concatenation is done just by matching this goal with the clause about **concat**, giving:

> **T1 = [d,e | T2]**
> **L = [a,b,c,d,e | T2] - T2**

Figure 8.1 Concatenation of lists represented by difference pairs. **L1** is represented by **A1-Z1**, **L2** by **A2-Z2**, and the result **L3** by **A1-Z2** when **Z1 = A2** must be true.

Due to its efficiency, this *difference lists* technique for list concatenation is very popular, although it cannot be used as flexibly as our usual conc procedure.

8.5.4 Improving the efficiency by asserting derived facts

Sometimes during computation the same goal has to be satisfied again and again. As Prolog has no special mechanism to discover such situations whole computation sequences are repeated.

As an example consider a program to compute the Nth Fibonacci number for a given N. The Fibonacci sequence is:

1, 1, 2, 3, 5, 8, 13, ...

Each number in the sequence, except for the first two, is the sum of the previous two numbers. We will define a predicate

fib(N, F)

to compute, for a given N, the Nth Fibonacci number, F. We count the numbers in the sequence starting with N = 1. The following fib program deals first with the first two Fibonacci numbers as two special cases, and then specifies the general rule about the Fibonacci sequence:

```
fib( 1, 1).              % 1st Fibonacci number

fib( 2, 1).              % 2nd Fibonacci number

fib( N, F) :-           % Nth Fib. number, N > 2
   N > 2,
   N1 is N - 1, fib( N1, F1),
   N2 is N - 2, fib( N2, F2),
   F is F1 + F2.        % Nth number is the sum of its two predecessors
```

This program tends to redo parts of the computation. This is easily seen if we trace the execution of the following goal:

?- fib(6, F).

Figure 8.2 illustrates the essence of this computational process. For example, the third Fibonacci number, *f(3)*, is needed in three places and the same computation is repeated each time.

This can be easily avoided by remembering each newly computed Fibonacci number. The idea is to use the built-in procedure assert and to add these (intermediate) results as facts to the database. These facts have to precede other clauses about fib to prevent the use of the general rule in cases

Figure 8.2   Computation of the 6th Fibonacci number by procedure **fib**.

where the result is already known. The modified procedure, **fib2**, differs from **fib** only in this assertion:

```
fib2( 1, 1).                    % 1st Fibonacci number

fib2( 2, 1).                    % 2nd Fibonacci number

fib2( N, F) :-                  % Nth Fib. number, N > 2
  N > 2,
  N1 is N - 1, fib2( N1, F1),
  N2 is N - 2, fib2( N2, F2),
  F is F1 + F2,
  asserta( fib2( N, F) ).       % Remember Nth number
```

This program will try to answer any **fib2** goal by first looking at stored facts about this relation, and only then resort to the general rule. As a result, when a goal **fib2(N, F)** is executed all Fibonacci numbers, up to the Nth number, will get tabulated. Figure 8.3 illustrates the computation of the 6th Fibonacci number by **fib2**. A comparison with Figure 8.2 shows the saving in the computational complexity. For greater N, the savings would be much more substantial.

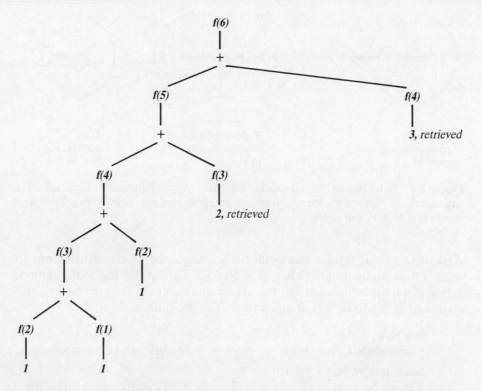

Figure 8.3 Computation of the 6th Fibonacci number by procedure **fib2**, which remembers previous results. This saves some computation in comparison with **fib**, see Figure 8.2.

Asserting intermediate results, also called caching, is a standard technique for avoiding repeated computations. It should be noted, however, that in the case of Fibonacci numbers we can also avoid repeated computation by using another algorithm, rather than by asserting intermediate results. This other algorithm will lead to a program that is more difficult to understand, but more efficient to execute. The idea this time is not to define the Nth Fibonacci number simply as the sum of its two predecessors and leave the recursive calls to unfold the whole computation 'downwards' to the two initial Fibonacci numbers. Instead, we can work 'upwards', starting with the initial two numbers, and compute the numbers in the sequence one by one in the forward direction. We have to stop when we have computed the Nth number. Most of the work in such a program is done by the procedure:

    forwardfib(M, N, F1, F2, F)

Here, F1 and F2 are the (M − 1)st and Mth Fibonacci numbers, and F is the Nth Fibonacci number. Figure 8.4 helps to understand the **forwardfib** relation.

Starting configuration, here M = 2

Transition from configuration M to M + 1

Final configuration, here M = N

Figure 8.4 Relations in the Fibonacci sequence. A 'configuration', depicted by a large circle, is defined by three things: an index M and two consecutive Fibonacci numbers $f(M - 1)$ and $f(M)$.

According to this figure, **forwardfib** finds a sequence of transformations to reach a final configuration (when M = N) from a given starting configuration. When **forwardfib** is invoked, all the arguments except F have to be instantiated, and M has to be less or equal to N. The program is:

```
fib3( N, F) :-
    forwardfib( 2, N, 1, 1, F).              % The first two Fib. numbers are 1

forwardfib( M, N, F1, F2, F2) :-
    M >= N.                                  % Nth Fibonacci number reached

forwardfib( M, N, F1, F2, F) :-
    M < N,                                   % Nth number not yet reached
    NextM is M + 1,
    NextF2 is F1 + F2,
    forwardfib( NextM, N, F2, NextF2, F).
```

EXERCISES

8.1 Procedures **sub1**, **sub2** and **sub3**, shown below, all implement the sublist relation. **sub1** is a more procedural definition whereas **sub2** and **sub3** are written in a more declarative style. Study the behaviour, with reference to efficiency, of these three procedures on some sample lists. Two of them behave nearly equivalently and have similar efficiency. Which two? Why is the remaining one less efficient?

```
sub1( List, Sublist) :-
    prefix( List, Sublist).

sub1( [_ | Tail], Sublist) :-
    sub1( Tail, Sublist).                    % Sublist is sublist of Tail
```

```
            prefix( _, [ ] ).
            prefix( [X | List1], [X | List2] ) :-
               prefix( List1, List2).
            sub2( List, Sublist) :-
               conc( List1, List2, List),
               conc( List3, Sublist, List1).
            sub3( List, Sublist) :-
               conc( List1, List2, List),
               conc( Sublist, _, List2).
```

8.2   Define the relation

            add_at_end(List, Item, NewList)

to add **Item** at the end of **List** producing **NewList**. Let both lists be
represented by difference pairs.

8.3   Define the relation

            reverse(List, ReversedList)

where both lists are represented by difference pairs.

8.4   Rewrite the **collect** procedure of Section 8.5.2 using difference pair
representation for lists so that the concatenation can be done more
efficiently.

SUMMARY

- There are several criteria for evaluating programs:

        correctness
        efficiency
        transparency, readability
        modifiability
        robustness
        documentation

- The principle of *stepwise refinement* is a good way of organizing the
program development process. Stepwise refinement applies to relations,
algorithms and data structures.

- In Prolog, the following techniques often help to find ideas for
refinements:

    Using recursion: identify boundary and general cases of a recursive
                definition.

    Generalization: consider a more general problem that may be easier to
                solve than the original one.

> *Using pictures*:   graphical representation may help to identify important relations.

- It is useful to conform to some stylistic conventions to reduce the danger of programming errors, make programs easier to read, debug and modify.

- Prolog systems usually provide program debugging aids. Trace facilities are most useful.

- There are many ways of improving the efficiency of a program. Simple techniques include:

  reordering of goals and clauses

  controlling backtracking by inserting cuts

  remembering (by assert) solutions that would otherwise be computed again

  More sophisticated and radical techniques aim at better algorithms (improving search efficiency in particular) and better data structures.

9 Operations on Data Structures

9.1 Representing and sorting lists
9.2 Representing sets by binary trees
9.3 Insertion and deletion in binary dictionary
9.4 Displaying trees
9.5 Graphs

One fundamental question in programming is how to represent complex data objects, such as sets, and efficiently implement operations on such objects. In general, we talk about selecting a proper data structure. The theme of this chapter is some frequently used data structures that belong to three big families: lists, trees and graphs. We will examine ways of representing these structures in Prolog, and develop programs for some operations on these structures, such as sorting a list, representing data sets by tree structures, storing data in trees and retrieving data from trees, path finding in graphs, etc. We will study several examples because these operations are extremely instructive for programming in Prolog.

9.1 Representing and sorting lists

9.1.1 Remarks on alternative representations of lists

The special Prolog notation for lists was introduced in Chapter 3 and is used throughout the text. This notation is, of course, only one way for representing lists. A *list* is, in general, defined as a structure that is either

- *empty*, or
- it consists of a *head* and a *tail*; the tail itself has to be a list too.

Therefore, to represent a list in general, we only need two things: a special symbol to represent the empty list, and a functor to combine a head and a tail. Thus one way to represent lists could be to choose

donothing

as the symbol that denotes the empty list, and the atom

then

as an infix operator to construct a list from a given head and tail. We can declare this operator, for example, as:

:- op(500, xfy, then).

The list

[enter, sit, eat]

can then be written in this notation as:

enter then sit then eat then donothing

It is important to notice that the special Prolog notation for lists and the alternative representations amount essentially to the same representation if properly abstracted. Typical operations on lists, such as

member(X, L)

conc(L1, L2, L3)

del(X, L1, L2)

that have been programmed for the special list notation, can be straight-forwardly rewritten into other, user-chosen representations. For example, the conc relation translates into the 'then–donothing' notation as follows. The definition that we have been using is:

```
conc( [ ], L, L).

conc( [X | L1], L2, [X | L3] ) :-
    conc( L1, L2, L3).
```

In our 'then–donothing' notation this becomes:

```
conc( donothing, L, L).

conc( X then L1, L2, X then L3) :-
    conc( L1, L2, L3).
```

This example illustrates how our definitions of relations regarding lists are easily generalized to the whole class of structures of this type. What notation for lists will be actually used in the program should be decided according to the meaning of the lists. If, for example, a list simply means a set of items, then the Prolog list notation is most convenient as it immediately indicates what the programmer had in mind. On the other hand, certain kinds of expressions can also be viewed as lists. For example, to represent a conjunction expression in propositional logic, a suitable list-like representation would be:

- true corresponds to the empty list
- & is the operator to combine the head and the tail, defined for example as:

```
:- op( 300, xfy, &)
```

Then the conjunction of a, b and c would be represented by:

```
a & b & c & true
```

All these examples of different notations for lists are essentially based on the same structure for lists. On the other hand, in Chapter 8 we discussed another, essentially different representation of lists, which affects computation on lists. The trick there was to represent the list by a pair of lists. The list represented by such a pair of lists is the difference between the two lists. It was shown that the difference-pair representation facilitates very efficient implementation of list concatenation.

The discussion in this section also further illuminates the difference between operators in mathematics and the operator notation in Prolog. In mathematics, actions are associated with operators whereas in Prolog the operator notation is simply used for representing structures.

EXERCISES

9.1 Define the predicate

list(Object)

to recognize whether Object is a standard Prolog list.

9.2 Define the list membership relation for lists represented in the 'then–donothing' notation of this section.

9.3 Define the relation

convert(StandardList, List)

for converting between lists, written in the standard list notation and the 'then–donothing' notation. For example:

convert([a,b], a then b then donothing)

9.4 Generalize the above convert relation to general representation of lists. The specific representation desired is then specified by a symbol to denote the empty list, and a functor to combine the head and the tail. To this end convert needs two additional arguments:

convert(StandardList, NewList, Functor, EmptyList)

Examples of using this relation are:

?- convert([a,b], L, then, donothing).
L = a then b then donothing
?- convert([a,b,c], L, +, 0).
L = a+(b+(c+0))

9.1.2 Sorting lists

Sorting is a frequent operation. A list can be sorted if there is an ordering relation between the items in the list. We will for the purpose of this discussion assume that there is an ordering relation

gt(X, Y)

meaning that X is *greater than* Y, whatever 'greater than' means. If our items are numbers then the gt relation will perhaps be defined as:

gt(X, Y) :- X > Y.

If the items are atoms then the gt relation can correspond to the alphabetical order.

Let

sort(List, Sorted)

denote a relation where List is a list of items and Sorted is a list of the same items sorted in the ascending order according to the gt relation. We will develop three definitions of this relation in Prolog, based on different ideas for sorting a list. The first idea is as follows:

> To sort a list, List:
>
> - Find two adjacent elements, X and Y, in List such that gt(X, Y) and swap X and Y in List, obtaining List1; then sort List1.
> - If there is no pair of adjacent elements, X and Y, in List such that gt(X, Y), then List is already sorted.

The purpose of swapping two elements, X and Y, that occur out of order, is that after the swapping the new list is closer to a sorted list. After a sufficient amount of swapping we should end up with all the elements in order. This principle of sorting is known as *bubble sort*. The corresponding Prolog procedure will be therefore called bubblesort:

```
bubblesort( List, Sorted) :-
    swap( List, List1), !,          % A useful swap in List?
    bubblesort( List1, Sorted).

bubblesort( Sorted, Sorted).        % Otherwise list is already sorted

swap( [X, Y | Rest], [Y, X | Rest] ) :-   % Swap first two elements
    gt( X, Y).

swap( [Z | Rest], [Z | Rest1] ) :-        % Swap elements in tail
    swap( Rest, Rest1).
```

Another simple sorting algorithm is *insertion sort*, which is based on the following idea:

> To sort a non-empty list, L = [X | T]:
>
> (1) Sort the tail T of L.
> (2) Insert the head, X, of L into the sorted tail at such a position that the resulting list is sorted. The result is the whole sorted list.

This translates into Prolog as the following **insertsort** procedure:

```
insertsort( [ ], [ ] ).

insertsort( [X | Tail], Sorted) :-
    insertsort( Tail, SortedTail),              % Sort the tail
    insert( X, SortedTail, Sorted).             % Insert X at proper place

insert( X, [Y | Sorted], [Y | Sorted1] ) :-
    gt( X, Y), !,
    insert( X, Sorted, Sorted1).

insert( X, Sorted, [X | Sorted] ).
```

The sorting procedures **bubblesort** and **insertsort** are simple, but inefficient. Of the two procedures, insertion sort is the more efficient one. However, the average time that **insertsort** requires for sorting a list of length n grows proportionally to n^2. For long lists, therefore, a much better sorting algorithm is *quicksort*. This is based on the following idea, which is illustrated in Figure 9.1.

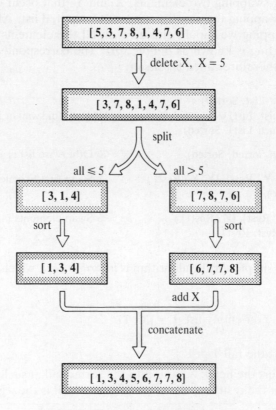

Figure 9.1 Sorting a list by *quicksort*.

To sort a non-empty list, L:

(1) Delete some element X from L and split the rest of L into two lists, called **Small** and **Big**, as follows: all elements in L that are greater than X belong to **Big**, and all others to **Small**.

(2) Sort **Small** obtaining **SortedSmall**.

(3) Sort **Big** obtaining **SortedBig**.

(4) The whole sorted list is the concatenation of **SortedSmall** and [X | SortedBig].

If the list to be sorted is empty then the result of sorting is also the empty list. A Prolog implementation of quicksort is shown in Figure 9.2. A particular detail of this implementation is that the element, X, that is deleted from L is always simply the head of L. The splitting is programmed as a four-argument relation:

split(X, L, Small, Big)

The time complexity of this algorithm depends on how lucky we are when splitting the list to be sorted. If the list is split into two lists of approximately equal lengths then the time complexity of this sorting procedure is of the order $n \log n$ where n is the length of the list to be sorted. If, on the contrary, splitting always results in one list far bigger than the other,

---

% quicksort(List, SortedList): sort List by the quicksort algorithm

```
quicksort( [ ], [ ] ).

quicksort( [X | Tail], Sorted) :-
    split( X, Tail, Small, Big),
    quicksort( Small, SortedSmall),
    quicksort( Big, SortedBig),
    conc( SortedSmall, [X | SortedBig], Sorted).

split( X, [ ], [ ], [ ] ).

split( X, [Y | Tail], [Y | Small], Big) :-
    gt( X, Y), !,
    split( X, Tail, Small, Big).

split( X, [Y | Tail], Small, [Y | Big] ) :-
    split( X, Tail, Small, Big).

conc( [ ], L, L).

conc( [X | L1], L2, [X | L3] ) :-
    conc( L1, L2, L3).
```

Figure 9.2 Quicksort.

then the complexity is in the order of n^2. Analysis would show that the average performance of quicksort is, fortunately, closer to the best case than to the worst case.

The program in Figure 9.2 can be further improved by a better implementation of the concatenation operation. Using the difference-pair representation of lists, introduced in Chapter 8, concatenation is reduced to triviality. To use this idea in our sorting procedure, the lists in the program of Figure 9.2 can be represented by pairs of lists of the form **A-Z** as follows:

SortedSmall   is represented by   **A1 - Z1**
SortedBig   is represented by   **A2 - Z2**

Then the concatenation of the lists **SortedSmall** and **[X | SortedBig]** corresponds to the concatenation of pairs:

A1 - Z1   and   **[X | A2] - Z2**

The resulting concatenated list is represented by:

A1 - Z2   where   **Z1 = [X | A2]**

The empty list is represented by any pair **Z-Z**. Introducing these changes systematically into the program of Figure 9.2 we get a more efficient implementation of quicksort, programmed as **quicksort2** in Figure 9.3. The procedure **quicksort** still uses the usual representation of lists, but the actual sorting is done by the more efficient **quicksort2**, which uses the difference-pair representation. The relation between the two procedures is:

```
quicksort( L, S) :-
  quicksort2( L, S - [ ] ).
```

```
% quicksort( List, SortedList): sort List with the quicksort algorithm

quicksort( List, Sorted) :-
  quicksort2( List, Sorted - [ ] ).

% quicksort2( List, SortedDiffList): sort List, result is represented as difference list

quicksort2( [ ], Z - Z).

quicksort2( [X | Tail], A1 - Z2) :-
  split( X, Tail, Small, Big),
  quicksort2( Small, A1 - [X | A2] ),
  quicksort2( Big, A2 - Z2).
```

Figure 9.3   A more efficient implementation of **quicksort** using difference-pair representation for lists. Relation **split(X, List, Small, Big)** is as defined in Figure 9.2.

EXERCISES

9.5 Write a procedure to merge two sorted lists producing a third list. For example:

> ?- merge([2,5,6,6,8], [1,3,5,9], L).
> L = [1,2,3,5,5,6,6,8,9]

9.6 The difference between the sorting programs of Figures 9.2 and 9.3 is in the representation of lists – the latter uses difference-lists. Transformation between plain lists and difference-lists is straight-forward and could be mechanized. Carry out the corresponding changes systematically in the program of Figure 9.2 to transform it into the program of Figure 9.3.

9.7 Our quicksort program performs badly when the list to be sorted is already sorted or almost sorted. Analyze why.

9.8 Another good idea for sorting a list that avoids the weakness of quicksort is based on dividing the list, then sorting smaller lists, and then merging these sorted smaller lists. Accordingly, to sort a list L:

- divide L into two lists, L1 and L2, of approximately equal length;
- sort L1 and L2 giving S1 and S2;
- merge S1 and S2 giving L sorted.

Implement this sorting principle and compare its efficiency with the quicksort program.

9.2 Representing sets by binary trees

One usual application of lists is to represent sets of objects. A disadvantage of using the list for representing a set is that the set membership testing is relatively inefficient. The predicate member(X, L) to test whether X is a member of a list L is usually programmed as:

> member(X, [X | L]).
>
> member(X, [Y | L]) :-
>   member(X, L).

To find X in a list L, this procedure scans the list element by element until X is found or the end of the list is encountered. This is very inefficient in the case of long lists.

For representing sets, there are various tree structures that facilitate more efficient implementation of the set membership relation. We will here consider binary trees.

A binary tree is either empty or it consists of three things:

- a root
- a left subtree
- a right subtree

The root can be anything, but the subtrees have to be binary trees again. Figure 9.4 shows an example. This tree represents the set {a, b, c, d}. The elements of the set are stored as nodes of the tree. In Figure 9.4, the empty subtrees are not pictured; for example, the node b has two subtrees that are both empty.

There are many ways to represent a binary tree by a Prolog term. One simple possibility is to make the root of a binary tree the principal functor of the term, and the subtrees its arguments. Accordingly, the example tree of Figure 9.4 would be represented by:

a(b, c(d))

Among other disadvantages, this representation requires another functor for each node of the tree. This can lead to troubles if nodes themselves are structured objects.

A better and more usual way to represent binary trees is as follows: we need a special symbol to represent the empty tree, and we need a functor to construct a non-empty tree from its three components (the root and the two subtrees). We will make the following choice regarding the functor and the special symbol:

- Let the atom **nil** represent the empty tree.
- Let the functor be **t** so the tree that has a root X, a left subtree L and a right subtree R is represented by the term t(L, X, R) (see Figure 9.5).

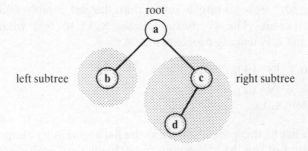

Figure 9.4   A binary tree.

Figure 9.5   A representation of binary trees.

In this representation, the example tree of Figure 9.4 is represented by the term:

   t(t(nil, b, nil), a, t(t(nil, d, nil), c, nil))

Let us now consider the set membership relation, here named **in**. A goal

   in(X, T)

is true if X is a node in a tree T. The **in** relation can be defined by the following rules:

X is in a tree T if:

   • the root of T is X, or
   • X is in the left subtree of T, or
   • X is in the right subtree of T.

These rules directly translate into Prolog:

   in(X, t(_, X, _)).
   in(X, t(L, _, _)) :-
      in(X, L).
   in(X, t(_, _, R)) :-
      in(X, R).

Obviously, the goal

   in(X, nil)

will fail for any X.

Let us investigate the behaviour of this procedure. In the following examples, T is the tree of Figure 9.4. The goal

   in(X, T)

will, through backtracking, find all the data in the set in the following order:

      X = a;   **X = b;**   **X = c;**   **X = d**

Now let us consider efficiency. The goal

      in(a, T)

succeeds immediately by the first clause of the procedure **in**. On the other hand, the goal

      in(d, T)

will cause several recursive calls of **in** before d is eventually found. Similarly, the goal

      in(e, T)

will fail only after the whole tree has been searched by recursive calls of **in** on all the subtrees of T.

This is, then, as inefficient as simply representing a set by a list. A major improvement can, however, be achieved if there is an ordering relation between the data in the set. Then the data in the tree can be ordered from left to right according to this relation. We say that a non-empty tree **t(Left, X, Right)** is ordered from left to right if:

(1)   all the nodes in the left subtree, **Left**, are less than X; and

(2)   all the nodes in the right subtree, **Right**, are greater than X; and

(3)   both subtrees are also ordered.

Such a binary tree will be called a *binary dictionary*. Figure 9.6 shows an example.

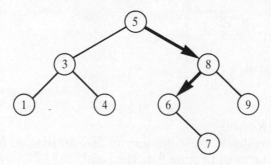

Figure 9.6 A binary dictionary. Item 6 is reached by following the indicated path $5 \rightarrow 8 \rightarrow 6$.

The advantage of ordering is that, to search for an object in a binary dictionary, it is always sufficient to search at most one subtree. The key to this economization when searching for X is that we can by comparing X and the root immediately discard at least one of the subtrees. For example, let us search for the item 6 in the tree of Figure 9.6. We start at the root, 5, compare 6 and 5, and establish $6 > 5$. As all the data in the left subtree must be less than 5, the only remaining possibility to find 6 is the right subtree. So we continue the search in the right subtree, moving to node 8, etc.

The general method for searching in the binary dictionary is:

To find an item X in a dictionary D:

- if X is the root of D then X has been found, otherwise
- if X is less than the root of D then search for
  X in the left subtree of D, otherwise
- search for X in the right subtree of D;
- if D is empty the search fails.

These rules are programmed as the procedure **in** in Figure 9.7. The relation gt(X, Y) means: X is greater than Y. If the items stored in the tree are numbers then this relation is simply $X > Y$.

In a way, the **in** procedure itself can be also used for *constructing* a binary dictionary. For example, the following sequence of goals will construct a dictionary D that contains the elements 5, 3, 8:

?- in(5, D), in(3, D), in(8, D).

D = t(t(D1, 3, D2), 5, t(D3, 8, D4)).

The variables D1, D2, D3 and D4 are in fact four unspecified subtrees. They can be anything and D will still contain the given items 3, 5 and 8. The dictionary that is constructed depends on the order of goals in the question (Figure 9.8).

% in(X, Tree): X in binary dictionary Tree

in(X, t(_, X, _)).

in(X, t(Left, Root, Right)) :-
  gt(Root, X),   % Root greater than X
  in(X, Left).   % Search left subtree

in(X, t(Left, Root, Right)) :-
  gt(X, Root),   % X greater than Root
  in(X, Right).   % Search right subtree

Figure 9.7 Finding an item X in a binary dictionary.

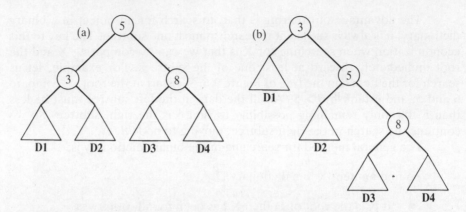

Figure 9.8 (a) Tree D that results from the sequence of goals: **in(5, D)**, **in(3, D)**, **in(8, D)**. (b) Tree resulting from: **in(3, D)**, **in(5, D)**, **in(8, D)**.

A comment is in order here on the search efficiency in dictionaries. Generally speaking, the search for an item in a dictionary is more efficient than searching in a list. What is the improvement? Let n be the number of items in our data set. If the set is represented by a list then the expected search time will be proportional to its length n. On average, we have to scan the list up to something like half-way through it. If the set is represented by a binary dictionary, the search time will be roughly proportional to the height of the tree. The height of a tree is the length of a longest path between the root and a leaf in the tree. The height, however, depends on the shape of the tree.

We say that a tree is (approximately) *balanced* if, for each node in the tree, its two subtrees accommodate approximately equal number of items. If a dictionary with n nodes is nicely balanced then its height is proportional to $\log n$. We say that a balanced tree has the *logarithmic complexity*. The difference between n and $\log n$ is the improvement of a balanced dictionary over a list. This holds, unfortunately, only when a tree is approximately balanced. If the tree gets out of balance its performance will degrade. In extreme cases of totally unbalanced trees, a tree is in effect reduced to a list. In such a case the tree's height is n, and the tree's performance is equally poor as that of a list. Therefore we are always interested in balanced dictionaries. Methods of achieving this objective will be discussed in Chapter 10.

EXERCISES

9.9 Define the predicates

(a) **binarytree(Object)**

(b) **dictionary(Object)**

to recognize whether **Object** is a binary tree or a binary dictionary respectively, written in the notation of this section.

9.10 Define the procedure

> **height(BinaryTree, Height)**

to compute the height of a binary tree. Assume that the height of the empty tree is 0, and that of a one-element tree is 1.

9.11 Define the relation

> **linearize(Tree, List)**

to collect all the nodes in **Tree** into a list.

9.12 Define the relation

> **maxelement(D, Item)**

so that **Item** is the largest element stored in the binary dictionary D.

9.13 Modify the procedure

> **in(Item, BinaryDictionary)**

by adding the third argument, **Path**, so that **Path** is the path between the root of the dictionary and **Item**.

9.3   Insertion and deletion in binary dictionary

When maintaining a dynamic set of data we may want to insert new items into the set and also delete some old items from the set. So one common repertoire of operations on a set of data, S, is:

in(X, S)	X is a member of S
add(S, X, S1)	Add X to S giving S1
del(S, X, S1)	Delete X from S giving S1

Let us now define the *add* relation. It is easiest to insert new data at the bottom level of the tree, so that a new item becomes a leaf of the tree at such a position that the ordering of the tree is preserved. Figure 9.9 shows changes in a tree during a sequence of insertions. Let us call this kind of insertion:

> **addleaf(D, X, D1)**

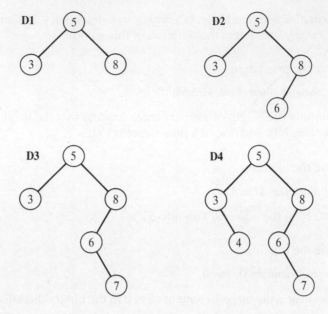

Figure 9.9 Insertion into a binary dictionary at the leaf level. The trees correspond to the following sequence of insertions: **add(D1, 6, D2)**, **add(D2, 7, D3)**, **add(D3, 4, D4)**.

Rules for adding at the leaf level are:

- The result of adding X to the empty tree is the tree **t(nil, X, nil)**.
- If X is the root of D then D1 = D (no duplicate item gets inserted).
- If the root of D is greater than X then insert X into the left subtree of D; if the root of D is less than X then insert X into the right subtree.

Figure 9.10 shows a corresponding program.

```
% addleaf( Tree, X, NewTree):
%    inserting X as a leaf into binary dictionary Tree gives NewTree
addleaf( nil, X, t( nil, X, nil) ).

addleaf( t( Left, X, Right), X, t( Left, X, Right) ).

addleaf( t( Left, Root, Right), X, t( Left1, Root, Right) ) :-
   gt( Root, X),
   addleaf( Left, X, Left1).

addleaf( t( Left, Root, Right), X, t( Left, Root, Right1) ) :-
   gt( X, Root),
   addleaf( Right, X, Right1).
```

Figure 9.10 Inserting an item as a leaf into the binary dictionary.

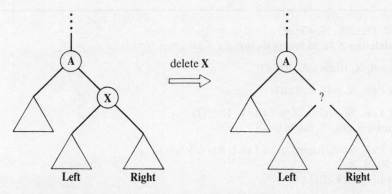

Figure 9.11   Deleting X from a binary dictionary. The problem is how to patch up the tree after X is removed.

Let us now consider the *delete* operation. It is easy to delete a leaf, but deleting an internal node is more complicated. The deletion of a leaf can be in fact defined as the inverse operation of inserting at the leaf level:

    delleaf(D1, X, D2) :-
        addleaf(D2, X, D1).

Unfortunately, if X is an internal node then this does not work because of the problem illustrated in Figure 9.11. X has two subtrees, **Left** and **Right**. After X is removed, we have a hole in the tree and **Left** and **Right** are no longer connected to the rest of the tree. They cannot both be directly connected to the father of X, A, because A can accommodate only one of them.

If one of the subtrees **Left** and **Right** is empty then the solution is simple: the non-empty subtree is connected to A. If they are both non-empty then one idea is as shown in Figure 9.12. The left-most node of **Right**, Y, is transferred from its current position upwards to fill the gap after X. After this transfer, the tree remains ordered. Of course, the same idea works symmetrically, with the transfer of the right-most node of **Left**.

According to these considerations, the operation to delete an item from the binary dictionary is programmed in Figure 9.13. The transfer of the

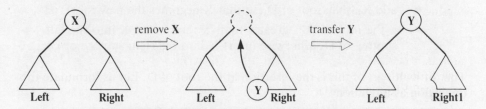

Figure 9.12   Filling the gap after removal of X.

% del(Tree, X, NewTree):
%   deleting X from binary dictionary Tree gives NewTree

del(t(nil, X, Right), X, Right).

del(t(Left, X, nil), X, Left).

del(t(Left, X, Right), X, t(Left, Y, Right1)) :-
  delmin(Right, Y, Right1).

del(t(Left, Root, Right), X, t(Left1, Root, Right)) :-
  gt(Root, X),
  del(Left, X, Left1).

del(t(Left, Root, Right), X, t(Left, Root, Right1)) :-
  gt(X, Root),
  del(Right, X, Right1).

% delmin(Tree, Y, NewTree):
%   delete minimal item Y in binary dictionary Tree producing NewTree

delmin(t(nil, Y, Right), Y, Right).

delmin(t(Left, Root, Right), Y, t(Left1, Root, Right)) :-
  delmin(Left, Y, Left1).

Figure 9.13   Deleting from the binary dictionary.

left-most node of the right subtree is accomplished by the relation

delmin(Tree, Y, Tree1)

where Y is the minimal (that is, the left-most) node of **Tree**, and **Tree1** is **Tree** with Y deleted.

There is another elegant solution to *add* and *delete*. The *add* relation can be defined non-deterministically so that a new item is inserted at any level of the tree, not just at the leaf level. The rules are:

> To add X to a binary dictionary D either:
>
> - add X at the root of D (so that X becomes the new root), or
> - if the root of D is greater than X then insert X into the left subtree of D, otherwise insert X into the right subtree of D.

The difficult part of this is the insertion at the root of D. Let us formulate this operation as a relation

addroot(D, X, D1)

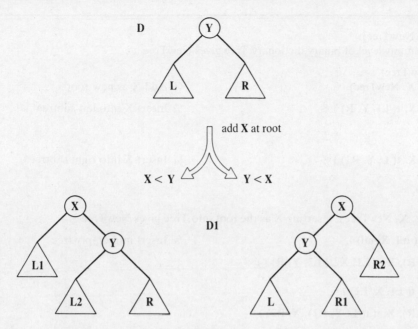

Figure 9.14   Inserting X at the root of a binary dictionary.

where X is the item to be inserted at the root of D and D1 is the resulting
dictionary with X as its root. Figure 9.14 illustrates the relations between X,
D and D1. The remaining question is now: What are the subtrees L1 and L2
in Figure 9.14 (or R1 and R2 alternatively)? The answer can be derived from
the following constraints:

- L1 and L2 must be binary dictionaries;
- the set of nodes in L1 and L2 is equal to the set of nodes in L;
- all the nodes in L1 are less than X, and all the nodes in L2 are greater
  than X.

The relation that imposes all these constraints is just our **addroot** relation.
Namely, if X were added as the root into L, then the subtrees of the resulting
tree would be just L1 and L2. In Prolog: L1 and L2 must satisfy the goal:

   addroot(L, X, t(L1, X, L2))

The same constraints apply to R1 and R2:

   addroot(R, X, t(R1, X, R2))

Figure 9.15 shows a complete program for the 'non-deterministic' insertion
into the binary dictionary.

```
% add( Tree, X, NewTree):
%    inserting X at any level of binary dictionary Tree gives NewTree
```

```
add( Tree, X, NewTree) :-
    addroot( Tree, X, NewTree).                    % Add X as new root

add( t( L, Y, R), X, t( L1, Y, R) ) :-             % Insert X into left subtree
    gt( Y, X),
    add( L, X, L1).

add( t( L, Y, R), X, t( L, Y, R1) ) :-             % Insert X into right subtree
    gt( X, Y),
    add( R, X, R1).
```

```
% addroot( Tree, X, NewTree): inserting X as the root into Tree gives NewTree
```

```
addroot( nil, X, t( nil, X, nil) ).                % Insert into empty tree

addroot( t( L, Y, R), X, t( L1, X, t( L2, Y, R) ) ) :-
    gt( Y, X),
    addroot( L, X, t( L1, X, L2) ).

addroot( t( L, Y, R), X, t( t( L, Y, R1), X, R2) ) :-
    gt( X, Y),
    addroot( R, X, t( R1, X, R2) ).
```

Figure 9.15 Insertion into the binary dictionary at any level of the tree.

The nice thing about this insertion procedure is that there is no restriction on the level of insertion. Therefore *add* can be used in the inverse direction in order to delete an item from the dictionary. For example, the following goal list constructs a dictionary D containing the items 3, 5, 1, 6, and then deletes 5 yielding a dictionary DD:

```
add( nil, 3, D1), add( D1, 5, D2), add( D2, 1, D3),
add( D3, 6, D), add( DD, 5, D)
```

9.4 Displaying trees

Like all data objects in Prolog, a binary tree, T, can be directly output by the built-in procedure **write**. However, the goal

```
write( T)
```

will only output all the information, but will not graphically indicate the actual tree structure. It can be rather tiring to imagine the actual tree structure from a Prolog term that represents that tree. Therefore it is often

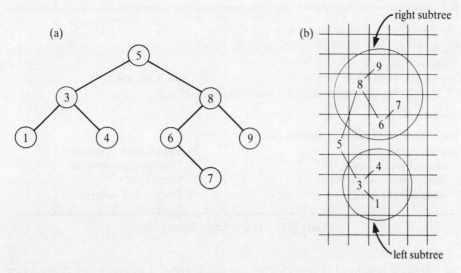

Figure 9.16   (a) A tree as normally pictured. (b) The same tree as typed out by the procedure **show** (arcs are added for clarity).

desirable to have a tree typed out in a way that graphically indicates its structure.

There is a relatively simple method for displaying trees in such a form. The trick is to display a tree growing from left to right, and not from top to bottom as trees are usually pictured. The tree is rotated to the left so that the root becomes the left-most element, and the leaves are moved to the right. Figure 9.16 illustrates.

Let us define a procedure

> **show(T)**

to display a tree T in the form indicated in Figure 9.16. The principle is:

> To show a non-empty tree, T:
>
> (1)   show the right subtree of T, indented by some distance, H, to the right;
> (2)   write the root of T;
> (3)   show the left subtree of T indented by distance H to the right.

The indentation distance H, which can be appropriately chosen, is an additional parameter for displaying trees. Introducing H we have the procedure

> **show2(T, H)**

```
% show( Tree): display binary tree

show( Tree) :-
  show2( Tree, 0).

% show2( Tree, Indent): display Tree indented by Indent

show2( nil, _).

show2( t( Left, X, Right), Indent) :-
  Ind2 is Indent + 2,                    % Indentation of subtrees
  show2( Right, Ind2),                    % Display right subtree
  tab( Indent), write( X), nl,            % Write root
  show2( Left, Ind2).                     % Display left subtree
```

Figure 9.17 Displaying a binary tree.

to display T indented H spaces from the left margin. The relation between the procedures **show** and **show2** is:

$$\text{show(T) :- show2(T, 0).}$$

The complete program, which indents by 2, is shown in Figure 9.17. The principle of achieving such an output format can be easily adopted for displaying other types of trees.

EXERCISE

9.14 Our procedure for displaying trees shows a tree in an unusual orientation, so that the root is on the left and the leaves of the tree are on the right. Write a (more difficult) procedure to display a tree in the usual orientation with the root at the top and the leaves at the bottom.

9.5 Graphs

9.5.1 Representing graphs

Graph structures are used in many applications, such as representing relations, situations or problems. A graph is defined by a set of *nodes* and a set of *edges*, where each edge is a pair of nodes. When the edges are directed they are also called *arcs*. Arcs are represented by *ordered* pairs. Such a graph is a *directed* graph. The edges can be attached costs, names, or any kind of labels, depending on the application. Figure 9.18 shows examples.

Graphs can be represented in Prolog in several ways. One method is to represent each edge or arc separately as one clause. The graphs in Figure 9.18 can be thus represented by sets of clauses, for example:

```
connected( a, b).
connected( b, c).
...

arc( s, t, 3).
arc( t, v, 1).
arc( u, t, 2).
...
```

Another method is to represent a whole graph as one data object. A graph can be thus represented as a pair of two sets: nodes and edges. Each set can be represented as a list; each edge is a pair of nodes. Let us choose the functor **graph** to combine both sets into a pair, and the functor e for edges. Then one way to represent the (undirected) graph in Figure 9.18 is:

G1 = graph([a,b,c,d], [e(a,b), e(b,d), e(b,c), e(c,d)])

To represent a directed graph we can choose the functors **digraph** and **a** (for arcs). The directed graph of Figure 9.18 is then:

G2 = digraph([s,t,u,v], [a(s,t,3), a(t,v,1), a(t,u,5), a(u,t,2), a(v,u,2)])

If each node is connected to at least one other node then we can omit the list of nodes from the representation as the set of nodes is then implicitly specified by the list of edges.

Yet another method is to associate with each node a list of nodes that are adjacent to that node. Then a graph is a list of pairs consisting of a node

Figure 9.18 (a) A graph. (b) A directed graph with costs attached to the arcs.

plus its adjacency list. Our example graphs can then, for example, be represented by:

> G1 = [a -> [b], b -> [a,c,d], c -> [b,d], d -> [b,c]]
>
> G2 = [s -> [t/3], t -> [u/5, v/1], u -> [t/2], v -> [u/2]]

The symbols '->' and '/' above are, of course, infix operators.

What will be the most suitable representation will depend on the application and on operations to be performed on graphs. Two typical operations are:

- find a path between two given nodes;
- find a subgraph, with some specified properties, of a graph.

Finding a spanning tree of a graph is an example of the latter operation. In the following sections we will look at some simple programs for finding a path and for finding a spanning tree.

9.5.2 Finding a path

Let G be a graph, and A and Z two nodes in G. Let us define a relation

> path(A, Z, G, P)

where P is an acyclic path between A and Z in G. P is represented as a list of nodes on the path. If G is the graph in the left-hand side of Figure 9.18 then:

> path(a, d, G, [a,b,d])
>
> path(a, d, G, [a,b,c,d])

Since a path must not contain any cycle, a node can appear in the path at most once. One method to find a path is:

> To find an acyclic path, P, between A and Z in a graph, G:
>
> If A = Z then P = [A], otherwise
> find an acyclic path, P1, from some node Y to Z, and find
> a path from A to Y avoiding the nodes in P1.

This formulation implies another relation: find a path under the restriction of avoiding some subset of nodes (P1 above). We will, accordingly, define another procedure:

> path1(A, Path1, G, Path)

Figure 9.19 The **path1** relation: **Path** is a path between A and Z; the last part of **Path** overlaps with **Path1**.

As illustrated in Figure 9.19, the arguments are:

- A is a node,
- G is a graph,
- **Path1** is a path in G,
- **Path** is an acyclic path in G that goes from A to the beginning of **Path1** and continues along **Path1** up to its end.

The relation between **path** and **path1** is:

> path(A, Z, G, Path) :- path1(A, [Z], G, Path).

Figure 9.19 suggests a recursive definition of **path1**. The boundary case arises when the start node of **Path1** (Y in Figure 9.19) coincides with the start node of **Path**, A. If the start nodes do not coincide then there must be a node, X, such that:

(1) Y is adjacent to X, and

(2) X is not in **Path1**, and

(3) **Path** must satisfy the relation **path1(A, [X | Path1], G, Path)**.

A complete program is shown in Figure 9.20. In this program, **member** is the list membership relation. The relation

> adjacent(X, Y, G)

means that there is an arc from X to Y in graph G. The definition of this relation depends on the representation of graphs. If G is represented as a pair of sets (nodes and edges),

> G = graph(Nodes, Edges)

% path(A, Z, Graph, Path): Path is an acyclic path from A to Z in Graph

path(A, Z, Graph, Path) :-
  path1(A, [Z], Graph, Path).

path1(A, [A | Path1], _, [A | Path1]).

path1(A, [Y | Path1], Graph, Path) :-
  adjacent(X, Y, Graph),
  not member(X, Path1),   % No-cycle condition
  path1(A, [X, Y | Path1], Graph, Path).

Figure 9.20   Finding an acyclic path, **Path**, from A to Z in **Graph**.

then:

```
adjacent( X, Y, graph( Nodes, Edges) ) :-
  member( e(X,Y), Edges)
;
  member( e(Y,X), Edges).
```

A classical problem on graphs is to find a Hamiltonian path; that is, an acyclic path comprising all the nodes in the graph. Using **path** this can be done as follows:

```
hamiltonian( Graph, Path) :-
  path( _, _, Graph, Path),
  covers( Path, Graph).

covers( Path, Graph) :-
  not ( node( N, Graph), not member( N, Path) ).
```

Here, **node(N, Graph)** means: N is a node in **Graph**.

We can attach costs to paths. The cost of a path is the sum of the costs of the arcs in the path. If there are no costs attached to the arcs then we can talk about the length instead, counting 1 for each arc in the path. Our **path** and **path1** relations can be modified to handle costs by introducing an additional argument, the cost, for each path:

```
path( A, Z, G, P, C)

path1( A, P1, C1, G, P, C)
```

Here, C is the cost of P and C1 is the cost of P1. The relation **adjacent** now also has an extra argument, the cost of an arc. Figure 9.21 shows a path-finding program that computes a path and its cost.

This procedure can be used for finding a minimum cost path. We can find such a path between two nodes, **node1** and **node2**, in some graph **Graph** by

% path(A, Z, Graph, Path, Cost):
%   Path is an acyclic path with cost Cost from A to Z in Graph

path(A, Z, Graph, Path, Cost) :-
  path1(A, [Z], 0, Graph, Path, Cost).

path1(A, [A | Path1], Cost1, Graph, [A | Path1], Cost1).

path1(A, [Y | Path1], Cost1, Graph, Path, Cost) :-
  adjacent(X, Y, CostXY, Graph),
  not member(X, Path1),
  Cost2 is Cost1 + CostXY,
  path1(A, [X, Y | Path1], Cost2, Graph, Path, Cost).

Figure 9.21   Path-finding in a graph: **Path** is an acyclic path with cost **Cost** from A to Z in **Graph**.

the goals:

      path(node1, node2, Graph, MinPath, MinCost),
      not (path(node1, node2, Graph, _, Cost), Cost < MinCost)

We can also find a maximum cost path between any pair of nodes in a graph **Graph** by the goals:

      path(_, _, Graph, MaxPath, MaxCost),
      not (path(_, _, Graph, _, Cost), Cost > MaxCost)

It should be noted that this is a very inefficient way for finding minimal or maximal paths. This method unselectively investigates possible paths and is completely unsuitable for large graphs because of its high time complexity. The path-finding problem frequently arises in Artificial Intelligence. We will study more sophisticated methods for finding optimal paths in Chapters 11 and 12.

9.5.3   Finding a spanning tree of a graph

A graph is said to be *connected* if there is a path from any node to any other node. Let G = (V, E) be a connected graph with the set of nodes V and the set of edges E. A *spanning tree* of G is a connected graph T = (V, E') where E' is a subset of E such that:

(1)   T is connected, and

(2)   there is no cycle in T.

These two conditions guarantee that T is a tree. For the left-hand side graph of Figure 9.18, there are three spanning trees, which correspond to three lists of edges:

Tree1 = [a-b, b-c, c-d]

Tree2 = [a-b, b-d, d-c]

Tree3 = [a-b, b-d, b-c]

Here each term of the form X-Y denotes an edge between nodes X and Y. We can pick any node in such a list as the root of a tree. Spanning trees are of interest, for example, in communication problems because they provide, with the minimum number of communication lines, a path between any pair of nodes.

We will define a procedure

stree(G, T)

where T is a spanning tree of G. We will assume that G is connected. We can imagine constructing a spanning tree algorithmically as follows: Start with the empty set of edges and gradually add new edges from G, taking care that a cycle is never created, until no more edge can be added because it would create a cycle. The resulting set of edges defines a spanning tree. The no-cycle condition can be maintained by a simple rule: an edge can be added only if one of its nodes is already in the growing tree, and the other node is not yet in the tree. A program that implements this idea is shown in Figure 9.22. The key relation in this program is:

spread(Tree1, Tree, G)

All the three arguments are sets of edges. G is a connected graph; Tree1 and Tree are subsets of G such that they both represent trees. Tree is a spanning tree of G obtained by adding zero or more edges of G to Tree1. We can say that 'Tree1 gets spread to Tree'.

It is interesting that we can also develop a working program for constructing a spanning tree in another, completely declarative way, by simply stating mathematical definitions. We will assume that both graphs and trees are represented by lists of their edges, as in the program of Figure 9.22. The definitions we need are:

(1) T is a spanning tree of G if:

- T is a subset of G, and
- T is a tree, and
- T 'covers' G; that is, each node of G is also in T.

```
% Finding a spanning tree of a graph
%
% Trees and graphs are represented by lists of their edges.
% For example: Graph = [a-b, b-c, b-d, c-d]

% stree( Graph, Tree): Tree is a spanning tree of Graph

stree( Graph, Tree) :-
  member( Edge, Graph),
  spread( [Edge], Tree, Graph).


% spread( Tree1, Tree, Graph): Tree1 'spreads to' spanning tree Tree of Graph

spread( Tree1, Tree, Graph) :-
  addedge( Tree1, Tree2, Graph),
  spread( Tree2, Tree, Graph).

spread( Tree, Tree, Graph) :-
  not addedge( Tree, _, Graph).       % No edge can be added without creating a cycle


% addedge( Tree, NewTree, Graph):
%    add an edge from Graph to Tree without creating a cycle

addedge( Tree, [A-B | Tree], Graph) :-
  adjacent( A, B, Graph),             % Nodes A and B adjacent in Graph
  node( A, Tree),                     % A in Tree
  not node( B, Tree).                 % A-B doesn't create a cycle in Tree

adjacent( Node1, Node2, Graph) :-
  member( Node1-Node2, Graph)
  ;
  member( Node2-Node1, Graph).

node( Node, Graph) :-                  % Node is a node in Graph if
  adjacent( Node, _, Graph).           %    Node is adjacent to anything in Graph
```

Figure 9.22 Finding a spanning tree of a graph: an 'algorithmic' program. The program assumes that the graph is connected.

(2)   A set of edges T is a tree if:

- T is connected, and
- T has no cycle.

Using our **path** program of the previous section, these definitions can be stated in Prolog as shown in Figure 9.23. It should be noted, however, that this program is, in this form, of little practical interest because of its inefficiency.

% Finding a spanning tree
% Graphs and trees are represented as lists of edges.

% stree(Graph, Tree): Tree is a spanning tree of Graph

stree(Graph, Tree) :-
  subset(Graph, Tree),
  tree(Tree),
  covers(Tree, Graph).

tree(Tree) :-
  connected(Tree),
  not hasacycle(Tree).

% connected(Graph): there is a path between any two nodes in Graph

connected(Graph) :-
  not (node(A, Graph), node(B, Graph), not path(A, B, Graph, _)).

hasacycle(Graph) :-
  adjacent(Node1, Node2, Graph),
  path(Node1, Node2, Graph, [Node1, X, Y | _]).   % Path of length > 1

% covers(Tree, Graph): every node of Graph is in Tree

covers(Tree, Graph) :-
  not (node(Node, Graph), not node(Node, Tree)).

% subset(List1, List2): List2 represents a subset of List1

subset([ ], [ ]).

subset([X | Set], Subset) :-   % X not in subset
  subset(Set, Subset).

subset([X | Set], [X | Subset]) :-   % X included in subset
  subset(Set, Subset).

Figure 9.23 Finding a spanning tree of a graph: a 'declarative' program. Relations **node** and **adjacent** are as in Figure 9.22.

EXERCISE

9.15 Consider spanning trees of graphs that have costs attached to edges. Let the *cost* of a spanning tree be defined as the sum of the costs of all the edges in the tree. Write a program to find a minimum-cost spanning tree of a given graph.

SUMMARY

In this chapter we studied Prolog implementations of some frequently used data structures and associated operations on them. These include:

- Lists:

  variations in representing lists
  sorting lists:
    bubble sort
    insertion sort
    quicksort
  efficiency of these procedures

- Representing sets as binary trees and binary dictionaries:

  searching for an item in a tree
  adding an item
  deleting an item
  adding as a leaf, adding as the root
  the balance of trees and its relation to the efficiency of these operations
  displaying trees

- Graphs:

  representing graphs
  finding a path in a graph
  finding a spanning tree of a graph

References

In this chapter we have tackled important topics of sorting and of maintaining data structures for representing sets. General description of structures and algorithms that were programmed in this chapter can be found, for example, in Aho, Hopcroft and Ullman (1974, 1983) or Baase (1978). The behaviour of these algorithms, in particular their time complexity, is also studied. Gonnet (1984) is a good and concise collection of many related algorithms and results of their mathematical analysis.

The Prolog program for insertion at any level of the binary tree (Section 9.3) was first shown to the author by M. van Emden (personal communication).

Aho, A.V., Hopcroft, J.E. and Ullman, J.D. (1974) *The Design and Analysis of Computer Algorithms*. Addison-Wesley.

Aho, A.V., Hopcroft, J.E. and Ullman, J.D. (1983) *Data Structures and Algorithms*. Addison-Wesley.

Baase, S. (1978) *Computer Algorithms*. Addison-Wesley.

Gonnet, G.H. (1984) *Handbook of Algorithms and Data Structures*. Addison-Wesley.

10 Advanced Tree Representations

10.1 The 2-3 dictionary
10.2 AVL-tree: an approximately balanced tree

In this chapter we look at advanced techniques for representing data sets by trees. The key idea is to keep the tree balanced, or approximately balanced, in order to prevent the tree from degenerating toward a list. Such tree-balancing schemes guarantee relatively fast, logarithmic-time data-access even in the worst case. Two such schemes are presented in this chapter: 2-3 trees and AVL-trees. (The knowledge of this chapter is not a prerequisite to any other chapter.)

10.1 The 2-3 dictionary

A binary tree is said to be well balanced if both its subtrees are of approximately equal height (or size) and they are also balanced. The height of a balanced tree is approximately $\log n$ where n is the number of nodes in the tree. The time needed to evaluate the relations **in**, **add** and **delete** on binary dictionaries grows proportionally with the height of the tree. On balanced dictionaries, then, all these operations can be done in time that is in the order of $\log n$. The logarithmic growth of the complexity of the set membership testing is a definite improvement over the list representation of sets, where the complexity grows linearly with the size of the data set. However, poor balance of a tree will degrade the performance of the dictionary. In extreme cases, the binary dictionary degenerates into a list, as shown in Figure 10.1. The form of the dictionary depends on the sequence in which the data is inserted. In the best case we get a good balance with performance in the order $\log n$, and in the worst case the performance is in the order n. Analysis shows that on average, assuming that any sequence of data is equally likely, the complexity of **in**, **add** and **delete** is still in the order $\log n$. So the average performance is, fortunately, closer to the best case than to the worst case. There are, however, several rather simple schemes for keeping good balance of the tree regardless of the data sequence. Such schemes guarantee the *worst case* performance of **in**, **add** and **delete** in the order $\log n$. One of them is the 2-3 tree; another scheme is the AVL-tree.

The *2-3* tree is defined as follows: it is either empty, or it consists of a single node, or it is a tree that satisfies the following conditions:

- each internal node has two or three children, and
- all the leaves are at the same level.

A 2-3 dictionary is a 2-3 tree in which the data items are stored in the leaves, ordered from left to right. Figure 10.2 shows an example. The internal nodes

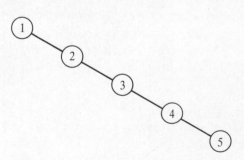

Figure 10.1 A totally unbalanced binary dictionary. Its performance is reduced to that of a list.

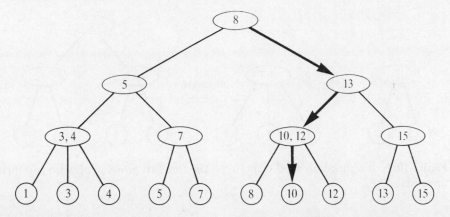

Figure 10.2   A 2-3 dictionary. The indicated path corresponds to searching for the item 10.

contain labels that specify the minimal elements of the subtrees as follows:

- if an internal node has two subtrees, this internal node contains the minimal element of the second subtree;
- if an internal node has three subtrees then this node contains the minimal elements of the second and of the third subtree.

To search for an item, X, in a 2-3 dictionary we start at the root and move toward the bottom level according to the labels in the internal nodes. Let the root contain the labels M1 and M2. Then:

- if X < M1 then continue the search in the left subtree, otherwise
- if X < M2 then continue the search in the middle subtree, otherwise
- continue the search in the right subtree.

If the root only contains one label, M, then proceed to the left subtree if X < M, and to the right subtree otherwise. This is repeated until the leaf level is reached, and at this point X is either successfully found or the search fails.

As all the leaves are at the same level, the 2-3 tree is perfectly balanced with respect to the heights of the subtrees. All search paths from the root to a leaf are of the same length which is of the order log n, where n is the number of items stored in the tree.

When inserting new data, the 2-3 tree can also grow in breadth, not only in depth. Each internal node that has two children can accommodate an additional child which results in the breadth-wise growth. If, on the other hand, a node with three children accepts another child then this node is split into two nodes, each of them taking over two of the total of four children. The so-generated new internal node gets incorporated further up in the tree. If

Figure 10.3 Inserting into a 2-3 dictionary. The tree first grows in breadth and then upwards.

this happens at the top level then the tree is forced to grow upwards. Figure 10.3 illustrates these principles.

Insertion into the 2-3 dictionary will be programmed as a relation

   add23(Tree, X, NewTree)

where **NewTree** is obtained by inserting X into **Tree**. The main burden of insertion will be transferred to two auxiliary relations, both called **ins**. The first one has three arguments:

   ins(Tree, X, NewTree)

where **NewTree** is the result of inserting X into **Tree**. **Tree** and **NewTree** have the *same height*. But, of course, it is not always possible to preserve the same height after insertion. Therefore we have another **ins** relation, with five arguments, to cater for this case:

   ins(Tree, X, NTa, Mb, NTb)

Here, when inserting X into **Tree**, **Tree** is split into two trees: **NTa** and **NTb**. Both **NTa** and **NTb** have the same height as **Tree**. **Mb** is the minimal element of **NTb**. Figure 10.4 shows an example.

In the program, a 2-3 tree will be represented, depending on its form, as follows:

- **nil** represents the empty tree.
- **l(X)** represents a single node tree, a leaf with item X.
- **n2(T1, M, T2)** represents a tree with two subtrees, T1 and T2; M is the minimal element of T2.
- **n3(T1, M2, T2, M3, T3)** represents a tree with three subtrees, T1, T2 and T3; M2 is the minimal element of T2, and M3 is the minimal element of T3.

Figure 10.4   The objects in the figure satisfy the relation
ins(Tree, 6, NTa, Mb, NTb).

T1, T2 and T3 are all 2-3 trees.

The relation between **add23** and **ins** is: if after insertion the tree does not grow upwards then simply:

```
add23( Tree, X, NewTree) :-
    ins( Tree, X, NewTree).
```

If, however, the height after insertion increases, then **ins** determines the two subtrees, T1 and T2, which are then combined into a bigger tree:

```
add23( Tree, X, n2( T1, M, T2) ) :-
    ins( Tree, X, T1, M, T2).
```

The **ins** relation is more complicated because it has to deal with many cases: inserting into the empty tree, a single node tree, a tree of type n2 or n3. Additional subcases arise from insertion into the first, second or third subtree. Accordingly, **ins** will be defined by a set of rules so that each clause about **ins** will deal with one of the cases. Figure 10.5 illustrates some of these cases. The cases in this figure translate into Prolog as follows:

Case a

```
ins( n2( T1, M, T2), X, n2( NT1, M, T2) ) :-
    gt( M, X),                          % M greater than X
    ins( T1, X, NT1).
```

Case b

```
ins( n2( T1, M, T2), X, n3( NT1a, Mb, NT1b, M, T2) ) :-
    gt( M, X),
    ins( T1, X, NT1a, Mb, NT1b).
```

Case c

```
ins( n3( T1, M2, T2, M3, T3), X,
    n2( NT1a, Mb, NT1b), M2, n2( T2, M3, T3) ) :-
    gt( M2, X),
    ins( T1, X, NT1a, Mb, NT1b).
```

Figure 10.5 Some cases of the **ins** relation.
(a) ins(n2(T1, M, T2), X, n2(NT1, M, T2));
(b) ins(n2(T1, M, T2), X, n3(NT1a, Mb, NT1b, M, T2));
(c) ins(n3(T1, M2, T2, M3, T3), X, n2(NT1a, Mb, NT1b), M2, n2(T2, M3, T3)).

Figure 10.6 shows the complete program for inserting into the 2-3 dictionary. Figure 10.7 shows a program for displaying 2-3 trees.

Our program occasionally does some unnecessary backtracking. If the three-argument **ins** fails then the five-argument **ins** is called, which redoes part

Figure 10.6 Inserting in the 2-3 dictionary. In this program, an attempt to insert a duplicate item will fail.

% Insertion in the 2-3 dictionary

```
add23( Tree, X, Tree1) :-             % Add X to Tree giving Tree1
  ins( Tree, X, Tree1).               % Tree grows in breadth

add23( Tree, X, n2( T1, M2, T2) ) :-  % Tree grows upwards
  ins( Tree, X, T1, M2, T2).

add23( nil, X, l(X) ).
```

(continues)

Figure 10.6 (cont.)

```
ins( l(A), X, l(A), X, l(X) ) :-
   gt( X, A).

ins( l(A), X, l(X), A, l(A) ) :-
   gt( A, X).

ins( n2( T1, M, T2), X, n2( NT1, M, T2) ) :-
   gt( M, X),
   ins( T1, X, NT1).

ins( n2( T1, M, T2), X, n3( NT1a, Mb, NT1b, M, T2) ) :-
   gt( M, X),
   ins( T1, X, NT1a, Mb, NT1b).

ins( n2( T1, M, T2), X, n2( T1, M, NT2) ) :-
   gt( X, M),
   ins( T2, X, NT2).

ins( n2( T1, M, T2), X, n3( T1, M, NT2a, Mb, NT2b) ) :-
   gt( X, M),
   ins( T2, X, NT2a, Mb, NT2b).

ins( n3( T1, M2, T2, M3, T3), X, n3( NT1, M2, T2, M3, T3) ) :-
   gt( M2, X),
   ins( T1, X, NT1).

ins( n3( T1, M2, T2, M3, T3), X, n2( NT1a, Mb, NT1b), M2, n2( T2, M3, T3) ) :-
   gt( M2, X),
   ins( T1, X, NT1a, Mb, NT1b).

ins( n3( T1, M2, T2, M3, T3), X, n3( T1, M2, NT2, M3, T3) ) :-
   gt( X, M2), gt( M3, X),
   ins( T2, X, NT2).

ins( n3( T1, M2, T2, M3, T3), X, n2( T1, M2, NT2a), Mb, n2( NT2b, M3, T3) ) :-
   gt( X, M2), gt( M3, X),
   ins( T2, X, NT2a, Mb, NT2b).

ins( n3( T1, M2, T2, M3, T3), X, n3( T1, M2, T2, M3, NT3) ) :-
   gt( X, M3),
   ins( T3, X, NT3).

ins( n3( T1, M2, T2, M3, T3), X, n2( T1, M2, T2), M3, n2( NT3a, Mb, NT3b) ) :-
   gt( X, M3),
   ins( T3, X, NT3a, Mb, NT3b).
```

% Displaying 2-3 dictionary

```
show( T) :-
   show( T, 0).

show( nil, _).

show( l(A), H) :-
   tab( H), write( A), nl.

show( n2( T1, M, T2), H) :-
   H1 is H + 5,
   show( T2, H1),
   tab( H), write( --), nl,
   tab( H), write( M), nl,
   tab( H), write( --), nl,
   show( T1, H1).

show( n3( T1, M2, T2, M3, T3), H) :-
   H1 is H + 5,
   show( T3, H1),
   tab( H), write( --), nl,
   tab( H), write( M3), nl,
   show( T2, H1),
   tab( H), write( M2), nl,
   tab( H), write( --), nl,
   show( T1, H1).
```

```
                                    15
                               --
                          15
                               --
                                    13
                     --
                13
                     --
                                    12
                          --
                     12
                                    10
                10
                     --
                                         8
      --
 8
      --
                                         7
                          --
                     7
                               --
                                    5
                --
           5
                --
                                    4
                     --
                4
                                    3
           3
                --
                                    1
```

Figure 10.7 Left: a program to display a 2-3 dictionary. Right: the dictionary of Figure 10.2 as displayed by this program.

of the work. This source of inefficiency can easily be eliminated by, for example, redefining **ins** as:

        ins2(Tree, X, NewTrees)

NewTrees is a list of length 1 or 3, as follows:

        NewTrees = [NewTree]   if   ins(Tree, X, NewTree)

        NewTrees = [NTa, Mb, NTb]   if   ins(Tree, X, NTa, Mb, NTb)

The add23 relation would be, accordingly, redefined as:

```
add23( T, X, T1) :-
    ins2( T, X, Trees),
    combine( Trees, T1).
```

The combine relation has to produce a single tree, T1, from the list Trees.

EXERCISES

10.1 Define the relation

in(Item, Tree)

to search for Item in a 2-3 dictionary Tree.

10.2 Modify the program of Figure 10.6 to avoid backtracking (define relations ins2 and combine).

10.2 AVL-tree: an approximately balanced tree

AVL-tree is a binary tree that has the following properties:

(1) Its left subtree and right subtree differ in height by 1 at the most.
(2) Both subtrees themselves are also AVL-trees.

This definition allows for trees that are slightly out of balance. It can be shown that the height of an AVL-tree is always, even in the worst case, roughly proportional to log n where n is the number of nodes in the tree. This guarantees the logarithmic performance for the operations in, add and del.

Operations on the AVL-dictionary are essentially the same as on binary dictionaries, with some additions to maintain approximate balance of the tree. If the tree gets out of approximate balance after an insertion or deletion then some additional mechanism will get it back into the required degree of balance. To implement this mechanism efficiently, we have to maintain some additional information about the balance of the tree. Essentially we only need the difference between the heights of its subtrees, which is either -1, 0 or $+1$. For the sake of simplicity of the operations involved we will, however, prefer to maintain the complete heights of trees and not only the differences.

We will define the insertion relation as

addavl(Tree, X, NewTree)

where both **Tree** and **NewTree** are AVL-dictionaries such that **NewTree** is **Tree** with X inserted. AVL-trees will be represented by terms of the form:

t(Left, A, Right)/Height

where A is the root, **Left** and **Right** are the subtrees, and **Height** is the height of the tree. The empty tree is represented by **nil/0**. Now let us consider the insertion of X into a non-empty AVL-dictionary:

Tree = t(L, A, R)/H

We will start our discussion by only considering the case that X is greater than A. Then X is to be inserted into R and we have the following relation:

addavl(R, X, t(R1, B, R2)/Hb)

Figure 10.8 illustrates the following ingredients from which **NewTree** is to be constructed:

L, A, R1, B, R2

What can be the heights of L, R, R1 and R2? L and R can only differ in height by 1 at the most. Figure 10.8 shows what the heights of R1 and R2 can be. As only one item, X, has been inserted into R, at most one of the subtrees R1 and R2 can have the height $h + 1$.

Figure 10.8 The problem of AVL insertion: (a) AVL-tree before inserting X, X > A; (b) AVL-tree after inserting X into R; (c) ingredients from which the new tree is to be constructed.

In the case that X is less than A then the situation is analogous with left and right subtrees interchanged. Therefore, in any case, we have to construct **NewTree** from three trees (let us call them **Tree1**, **Tree2** and **Tree3**), and two single items, A and B. Let us now consider the question: How can we combine these five ingredients to make **NewTree** so that **NewTree** is an AVL-dictionary? The order from left to right in **NewTree** has to be:

Tree1, A, Tree2, B, Tree3

We have to consider three cases:

(1)   The middle tree, **Tree2**, is taller than both other trees.
(2)   **Tree1** is at least as tall as **Tree2** and **Tree3**.
(3)   **Tree3** is at least as tall as **Tree2** and **Tree1**.

Figure 10.9 shows how **NewTree** can be constructed in each of these cases. In case 1, the middle tree **Tree2** has to be decomposed and its parts incorporated

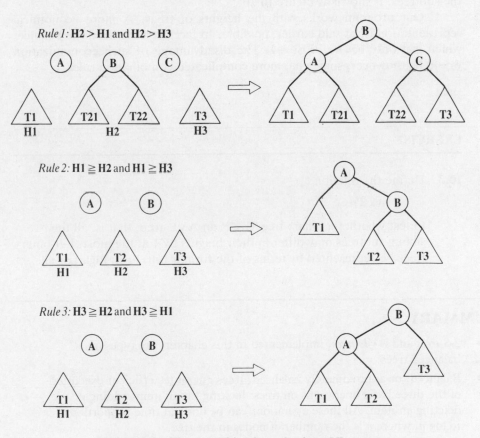

Figure 10.9   Three combination rules for AVL-trees.

into **NewTree**. The three rules of Figure 10.9 are easily translated into Prolog as a relation:

> combine(Tree1, A, Tree2, B, Tree3, NewTree)

The last argument, **NewTree**, is an AVL-tree constructed from five ingredients, the first five arguments. Rule 1, for example, becomes:

```
combine(
   T1/H1, A, t(T21,B,T22)/H2, C, T3/H3,        % Five ingredients
   t( t(T1/H1,A,T21)/Ha, B, t(T22,C,T3/H3)/Hc)/Hb) :- % Their combination

   H2 > H1, H2 > H3,                            % Middle tree is tallest
   Ha is H1 + 1,                                % Height of left subtree
   Hc is H3 + 1,                                % Height of right subtree
   Hb is Ha + 1.                                % Height of the whole tree
```

A complete **addavl** program, which also computes the heights of the tree and the subtrees, is shown as Figure 10.10.

Our program works with the heights of trees. A more economical representation is, as said earlier, possible. In fact, we only need the balance, which can only be -1, 0 or $+1$. The disadvantage of such economization would be, however, somewhat more complicated combination rules.

EXERCISE

10.3 Define the relation

> avl(Tree)

to test whether a binary tree **Tree** is an AVL-tree; that is, all the sibling subtrees may differ in their heights by 1 at the most. Let binary trees be represented by terms of the form t(**Left, Root, Right**) or **nil**.

SUMMARY

- *2-3 trees* and *AVL-trees*, implemented in this chapter, are types of balanced trees.
- Balanced, or approximately balanced, trees guarantee efficient execution of the three basic operations on trees: looking for an item, adding or deleting an item. All these operations can be done in time proportional to log n, where n is the number of nodes in the tree.

```
% addavl( Tree, X, NewTree): insertion into AVL-dictionary
%     Tree = t( Left, Root, Right)/HeightOfTree
%     Empty tree = nil/0
```

addavl(nil/0, X, t(nil/0, X, nil/0)/1).   % Add X to empty tree

addavl(t(L, Y, R)/Hy, X, NewTree) :-   % Add X to non-empty tree
  gt(Y, X),
  addavl(L, X, t(L1, Z, L2)/_),   % Add into left subtree
  combine(L1, Z, L2, Y, R, NewTree).   % Combine ingredients of NewTree

addavl(t(L, Y, R)/Hy, X, NewTree) :-
  gt(X, Y),
  addavl(R, X, t(R1, Z, R2)/_),   % Add into right subtree
  combine(L, Y, R1, Z, R2, NewTree).

```
% combine( Tree1, A, Tree2, B, Tree3, NewTree):
%     combine Tree1, Tree2, Tree3 and nodes A and B into an AVL-tree
```

combine(T1/H1, A, t(T21, B, T22)/H2, C, T3/H3,
      t(t(T1/H1,A,T21)/Ha, B, t(T22,C,T3/H3)/Hc)/Hb) :-
H2 > H1, H2 > H3,   % Middle subtree tallest
Ha is H1 + 1,
Hc is H3 + 1,
Hb is Ha + 1.

combine(T1/H1, A, T2/H2, C, T3/H3, t(T1/H1, A, t(T2/H2,C,T3/H3)/Hc)/Ha) :-
H1 >= H2, H1 >= H3,   % Tall left subtree
max1(H2, H3, Hc),
max1(H1, Hc, Ha).

combine(T1/H1, A, T2/H2, C, T3/H3, t(t(T1/H1,A,T2/H2)/Ha, C, T3/H3)/Hc) :-
H3 >= H2, H3 >= H1,   .   % Tall right subtree
max1(H1, H2, Ha),
max1(Ha, H3, Hc).

max1(U, V, M) :-   % M is 1 + max. of U and V
  U > V, !, M is U + 1
  ;
  M is V + 1.

Figure 10.10 AVL-dictionary insertion. In this program, an attempt to insert a duplicate will fail. See Figure 10.9 for **combine**.

References

2-3 trees are described in detail by, for example, Aho, Hopcroft and Ullman (1974, 1983). In their 1983 book an implementation in Pascal is also given. Wirth (1976) gives a Pascal program to handle AVL-trees. 2-3 trees are a special case of more general B-trees. This and several other variations or data structures related to 2-3 trees and AVL-trees are covered by Gonnet (1984) together with various results on the behaviour of these structures.

A program for AVL-tree insertion that only uses tree-bias information (that is, the difference between the heights of the subtrees −1, 0 or +1, and not the complete height) was published by van Emden (1981).

Aho, A.V., Hopcroft, J.E. and Ullman, J.D. (1974) *The Design and Analysis of Computer Algorithms*. Addison-Wesley.

Aho, A.V., Hopcroft, J.E. and Ullman, J.D. (1983) *Data Structures and Algorithms*. Addison-Wesley.

Gonnet, G.H. (1984) *Handbook of Algorithms and Data Structures*. Addison-Wesley.

van Emden, M. (1981) *Logic Programming Newsletter* **2**.

Wirth, N. (1976) *Algorithms + Data Structures = Programs*. Prentice-Hall.

Part II

Prolog in Artificial Intelligence

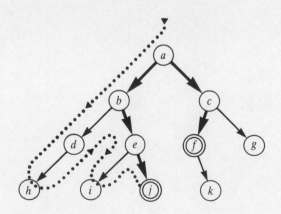

11 Basic Problem-Solving Strategies

11.1 Introductory concepts and examples
11.2 Depth-first search and iterative deepening
11.3 Breadth-first search
11.4 Comments on searching graphs, on optimality and on search complexity

This chapter is centred around a general scheme, called *state space*, for representing problems. A state space is a graph whose nodes correspond to problem situations, and a given problem is reduced to finding a path in this graph. We will study examples of formulating problems using the state-space approach, and discuss general methods for solving problems represented in this formalism. Problem solving involves graph searching and typically leads to the problem of dealing with alternatives. Two basic strategies for exploring alternatives, presented in this chapter, are the depth-first search and the breadth-first search.

11.1 Introductory concepts and examples

Let us consider the example in Figure 11.1. The problem is to find a plan for rearranging a stack of blocks as shown in the figure. We are only allowed to move one block at a time. A block can be grasped only when its top is clear. A block can be put on the table or on some other block. To find a required plan, we have to find a sequence of moves that accomplish the given transformation.

We can think of this problem as a problem of exploring among possible alternatives. In the initial problem situation we are only allowed one alternative: put block C on the table. After C has been put on the table, we have three alternatives:

- put A on table, or
- put A on C, or
- put C on A.

We will not seriously consider putting C on the table as this clearly has no effect on the situation.

As this example illustrates, we have, in such a problem, two types of concept:

(1) Problem situations.
(2) Legal moves, or actions, that transform problem situations into other situations.

Problem situations and possible moves form a directed graph, called a *state space*. A state space for our example problem is shown in Figure 11.2. The nodes of the graph correspond to problem situations, and the arcs correspond to legal transitions between states. The problem of finding a solution plan is equivalent to finding a path between the given initial situation (the start node) and some specified final situation, also called a *goal node*.

Figure 11.1 A blocks rearrangement problem.

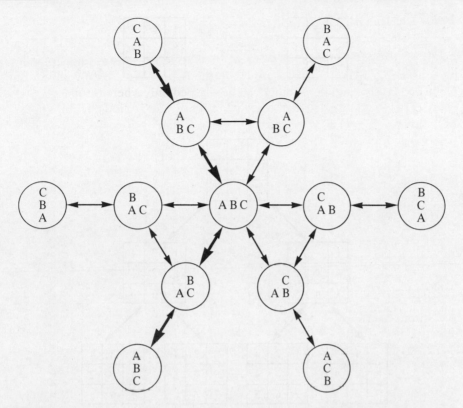

Figure 11.2 A state-space representation of the block manipulation problem. The indicated path is a solution to the problem in Figure 11.1.

Figure 11.3 shows another example problem: an eight puzzle and its representation as a path-finding problem. The puzzle consists of eight sliding tiles, numbered by digits from 1 to 8, and arranged in a 3 by 3 array of nine cells. One of the cells is always empty, and any adjacent tile can be moved into the empty cell. We can say that the empty cell is allowed to move around, swapping its place with any of the adjacent tiles. The final situation is some special arrangement of tiles, as shown for example in Figure 11.3.

It is easy to construct similar graph representations for other popular puzzles. Straightforward examples are the Tower of Hanoi, or getting fox, goose and grain across the river. In the latter problem, the boat can only hold the farmer and one other object, and the farmer has to protect the goose from the fox, and the grain from the goose. Many practical problems also naturally fit this paradigm. Among them is the travelling salesman problem which is the formal model of many practical optimization problems. The problem is defined by a map with n cities and road distances between the cities. The task is to find a shortest route from some starting city, visiting all the cities and

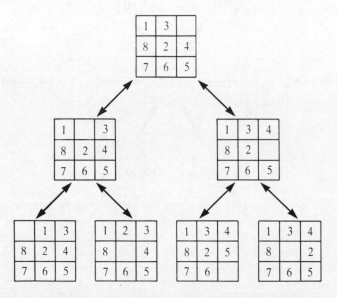

Figure 11.3 An eight puzzle and a corresponding state-space representation.

ending in the starting city. No city, with the exception of the starting one, may appear in the tour twice.

Let us summarize the concepts introduced by these examples. The state space of a given problem specifies the 'rules of the game': nodes in the state space correspond to situations, and arcs correspond to 'legal moves', or actions, or solution steps. A particular problem is defined by:

- a state space,
- a start node,
- a goal condition (a condition to be reached); 'goal nodes' are those nodes that satisfy this condition.

We can attach costs to legal moves or actions. For example, costs attached to moving blocks in the block manipulation problem would indicate that some blocks are harder to move than others. In the travelling salesman problem, moves correspond to direct city-to-city journeys. Naturally, the costs of such moves are the distances between the cities.

In cases where costs are attached to moves, we are normally interested in minimum cost solutions. The cost of a solution is the sum of the costs of the arcs along the solution path. Even if no costs are given we may have an optimization problem: we may be interested in shortest solutions.

Before presenting some programs that implement classical algorithms for searching state spaces, let us first discuss how a state space can be represented in a Prolog program.

We will represent a state space by a relation

s(X, Y)

which is true if there is a legal move in the state space from a node X to a node Y. We will say that Y is a *successor* of X. If there are costs associated with moves then we will add a third argument, the cost of the move:

s(X, Y, Cost)

This relation can be represented in the program explicitly by a set of facts. For typical state spaces of any significant complexity this would be, however, impractical or impossible. Therefore the successor relation, s, is usually defined implicitly by stating the rules for computing successor nodes of a given node.

Another question of general importance is, how to represent problem situations, that is nodes themselves. The representation should be compact, but it should also enable efficient execution of operations required; in particular, the evaluation of the successor relation, and possibly the associated costs.

As an example, let us consider the block manipulation problem of Figure 11.1. We will consider a more general case, so that there are altogether any number of blocks that are arranged in one or more stacks. The number of stacks will be limited to some given maximum to make the problem more interesting. This may also be a realistic constraint because a robot that manipulates blocks may be only given a limited working space on the table.

A problem situation can be represented as a list of stacks. Each stack can be, in turn, represented by a list of blocks in that stack ordered so that the top block in the stack is the head of the list. Empty stacks are represented by empty lists. The initial situation of the problem in Figure 11.1 can be thus represented by:

[[c,a,b], [ ], [ ]]

A goal situation is any arrangement with the ordered stack of all the blocks. There are three such situations:

[[a,b,c], [ ], [ ]]

[[ ], [a,b,c], [ ]]

[[ ], [ ], [a,b,c]]

The successor relation can be programmed according to the following rule: **Situation2** is a successor of **Situation1** if there are two stacks, **Stack1** and **Stack2**, in **Situation1**, and the top block of **Stack1** can be moved to **Stack2**. As all situations are represented as lists of stacks, this is translated into Prolog as:

```
s( Stacks, [Stack1, [Top1 | Stack2] | OtherStacks] ) :-   % Move Top1 to Stack2
    del( [Top1 | Stack1], Stacks, Stacks1),                % Find first stack
    del( Stack2, Stacks1, OtherStacks).                    % Find second stack

del( X, [X | L], L).

del( X, [Y | L], [Y | L1] ) :-
    del( X, L, L1).
```

The goal condition for our example problem is:

```
goal( Situation) :-
    member( [a,b,c], Situation).
```

We will program search algorithms as a relation

```
solve( Start, Solution)
```

where **Start** is the start node in the state space, and **Solution** is a path between **Start** and any goal node. For our block manipulation problem the corresponding call can be:

```
?- solve( [ [c,a,b], [], [] ], Solution).
```

As the result of a successful search, **Solution** is instantiated to a list of block arrangements. This list represents a plan for transforming the initial state into a state in which all the three blocks are in one stack arranged as [a,b,c].

11.2   Depth-first search and iterative deepening

Given a state-space formulation of a problem, there are many approaches to finding a solution path. Two basic search strategies are: *depth-first* search and *breadth-first* search. In this section we will implement the first of them.

We will start the development of this algorithm and its variations with a simple idea:

> To find a solution path, **Sol**, from a given node, N, to some goal node:
>
> - if N is a goal node then **Sol** = [N], or
> - if there is a successor node, N1, of N, such that there is a path **Sol1** from N1 to a goal node, then **Sol** = [N | Sol1].

This translates into Prolog as:

```
solve( N, [N] ) :-
  goal( N).

solve( N, [ N | Sol1] ) :-
  s( N, N1),
  solve( N1, Sol1).
```

This program is in fact an implementation of the depth-first strategy. It is called 'depth-first' because of the order in which the alternatives in the state space are explored. Whenever the depth-first algorithm is given a choice of continuing the search from several nodes it always decides to choose a deepest one. A 'deepest' node is one that is farthest from the start node. Figure 11.4 illustrates the order in which the nodes are visited. This order corresponds to tracing the way that Prolog answers the question:

```
?- solve( a, Sol).
```

The depth-first search is most amenable to the recursive style of programming in Prolog. The reason for this is that Prolog itself, when executing goals, explores alternatives in the depth-first fashion.

The depth-first search is simple and easy to program, and may work well in certain cases. The eight queens programs of Chapter 4 were, in fact, examples of depth-first search. A state-space formulation of the eight queens problem that could be used by the **solve** procedure above can be as follows:

- nodes are board positions with zero or more queens placed in consecutive files of the board;

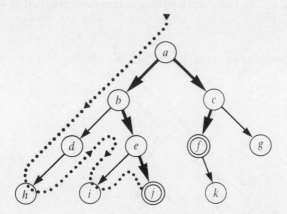

Figure 11.4 A simple state space: *a* is the start node, *f* and *j* are goal nodes. The order in which the depth-first strategy visits the nodes in this state space is: *a, b, d, h, e, i, j*. The solution found is: **[a,b,e,j]**. On backtracking, the other solution is discovered: **[a,c,f]**.

- a successor node is obtained by placing another queen into the next file so that she does not attack any of the existing queens;
- the start node is the empty board represented by the empty list;
- a goal node is any position with eight queens (the successor rule guarantees that the queens do not attack each other).

Representing the board position as a list of Y-coordinates of the queens, this can be programmed as:

```
s( Queens, [Queen | Queens] ) :-
    member( Queen, [1,2,3,4,5,6,7,8] ),      % Place Queen into any row
    noattack( Queen, Queens).

goal( [_, _, _, _, _, _, _, _] ).            % Position with 8 queens
```

The **noattack** relation requires that **Queen** does not attack any of the **Queens**; it can be easily programmed as in Chapter 4. The question

```
?- solve( [ ], Solution).
```

will produce a list of board positions with increasing number of queens. The list will end with a safe configuration of eight queens. It will also find alternative solutions through backtracking.

The depth-first search often works well, as in this example, but there are many ways in which our simple **solve** procedure can run into trouble. Whether this will actually happen or not depends on the state space. To embarrass our **solve** procedure with the problem of Figure 11.4, a slight modification of this problem is sufficient: add an arc from h to d, thus creating a cycle (Figure 11.5). The search would in this case proceed as follows: start at

Figure 11.5 Starting at a, the depth-first search ends in cycling between d and h: $a, b, d, h, d, h, d \ldots$.

a and descend to *h* following the left-most branch of the graph. At this point, in contrast with Figure 11.4, *h* has a successor, *d*. Therefore the execution will *not backtrack* from *h*, but *proceed* to *d* instead. Then the successor of *d*, *h*, will be found, etc., resulting in cycling between *d* and *h*.

An obvious improvement of our depth-first program is to add a cycle-detection mechanism. Accordingly, any node that is already in the path from the start node to the current node should not be considered again. We can formulate this as a relation:

depthfirst(Path, Node, Solution)

As illustrated in Figure 11.6, **Node** is the state from which a path to a goal state is to be found; **Path** is a path (a list of nodes) between the start node and **Node**; **Solution** is **Path** extended via **Node** to a goal node.

For the sake of ease of programming, paths will be in our program represented by lists in the *inverse* order. The argument **Path** can be used for two purposes:

(1)   to prevent the algorithm from considering those successors of **Node** that have already been encountered (cycle detection);

(2)   to construct a solution path **Solution**.

A corresponding depth-first search program is shown in Figure 11.7.

With the cycle-detection mechanism, our depth-first procedure will find solution paths in state spaces such as that in Figure 11.5. There are, however, state spaces in which this program will still easily get lost. Many state spaces are infinite. In such a space, the depth-first algorithm may miss a goal node, proceeding along an infinite branch of the graph. The program may then indefinitely explore this infinite part of the space never getting closer to a goal. The eight queens state space, as defined in this section, may seem to be susceptible to this kind of trap. However, this space is,

Figure 11.6   Relation **depthfirst(Path, Node, Solution)**.

```
% solve( Node, Solution):
%     Solution is an acyclic path (in reverse order) between Node and a goal

solve( Node, Solution) :-
  depthfirst( [ ], Node, Solution).

% depthfirst( Path, Node, Solution):
%     extending the path [Node | Path] to a goal gives Solution

depthfirst( Path, Node, [Node | Path] ) :-
  goal( Node).

depthfirst( Path, Node, Sol) :-
  s( Node, Node1),
  not member( Node1, Path),                          % Prevent a cycle
  depthfirst( [Node | Path], Node1, Sol).
```

Figure 11.7   A depth-first search program that avoids cycling.

incidentally, finite, because by the limited choice of Y-coordinates eight queens at most can be placed safely.

To avoid aimless infinite (non-cyclic) branches, we can add another refinement to the basic depth-first search procedure: limiting the depth of search. We then have the following arguments for the depth-first search procedure:

> **depthfirst2(Node, Solution, Maxdepth)**

The search is not allowed to go in depth beyond **Maxdepth**. This constraint can be programmed by decreasing the depth limit at each recursive call, and not allowing this limit to become negative. The resulting program is shown in Figure 11.8.

A difficulty with the depth-limited program in Figure 11.8 is that we have to guess a suitable limit in advance. If we set the limit too low – that is, less than any solution path – then the search will fail. If we set the limit too high, the search will become too complex. To circumvent this difficulty, we can execute the depth-limited search iteratively, varying the depth limit: start with a very low depth limit and gradually increase the limit until a solution is found. This technique is called *iterative deepening*. It can be implemented by modifying the program of Figure 11.8 in the following way. The **depthfirst2** procedure can be called from another procedure which would, on each recursive call, increase the limit by 1.

There is, however, a more elegant implementation based on a procedure

> **path(Node1, Node2, Path)**

```
% depthfirst2( Node, Solution, Maxdepth):
%    Solution is a path, not longer than Maxdepth, from Node to a goal

depthfirst2( Node, [Node], _) :-
  goal( Node).

depthfirst2( Node, [Node | Sol], Maxdepth) :-
  Maxdepth > 0,
  s( Node, Node1),
  Max1 is Maxdepth − 1,
  depthfirst2( Node1, Sol, Max1).
```

Figure 11.8   A depth-limited, depth-first search program.

where **Path** is an acyclic path between nodes **Node1** and **Node2** in the state space. Let the path be represented as a list of nodes in the inverse order. Then **path** can be written as:

```
path( Node, Node, [Node] ).              % Single node path

path( FirstNode, LastNode, [LastNode | Path] ) :-
  path( FirstNode, OneButLast, Path),    % Path up to one-but-last node
  s( OneButLast, LastNode),              % Last step
  not member( LastNode, Path).           % No cycle
```

Let us find some paths starting with node a in the state space of Figure 11.4:

```
?- path( a, Last, Path).

Last = a
Path = [a];

Last = b
Path = [b,a];

Last = c
Path = [c,a];

Last = d
Path = [d,b,a];

...
```

The **path** procedure generates, for the given initial node, all possible acyclic paths of increasing length. This is exactly what we need in the iterative deepening approach: generate paths of increasing length until a path is generated that ends with a goal node. This immediately gives a depth-first iterative deepening search program:

```
depth_first_iterative_deepening( Node, Solution) :-
  path( Node, GoalNode, Solution),
  goal( GoalNode).
```

This procedure is in fact quite useful in practice, as long as the combinatorial complexity of the problem does not require the use of problem-specific heuristics. The procedure is simple and, even if it does not do anything very clever, it does not waste much time or space. In comparison with some other search strategies, such as breadth first, the main advantage of iterative deepening is that it requires relatively little memory space. At any point of execution, the space requirements are basically reduced to *one path* between the start node of the search and the current node. Paths are generated, checked and forgotten, which is in contrast to some other search procedures (like breadth-first search) that, during search, keep many candidate paths at the same time. A disadvantage of iterative deepening is the consequence of its main strength: on each iteration, when the depth limit is increased, the paths previously computed have to be recomputed and extended to the new limit. In typical search problems, however, this recomputation does not critically affect the overall computation time. Typically, most computation is done at the deepest level of search; therefore, repeated computation at upper levels adds relatively little to the total time.

EXERCISES

11.1 Write a depth-first search procedure (with cycle detection)

> depthfirst1(CandidatePath, Solution)

to find a solution path **Solution** as an extension of **CandidatePath**. Let both paths be represented as lists of nodes in the inverse order, so that the goal node is the head of **Solution**.

11.2 Write a depth-first procedure that combines both the cycle-detection and the depth-limiting mechanisms of the procedures in Figures 11.7 and 11.8.

11.3 Experiment with the depth-first programs of this section in the blocks world planning problem of Figure 11.1.

11.4 Write a procedure

> show(Situation)

to display a problem state, **Situation**, in the blocks world. Let **Situation** be a list of stacks, and a stack in turn a list of blocks. The goal

> show([[a], [e,d], [c,b]])

should display the corresponding situation; for example, as:

11.3   Breadth-first search

In contrast to the depth-first search strategy, the breadth-first search strategy chooses to first visit those nodes that are closest to the start node. This results in a search process that tends to develop more into breadth than into depth, as illustrated by Figure 11.9.

The breadth-first search is not so easy to program as the depth-first search. The reason for this difficulty is that we have to maintain a *set* of alternative candidate nodes, not just one as in depth-first search. This set of candidates is the whole growing bottom edge of the search tree. However, even this set of nodes is not sufficient if we also want to extract a solution path from the search process. Therefore, instead of maintaining a set of candidate nodes, we maintain a set of candidate *paths*. Then,

> breadthfirst(Paths, Solution)

is true if some path from a candidate set **Paths** can be extended to a goal node. **Solution** is such an extended path.

We will use the following representation for the set of candidate paths. The set will be represented as a list of paths, and each path will be a list of nodes in the inverse order; that is, the head will be the most recently generated node, and the last element of the list will be the start node of the search. The search is initiated with a single element candidate set:

> [[StartNode]]

Figure 11.9   A simple state space: a is the start node, f and j are goal nodes. The order in which the breadth-first strategy visits the nodes in this state space is: a, b, c, d, e, f. The shorter solution **[a,c,f]** is found before the longer one **[a,b,e,j]**.

An outline for breadth-first search is:

> To do the breadth-first search when given a set of candidate paths:
>
> - if the first path contains a goal node as its head then this is a solution of the problem, otherwise
> - remove the first path from the candidate set and generate the set of all possible one-step extensions of this path, adding this set of extensions at the end of the candidate set, and execute breadth-first search on this updated set.

For our example problem of Figure 11.9, this process develops as follows:

(1) Start with the initial candidate set:

[[a]]

(2) Generate extensions of [a]:

[[b,a], [c,a]]

(Note that all paths are represented in the inverse order.)

(3) Remove the first candidate path, [b,a], from the set and generate extensions of this path:

[[d,b,a], [e,b,a]]

Add the list of extensions to the end of the candidate set:

[[c,a], [d,b,a], [e,b,a]]

(4) Remove [c,a] and add its extensions to the end of the candidate set, producing:

[[d,b,a], [e,b,a], [f,c,a], [g,c,a]]

In further steps, [d,b,a] and [e,b,a] are extended and the modified candidate set becomes:

[[f,c,a], [g,c,a], [h,d,b,a], [i,e,b,a], [j,e,b,a]]

Now the search process encounters [f,c,a] which contains a goal node, f. Therefore this path is returned as a solution.

A program that carries out this process is shown in Figure 11.10. In this program all one-step extensions are generated by using the built-in procedure **bagof**. A test to prevent the generation of cyclic paths is also made. Note that in the case that no extension is possible, **bagof** fails and therefore an alternative call to **breadthfirst** is provided. **member** and **conc** are the list membership and list concatenation relations respectively.

A drawback of this program is the inefficiency of the **conc** operation. This can be rectified by using the difference-pair representation of lists introduced in Chapter 8. The set of candidate paths would then be represented

```
% solve( Start, Solution):
%    Solution is a path (in reverse order) from Start to a goal

solve( Start, Solution) :-
   breadthfirst( [ [Start] ], Solution).

% breadthfirst( [ Path1, Path2, ...], Solution):
%    Solution is an extension to a goal of one of paths

breadthfirst( [ [Node | Path] | _], [Node | Path]) :-
   goal( Node).

breadthfirst( [Path | Paths], Solution) :-
   extend( Path, NewPaths),
   conc( Paths, NewPaths, Paths1),
   breadthfirst( Paths1, Solution).

extend( [Node | Path], NewPaths) :-
   bagof( [NewNode, Node | Path],
      ( s( Node, NewNode), not member( NewNode, [Node | Path] ) ),
      NewPaths),
   !.

extend( Path, [ ] ).                    % bagof failed: Node has no successor
```

Figure 11.10   An implementation of breadth-first search.

by a pair of lists, **Paths** and **Z**, written as:

   Paths - Z

Introducing this representation into the program of Figure 11.10, it can be systematically transformed into the program shown in Figure 11.11. This transformation is left as an exercise for the reader.

```
% solve( Start, Solution):
%    Solution is a path (in reverse order) from Start to a goal

solve( Start, Solution) :-
   breadthfirst( [ [Start] | Z] - Z, Solution).

breadthfirst( [ [Node | Path] | _] - _, [Node | Path] ) :-
   goal( Node).

breadthfirst( [Path | Paths] - Z, Solution) :-
   extend( Path, NewPaths),
   conc( NewPaths, Z1, Z),        % Add NewPaths at end
   Paths \== Z1,                  % Set of candidates not empty
   breadthfirst( Paths - Z1, Solution).
```

Figure 11.11   A more efficient program than that of Figure 11.10 for the breadth-first search. The improvement is based on using the difference-pair representation for the list of candidate paths. Procedure **extend** is as in Figure 11.10.

EXERCISES

11.5 Rewrite the breadth-first program of Figure 11.10 using the difference-pair representation for the list of candidate paths, and show that the result can be the program in Figure 11.11. In Figure 11.11, what is the purpose of the goal:

   Paths \ = = Z1

Test what happens if this goal is omitted on the state space of Figure 11.9. The difference should only show when trying to find more solutions when there are none left.

11.6 How can the search programs of this section be used for searching from a *starting set* of nodes instead of a single start node?

11.7 How can the search programs of this chapter be used to search in the backward direction; that is, starting from a goal node and progressing toward the start node (or *a* start node in the case of multiple start nodes). Hint: Redefine the s relation. In what situations would the backward search be advantageous over the forward search?

11.8 Sometimes it is beneficial to search *bidirectionally*; that is, to work from both ends, the start and the goal. The search ends when both ends come together. Define the search space (relation s) and the goal relation for a given graph so that our search procedures would in effect perform bidirectional search.

11.9 Experiment with various search techniques in the blocks world planning problem.

11.10 The breadth-first programs of this chapter only check for repeated nodes that appear in the same candidate path. In graphs, a node can be reached by different paths. This is not detected by our programs, which, therefore, duplicate the search below such nodes. Modify the programs of Figures 11.10 and 11.11 to prevent this unnecessary work.

11.4 Comments on searching graphs, on optimality and on search complexity

At this point it is appropriate to make some comments on our search programs so far: first, on searching graphs; second, on the optimality of solutions produced; and third, on the complexity of search.

Examples so far might have made the wrong impression that our breadth-first programs only work for state spaces that are trees and not general graphs. When a graph is searched it, in effect, unfolds into a tree so that some paths are possibly copied in other parts of the tree. Figure 11.12 illustrates. So our programs work on graphs as well, although they may unnecessarily duplicate some work in cases where a node is reached by various paths. This can be prevented by checking for repetition of a node in *all* the candidate paths, and not only in the path in which the node was generated. Of course, such checking is only possible in our breadth-first programs where alternative paths are available for checking.

Our breadth-first search programs generate solution paths, one after another, ordered according to their lengths: shortest solutions come first. This is important if optimality (with respect to length) is a concern. The breadth-first strategy is guaranteed to produce a shortest solution first. This is, of course, not true for the depth-first strategy. However, depth-first iterative deepening performs depth-first search to increasing depth limits and is thus bound to find the shortest solutions first. As regards space requirements, depth-first search is much more economical than breadth-first search. Depth-first iterative deepening with its space economy and overall breadthfirst-like behaviour is therefore a good compromise, especially since space limitations are usually, in practice, most critical. It has been shown by mathematical analysis (Korf 1985) that iterative deepening is in a certain sense in fact optimal with respect to both time and space complexity.

Our programs do not, however, take into account any costs associated with the arcs in the state space. If the minimal cost of the solution path is the optimization criterion (and not its length) then the breadth-first search is not sufficient. The best-first search of Chapter 12 will aspire to optimize the cost.

Another typical problem associated with searching problem spaces is that of the *combinatorial complexity*. For non-trivial problem domains the

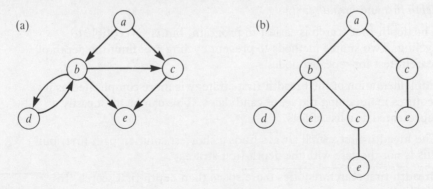

Figure 11.12 (a) A state space: *a* is the start node. (b) The tree of all possible non-cyclic paths from *a* as effectively developed by the breadth-first search program of Figure 11.10.

number of alternatives to be explored is so high that the problem of complexity often becomes critical. It is easy to understand why this happens: If each node in the state space has b successors then the number of paths of length l from the start node is b^l (we assume no cycles). Thus the set of candidate solution paths grows *exponentially* with their length, which leads to what is called the *combinatorial explosion*. The depth-first and breadth-first strategies do not do anything clever against this complexity: they non-selectively treat all candidates as equally promising.

A more sophisticated search procedure should use some problem-specific information to decide what is the most promising way to proceed at each stage of the search. This should have the effect of drawing the search process toward a goal node, avoiding aimless paths. Problem-specific information that can be thus used for guiding the search is called *heuristic*. Algorithms that use heuristics are said to be *heuristically guided*: they perform *heuristic search*. The next chapter presents such a search method.

SUMMARY

- *State space* is a formalism for representing problems.

- State space is a directed graph whose nodes correspond to problem situations and arcs to possible moves. A particular problem is defined by a *start node* and a *goal condition*. A solution of the problem then corresponds to a path in the graph. Thus problem solving is reduced to searching for a path in a graph.

- Optimization problems can be modelled by attaching costs to the arcs of a state space.

- Two basic search strategies that systematically explore a state space are *depth first* and *breadth first*.

- The depth-first search is easiest to program, but is susceptible to cycling. Two simple methods to prevent cycling are: limit the depth of search; test for repeated nodes.

- Implementation of the breadth-first strategy is more complicated as it requires maintaining the set of candidates. This can be most easily represented as a list of lists.

- The breadth-first search always finds a shortest solution path first, but this is not the case with the depth-first strategy.

- Breadth-first search requires more space than depth-first search. In practice, space is often the critical limitation.

- Depth-first iterative deepening combines the desirable properties of depth-first and breadth-first search.

- In the case of large state spaces there is the danger of *combinatorial explosion*. Both depth-first and breadth-first strategies are poor tools in combatting this difficulty. Heuristic guidance is required in such cases.

- Concepts introduced in this chapter are:

  state space
  start node, goal condition, solution path
  search strategy
  depth-first search, breadth-first search, iterative deepening
  heuristic search

References

Depth-first and breadth-first search are basic search strategies described in any general text on Artificial Intelligence; see, for example, Nilsson (1971, 1980) or Winston (1984). Kowalski (1980) showed how logic can be used for implementing these principles. Korf (1985) analyzed the comparative advantages of iterative deepening.

Korf, R.E. (1985) Depth-first iterative deepening: an optimal admissible tree search. *Artificial Intelligence* **27**: 97–109.

Kowalski, R. (1980) *Logic for Problem Solving*. North-Holland.

Nilsson, N.J. (1971) *Problem Solving Methods in Artificial Intelligence*. McGraw-Hill.

Nilsson, N.J. (1980) *Principles of Artificial Intelligence*. Tioga; also Springer-Verlag, 1981.

Winston, P.H. (1984) *Artificial Intelligence* (second edition). Addison-Wesley.

12 Best First: A Heuristic Search Principle

12.1 Best-first search
12.2 Best-first search applied to the eight puzzle
12.3 Best-first search applied to scheduling

Graph searching in problem solving typically leads to the problem of combinatorial complexity due to the proliferation of alternatives. Heuristic search aspires to fight this problem efficiently. One way of using heuristic information about a problem is to compute numerical *heuristic estimates* for the nodes in the state space. Such an estimate of a node indicates how promising a node is with respect to reaching a goal node. The idea is to continue the search always from the most promising node in the candidate set. The best-first search program of this chapter is based on this principle.

12.1   Best-first search

A best-first search program can be derived as a refinement of a breadth-first search program. The best-first search also starts at the start node and maintains the set of candidate paths. The breadth-first search always chooses for expansion a shortest candidate path (that is, shallowest tip nodes of the search). The best-first search refines this principle by computing a heuristic estimate for each candidate and chooses for expansion the best candidate according to this estimate.

We will from now on assume that a cost function is defined for the arcs of the state space. So $c(n,n')$ is the cost of moving from a node n to its successor n' in the state space.

Let the heuristic estimator be a function f, such that for each node n of the space, $f(n)$ estimates the 'difficulty' of n. Accordingly, the most promising current candidate node is the one that minimizes f. We will use here a specially constructed function f which leads to the well-known A* algorithm. $f(n)$ will be constructed so as to estimate the cost of a best solution path from the start node, s, to a goal node, under the constraint that this path goes through n. Let us suppose that there is such a path and that a goal node that minimizes its cost is t. Then the estimate $f(n)$ can be constructed as the sum of two terms, as illustrated in Figure 12.1:

$$f(n) = g(n) + h(n)$$

$g(n)$ is an estimate of the cost of an optimal path from s to n; $h(n)$ is an estimate of the cost of an optimal path from n to t.

When a node n is encountered by the search process we have the following situation: a path from s to n must have already been found, and its cost can be computed as the sum of the arc costs on the path. This path is not necessarily an optimal path from s to n (there may be a better path from s to n not, yet, found by the search), but its cost can serve as an estimate $g(n)$ of the minimal cost from s to n. The other term, $h(n)$, is more problematic because the 'world' between n and t has not been explored by the search until this point. Therefore, $h(n)$ is typically a real heuristic guess, based on the algorithm's general knowledge about the particular problem. As h depends on the problem domain there is no universal method for constructing h. Concrete examples of how such a heuristic guess can be made will be shown later. But let us assume for now that a function h is given, and concentrate on details of our best-first program.

We can imagine the best-first search to work as follows. The search process consists of a number of competing subprocesses, each of them exploring its own alternative; that is, exploring its own subtree. Subtrees have subtrees: these are explored by subprocesses of subprocesses, etc. Among all these competing processes, only one is active at each time: the one that deals with the currently most promising alternative; that is, the alternative with the lowest f-value. The remaining processes have to wait quietly until the current

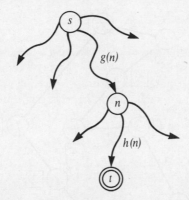

Figure 12.1   Construction of a heuristic estimate *f(n)* of the cost of the cheapest path from *s* to *t* via *n*: *f(n) = g(n) + h(n)*.

f-estimates change so that some other alternative becomes more promising. Then the activity is switched to this alternative. We can imagine this activate–deactivate mechanism as functioning as follows: the process working on the currently top-priority alternative is given some budget and the process is active until this budget is exhausted. During this activity, the process keeps expanding its subtree and reports a solution if a goal node was encountered. The budget for this run is defined by the heuristic estimate of the closest competing alternative.

Figure 12.2 shows an example of such behaviour. Given a map, the task is to find the shortest route between the start city *s* and the goal city *t*. In estimating the cost of the remaining route distance from a city *X* to the goal we simply use the straight-line distance denoted by *dist(X,t)*. So:

$$f(X) = g(X) + h(X) = g(X) + dist(X,t)$$

In this example, we can imagine the best-first search as consisting of two processes, each of them exploring one of the two alternative paths: Process 1 the path via *a*, Process 2 the path via *e*. In initial stages, Process 1 is more active because *f*-values along its path are lower than along the other path. At the moment that Process 1 is at *c* and Process 2 still at *e*, the situation changes:

$$f(c) = g(c) + h(c) = 6 + 4 = 10$$
$$f(e) = g(e) + h(e) = 2 + 7 = 9$$

So *f(e) < f(c)*, and now Process 2 proceeds to *f* and Process 1 waits. Here, however,

$$f(f) = 7 + 4 = 11$$
$$f(c) = 10$$
$$f(c) < f(f)$$

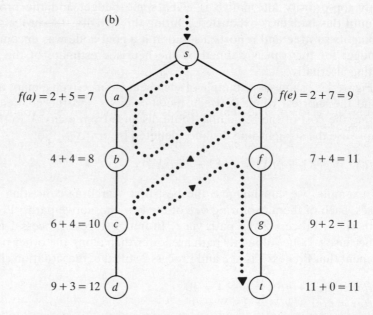

Figure 12.2 Finding the shortest route from s to t in a map. (a) The map with links labelled by their lengths; the numbers in the boxes are straight-line distances to t. (b) The order in which the map is explored by a best-first search. Heuristic estimates are based on straight-line distances. The dotted line indicates the switching of activity between alternate paths. The line shows the ordering of nodes according to their f-values; that is, the order in which the nodes are *expanded* (not the order in which they are generated).

Therefore Process 2 is stopped and Process 1 is allowed to proceed, but only to d when $f(d) = 12 > 11$. Process 2, invoked at this point, now runs smoothly up to the goal t.

The search thus outlined, starting with the start node, keeps generating new successor nodes, always expanding in the most promising direction according to the f-values. During this process, a search tree is generated whose root is the start node of the search. Our best-first search program will thus keep expanding this search tree until a solution is found. This tree will be represented in the program by terms of two forms:

(1) l(N, F/G) represents a single node tree (a leaf); N is a node in the state space, G is $g(\mathrm{N})$ (cost of the path found from the start node to N); F is $f(\mathrm{N}) = \mathrm{G} + h(\mathrm{N})$.

(2) t(N, F/G, Subs) represents a tree with non-empty subtrees; N is the root of the tree, Subs is a list of its subtrees; G is $g(\mathrm{N})$; F is the *updated* f-value of N – that is, the f-value of the most promising successor of N; the list Subs is ordered according to increasing f-values of the subtrees.

For example, consider the search in Figure 12.2 again. At the moment that the node s has been expanded, the search tree consists of three nodes: the root s and its children, a and e. In our program this search tree will be represented by the term:

t(s, 7/0, [l(a,7/2), l(e,9/2)])

The f-value of the root s is equal to 7, that is the f-value of the root's most promising successor a. The search tree is now expanded by expanding the most promising subtree a. The closest competitor to a is e whose f-value is 9. Therefore, a is allowed to expand as long as the f-value of a does not exceed 9. Thus, the nodes b and c are generated. $f(c) = 10$, so the bound for expansion has been exceeded and alternative a is no longer allowed to grow. At this moment, the search tree is:

t(s, 9/0, [l(e,9/2), t(a,10/2, [t(b,10/4, [l(c,10/6)])])])

Notice that now the f-value of node a is 10 while that of node s is 9. They have been updated because new nodes, b and c, have been generated. Now the most promising successor of s is e, whose f-value is 9.

The updating of the f-values is necessary to enable the program to recognize the most promising subtree at each level of the search tree (that is, the tree that contains the most promising tip node). This modification of f-estimates leads, in fact, to a generalization of the definition of f. The generalization extends the definition of the function f from nodes to trees. For a single node tree (a leaf), n, we have the original definition:

$$f(n) = g(n) + h(n)$$

Figure 12.3 A best-first search program.

```
% bestfirst( Start, Solution): Solution is a path from Start to a goal

bestfirst( Start, Solution) :-
    expand( [ ], l( Start, 0/0), 9999, _, yes, Solution).        % Assume 9999 is greater than any f-value

% expand( Path, Tree, Bound, Tree1, Solved, Solution):
%     Path is path between start node of search and subtree Tree,
%     Tree1 is Tree expanded within Bound,
%     if goal found then Solution is solution path and Solved = yes

% Case 1: goal leaf-node, construct a solution path

expand( P, l( N, _), _, _, yes, [N | P] ) :-
    goal(N).

% Case 2: leaf-node, f-value less than Bound
% Generate successors and expand them within Bound

expand( P, l(N, F/G), Bound, Tree1, Solved, Sol) :-
    F =< Bound,
    ( bagof( M/C, ( s(N, M, C), not member(M, P) ), Succ),
        !,
        succlist( G, Succ, Ts),                      % Make subtrees Ts
        bestf( Ts, F1),                              % f-value of best successor
        expand( P, t(N, F1/G, Ts), Bound, Tree1, Solved, Sol)
        ;
        Solved = never                               % N has no successors – dead end
    ).

% Case 3: non-leaf, f-value less than Bound
% Expand the most promising subtree; depending on
% results, procedure continue will decide how to proceed

expand( P, t(N, F/G, [T | Ts]), Bound, Tree1, Solved, Sol) :-
    F =< Bound,
    bestf( Ts, BF), min( Bound, BF, Bound1),
    expand( [N | P], T, Bound1, T1, Solved1, Sol),
    continue( P, t(N, F/G, [T1 | Ts]), Bound, Tree1, Solved1, Solved, Sol).

% Case 4: non-leaf with empty subtrees
% This is a dead end which will never be solved

expand( _, t(_, _, [ ]), _, _, never, _) :- !.

% Case 5: value greater than Bound
% Tree may not grow

expand( _, Tree, Bound, Tree, no, _) :-
    f( Tree, F), F > Bound.
```

Figure 12.3 (cont.)

```
% continue( Path, Tree, Bound, NewTree, SubtreeSolved, TreeSolved, Solution)

continue( _, _, _, _, yes, yes, Sol).

continue( P, t(N, F/G, [T1 | Ts]), Bound, Tree1, no, Solved, Sol) :-
   insert( T1, Ts, NTs),
   bestf( NTs, F1),
   expand( P, t(N, F1/G, NTs), Bound, Tree1, Solved, Sol).

continue( P, t(N, F/G, [_ | Ts]), Bound, Tree1, never, Solved, Sol) :-
   bestf( Ts, F1),
   expand( P, t(N, F1/G, Ts), Bound, Tree1, Solved, Sol).

% succlist( G0, [Node1/Cost1, ... ], [l(BestNode, BestF/G), ... ] ):
%    make list of search leaves ordered by their f-values

succlist( _, [ ], [ ] ).

succlist( G0, [N/C | NCs], Ts) :-
   G is G0 + C,
   h( N, H),                                           % Heuristic term h(N)
   F is G + H,
   succlist( G0, NCs, Ts1),
   insert( l(N, F/G), Ts1, Ts).

% Insert T into list of trees Ts preserving order with respect to f-values

insert( T, Ts, [T | Ts] ) :-
   f( T, F), bestf( Ts, F1),
   F =< F1, !.

insert( T, [T1 | Ts], [T1 | Ts1] ) :-
   insert( T, Ts, Ts1).

% Extract f-value

f( l(_, F/_), F).                                      % f-value of a leaf

f( t(_, F/_, _), F).                                   % f-value of a tree

bestf( [T | _], F) :-                                  % Best f-value of a list of trees
   f( T, F).

bestf( [ ], 9999).                                     % No trees: bad f-value

min( X, Y, X) :-
   X =< Y, !.

min( X, Y, Y).
```

For a tree, T, whose root is n, and n's subtrees are S_1, S_2, etc.,

$$f(T) = \min_i f(S_i)$$

A best-first program along these lines is shown as Figure 12.3. Some more explanation of this program follows.

The key procedure is **expand**, which has six arguments:

expand(P, Tree, Bound, Tree1, Solved, Solution)

It expands a current (sub)tree as long as the f-value of this tree remains less or equal to **Bound**. The arguments of **expand** are:

P	Path between the start node and **Tree**.
Tree	Current search (sub)tree.
Bound	f-limit for expansion of **Tree**.
Tree1	**Tree** expanded within **Bound**; consequently, the f-value of **Tree1** is greater than **Bound** (unless a goal node has been found during the expansion).
Solved	Indicator whose value is 'yes', 'no' or 'never'.
Solution	A solution path from the start node 'through **Tree1**' to a goal node within **Bound** (if such a goal node exists).

P, **Tree** and **Bound** are 'input' parameters to **expand**; that is, they are already instantiated whenever **expand** is called. **expand** produces three kinds of results, which is indicated by the value of the argument **Solved** as follows:

(1)   **Solved** = **yes**.
       Solution = a solution path found by expanding **Tree** within **Bound**.
       Tree1 = uninstantiated.

(2)   **Solved** = **no**.
       Tree1 = **Tree** expanded so that its f-value exceeds **Bound** (Figure 12.4 illustrates).
       Solution = uninstantiated.

(3)   **Solved** = **never**.
       Tree1 and **Solution** = uninstantiated.

The last case indicates that **Tree** is a 'dead' alternative and should never be given another chance by reactivating its exploration. This case arises when the f-value of **Tree** is less or equal to **Bound**, but the tree cannot grow because no leaf in it has any successor at all, or such a successor would create a cycle.

start node

P

N

Tree

Tree1

$f >$**Bound**

Figure 12.4 The **expand** relation: expanding **Tree** until the f-value exceeds **Bound** results in **Tree1**.

Some clauses about **expand** deserve explanation. The clause that deals with the most complicated case when **Tree** has subtrees – that is,

> **Tree = t(N, F/G, [T | Ts])**

says the following. First, the most promising subtree, T, is expanded. This expansion is not given the bound **Bound**, but possibly some lower value, depending on the f-values of the other competing subtrees, **Ts**. This ensures that the currently growing subtree is always the most promising subtree. The expansion process then switches between the subtrees according to their f-values. After the best candidate has been expanded, an auxiliary procedure **continue** decides what to do next; this depends on the type of result produced by this expansion. If a solution was found then this is returned, otherwise expansion continues.

The clause that deals with the case

> **Tree = l(N, F/G)**

generates successor nodes of N together with the costs of the arcs between N and successor nodes. Procedure **succlist** makes a list of subtrees from these successor nodes, also computing their g-values and f-values as shown in

$$g(M) = g(N) + C$$
$$f(M) = g(M) + h(M)$$

Figure 12.5 Relation between the g-value of node N, and the f- and g-values of its children in the search space.

Figure 12.5. The resulting tree is then further expanded as far as **Bound** permits. If, on the other hand, there were no successors, then this leaf is abandoned for ever by instantiating **Solved** = 'never'.

Other relations are:

s(N, M, C)   M is a successor node of N in the state space; C is the cost of the arc from N to M.

h(N, H)   H is a heuristic estimate of the cost of the best path from node N to a goal node.

Application of this best-first search program to some example problems will be shown in the next section. But first some general, concluding comments on this program. It is a variation of a heuristic algorithm known in the literature as the A* algorithm (see references at the end of the chapter). Usually, in practice, the program's space complexity is more critical than its time complexity. The space problem can be alleviated by applying iterative deepening (see Section 11.2) to best-first search.

A* has attracted a great deal of attention; we will mention here an important result from the mathematical analysis of A*:

> A search algorithm is said to be *admissible* if it always produces an optimal solution (that is, a minimum-cost path) provided that a solution exists at all. Our implementation, which produces all solutions through backtracking, can be considered admissible if the *first* solution found is optimal. Let, for each node n in the state space, $h^*(n)$ denote the cost of an optimal path from n to a goal node. A theorem about the admissibility of A* says: an A* algorithm that uses a heuristic function h such that for all nodes n in the state space
>
> $$h(n) \leq h*(n)$$
>
> is admissible.

This result is of great practical value. Even if we do not know the exact value of h^* we just have to find a lower bound of h^* and use it as h in A*. This is sufficient guarantee that A* will produce an optimal solution.

There is a trivial lower bound, namely:

$h(n) = 0,$ for all n in the state space

This indeed guarantees admissibility. The disadvantage of $h = 0$ is, however, that it has no heuristic power and does not provide any guidance for the search. A* using $h = 0$ behaves similarly to the breadth-first search. It in fact reduces to the breadth-first search in the case that the arc-cost function $c(n,n') = 1$ for all arcs (n,n') in the state space. The lack of heuristic power results in high complexity. We would therefore like to have h, which is a lower bound of h^* (to ensure admissibility), and which is also as close as possible to h^* (to ensure efficiency). Ideally, if we knew h^*, we would use h^* itself: A* using h^* finds an optimal solution directly, without any backtracking at all.

EXERCISE

12.1   Define the problem-specific relations s, goal and h for the route-finding problem of Figure 12.2. Inspect the behaviour of our best-first search program on this problem.

12.2   Best-first search applied to the eight puzzle

If we want to apply the best-first search program of Figure 12.3 to some particular problem we have to add problem-specific relations. These relations define the particular problem ('rules of the game') and also convey heuristic information about how to solve that problem. This heuristic information is supplied in the form of a heuristic function.

Problem-specific predicates are:

s(Node, Node1, Cost)

This is true if there is an arc, costing Cost, between Node and Node1 in the state space.

goal(Node)

is true if Node is a goal node in the state space.

h(Node, H)

H is a heuristic estimate of the cost of a cheapest path from Node to a goal node.

In this and the following sections we will define these relations for two example problem domains: the eight puzzle (described in Section 11.1) and the task-scheduling problem.

Problem-specific relations for the eight puzzle are shown in Figure 12.6. A node in the state space is some configuration of the tiles on the board. In the program, this is represented by a list of the current positions of the tiles. Each position is specified by a pair of coordinates: X/Y. The order of items in the list is as follows:

(1)   the current position of the empty square,

(2)   the current position of tile 1,

(3)   the current position of tile 2,

    . . .

The goal situation (see Figure 11.3) is defined by the clause:

goal([2/2,1/3,2/3,3/3,3/2,3/1,2/1,1/1,1/2]).

An auxiliary relation is:

mandist(S1, S2, D)

D is the 'Manhattan distance' between squares S1 and S2; that is, the distance between S1 and S2 in the horizontal direction plus the distance between S1 and S2 in the vertical direction.

We want to minimize the *length* of solutions. Therefore, we define the cost of all the arcs in the state space to equal 1. In the program of Figure 12.6, three example starting positions from Figure 12.7 are also defined.

The heuristic function, h, is programmed as:

h(Pos, H)

Pos is a board position; H is a combination of two measures:

(1)   totdist: the 'total distance' of the eight tiles in Pos from their 'home squares'. For example, in the starting position of the puzzle in Figure 12.7(a), totdist = 4.

Figure 12.6 Problem-specific procedures for the eight puzzle, to be used in best-first search of Figure 12.3.

```
/* Problem-specific procedures for the eight puzzle
```

Current situation is represented as a list of positions of the tiles, with first item in the list corresponding to the empty square.

Example:

```
3 | 1 2 3
2 | 8   4
1 | 7 6 5
  ─────────
    1 2 3
```

This position is represented by:

[2/2, 1/3, 2/3, 3/3, 3/2, 3/1, 2/1, 1/1, 1/2]

'Empty' can move to any of its neighbours which means that 'empty' and its neighbour interchange their positions.

```
*/
```

```
% s( Node, SuccessorNode, Cost)

s( [Empty | Tiles], [Tile | Tiles1], 1) :-        % All arc costs are 1
    swap( Empty, Tile, Tiles, Tiles1).            % Swap Empty and Tile in Tiles

swap( Empty, Tile, [Tile | Ts], [Empty | Ts] ) :-
    mandist( Empty, Tile, 1).                     % Manhattan distance = 1

swap( Empty, Tile, [T1 | Ts], [T1 | Ts1] ) :-
    swap( Empty, Tile, Ts, Ts1).

mandist( X/Y, X1/Y1, D) :-                        % D is Manh. dist. between two squares
    dif( X, X1, Dx),
    dif( Y, Y1, Dy),
    D is Dx + Dy.

dif( A, B, D) :-                                  % D is |A-B|
    D is A-B, D >= 0, !
    ;
    D is B-A.

% Heuristic estimate h is the sum of distances of each tile
% from its 'home' square plus 3 times 'sequence' score

h( [Empty | Tiles], H) :-
    goal( [Empty1 | GoalSquares] ),
    totdist( Tiles, GoalSquares, D),              % Total distance from home squares
    seq( Tiles, S),                               % Sequence score
    H is D + 3*S.

totdist( [ ], [ ], 0).

totdist( [Tile | Tiles], [Square | Squares], D) :-
    mandist( Tile, Square, D1),
    totdist( Tiles, Squares, D2),
    D is D1 + D2.
```

(continues)

Figure 12.6 (cont.)

```
% seq( TilePositions, Score): sequence score

seq( [First | OtherTiles], S) :-
  seq( [First | OtherTiles ], First, S).

seq( [Tile1, Tile2 | Tiles], First, S) :-
  score( Tile1, Tile2, S1),
  seq( [Tile2 | Tiles], First, S2),
  S is S1 + S2.

seq( [Last], First, S) :-
  score( Last, First, S).

score( 2/2, _, 1) :- !.                              % Tile in centre scores 1

score( 1/3, 2/3, 0) :- !.                            % Proper successor scores 0
score( 2/3, 3/3, 0) :- !.
score( 3/3, 3/2, 0) :- !.
score( 3/2, 3/1, 0) :- !.
score( 3/1, 2/1, 0) :- !.
score( 2/1, 1/1, 0) :- !.
score( 1/1, 1/2, 0) :- !.
score( 1/2, 1/3, 0) :- !.

score( _, _, 2).                                     % Tiles out of sequence score 2

goal( [2/2,1/3,2/3,3/3,3/2,3/1,2/1,1/1,1/2] ).       % Goal squares for tiles

% Display a solution path as a list of board positions

showsol( [ ] ).

showsol( [P | L] ) :-
  showsol( L),
  nl, write( '---'),
  showpos( P).

% Display a board position

showpos( [S0,S1,S2,S3,S4,S5,S6,S7,S8] ) :-
  member( Y, [3,2,1] ),                              % Order of Y-coordinates
  nl, member( X, [1,2,3] ),                          % Order of X-coordinates
  member( Tile-X/Y,                                  % Tile on square X/Y
          [' '-S0,1-S1,2-S2,3-S3,4-S4,5-S5,6-S6,7-S7,8-S8] ),
  write( Tile),
  fail                                               % Backtrack to next square
  ;
  true.                                              % All squares done
```

Figure 12.6 (cont.)

% Starting positions for some puzzles

start1([2/2,1/3,3/2,2/3,3/3,3/1,2/1,1/1,1/2]).   % Requires 4 steps

start2([2/1,1/2,1/3,3/3,3/2,3/1,2/2,1/1,2/3]).   % Requires 5 steps

start3([2/2,2/3,1/3,3/1,1/2,2/1,3/3,1/1,3/2]).   % Requires 18 steps

% An example query: ?- start1(Pos), bestfirst(Pos, Sol), showsol(Sol).

(2)   seq: the 'sequence score' that measures the degree to which the tiles are
       already ordered in the current position with respect to the order
       required in the goal configuration. seq is computed as the sum of scores
       for each tile according to the following rules:

- a tile in the centre scores 1;
- a tile on a non-central square scores 0 if the tile is, in the
  clockwise direction, followed by its proper successor;
- such a tile scores 2 if it is not followed by its proper successor.

For example, for the starting position of the puzzle in Figure 12.7(a),
seq = 6.

The heuristic estimate, H, is computed as:

$$H = totdist + 3 * seq$$

This heuristic function works well in the sense that it very efficiently directs
the search toward the goal. For example, when solving the puzzles of Figure
12.7(a) and (b), no node outside the shortest solution path is ever expanded
before the first solution is found. This means that the shortest solutions are
found directly in these cases without any backtracking. Even the difficult
puzzle of Figure 12.7(c) is solved almost directly. A drawback of this heuristic

1	3	4
8		2
7	6	5

(a)

2	8	3
1	6	4
7		5

(b)

2	1	6
4		8
7	5	3

(c)

Figure 12.7 Three starting positions for the eight puzzle: (a) requires four steps;
(b) requires five steps; (c) requires 18 steps.

is, however, that it is not admissible: it does not guarantee that the shortest solution path will always be found before any longer solution. The h function used does not satisfy the admissibility condition: $h \leq h^*$ for all the nodes. For example, for the initial position in Figure 12.7(a),

$$h = 4 + 3 * 6 = 22, \quad h^* = 4$$

On the other hand, the 'total distance' measure itself is admissible: for all positions:

totdist $\leq h^*$

This relation can be easily proved by the following argument: if we relaxed the problem by allowing the tiles to climb on top of each other, then each tile could travel to its home square along a trajectory whose length is exactly the Manhattan distance between the tile's initial square and its home square. So the optimal solution in the relaxed puzzle would be exactly of length totdist. In the original problem, however, there is interaction between the tiles and they are in each other's way. This can prevent the tiles from moving along the shortest trajectories, which ensues our optimal solution's length be equal or greater than totdist.

EXERCISE

12.2 Modify the best-first search program of Figure 12.3 to count the number of nodes generated in the search. One easy way is to keep the current number of nodes asserted as a fact, and update it by retract and assert whenever new nodes are generated. Experiment with various heuristic functions for the eight puzzle with respect to their heuristic power, which is reflected in the number of nodes generated.

12.3 Best-first search applied to scheduling

Let us consider the following task-scheduling problem. We are given a collection of *tasks*, $t_1, t_2, \ldots$, with their execution times $D_1, D_2, \ldots$ respectively. The tasks are to be executed on a set of m identical *processors*. Any task can be executed on any processor, but each processor can only execute one task at a time. There is a precedence relation between tasks which tells what tasks, if any, have to be completed before some other task can be started. The

Figure 12.8 A task-scheduling problem with seven tasks and three processors. The top part of the diagram shows the task precedence relation and the duration of the tasks. Task t_5, for example, requires 20 time units, and its execution can only start after three other tasks, t_1, t_2 and t_3, have been completed. Two permissible schedules are shown; an optimal one with the finishing time 24, and a suboptimal one with the finishing time 33. In this problem any optimal schedule has to include idle time. Coffman/Denning, *Operating Systems Theory*, © 1973, p. 86. Adapted by permission of Prentice-Hall, Englewood Cliffs, New Jersey.

scheduling problem is to assign tasks to processors so that the precedence relation is not violated and that all the tasks together are processed in the shortest possible time. The time that the last task in a schedule is completed is called the *finishing time* of the schedule. We want to minimize the finishing time over all permissible schedules.

Figure 12.8 shows such a task-scheduling problem and two permissible schedules, one of which is optimal. This example shows an interesting property of optimal schedules; namely, that they may include 'idle time' for processors. In the optimal schedule of Figure 12.8, processor 2 after having executed task t_2 waits for two time units although it could start executing task t_7.

One way to construct a schedule is roughly as follows. We start with the empty schedule (with void time slots for each processor) and gradually insert tasks one by one into the schedule until all the tasks have been inserted. Usually there are alternatives at any such insertion step because there are several candidate tasks waiting to be processed. Therefore, the scheduling problem is one of search. Accordingly, we can formulate the scheduling problem as a state-space search problem as follows:

- states are partial schedules;
- a successor state of some partial schedule is obtained by adding a not yet scheduled task to this schedule; another possibility is to leave a processor that has completed its current task idle;
- the start state is the empty schedule;
- any schedule that includes all the tasks in the problem is a goal state;
- the cost of a solution (which is to be minimized) is the finishing time of a goal schedule;
- accordingly, the cost of a transition between two (partial) schedules whose finishing times are F_1 and F_2 respectively is the difference $F_2 - F_1$.

Some refinements are needed to this rough scenario. First, we decide to fill the schedule according to increasing times so that tasks are inserted into the schedule from left to right. Also, each time a task is added, the precedence constraint has to be checked. Further, there is no point in leaving a processor idle indefinitely if there are still some candidate tasks waiting. So we decide to leave a processor idle only until some other processor finishes its current task, and then consider again assigning a task to it.

Now let us decide on the representation of problem situations – that is, partial schedules. We need the following information:

(1)   list of waiting tasks and their execution times,
(2)   current engagements of the processors;

We will also add for convenience:

(3)   the finishing time of the (partial) schedule; that is, the latest end-time of the current engagements of the processors.

The list of waiting tasks and their execution times will be represented in the program as a list of the form:

[Task1/D1, Task2/D2, ...]

The current engagements of the processors will be represented by a list of tasks currently being processed; that is, pairs of the form:

Task/FinishingTime

There are m such pairs in the list, one for each processor. We will always add a new task to a schedule at the moment that the first current execution is completed. To this end, the list of current engagements will be kept ordered according to increasing finishing times. The three components of a partial schedule (waiting tasks, current engagements and finishing time) will be combined in the program into a single expression of the form:

WaitingList * ActiveTasks * FinishingTime

In addition to this information we have the precedence constraint which will be specified in the program as a relation:

prec(TaskX, TaskY)

Now let us consider a heuristic estimate. We will use a rather straightforward heuristic function, which will not provide a very efficient guidance to the search algorithm. The function will be admissible and will hence guarantee an optimal schedule. It should be noted, however, that a much more powerful heuristic would be needed for large scheduling problems.

Our heuristic function will be an optimistic estimate of the finishing time of a partial schedule completed with all currently waiting tasks. This optimistic estimate will be computed under the assumption that two constraints on the actual schedule be relaxed:

(1) remove the precedence constraint;
(2) allow (unrealistically) that a task can be executed in a distributed fashion on several processors, and that the sum of the execution times of this task over all these processors is equal to the originally specified execution time of this task on a single processor.

Let the execution times of the currently waiting tasks be $D_1, D_2, \ldots$, and the finishing times of the current processors engagements be $F_1, F_2, \ldots$. Such an optimistically estimated finishing time, *Finall*, to complete all the currently active and all the waiting tasks, is:

$$Finall = (\sum_i D_i + \sum_j F_j)/m$$

where m is the number of processors. Let the finishing time of the current partial schedule be:

$$Fin = \max_j(F_j)$$

Then the heuristic estimate H (an extra time needed to complete the partial schedule with the waiting tasks) is:

if *Finall* > *Fin* then $H = Finall - Fin$ else $H = 0$

A complete program that defines the state-space relations for task scheduling as outlined above is shown in Figure 12.9. The figure also includes a specification of the particular scheduling problem of Figure 12.8. These definitions can now be used by the best-first search program of Figure 12.3. One of the optimal solutions produced by best-first search in the thus specified problem space is an optimal schedule of Figure 12.8.

Figure 12.9   Problem-specific relations for the task-scheduling problem. The particular scheduling problem of Figure 12.8 is also defined by its precedence graph and an initial (empty) schedule as a start node for search.

```
/* Problem-specific relations for task scheduling

Nodes in the state space are partial schedules specified by:

[ WaitingTask1/D1, WaitingTask2/D2, ...] * [ Task1/F1, Task2/F2, ...] * FinTime

The first list specifies the waiting tasks and their durations; the second list specifies the currently
executed tasks and their finishing times, ordered so that F1 ≤ F2, F2 ≤ F3 .... Fintime is the
latest completion time of current engagements of the processors.
*/

% s( Node, SuccessorNode, Cost)

s( Tasks1 * [_/F | Active1] * Fin1, Tasks2 * Active2 * Fin2, Cost) :-
   del( Task/D, Tasks1, Tasks2),                      % Pick a waiting task
   not ( member( T/_, Tasks2), before( T, Task) ),    % Check precedence
   not ( member( T1/F1, Active1), F < F1, before( T1, Task) ),   % Active tasks too
   Time is F + D,                                      % Finishing time of activated task
   insert( Task/Time, Active1, Active2, Fin1, Fin2),
   Cost is Fin2 - Fin1.

s( Tasks * [_/F | Active1] * Fin, Tasks * Active2 * Fin, 0) :-
   insertidle( F, Active1, Active2).                   % Leave processor idle

before( T1, T2) :-                                     % Task T1 before T2
   prec( T1, T2).                                      % according to precedence

before( T1, T2) :-
   prec( T, T2),
   before( T1, T).

insert( S/A, [T/B | L], [S/A, T/B | L], F, F) :-       % Task lists are ordered
   A =< B, !.
```

Figure 12.9 (cont.)

```
insert( S/A, [T/B | L], [T/B | L1], F1, F2) :-
   insert( S/A, L, L1, F1, F2).

insert( S/A, [ ], [S/A], _, A).

insertidle( A, [T/B | L], [idle/B, T/B | L] ) :-      % Leave processor idle
   A < B, !.                                           % until first greater finishing time

insertidle( A, [T/B | L], [T/B | L1] ) :-
   insertidle( A, L, L1).

del( A, [A | L], L).                                    % Delete item from list

del( A, [B | L], [B | L1] ) :-
   del( A, L, L1).

goal( [ ] * _ * _)                                      % Goal state: no task waiting
```

% Heuristic estimate of a partial schedule is based on an
% optimistic estimate of the final finishing time of this
% partial schedule extended by all the remaining waiting tasks.

```
h( Tasks * Processors * Fin, H) :-
   totaltime( Tasks, Tottime),                          % Total duration of waiting tasks
   sumnum( Processors, Ftime, N),                       % Ftime is sum of finishing times
                                                        % of processors, N is their number
   Finall is ( Tottime + Ftime)/N,
   ( Finall > Fin, !, H is Finall − Fin
   ;
     H = 0
   ).

totaltime( [ ], 0).

totaltime( [_/D | Tasks], T) :-
   totaltime( Tasks, T1),
   T is T1 + D.

sumnum( [ ], 0, 0).

sumnum( [_/T | Procs], FT, N) :-
   sumnum( Procs, FT1, N1),
   N is N1 + 1,
   FT is FT1 + T.
```

% A task-precedence graph

```
prec( t1, t4).   prec( t1, t5).   prec( t2, t4).   prec( t2, t5).
prec( t3, t5).   prec( t3, t6).   prec( t3, t7).
```

% A start node

```
start( [t1/4, t2/2, t3/2, t4/20, t5/20, t6/11, t7/11] * [idle/0, idle/0, idle/0] * 0).
```

% An example query: ?- start(Problem), bestfirst(Problem, Sol).

Project

In general, scheduling problems are known to be combinatorially difficult. Our simple heuristic function does not provide very powerful guidance. Propose other functions and experiment with them.

SUMMARY

- Heuristic information can be used to estimate how far a node is from a nearest goal node in the state space. This chapter considered numerical heuristic estimates.

- The *best-first* heuristic principle guides the search process so as to always expand the node that is currently the most promising, according to the heuristic estimates.

- The search algorithm, known as A*, that uses this principle, was programmed in this chapter.

- To use A* for solving a concrete problem, a state space, a goal predicate, and a heuristic function have to be defined to be used by A*. For complex problems, the difficult part is to find a good heuristic function.

- The *admissibility theorem* helps to establish whether A*, using a particular heuristic function, will always find an optimal solution.

References

The best-first search program of this chapter is a variation of many similar algorithms of which A* is the most popular. General descriptions of A* can be found in Nilsson (1971, 1980) or Winston (1984). The admissibility theorem was discovered by Hart, Nilsson and Raphael (1968). An excellent and rigorous treatment of many variations of best-first search algorithms and related mathematical results is provided by Pearl (1984). Doran and Michie (1966) originated the best-first search guided by distance-to-goal estimate. Kanal and Kumar (1988) edited a collection of interesting papers dealing with various advanced aspects of search.

The eight puzzle was used in Artificial Intelligence as a test problem for studying heuristic principles by several researchers – for example, Doran and Michie (1966), Michie and Ross (1970), and Gaschnig (1979).

Our task-scheduling problem and its variations arise in numerous applications in which servicing of requests for resources is to be planned. An example is computer operating systems. Task-scheduling problems with reference to this application are treated by Coffman and Denning (1973).

Finding good heuristics is important and difficult, therefore the study of heuristics is one of the central themes of Artificial Intelligence. There are, however, also some limitations on how far we can get in the refinement of heuristics. It may appear that to solve any combinatorial problem efficiently we only have to find a powerful heuristic. However, there are problems (including many scheduling problems) for which no general heuristic exists that would guarantee both efficiency and admissibility in all cases. Many theoretical results that pertain to this limitation issue are collected in Garey and Johnson (1979).

Coffman, E.G. and Denning, P.J. (1973) *Operating Systems Theory*. Prentice-Hall.

Doran, J. and Michie, D. (1966) Experiments with the graph traverser program. *Proc. Royal Society of London* **294(A)**: 235–259.

Garey, M.R. and Johnson, D.S. (1979) *Computers and Intractability*. W.H. Freeman.

Gaschnig, J. (1979) Performance measurement and analysis of certain search algorithms. Carnegie-Mellon University: Computer Science Department. Technical Report CMU-CS-79-124 (Ph.D. Thesis).

Hart, P.E., Nilsson, N.J. and Raphael, B. (1968) A formal basis for the heuristic determination of minimum cost paths. *IEEE Transactions on Systems Sciences and Cybernetics* **SSC-4(2)**: 100–107.

Kanal, L. and Kumar, V. (1988, eds.) *Search in Artificial Intelligence*. Springer-Verlag.

Michie, D. and Ross, R. (1970) Experiments with the adaptive graph traverser. *Machine Intelligence* **5**: 301–308.

Nilsson, N.J. (1971) *Problem Solving Methods in Artificial Intelligence*. McGraw-Hill.

Nilsson, N.J. (1980) *Principles of Artificial Intelligence*. Tioga; also Springer-Verlag.

Pearl, J. (1984) *Heuristics: Intelligent Search Strategies for Computer Problem Solving*. Addison-Wesley.

Winston, P.H. (1984) *Artificial Intelligence* (second edition). Addison-Wesley.

13 Problem Reduction and AND/OR Graphs

AND/OR graphs are a suitable representation for problems that can be naturally decomposed into mutually independent subproblems. Examples of such problems include route finding, symbolic integration, game playing, theorem proving, etc. In this chapter we will develop programs for searching AND/OR graphs, including a heuristically guided best-first AND/OR search.

13.1 AND/OR graph representation of problems

In Chapters 11 and 12, problem solving was centred around the state-space representation of problems. Accordingly, problem solving was reduced to finding a path in a state-space graph. Another representation, the AND/OR graph representation, more naturally suits certain categories of problems. This representation relies on the decomposition of problems into sub-problems. Decomposition into subproblems is advantageous if the sub-problems are mutually independent, and can therefore be solved independently of each other.

Let us illustrate this with an example. Consider the problem of finding a route in a road map between two given cities, as shown in Figure 13.1. We will disregard path lengths for the moment. The problem could, of course, be formulated as path finding in a state space. The corresponding state space would look just like the map: the nodes in the state space correspond to cities, the arcs correspond to direct connections between cities, arc costs correspond to distances between cities. However, let us construct another representation of this problem, based on a natural decomposition of the problem.

In the map of Figure 13.1, there is also a river. Let us assume that there are only two bridges at which the river can be crossed, one bridge at city f and the other at city g. Obviously, our route will have to include one of the

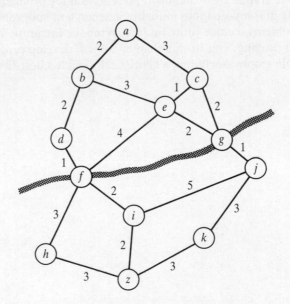

Figure 13.1 Finding a route from a to z in a road map. The river has to be crossed at f or g. An AND/OR representation of this problem is shown in Figure 13.2.

bridges; so it will have to go through *f* or through *g*. We have, then, two major alternatives:

To find a path between *a* and *z*, find *either*

(1) a path from *a* to *z* via *f*, *or*
(2) a path from *a* to *z* via *g*.

Each of these two alternative problems can now be decomposed as follows:

(1) To find a path from *a* to *z* via *f*:
  1.1 find a path from *a* to *f*, *and*
  1.2 find a path from *f* to *z*.

(2) To find a path from *a* to *z* via *g*:
  2.1 find a path from *a* to *g*, *and*
  2.2 find a path from *g* to *z*.

To summarize, we have two main alternatives for solving the original problem: (1) via *f* or (2) via *g*. Further, each of these alternatives can be *decomposed* into two subproblems (1.1 and 1.2, or 2.1 and 2.2 respectively). What is important here is that (in both alternatives) each of the subproblems can be solved independently of the other. Such a decomposition can be pictured as an *AND/OR graph* (Figure 13.2). Notice the curved arcs which indicate the AND relationship between subproblems. Of course, the graph in Figure 13.2 is only the top part of a corresponding AND/OR tree. Further decomposition of subproblems could be based on the introduction of additional intermediate cities.

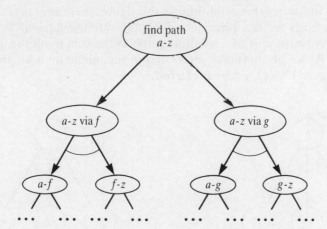

Figure 13.2 An AND/OR representation of the route-finding problem of Figure 13.1. Nodes correspond to problems or subproblems, and curved arcs indicate that all (both) subproblems have to be solved.

What are goal nodes in such an AND/OR graph? Goal nodes correspond to subproblems that are trivial or 'primitive'. In our example, such a subproblem would be 'find a route from a to c', for there is a direct connection between cities a and c in the road map.

Some important concepts have been introduced in this example. An AND/OR graph is a directed graph in which nodes correspond to problems, and arcs indicate relations between problems. There are also relations among arcs themselves. These relations are AND and OR, depending on whether we have to solve just one of the successor problems or several (see Figure 13.3). In principle, a node can issue both AND-related arcs and OR-related arcs. We will, however, assume that each node has either only AND successors or only OR successors. Each AND/OR graph can be transformed into this form by introducing auxiliary OR nodes if necessary. Then, a node that only issues AND arcs is called an AND node; a node that only issues OR arcs is called an OR node.

In the state-space representation, a solution to the problem was a path in the state space. What is a solution in the AND/OR representation? A solution, of course, has to include all the subproblems of an AND node. Therefore, a solution is not a path any more, but it is a tree. Such a solution tree, T, is defined as follows:

- the original problem, P, is the root node of T;
- if P is an OR node then exactly one of its successors (in the AND/OR graph), together with its own solution tree, is in T;
- if P is an AND node then all of its successors (in the AND/OR graph), together with their solution trees, are in T.

Figure 13.4 illustrates this definition. In this figure, there are costs attached to arcs. Using costs we can formulate an optimization criterion. We can, for example, define the cost of a solution graph as the sum of all the arc costs in the graph. As we are normally interested in the minimum cost, the solution graph in Figure 13.4(c) will be preferred.

Figure 13.3 (a) To solve P solve any of P_1 or P_2 or .... (b) To solve Q solve all Q_1 and Q_2 ....

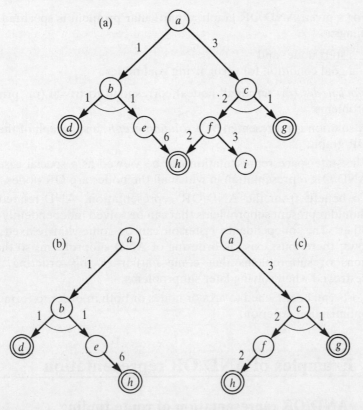

Figure 13.4 (a) An AND/OR graph; d, g and h are goal nodes; a is the problem to be solved. (b) and (c) Two solution trees whose costs are 9 and 8 respectively. The cost of a solution tree is here defined as the sum of all the arc costs in the solution tree.

But we do not have to base our optimization measure on the costs of arcs. Sometimes it is more natural to associate costs with nodes rather than arcs, or with both arcs and nodes.

To summarize:

- AND/OR representation is based on the philosophy of reducing a problem to subproblems.

- Nodes in an AND/OR graph correspond to problems; links between nodes indicate relations between problems.

- A node that issues OR links is an OR node. To solve an OR node, one of its successor nodes has to be solved.

- A node that issues AND links is an AND node. To solve an AND node, all of its successors have to be solved.

- For a given AND/OR graph, a particular problem is specified by two things:

  a start node, and
  a goal condition for recognizing goal nodes.

- *Goal nodes* (or 'terminal' nodes) correspond to trivial (or 'primitive') problems.

- A solution is represented by a *solution graph*, a subgraph of the AND/OR graph.

- The state-space representation can be viewed as a special case of the AND/OR representation in which all the nodes are OR nodes.

- To benefit from the AND/OR representation, AND-related nodes should represent subproblems that can be solved independently of each other. The independency criterion can be somewhat relaxed, as follows: there must exist an ordering of AND subproblems so that solutions of subproblems that come earlier in this ordering are not destroyed when solving later subproblems.

- Costs can be attached to arcs or nodes or both in order to formulate an optimization criterion.

13.2   Examples of AND/OR representation

13.2.1   AND/OR representation of route finding

For the shortest route problem of Figure 13.1, an AND/OR graph including a cost function can be defined as follows:

- OR nodes are of the form X-Z, meaning: find a shortest path from X to Z.

- AND nodes are of the form

  X-Z via Y

  meaning: find a shortest path from X to Z under the constraint that the path goes through Y.

- A node X-Z is a goal node (primitive problem) if X and Z are directly connected in the map.

- The cost of each goal node X-Z is the given road distance between X and Z.

- The costs of all other (non-terminal) nodes are 0.

The cost of a solution graph is the sum of the costs of all the nodes in the solution graph (in our case, this is just the sum over the terminal nodes). For the problem of Figure 13.1, the start node is a-z. Figure 13.5 shows a solution

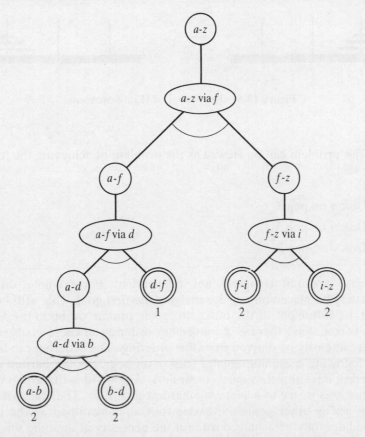

Figure 13.5 The cheapest solution tree for the route problem of Figure 13.1 formulated as an AND/OR graph.

tree of cost 9. This tree corresponds to the path **[a,b,d,f,i,z]**. This path can be reconstructed from the solution tree by visiting all the leaves in this tree in the left-to-right order.

13.2.2   The Tower of Hanoi problem

The Tower of Hanoi problem, shown in Figure 13.6, is another, classical example of effective application of the AND/OR decomposition scheme. For simplicity, we will consider a simple version of this problem, containing three disks only:

> There are three pegs, 1, 2 and 3, and three disks, *a*, *b* and *c* (*a* being the smallest and *c* being the biggest). Initially, all the disks are stacked on peg 1. The problem is to transfer them all on to peg 3. Only one disk can be moved at a time, and no disk can ever be placed on top of a smaller disk.

Figure 13.6 The Tower of Hanoi problem.

This problem can be viewed as the problem of achieving the following set of goals:

(1)   Disk *a* on peg 3.
(2)   Disk *b* on peg 3.
(3)   Disk *c* on peg 3.

These goals are, unfortunately, not independent. For example, disk *a* can immediately be placed on peg 3, satisfying the first goal. This will, however, prevent the fulfilment of the other two goals (unless we undo the first goal again). Fortunately, there is a convenient ordering of these goals so that a solution can easily be derived from this ordering. The ordering can be found by the following reasoning: goal 3 (disk *c* on peg 3) is the hardest because moving disk *c* is subject to most constraints. A good idea that often works in such situations is: try to achieve the hardest goal first. The logic behind this principle is: as other goals are easier (not as constrained as the hardest) they can hopefully be achieved without the necessity of undoing this hardest goal.

The problem-solving strategy that results from this principle in our task is:

> First satisfy the goal 'disk *c* on peg 3',
> then satisfy the remaining goals.

But the first goal cannot immediately be achieved: disk *c* cannot move in the initial situation. Therefore, we first have to prepare this move and our strategy is refined to:

(1)   Enable moving disk *c* from 1 to 3.
(2)   Move disk *c* from 1 to 3.
(3)   Achieve remaining goals: *a* on 3, and *b* on 3.

Disk *c* can only move from 1 to 3 if both *a* and *b* are stacked on peg 2. Then, our initial problem of moving *a*, *b* and *c* from peg 1 to peg 3 is reduced to three subproblems:

> To move *a*, *b* and *c* from 1 to 3:
>
> (1)   move *a* and *b* from 1 to 2, *and*
>
> (2)   move *c* from 1 to 3, *and*
>
> (3)   move *a* and *b* from 2 to 3.

Problem 2 is trivial (one-step solution). The other two subproblems can be solved independently of problem 2 because disks *a* and *b* can be moved regardless of the position of disk *c*. To solve problems 1 and 3, the same decomposition principle can be applied (disk *b* is the hardest this time). Accordingly, problem 1 is reduced to three trivial subproblems:

> To move *a* and *b* from 1 to 2:
>
> (1)   move *a* from 1 to 3, *and*
>
> (2)   move *b* from 1 to 2, *and*
>
> (3)   move *a* from 3 to 2.

13.2.3   AND/OR formulation of game playing

Games like chess and checkers can naturally be viewed as problems, represented by AND/OR graphs. Such games are called two-person, perfect-information games, and we will assume here that there are only two possible outcomes: WIN or LOSS. (We can think of games with three outcomes – WIN, LOSS and DRAW – as also having just two outcomes: WIN and NO-WIN.) As the two players move in turn we have two kinds of positions, depending on who is to move. Let us call the two players 'us' and 'them', so the two kinds of positions are: 'us-to-move' positions and 'them-to-move' positions. Assume that the game starts in an us-to-move position P. Each alternative us-move in this position leads to one of them-to-move positions $Q_1, Q_2, \ldots$ (Figure 13.7). Further, each alternative them-move in Q_1 leads to one of the positions $R_{11}, R_{12}, \ldots$. In the AND/OR tree of Figure 13.7, nodes correspond to positions, and arcs correspond to possible moves. Us-to-move levels alternate with them-to-move levels. To win in the initial position, P, we have to find a move from P to Q_i, for some i, so that the position Q_i is won. Thus, P is won if Q_1 or Q_2 or ... is won. Therefore position P is an OR node. For all i, position Q_i is a them-to-move position, so if it is to be won for us it has to be won after *each* them-move. Thus Q_i is won if all R_{i1} and R_{i2} and ... are won. Accordingly, all them-to-move positions are AND nodes. Goal nodes are those positions that are won by the rules of the game; for example, their king checkmated in chess. Those positions that are lost by the rules of the game correspond to unsolvable problems. To solve the game we have to find a solution tree that guarantees our victory regardless of the opponent's

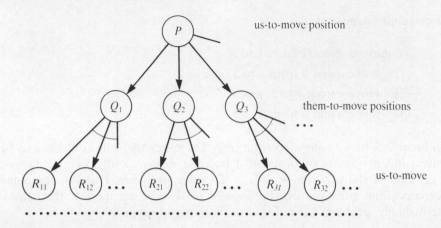

Figure 13.7 An AND/OR formulation of a two-person game; the players are 'us' and 'them'.

replies. Such a solution tree, then, is a complete strategy for winning the game: for each possible continuation that can be chosen by the opponent, there is a move in such a strategy tree that forces a win.

13.3 Basic AND/OR search procedures

In this section we will only be interested in finding *some* solution of the problem, regardless of its cost. So for the purposes of this section we can ignore the costs of links or nodes in an AND/OR graph.

The simplest way of searching AND/OR graphs in Prolog is to use Prolog's own search mechanism. This happens to be trivial as Prolog's procedural meaning itself is nothing but a procedure for searching AND/OR graphs. For example, the AND/OR graph of Figure 13.4 (ignoring the arc costs) can be specified by the following clauses:

a :- b.   % a is an OR node with two successors, b and c

a :- c.

b :- d, e.   % b is an AND node with two successors, d and e

e :- h.

c :- f, g.

f :- h; i.

d.   g.   h.   % d, g and h are goal nodes

To ask whether problem **a** can be solved we can simply ask:

    ?- a.

Now Prolog will effectively search the tree of Figure 13.4 in the depth-first fashion and answer 'yes', after having visited that part of the search graph corresponding to the solution tree in Figure 13.4(b).

The advantage of this approach to programming AND/OR search is its simplicity. There are disadvantages, however:

- We only get an answer 'yes' or 'no', not a solution tree as well. We could reconstruct the solution tree from the program's trace, but this can be awkward and insufficient if we want a solution tree explicitly accessible as an object in the program.

- This program is hard to extend so as to be able to handle costs as well.

- If our AND/OR graph were a general graph, containing cycles, then Prolog with its depth-first strategy could enter an indefinite recursive loop.

Let us rectify these deficiencies gradually. We will first define our own depth-first search procedure for AND/OR graphs.

To begin with, we will change the representation of AND/OR graphs in the program. For that we will introduce a binary relation represented in the infix notation with the operator '--->'. For example, node *a* linked to its two OR successors will be represented by the clause:

    a ---> or : [b,c].

The symbols '--->' and ':' are both infix operators that can be defined by:

    :- op(600, xfx, --->).

    :- op(500, xfx, :).

The complete AND/OR graph of Figure 13.4 is thus specified by the clauses:

    a ---> or : [b,c].
    b ---> and : [d,e].
    c ---> and : [f,g].
    e ---> or : [h].
    f ---> or : [h,i].

    goal(d).   goal(g).   goal(h).

The depth-first AND/OR procedure can be constructed from the following principles:

To solve a node, N, use the following rules:

(1) If N is a goal node then it is trivially solved.

(2) If N has OR successors then solve one of them (attempt them one after another until a solvable one is found).

(3) If N has AND successors then solve all of them (attempt them one after another until they have all been solved).

If the above rules do not produce a solution then assume the problem cannot be solved.

A corresponding program can be as follows:

```
solve( Node) :-
    goal( Node).

solve( Node) :-
    Node ---> or : Nodes,          % Node is an OR node
    member( Node1, Nodes),         % Select a successor Node1 of Node
    solve( Node1).

solve( Node) :-
    Node ---> and : Nodes,         % Node is an AND node
    solveall( Nodes).              % Solve all Node's successors

solveall( [ ] ).

solveall( [Node | Nodes] ) :-
    solve( Node),
    solveall( Nodes).
```

member is the usual list membership relation.

This program still has the following disadvantages:

- it does not produce a solution tree, and
- it is susceptible to infinite loops, depending on the properties of the AND/OR graph (cycles).

The program can easily be modified to produce a solution tree. We have to modify the **solve** relation so that it has two arguments:

```
solve( Node, SolutionTree)
```

Let us represent a solution tree as follows. We have three cases:

(1) If **Node** is a goal node then the corresponding solution tree is **Node** itself.

(2)   If **Node** is an OR node then its solution tree has the form:

     Node ---> Subtree

where **Subtree** is a solution tree for one of the successors of **Node**.

(3)   If **Node** is an AND node then its solution tree has the form:

     Node ---> and : Subtrees

where **Subtrees** is the list of solution trees of all of the successors of **Node**.

For example, in the AND/OR graph of Figure 13.4, the first solution of the top node a is represented by:

    a ---> b ---> and : [d, e ---> h]

The three forms of a solution tree correspond to the three clauses about our **solve** relation. So our initial **solve** procedure can be altered by simply modifying each of the three clauses; that is, by just adding solution tree as the second argument to **solve**. The resulting program is shown as Figure 13.8. An additional procedure in this program is **show** for displaying solution trees. For example, the solution tree of Figure 13.4 is displayed by **show** in the following form:

    a ---> b ---> d
               e ---> h

The program of Figure 13.8 is still prone to infinite loops. One simple way to prevent infinite loops is to keep trace of the current depth of the search and prevent the program from searching beyond some depth limit. We can do this by simply introducing another argument to the **solve** relation:

    solve(Node, SolutionTree, MaxDepth)

As before, **Node** represents a problem to be solved, and **SolutionTree** is a solution not deeper than **MaxDepth**. **MaxDepth** is the allowed depth of search in the graph. In the case that **MaxDepth** = 0 no further expansion is allowed; otherwise, if **MaxDepth** > 0 then **Node** can be expanded and its successors are attempted with a lower depth limit **MaxDepth** − 1. This can easily be incorporated into the program of Figure 13.8. For example, the second clause about **solve** becomes:

```
solve( Node, Node ---> Tree, MaxDepth) :-
    MaxDepth > 0,
    Node ---> or : Nodes,           % Node is an OR node
    member( Node1, Nodes),          % Select a successor Node1 of Node
    Depth1 is MaxDepth − 1,         % New depth limit
    solve( Node1, Tree, Depth1).    % Solve successor with lower limit
```

```
% Depth-first AND/OR search
% solve( Node, SolutionTree):
%    find a solution tree for Node in an AND/OR graph
```

```
solve( Node, Node) :-                            % Solution tree of goal node is Node itself
  goal( Node).
```

```
solve( Node, Node ---> Tree) :-
  Node ---> or : Nodes,                          % Node is an OR node
  member( Node1, Nodes),                         % Select a successor Node1 of Node
  solve( Node1, Tree).
```

```
solve( Node, Node ---> and : Trees) :-
  Node ---> and : Nodes,                         % Node is an AND node
  solveall( Nodes, Trees).                       % Solve all Node's successors
```

```
% solveall( [Node1, Node2, ...], [SolutionTree1, SolutionTree2, ...] )
```

```
solveall( [ ], [ ] ).
```

```
solveall( [Node | Nodes], [Tree | Trees] ) :-
  solve( Node, Tree),
  solveall( Nodes, Trees).
```

```
show( Tree) :-                                   % Display solution tree
  show( Tree, 0).                                % Indented by 0
```

```
% show( Tree, H): display solution tree indented by H
```

```
show( Node ---> Tree, H) :- !,
  write( Node), write( ' ---> '),
  H1 is H + 7,
  show( Tree, H1).
```

```
show( and : [ ], H) :- !.                        % Display empty AND list of trees
```

```
show( and : [T | Ts], H) :- !,                   % Display AND list of solution trees
  show( T, H),
  tab( H),
  show( and : Ts, H).
```

```
show( Node, H) :-
  write( Node), nl.
```

Figure 13.8 Depth-first search for AND/OR graphs. This program does not avoid infinite cycling. Procedure **solve** finds a solution tree and procedure **show** displays such a tree. **show** assumes that each node only takes one character on output.

This depth-limited, depth-first procedure can also be used in the iterative deepening regime, thereby simulating the breadth-first search. The idea is to do the depth-first search repetitively, each time with a greater depth limit, until a solution is found. That is, try to solve the problem with depth limit 0, then with 1, then with 2, etc. Such a program is:

```
iterative_deepening( Node, SolTree) :-
    trydepths( Node, SolTree, 0).          % Try search with increasing
                                           % depth limit, start with 0

trydepths( Node, SolTree, Depth) :-
    solve( Node, SolTree, Depth)
    ;
    Depth1 is Depth + 1,                   % Get new depth limit
    trydepths( Node, SolTree, Depth1).     % Try higher depth limit
```

As with iterative deepening in state space (see Chapter 11), a disadvantage of this breadth-first simulation is that the program researches top parts of the search space each time that the depth limit is increased. On the other hand, the important advantage as compared with genuine breadth-first search is space economy.

EXERCISES

13.1 Complete the depth-limited, depth-first AND/OR search program according to the procedure outlined in this section.

13.2 Define in Prolog an AND/OR space for the Tower of Hanoi problem and use this definition with the search procedures of this section.

13.3 Consider some simple two-person, perfect-information game without chance and define its AND/OR representation. Use a depth-first AND/OR search program to find winning strategies in the form of AND/OR trees.

13.4 Best-first AND/OR search

13.4.1 Heuristic estimates and the search algorithm

The basic search procedures of the previous section search AND/OR graphs systematically and exhaustively, without any heuristic guidance. For complex problems such procedures are too inefficient due to the combinatorial complexity of the search space. Heuristic guidance that aims to reduce the complexity by avoiding useless alternatives becomes necessary. The heuristic guidance introduced in this section will be based on numerical heuristic estimates of the difficulty of problems in the AND/OR graph. The program that we shall develop can be viewed as a generalization of the best-first search program for the state-space representation of Chapter 12.

Let us begin by introducing an optimization criterion based on the costs of arcs in the AND/OR graph. First, we extend our representation of AND/OR graphs to include arc costs. For example, the AND/OR graph of Figure 13.4 can be represented by the following clauses:

```
a ---> or : [b/1, c/3].
b ---> and : [d/1, e/1].
c ---> and : [f/2, g/1].
e ---> or : [h/6].
f ---> or : [h/2, i/3].

goal( d).     goal( g).     goal( h).
```

We shall define the cost of a solution tree as the sum of all the arc costs in the tree. The optimization objective is to find a minimum-cost solution-tree. For illustration, see Figure 13.4 again.

It is useful to define the *cost of a node* in the AND/OR graph as the cost of the node's optimal solution tree. So defined, the cost of a node corresponds to the difficulty of the node.

We shall now assume that we can estimate the costs of nodes (without knowing their solution trees) in the AND/OR graph with some heuristic function h. Such estimates will be used for guiding the search. Our heuristic search program will begin the search with the start node and, by expanding already visited nodes, gradually grow a search tree. This process will grow a *tree* even in cases that the AND/OR graph itself is not a tree; in such a case the graph unfolds into a tree by duplicating parts of the graph.

The search process will at any time of the search select the 'most promising' candidate solution tree for the next expansion. Now, how is the function h used to estimate how promising a candidate solution tree is? Or, how promising a node (the root of a candidate solution tree) is?

For a node N in the search tree, $H(N)$ will denote its estimated difficulty. For a tip node N of the current search tree, $H(N)$ is simply $h(N)$. On the other hand, for an interior node of the search tree we do not have to use function h directly because we already have some additional information about such a node; that is, we already know its successors. Therefore, as Figure 13.9 shows, for an interior OR node N we approximate its difficulty as:

$$H(N) = \min_{i} (\, cost(N,N_i) + H(N_i) \,)$$

where $cost(N,N_i)$ is the cost of the arc from N to N_i. The minimization rule in this formula is justified by the fact that, to solve N, we just have to solve one of its successors.

Figure 13.9 Estimating the difficulty, H, of problems in the AND/OR graph.

The difficulty of an AND node N is approximated by:

$$H(N) = \sum_i (\ cost(N,N_i) + H(N_i) \ )$$

We say that the H-value of an interior node is a 'backed-up' estimate.

In our search program, it will be more practical to use (instead of the H-values) another measure, F, defined in terms of H, as follows. Let a node M be the predecessor of N in the search tree, and the cost of the arc from M to N be $cost(M,N)$, then we define:

$$F(N) = cost(M,N) + H(N)$$

Accordingly, if M is the parent node of N, and N_1, N_2, ... are N's children, then:

$$F(N) = cost(M,N) + \min_i F(N_i), \qquad \text{if } N \text{ is an OR node}$$

$$F(N) = cost(M,N) + \sum_i F(N_i), \qquad \text{if } N \text{ is an AND node}$$

The start node S of the search has no predecessor, but let us choose the cost of its (virtual) incoming arc as 0. Now, if h for all goal nodes in the AND/OR graph is 0, and an optimal solution tree has been found, then $F(S)$ is just the cost of this solution tree (that is, the sum of all the costs of its arcs).

At any stage of the search, each successor of an OR node represents an alternative candidate solution subtree. The search process will always decide to continue the exploration at that successor whose *F*-value is minimal. Let us return to Figure 13.4 again and trace such a search process when searching the AND/OR graph of this figure. Initially, the search tree is just the start node *a*, and then the tree grows until a solution tree is found. Figure 13.10 shows

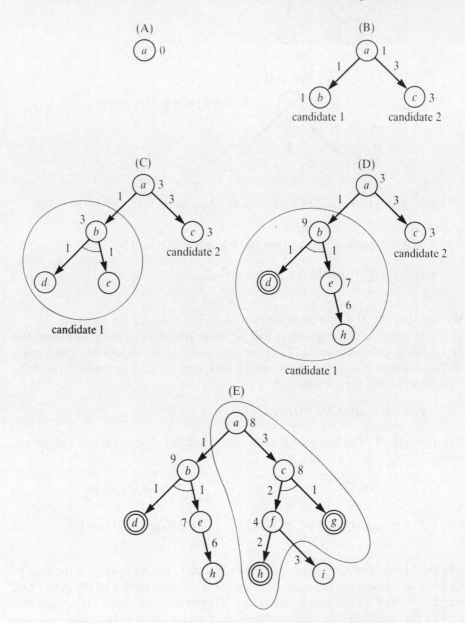

Figure 13.10 A trace of a best-first AND/OR search (using *h* = 0) solving the problem of Figure 13.4.

some snapshots taken during the growth of the search tree. We shall assume for simplicity that $h = 0$ for all the nodes. Numbers attached to nodes in Figure 13.10 are the F-values of the nodes (of course, these change during the search as more information is accumulated). Here are some explanatory remarks to Figure 13.10.

Expanding the initial search tree (snapshot A) produces tree B. Node a is an OR node, so we now have two candidate solution trees: b and c. As $F(b) = 1 < 3 = F(c)$, alternative b is selected for expansion. Now, how far can alternative b be expanded? The expansion can proceed until either:

(1)   the F-value of node b has become greater than that of its competitor c, or

(2)   it has become clear that a solution tree has been found.

So candidate b starts to grow with the upper bound for $F(b)$: $F(b) \leq 3 = F(c)$. First, b's successors d and e are generated (snapshot C) and the F-value of b is increased to 3. As this does not exceed the upper bound, the candidate tree rooted in b continues to expand. Node d is found to be a goal node, and then node e is expanded resulting in snapshot D. At this point $F(b) = 9 > 3$ which stops the expansion of alternative b. This prevents the process from realizing that h is also a goal node and that a solution tree has already been generated. Instead, the activity now switches to the competing alternative c. The bound on $F(c)$ for expanding this alternative is set to 9, since at this point $F(b) = 9$. Within this bound the candidate tree rooted in c is expanded until the situation of snapshot E is reached. Now the process realizes that a solution tree (which includes goal nodes h and g) has been found, and the whole process terminates. Notice that the cheaper of the two possible solution trees was reported a solution by this process – that is, the solution tree in Figure 13.4(c).

13.4.2   Search program

A program that implements the ideas of the previous section is given in Figure 13.12. Before explaining some details of this program, let us consider the representation of the search tree that this program uses.

There are several cases, as shown in Figure 13.11. The different forms of the search tree arise from combining the following possibilities with respect to the tree's size and 'solution status':

- Size:
    - (1)   the tree is either a single node tree (a leaf), or
    - (2)   it has a root and (non-empty) subtrees.
- Solution status:
    - (1)   the tree has already been discovered to be solved (the tree is a solution tree), or
    - (2)   it is still just a *candidate* solution tree.

Case 1: Search leaf

leaf(N, F, C)

Case 2: Search tree with OR subtrees

tree(N, F, C, or : [T1, T2, ...])

Case 3: Search tree with AND subtrees

tree(N, F, C, and : [T1, T2, ...])

Case 4: Solved leaf

solvedleaf (N, F)

Case 5: Solution tree rooted at OR node

solvedtree(N, F, T)

Case 6: Solution tree rooted at AND node

solvedtree(N, F, and : [T1, T2, ...])

Figure 13.11   Representation of the search tree.

The principal functor used to represent the tree indicates a combination of these possibilities. This can be one of the following:

leaf   solvedleaf   tree   solvedtree

Further, the representation comprises some or all of the following information:

- root node of the tree,
- *F*-value of the tree,
- the cost C of the arc in the AND/OR graph pointing to the tree,
- list of subtrees,
- relation among subtrees (AND or OR).

The list of subtrees is always ordered according to increasing *F*-values. A subtree can already be solved. Such subtrees are accommodated at the end of the list.

Now to the program of Figure 13.12. The top-level relation is

andor(Node, SolutionTree)

where **Node** is the start node of the search. The program produces a solution tree (if one exists) with the aspiration that this will be an optimal solution.

Figure 13.12   Best-first AND/OR search program.

/* BEST-FIRST AND/OR SEARCH

This program only generates one solution. This solution is guaranteed to be a cheapest one if the heuristic function used is a lower bound of the actual costs of solution trees.

Search tree is either:

tree(Node, F, C, SubTrees)	tree of candidate solutions
leaf(Node, F, C)	leaf of a search tree
solvedtree(Node, F, SubTrees)	solution tree
solvedleaf(Node, F)	leaf of solution tree

C is the cost of the arc pointing to Node

F = C + H, where H is the heuristic estimate of an optimal solution subtree rooted in Node

SubTrees are always ordered so that:
(1) all solved subtrees are at the end of a list;
(2) other (unsolved subtrees) are ordered according to ascending F-values.
*/

(continues)

Figure 13.12 (cont.)

```
:- op( 500, xfx, :).

:- op( 600, xfx, --->).

andor( Node, SolutionTree) :-
    expand( leaf( Node, 0, 0), 9999, SolutionTree, yes).    % Assuming 9999 > any F-value

% Procedure expand( Tree, Bound, NewTree, Solved)
% expands Tree with Bound producing NewTree whose
% 'solution-status' is Solved

% Case 1: bound exceeded

expand( Tree, Bound, Tree, no) :-
    f( Tree, F), F > Bound, !.                              % Bound exceeded

% In all remaining cases F ≦ Bound
% Case 2: goal encountered

expand( leaf( Node, F, C), _, solvedleaf( Node, F), yes) :-
    goal( Node), !.

% Case 3: expanding a leaf

expand( leaf( Node, F, C), Bound, NewTree, Solved) :-
    expandnode( Node, C, Tree1), !,
    expand( Tree1, Bound, NewTree, Solved)
    ;
    Solved = never, !.                                      % No successors, dead end

% Case 4: expanding a tree

expand( tree( Node, F, C, SubTrees), Bound, NewTree, Solved) :-
    Bound1 is Bound - C,
    expandlist( SubTrees, Bound1, NewSubs, Solved1),
    continue( Solved1, Node, C, NewSubs, Bound, NewTree, Solved).

% expandlist( Trees, Bound, NewTrees, Solved)
% expands tree list Trees with Bound producing
% NewTrees whose 'solved-status' is Solved

expandlist( Trees, Bound, NewTrees, Solved) :-
    selecttree( Trees, Tree, OtherTrees, Bound, Bound1),
    expand( Tree, Bound1, NewTree, Solved1),
    combine( OtherTrees, NewTree, Solved1, NewTrees, Solved).

% 'continue' decides how to continue after expanding a tree list

continue( yes, Node, C, SubTrees, _, solvedtree( Node, F, SubTrees), yes) :-
    backup( SubTrees, H), F is C + H, !.
```

Figure 13.12 (cont.)

---

continue(never, _, _, _, _, _, never) :- !.

continue(no, Node, C, SubTrees, Bound, NewTree, Solved) :-
  backup(SubTrees, H), F is C + H, !,
  expand(tree(Node, F, C, SubTrees), Bound, NewTree, Solved).

% 'combine' combines results of expanding a tree and a tree list

combine(or : _, Tree, yes, Tree, yes) :- !.   % OR list solved

combine(or : Trees, Tree, no, or : NewTrees, no) :-
  insert(Tree, Trees, NewTrees), !.   % OR list still unsolved

combine(or : [ ], _, never, _, never) :- !.   % No more candidates

combine(or : Trees, _, never, or : Trees, no) :- !.   % There are more candidates.

combine(and : Trees, Tree, yes, and : [Tree | Trees], yes) :-
  allsolved(Trees), !.   % AND list solved

combine(and : _, _, never, _, never) :- !.   % AND list unsolvable

combine(and : Trees, Tree, YesNo, and : NewTrees, no) :-
  insert(Tree, Trees, NewTrees), !.   % AND list still unsolved

% 'expandnode' makes a tree of a node and its successors

expandnode(Node, C, tree(Node, F, C, Op : SubTrees)) :-
  Node ---> Op : Successors,
  evaluate(Successors, SubTrees),
  backup(Op : SubTrees, H), F is C + H.

evaluate([ ], [ ]).

evaluate([Node/C | NodesCosts], Trees) :-
  h(Node, H), F is C + H,
  evaluate(NodesCosts, Trees1),
  insert(leaf(Node, F, C), Trees1, Trees).

% 'allsolved' checks whether all trees in a tree list are solved

allsolved([ ]).

allsolved([Tree | Trees]) :-
  solved(Tree),
  allsolved(Trees).

solved(solvedtree(_, _, _)).

solved(solvedleaf(_, _)).

f(Tree, F) :-   % Extract F-value of a tree
  arg(2, Tree, F), !.   % F is the 2nd argument in Tree

(continues)

Figure 13.12 (cont.)

% insert(Tree, Trees, NewTrees) inserts Tree into
% tree list Trees producing NewTrees

insert(T, [ ], [T]) :- !.

insert(T, [T1 | Ts], [T, T1 | Ts]) :-
  solved(T1), !.

insert(T, [T1 | Ts], [T1 | Ts1]) :-
  solved(T),
  insert(T, Ts, Ts1), !.

insert(T, [T1 | Ts], [T, T1 | Ts]) :-
  f(T, F), f(T1, F1), F =< F1, !.

insert(T, [T1 | Ts], [T1 | Ts1]) :-
  insert(T, Ts, Ts1).

% 'backup' finds the backed-up F-value of AND/OR tree list

backup(or : [Tree | _], F) :-   % First tree in OR list is best
  f(Tree, F), !.

backup(and : [ ], 0) :- !.

backup(and : [Tree1 | Trees], F) :-
  f(Tree1, F1),
  backup(and : Trees, F2),
  F is F1 + F2, !.

backup(Tree, F) :-
  f(Tree, F).

% Relation selecttree(Trees, BestTree, OtherTrees, Bound, Bound1):
% OtherTrees is an AND/OR list Trees without its best member
% BestTree; Bound is expansion bound for Trees, Bound1 is
% expansion bound for BestTree

selecttree(Op : [Tree], Tree, Op : [ ], Bound, Bound) :- !.   % The only candidate

selecttree(Op : [Tree | Trees], Tree, Op : Trees, Bound, Bound1) :-
  backup(Op : Trees, F),
  (Op = or, !, min(Bound, F, Bound1);
    Op = and, Bound1 is Bound - F).

min(A, B, A) :- A < B, !.

min(A, B, B).

Whether it will really be a cheapest solution depends on the heuristic function h used by the algorithm. There is a theorem that talks about this dependance on h. The theorem is similar to the admissibility theorem about the state-space, best-first search of Chapter 12. Let $COST(N)$ denote the cost of a cheapest solution tree of a node N. If for each node N in the AND/OR graph the heuristic estimate $h(N) \leq COST(N)$ then andor is guaranteed to find an optimal solution. If h does not satisfy this condition then the solution found may be suboptimal. A trivial heuristic function that satisfies the admissibility condition is $h = 0$ for all the nodes. The disadvantage of this function is, of course, lack of heuristic power.

The key relation in the program of Figure 13.12 is:

expand(Tree, Bound, Tree1, Solved)

Tree and Bound are 'input' arguments, and Tree1 and Solved are 'output' arguments. Their meaning is:

Tree is a search tree that is to be expanded.
Bound is a limit for the F-value within which Tree is allowed to expand.
Solved is an indicator whose value indicates one of the following three cases:

(1) Solved = yes: Tree can be expanded within bound so as to comprise a solution tree Tree1;
(2) Solved = no: Tree can be expanded to Tree1 so that the F-value of Tree1 exceeds Bound, and there was no solution subtree before the F-value overstepped Bound;
(3) Solved = never: Tree is unsolvable.

Tree1 is, depending on the cases above, either a solution tree, an extension of Tree just beyond Bound, or uninstantiated in the case Solved = never.

Procedure

expandlist(Trees, Bound, Trees1, Solved)

is similar to expand. As in expand, Bound is a limit of the expansion of a tree, and Solved is an indicator of what happened during the expansion ('yes', 'no' or 'never'). The first argument is, however, a *list* of trees (an AND list or an OR list):

Trees = or : [T1, T2, ...]   or   Trees = and : [T1, T2, ...]

expandlist selects the most promising tree T (according to F-values) in Trees. Due to the ordering of the subtrees this is always the first tree in Trees. This most promising subtree is expanded with a new bound Bound1. Bound1 depends on **Bound** and also on the other trees in **Trees**. If **Trees** is an OR list then **Bound1** is the lower of **Bound** and the *F*-value of the next best tree in **Trees**. If **Trees** is an AND list then **Bound1** is **Bound** minus the sum of the *F*-values of the remaining trees in **Trees**. **Trees1** depends on the case indicated by **Solved**. In the case **Solved** = no, **Trees1** is the list **Trees** with the most promising tree in **Trees** expanded with **Bound1**. In the case **Solved** = yes, **Trees1** is a solution of the list **Trees** (found within **Bound**). If **Solved** = never, **Trees1** is uninstantiated.

The procedure **continue**, which is called after expanding a tree list, decides what to do next, depending on the results of **expandlist**. It either constructs a solution tree, or updates the search tree and continues its expansion, or signals 'never' in the case that the tree list was found unsolvable.

Another procedure,

> combine(OtherTrees, NewTree, Solved1, NewTrees, Solved)

relates several objects dealt with in **expandlist**. **NewTree** is the expanded tree in the tree list of **expandlist**, **OtherTrees** are the remaining, unchanged trees in the tree list, and **Solved1** indicates the 'solution-status' of **NewTree**. **combine** handles several cases, depending on **Solved1** and on whether the tree list is an AND list or an OR list. For example, the clause

> combine(or : _, Tree, yes, Tree, yes).

says: in case that the tree list is an OR list, and the just expanded tree was solved, and its solution tree is **Tree**, then the whole list has also been solved, and its solution is **Tree** itself. Other cases are best understood from the code of **combine** itself.

For displaying a solution tree, a procedure similar to **show** of Figure 13.8 can be defined. This procedure is left as an exercise for the reader.

13.4.3 Example of problem-defining relations: route finding

Let us now formulate the route-finding problem as an AND/OR search so that this formulation can be directly used by our **andor** procedure of Figure 13.12. We shall assume that the road map is represented by a relation

> s(City1, City2, D)

meaning that there is a direct connection between **City1** and **City2** of distance D. Further, we shall assume there is a relation

> key(City1 - City2, City3)

meaning: to find a route from **City1** to **City2** we should consider paths that go through **City3** (**City3** is a 'key point' between **City1** and **City2**). For example, in the map of Figure 13.1, f and g are key points between a and z:

> key(a-z, f).   key(a-z, g).

We shall implement the following principles of route finding:

> To find a route between two cities X and Z:

> (1) if there are key points Y1, Y2, ... between X and Z then find either

>> • route from A to Z via Y1, or
>> • route from A to Z via Y2, or
>> ...

> (2) if there is no key point between X and Z then simply find some neighbour city Y of X such that there is a route from Y to Z.

We have, then, two kinds of problems that will be represented as:

(1)   X-Z   find a route from X to Z
(2)   X-Z via Y   find a route from X to Z through Y

Here 'via' is an infix operator with precedence higher than that of '-' and lower than that of '--->'. The corresponding AND/OR graph can now be implicitly defined by the following piece of program:

```
:- op( 560, xfx, via).

% Expansion rule for problem X-Z when
% there are key points between X and Z,
% costs of all arcs are equal 0

X-Z ---> or : ProblemList
 :- bagof( ( X-Z via Y)/0, key( X-Z, Y), ProblemList), !.

% Expansion rule for problem X-Z with no key points

X-Z ---> or : ProblemList
 :- bagof( ( Y-Z)/D, s( X, Y, D), ProblemList).

% Reduce a 'via problem' to two AND-related subproblems

X-Z via Y ---> and : [( X-Y)/0, ( Y-Z)/0].

goal( X-X).                          % To go from X to X is trivial
```

The function h could be defined, for example, as the air distance between cities.

EXERCISE

13.4 Write a procedure

show2(SolutionTree)

to display a solution tree found by the **andor** program of Figure 13.12. Let the display format be similar to that of the **show** procedure of Figure 13.8, so that **show2** can be written as a modification of **show**, using a different tree representation. Another useful modification would be to replace the goal **write(Node)** in **show** by a user-defined procedure

writenode(Node, H)

which outputs **Node** in some suitable form, and instantiates H to the number of characters that **Node** takes if output in this form. H is then used for proper indentation of subtrees.

SUMMARY

- AND/OR graph is a formalism for representing problems. It naturally suits problems that are decomposable into independent subproblems. Game playing is an example of such problems.

- Nodes of an AND/OR graph are of two types: AND nodes and OR nodes.

- A concrete problem is defined by a start node and a goal condition. A solution of a problem is represented by a solution graph.

- Costs of arcs and nodes can be introduced into an AND/OR graph to model optimization problems.

- Solving a problem, represented by an AND/OR graph, involves searching the graph. The depth-first strategy searches the graph systematically and is easy to program. However, it may suffer from inefficiency due to combinatorial explosion.

- Heuristic estimates can be introduced to estimate the difficulty of problems, and the best-first heuristic principle can be used to guide the search. Implementing this strategy is more difficult.

- Prolog programs for depth-first search, depth-first iterative deepening and best-first search of AND/OR graphs were developed in this chapter.

- Concepts introduced in this chapter are:

    AND/OR graphs
    AND arcs, OR arcs
    AND nodes, OR nodes

solution graph, solution tree
arc costs, node costs
heuristic estimates in AND/OR graphs, backed-up estimates
depth-first search in AND/OR graphs
iterative deepening in AND/OR graphs
best-first search in AND/OR graphs

References

AND/OR graphs and related search algorithms are part of the classical Artificial Intelligence problem-solving and game-playing machinery. An early example of their application is a symbolic integration program (Slagle 1963). Prolog itself does AND/OR search. A general treatment of AND/OR graphs and the best-first AND/OR search algorithm can be found in general books on Artificial Intelligence (Nilsson 1971; Nilsson 1980). Our best-first AND/OR program is a variation of an algorithm known as AO*. Formal properties of AO* (including its admissibility) have been studied by several authors; Pearl (1984) gives a comprehensive account of these results.

Nilsson, N.J. (1971) *Problem-Solving Methods in Artificial Intelligence*. McGraw-Hill.
Nilsson, N.J. (1980) *Principles of Artificial Intelligence*. Tioga; also Springer-Verlag.
Pearl, J. (1984) *Heuristics: Intelligent Search Strategies for Computer Problem Solving*. Addison-Wesley.
Slagle, J.R. (1963) A heuristic program that solves symbolic integration problems in freshman calculus. In: *Computers and Thought* (E. Feigenbaum, J. Feldman, eds.). McGraw-Hill.

14 Expert Systems and Knowledge Representation

An expert system is a program that behaves like an expert for some problem domain. It should be capable of *explaining* its decisions and the underlying reasoning. Often an expert system is expected to be able to deal with uncertain and incomplete information. In this chapter we will review basic concepts in representing knowledge and building expert systems.

14.1 Functions of an expert system

An *expert system* is a program that behaves like an expert in some, usually narrow, domain of application. Typical applications include tasks such as medical diagnosis, locating a failure in certain kind of equipment, or interpreting measurement data. Expert systems have to be capable of solving problems that require expert knowledge in a particular domain. They should possess that knowledge in some form. Therefore they are also called *knowledge-based systems*. However, not every knowledge-based system can be considered an expert system. An expert system also has to be capable, in some way, of *explaining* its behaviour and its decisions to the user, as human experts do. Such an explanation feature is especially necessary in uncertain domains (such as medical diagnosis) in order to enhance the user's confidence in the system's advice, or to enable the user to detect a possible flaw in the system's reasoning. Therefore, expert systems have to have a friendly user-interaction capability that will make the system's reasoning transparent to the user.

An additional feature that is often required of an expert system is the ability to deal with uncertainty and incompleteness. Information about the problem to be solved can be incomplete or unreliable; relations in the problem domain can be approximate. For example, we may not be quite sure that some symptom is present in the patient, or that some measurement data is absolutely correct; some drug *may* cause some problem, but *usually* does not. All this requires probabilistic reasoning.

To build an expert system we have, in general, to develop the following functions:

- *problem-solving* function capable of using domain-specific knowledge – this may require *dealing with uncertainty*
- *user-interaction* function, which includes explanation of the system's intentions and decisions during and after the problem-solving process.

Each of these functions can be very complicated, and can depend on the domain of application and practical requirements. Various intricate problems

Figure 14.1 Structure of expert systems.

may arise in the design and implementation. This involves the representation of knowledge and associated reasoning. In this chapter we will develop a framework of basic ideas that can be further refined. In Chapter 15 we will implement a complete expert system shell. The main difficulty there will be maintaining smooth interaction with the user during the reasoning process.

14.2   Main structure of an expert system

It is convenient to divide the development of an expert system into three main modules, as illustrated in Figure 14.1:

(1)   a knowledge base,
(2)   an inference engine,
(3)   a user interface.

A *knowledge-base* comprises the knowledge that is specific to the domain of application, including such things as simple facts about the domain, rules that describe relations or phenomena in the domain, and possibly also methods, heuristics and ideas for solving problems in this domain. An *inference engine* knows how to actively use the knowledge in the base. A *user interface* caters for smooth communication between the user and the system, also providing the user with an insight into the problem-solving process carried out by the inference engine. It is convenient to view the inference engine and the interface as one module, usually called an *expert system shell*, or simply a *shell* for brevity.

The foregoing scheme separates knowledge from algorithms that use the knowledge. This division is suitable for the following reasons: the knowledge base clearly depends on the application. On the other hand, the shell is, in principle at least, domain independent. Thus a rational way of developing expert systems for several applications consists of developing a shell that can be used universally, and then to plug in a new knowledge base for each application. Of course, all the knowledge bases will have to conform to the same formalism that is 'understood' by the shell. According to practical experience in complex expert systems the scenario with one shell and many knowledge bases will not work quite so smoothly unless the application domains are indeed very similar. Nevertheless, even if modifications of the shell from one domain to another are necessary, at least the main principles can be retained.

This chapter presents some basic expert systems techniques. In particular, we will look at representing knowledge with *if-then* rules, basic inference mechanisms in rule-based expert systems (such as forward or backward chaining), enhancing rule-based representation with uncertainty, semantic network representation and frame-based representation of knowledge.

14.3 Representing knowledge with *if-then* rules

In principle, any consistent formalism in which we can express knowledge about some problem domain can be considered for use in an expert system. However, the language of *if-then* rules, also called *production* rules, is by far the most popular formalism for representing knowledge. In general, such rules are conditional statements, but they can have various interpretations. Examples are:

- *if* precondition P *then* conclusion C
- *if* situation S *then* action A
- *if* conditions C1 and C2 hold *then* condition C does not hold

If-then rules usually turn out to be a natural form of expressing knowledge, and have the following additional desirable features:

- *Modularity*: each rule defines a small, relatively independent piece of knowledge.
- *Incrementability*: new rules can be added to the knowledge base relatively independently of other rules.
- *Modifiability* (as a consequence of modularity): old rules can be changed relatively independently of other rules.
- Support system's *transparency*.

This last property is an important and distinguishing feature of expert systems. By transparency of the system we mean the system's ability to explain its decisions and solutions. If-then rules facilitate answering the following basic types of user's questions:

(1) 'How' questions: *How* did you reach this conclusion?
(2) 'Why' questions: *Why* are you interested in this information?

Mechanisms, based on if-then rules, for answering such questions will be discussed later.

If-then rules often define logical relations between concepts of the problem domain. Purely logical relations can be characterized as belonging to 'categorical knowledge', 'categorical' because they are always meant to be absolutely true. However, in some domains, such as medical diagnosis, 'soft' or probabilistic knowledge prevails. It is 'soft' in the sense that empirical regularities are usually only valid to a certain degree (often but not always). In such cases if-then rules may be modified by adding a likelihood qualification to their logical interpretation. For example:

if condition A *then* conclusion B follows *with certainty* F *if*

    1   the infection is primary bacteremia, and
    2   the site of the culture is one of the sterilesites, and
    3   the suspected portal of entry of the organism is the gastrointestinal
       tract

then

    there is suggestive evidence (0.7) that the identity of the organism is
    bacteroides.

Figure 14.2   An if-then rule from the MYCIN system for medical consultation (Shortliffe 1976). The parameter 0.7 says to what degree the rule can be trusted.

Figures 14.2, 14.3 and 14.4 give an idea of the variety of ways of expressing knowledge by if-then rules. They show example rules from three different knowledge-based systems: MYCIN for medical consultation, AL/X for diagnosing equipment failures and AL3 for problem solving in chess.

In general, if you want to develop a serious expert system for some chosen domain then you have to consult actual experts for that domain and learn a great deal about it yourself. Extracting some understanding of the domain from experts and literature, and moulding this understanding into a chosen knowledge-representation formalism is called *knowledge elicitation*. This is, as a rule, a complex effort that we cannot go into here. But we do need some domain and some knowledge base as material to carry out our examples. Consider the toy knowledge base shown in Figure 14.5. It is concerned with diagnosing the problem of water leaking in a flat. A problem

if

    the pressure in V-01 reached relief valve lift pressure

then

    the relief valve on V-01 has lifted [$N = 0.005, S = 400$]

if

    NOT the pressure in V-01 reached relief valve lift pressure,
    and the relief valve on V-01 has lifted

then

    the V-01 relief valve opened early (the set pressure has drifted)
    [$N = 0.001, S = 2000$]

Figure 14.3   Two rules from an AL/X demonstration knowledge base for fault diagnosis (Reiter 1980). N and S are the 'necessity' and 'sufficiency' measures described in detail in Section 15.4. S estimates to what degree the condition part of a rule implies the conclusion part. N estimates to what degree the truth of the condition part is necessary for the conclusion to be true.

if

1   there is a hypothesis, H, that a plan P succeeds, and
2   there are two hypotheses,
H_1, that a plan R_1 refutes plan P, and
H_2, that a plan R_2 refutes plan P, and
3   there are facts: H_1 *is false*, and H_2 *is false*

then

1   generate the hypothesis, H_3, that the combined plan 'R_1 *or* R_2' refutes plan P, and
2   generate the fact: H_3 *implies not*(H)

Figure 14.4   A rule for plan refinement in chess problem solving from the AL3 system (Bratko 1982).

can arise either in the bathroom or the kitchen. In either case, the leakage also causes a problem (water on the floor) in the hall. Apart from its overall naïveté, this knowledge base only assumes single faults; that is, the problem may be in the bathroom or the kitchen, but not in both of them at the same time. This knowledge base is shown in Figure 14.5 as an *inference network*. Nodes in the network correspond to propositions and links correspond to rules in the knowledge base. Arcs that connect some of the links indicate the conjunctive connection between the corresponding propositions. Accordingly, the rule about a problem in the kitchen in this network is:

if hall_wet *and* bathroom_dry *then* problem_in_kitchen

Figure 14.5   A toy knowledge base to diagnose leaks in water appliances in the flat shown.

The network representation of Figure 14.5 is in fact an AND/OR graph as discussed in Chapter 13. This indicates the relevance of AND/OR representation of problems in the context of expert systems.

14.4 Forward and backward chaining in rule-based systems

Once knowledge is represented in some form, we need a reasoning procedure to draw conclusions from the knowledge base. For if-then rules, there are two basic ways of reasoning:

- backward chaining, and
- forward chaining.

Both of these procedures are very easily implemented in Prolog. In fact, procedures for searching AND/OR graphs, presented in Chapter 13, can be used here. The more advanced search techniques for AND/OR graphs are in a way even more sophisticated than those usually used in expert systems. On the other hand, there is often an emphasis in expert systems on the style of search, from its semantic point of view, in relation to the human reasoning; that is, it is desirable to sequence the reasoning in ways that humans find natural in the domain of application. This is important when interaction with the user occurs during the reasoning process and we want to make this process transparent to the user. This section sketches, in Prolog, the basic reasoning procedures as they appear in the context of expert systems, although they are similar to searching AND/OR graphs.

14.4.1 Backward chaining

With our example knowledge base of Figure 14.5, reasoning in the backward chaining style may proceed as follows. We start with a hypothesis – for example, leak_in_kitchen – then we reason backwards in the inference network. To confirm the hypothesis, we need problem_in_kitchen and no_water_from_outside to be true. The former is confirmed if we find that the hall is wet and the bathroom is dry. The latter is confirmed, for example, if we find that the window was closed.

This style of reasoning is called backward chaining because we follow a chain of rules from the hypothesis (leak_in_kitchen) to the pieces of evidence (hall_wet, etc.). This is trivially programmed in Prolog – this is, in fact, Prolog's own built-in style of reasoning. The straightforward way is to state the rules in the knowledge base as Prolog rules:

```
leak_in_bathroom :-
    hall_wet,
    kitchen_dry.
```

```
problem_in_kitchen :-
    hall_wet,
    bathroom_dry.

no_water_from_outside :-
    window_closed
    ;
    no_rain.

leak_in_kitchen :-
    ...
```

The observed pieces of evidence can be stated as Prolog facts:

```
hall_wet.
bathroom_dry.
window_closed.
```

The hypothesis can now be checked by:

```
?- leak_in_kitchen.

yes
```

Using Prolog's own syntax for rules, as in the foregoing, has certain disadvantages however:

(1)   This syntax may not be the most suitable for a user unfamiliar with Prolog; for example, the domain expert who should be able to read the rules, specify new rules and modify them.

(2)   The knowledge base is, therefore, not syntactically distinguishable from the rest of the program; a more explicit distinction between the knowledge base and the rest of the program may be desirable.

It is easiest to tailor the syntax of expert rules to our taste by using Prolog operator notation. For example, we can choose to use 'if', 'then', 'and' and 'or' as operators, appropriately declared as:

```
:- op( 800, fx, if).
:- op( 700, xfx, then).
:- op( 300, xfy, or).
:- op( 200, xfy, and).
```

This suffices to write our example rules of Figure 14.5 as:

```
if
    hall_wet and kitchen_dry
then
    leak_in_bathroom.
```

```
if
     hall_wet and bathroom_dry
then
     problem_in_kitchen.

if
     window_closed or no_rain
then
     no_water_from_outside.

...
```

Let the observable findings be stated as a procedure **fact**:

```
fact( hall_wet).
fact( bathroom_dry).
fact( window_closed).
```

Of course, we now need a new interpreter for rules in the new syntax. Such an interpreter can be defined as the procedure

```
is_true( P)
```

where proposition **P** is either given in procedure **fact** or can be derived using rules. The new rule interpreter is given in Figure 14.6. Note that it still does

---

```
% A simple backward chaining rule interpreter

:- op( 800, fx, if).
:- op( 700, xfx, then).
:- op( 300, xfy, or).
:- op( 200, xfy, and).

is_true( P) :-
  fact( P).

is_true( P) :-
  if Condition then P,          % A relevant rule
  is_true( Condition).          % whose condition is true

is_true( P1 and P2) :-
  is_true( P1),
  is_true( P2).

is_true( P1 or P2) :-
  is_true( P1)
  ;
  is_true( P2).
```

Figure 14.6 A backward chaining interpreter for if-then rules.

backward chaining in the depth-first manner. The interpreter can now be called by the question:

```
?- is_true( leak_in_kitchen).

yes
```

A major practical disadvantage of the simple inference procedures of this section is that the user has to state all the relevant information as facts in advance, before the reasoning process is started. So the user may state too much or too little. Therefore, it would be better for the information to be provided by the user interactively in a dialogue when it is needed. Such a dialogue facility will be programmed in Chapter 15.

14.4.2   Forward chaining

In backward chaining we start with a hypothesis (such as leak in the kitchen) and work backwards, according to the rules in the knowledge base, toward easily confirmed findings (such as the hall is wet). Sometimes it is more natural to reason in the opposite direction, from the 'if' part to the 'then' part. Forward chaining does not start with a hypothesis, but with some confirmed findings. Once we have observed that the hall is wet and the bathroom is dry, we conclude that there is a problem in the kitchen; also, having noticed the kitchen window is closed, we infer that no water came from the outside; this leads to the final conclusion that there is a leak in the kitchen.

Programming simple forward chaining in Prolog is still easy if not exactly as trivial as backward chaining. Figure 14.7 shows a forward chaining interpreter, assuming that rules are, as before, in the form:

if Condition then Conclusion

where **Condition** can be an AND/OR expression. For simplicity we assume throughout this chapter that rules do not contain variables. This interpreter starts with what is already known (stated in the **fact** relation), derives all conclusions that follow from this and adds (using **assert**) the conclusions to the **fact** relation. Our example knowledge base is run by this interpreter thus:

```
?- forward.

Derived: problem_in_kitchen
Derived: no_water_from_outside
Derived: leak_in_kitchen
No more facts
```

```
% Simple forward chaining in Prolog

forward :-
    new_derived_fact( P),                           % A new fact
    !,
    write( 'Derived: '), write( P), nl,
    assert( fact( P)),
    forward                                         % Continue
    ;
    write( 'No more facts').                         % All facts derived

new_derived_fact( Concl) :-
    if Cond then Concl,                             % A rule
    not fact( Concl),                               % Rule's conclusion not yet a fact
    composed_fact( Cond).                           % Condition true?

composed_fact( Cond) :-
    fact( Cond).                                    % Simple fact

composed_fact( Cond1 and Cond2) :-
    composed_fact( Cond1),
    composed_fact( Cond2).                          % Both conjuncts true

composed_fact( Cond1 or Cond2) :-
    composed_fact( Cond1)
    ;
    composed_fact( Cond2).
```

Figure 14.7 A forward chaining rule interpreter.

14.4.3 Forward chaining vs. backward chaining

If-then rules form chains that, in Figure 14.5, go from left to right. The elements on the left-hand side of these chains are input information, while those on the right-hand side are derived information:

> input information → ... → derived information

These two kinds of information have a variety of names, depending on the context in which they are used. Input information can be called *data* (for example, measurement data) or *findings* or *manifestations*. Derived information can be called *hypotheses* to be proved, or *causes* of manifestations, or *diagnoses*, or *explanations* that explain findings. So chains of inference steps connect various types of information, such as:

> data → ... → goals
> evidence → ... → hypotheses
> findings, observations → ... → explanations, diagnoses
> manifestations → ... → diagnoses, causes

Both forward and backward chaining involve search, but they differ in the direction of search. Backward chaining searches from goals to data, from diagnoses to findings, etc. In contrast, forward chaining searches from data to goals, from findings to explanations or diagnoses, etc. Because backward chaining starts with goals we say that it is *goal driven*. Similarly, since forward chaining starts with data we say that it is *data driven*.

An obvious question is: Which is better, forward or backward chaining? This question is similar to the dilemma between forward and backward search in state space (see Chapter 11). As there, the answer here also depends on the problem. If we want to check whether a particular hypothesis is true then it is more natural to chain backward, starting with the hypothesis in question. On the other hand, if there are many competing hypotheses, and there is no reason to start with one rather than another, it may be better to chain forward. In particular, forward chaining is more natural in monitoring tasks where the data are acquired continuously and the system has to detect whether an anomalous situation has arisen; a change in the input data can be propagated in the forward chaining fashion to see whether this change indicates some fault in the monitored process or a change in the performance level. In choosing between forward or backward chaining, simply the shape of the rule network can also help. If there are a few data nodes (the left flank of the network) and many goal nodes (right flank) then forward chaining looks more appropriate; if there are few goal nodes and many data nodes then vice versa.

Expert tasks are usually more intricate and call for a combination of chaining in both directions. In medicine, for example, some initial observations in the patient typically trigger doctor's reasoning in the forward direction to generate some initial hypothesized diagnosis. This initial hypothesis has to be confirmed or rejected by additional evidence, which is done in the backward chaining style. In our example of Figure 14.5, observing the hall wet may trigger the following inference steps:

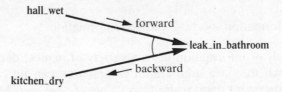

EXERCISE

14.1 Write a program that combines forward and backward chaining in the style discussed in this section.

14.5 Generating explanation

There are standard ways of generating explanation in rule-based systems. Of the two usual types of explanation, 'how' and 'why', let us consider first the 'how' explanation. When the system comes up with an answer, the user may ask: *How* did you find this answer? The typical explanation consists of presenting the user with the trace of *how* the answer was derived. Suppose the system has just found that there is a leak in the kitchen and the user is asking 'How?'. The explanation can be along the following line:

Because:

(1) there is a problem in the kitchen, which was concluded from hall wet and bathroom dry, and
(2) no water came from outside, which was concluded from window closed.

Such an explanation is in fact a *proof tree* of how the final conclusion follows from rules and facts in the knowledge base. Let '<=' be defined as an infix operator. Then we can choose to represent the proof tree of a proposition in one of the following forms, depending on the case:

(1) If P is a fact then the proof tree is P.
(2) If P was derived using a rule

   if Cond then P

then the proof tree is

   P <= ProofCond

where **ProofCond** is a proof tree of **Cond**.

(3) Let **P1** and **P2** be propositions whose proof trees are **Proof1** and **Proof2**. If P is **P1 and P2** then the proof tree is **Proof1 and Proof2**. If P is **P1 or P2** then the proof tree is either **Proof1** or **Proof2**.

Constructing proof trees in Prolog is straightforward and can be achieved by modifying the predicate **is_true** of Figure 14.6 according to the three cases above. Figure 14.8 shows such a modified **is_true** predicate. Notice that proof trees of this kind are essentially the same as solution trees for problems represented by AND/OR graphs. Displaying proof trees in some user-friendly format can be programmed similarly to displaying AND/OR solution trees. More sophisticated output formatting of proof trees is part of the shell program in Chapter 15.

In contrast, the 'why' explanation is required *during* the reasoning process, not at the end of it. This requires user interaction with the reasoning process. The system asks the user for information at the moment that the

```
% is_true( P, Proof) if Proof is a proof that P is true

:- op( 800, xfx, <=).

is_true( P, P) :-
   fact( P).

is_true( P, P <= CondProof) :-
   if Cond then P,
   is_true( Cond, CondProof).

is_true( P1 and P2, Proof1 and Proof2) :-
   is_true( P1, Proof1),
   is_true( P2, Proof2).

is_true( P1 or P2, Proof) :-
   is_true( P1, Proof)
   ;
   is_true( P2, Proof).
```

Figure 14.8   Generating proof trees.

information is needed. When asked, the user may answer 'Why?', thus triggering the 'why' explanation. This kind of interaction and 'why' explanation is programmed as part of the shell in Chapter 15.

14.6   Introducing uncertainty

In the foregoing discussion, the representation assumes problem domains that are *categorical*; that is, answers to all questions are either true or false, not somewhere between. As data, rules were also categorical: 'categorical implications'. However, many expert domains are not categorical. Typical expert behaviour is full of guesses (although highly articulated) that are usually true, but there can be exceptions. Both data about a particular problem and general rules can be less than certain. We can model uncertainty by assigning some qualification, other than just true or false, to assertions. Such qualification can be expressed by descriptors – for example, *true*, *highly likely*, *likely*, *unlikely*, *impossible*. Alternatively, the degree of belief can be expressed by a real number in some interval – for example, between 0 and 1 or −5 and +5. Such numbers are known by a variety of names, such as 'certainty factor', 'measure of belief' or 'subjective certainty'.

   In this section we will extend our rule-based representation with a simple uncertainty scheme. Each proposition is simply added a number between 0 and 1 as a certainty qualification. We will choose to represent this as a pair of the form:

>Proposition : CertaintyFactor

This notation applies to rules as well. So the following form defines a rule and the degree of certainty to which the rule is valid:

>if Condition then Conclusion : Certainty.

In any representation with uncertainty we need a way of combining the certainties of propositions and rules. For example, let there be two propositions $P1$ and $P2$ whose certainties are $C1$ and $C2$. What is the certainty of logical combinations $P1$ *and* $P2$, $P1$ *or* $P2$? The following is one simple scheme for combining certainties. Let $P1$ and $P2$ be propositions, and $c(P1)$ and $c(P2)$ denote their certainties. Then:

$$c(P1 \ and \ P2) = min(c(P1), c(P2))$$
$$c(P1 \ or \ P2) = max(c(P1), c(P2))$$

If there is a rule

>if P1 then P2 : C

then

$$c(P2) = c(P1) * C$$

For simplicity we assume that no more than one rule ever bears on the same assertion. If there were two rules bearing on the same assertion in the knowledge base, they could be transformed using *or* into equivalent rules that satisfy this assumption. Figure 14.9 shows a rule interpreter for this uncertainty scheme. The interpreter assumes that the user specifies the certainty estimates for the observables (left-most nodes in the rule network) by the relation

>given(Proposition, Certainty)

Now we can 'soften' some rule in our knowledge base of Figure 14.5. For example:

>if
>>hall_wet and bathroom_dry
>
>then
>>problem_in_kitchen : 0.9.

```
% Rule interpreter with certainties
% certainty( Proposition, Certainty)

certainty( P, Cert) :-
    given( P, Cert).

certainty( Cond1 and Cond2, Cert) :-
    certainty( Cond1, Cert1),
    certainty( Cond2, Cert2),
    minimum( Cert1, Cert2, Cert).

certainty( Cond1 or Cond2, Cert) :-
    certainty( Cond1, Cert1),
    certainty( Cond2, Cert2),
    maximum( Cert1, Cert2, Cert).

certainty( P, Cert) :-
    if Cond then P : C1,
    certainty( Cond, C2),
    Cert is C1 * C2.
```

Figure 14.9   An interpreter for rules with certainties.

A situation in which the hall is wet, the bathroom is dry, the kitchen is not dry, the window is not closed and we think that there was no rain but are not quite sure can be specified as:

given(hall_wet, 1).	% Hall is wet
given(bathroom_dry, 1).	% Bathroom is dry
given(kitchen_dry, 0).	% Kitchen is not dry
given(no_rain, 0.8).	% Probably no rain, but not sure
given(window_closed, 0).	% Window not closed

Now we can ask about a leak in the kitchen:

   ?- certainty(leak_in_kitchen, C).

   C = 0.8

This is obtained as follows. The facts that the hall is wet and the bathroom is dry indicate a problem in the kitchen with certainty 0.9. Since there was some possibility of rain, the certainty of no_water_from_outside is 0.8. Finally, the certainty of leak_in_kitchen is min(0.8, 0.9) = 0.8.

14.7 Difficulties in handling uncertainty

The question of handling uncertainty in expert systems has been much researched and debated. Typical controversial issues have been the usefulness of probability theory in handling uncertainty in expert systems on the one hand and drawbacks of *ad hoc* uncertainty schemes on the other. Our ultra-simple approach in Section 14.6 can be easily criticized. For example, suppose the certainty of *a* is 0.5 and that of *b* is 0. Then in our scheme the certainty of *a or b* is 0.5. Now suppose that the certainty of *b* increases to 0.5. In our scheme this change will not affect the certainty of *a or b* at all, which is counter-intuitive. Many schemes for handling uncertainty have been proposed, used and investigated. In Chapter 15, a more sophisticated scheme is described, although it too suffers from the most common problem with such approaches. The problem in such schemes typically stems from ignoring some dependencies between propositions. For example, let there be a rule:

> *if a or b then c*

The certainty of *c* should not only depend on the certainty of *a* and *b*, but also on any correlation between *a* and *b*; that is, whether they tend to occur together or they depend on each other in some other way. Completely correct treatment of these dependencies is more complicated than it is often considered acceptable and may require information that is not normally available. The debatable short-cut usually taken is the assumption of *independence* of events, such as *a* and *b* in the foregoing example. Unfortunately, this assumption is not generally justifiable and in practice is often simply not true, and may therefore lead to incorrect and counter-intuitive results. It has often been admitted that such departures from mathematically sound handling of uncertainty may be unsafe in general, but it has also been argued that they are solutions that work in practice. Along with this, it has been argued that probability theory, although mathematically sound, is impractical and not really appropriate for the following reasons:

- Human experts seem to have trouble thinking in terms of actual probabilities; their likelihood estimates do not quite correspond to probabilities as defined mathematically.
- Mathematically correct probabilistic treatment requires either information that is not available or some simplification assumptions that are not really quite justified in a practical application. In the latter case, the treatment would become mathematically unsound again.

Conversely, there have been equally eager arguments in favour of mathematically well-justified approaches based on the probability theory. For example, Pearl (1989) convincingly answers both of the foregoing objections regarding probability, while at the same time reporting on real dangers that arise in schemes that 'work in practice'. Dangers clearly arise from simplifications that involve unsafe assumptions. It seems that, in the light of the strength of these arguments, some mathematically sound schemes will eventually prevail, although debatable simplifications may remain in common practice for a long time.

14.8 Semantic networks and frames

In this section we look at two other frameworks for representing knowledge: *semantic networks* and *frames*. These differ from rule-based representations in that they are directed to representing, in a structured way, large sets of facts. The set of facts is structured and possibly compressed: facts can be abstracted away when they can be reconstructed through inference.

Semantic networks and frames can be easily implemented in Prolog. Essentially, this amounts to adopting, in a disciplined way, a particular style of programming and organizing a program.

14.8.1 Semantic networks

A semantic network consists of entities and relations between the entities. It is customary to represent a semantic network as a graph. There are various types of semantic network with various conventions, but usually nodes of the graph correspond to entities, while relations are shown as links labelled by the names of relations. Figure 14.10 shows such a network. The relation name isa stands for 'is a'. This network represents the following facts:

- A bird is a kind of animal.
- Flying is the normal moving method of birds.
- An albatross is a bird.
- Albert is an albatross, and so is Ross.

Notice that isa sometimes relates a class of objects with the superclass of the class (animal is a superclass of bird), and sometimes an *instance* of a class with the class itself (Albert is an albatross).

A network of this kind is immediately translated into Prolog facts; for example, as:

```
isa( bird, animal).
isa( ross, albatross).
moving_method( bird, fly).
moving_method( kiwi, walk).
```

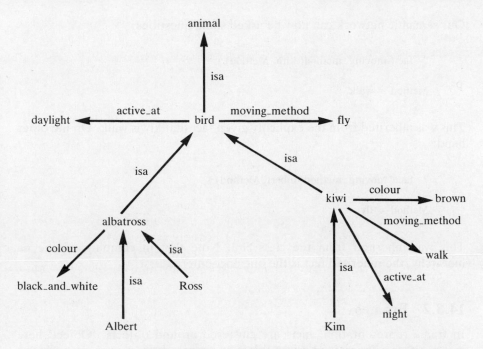

Figure 14.10 A semantic network.

In addition to these facts, which are explicitly stated, some other facts can be inferred from the network. Ways of inferring other facts are built into a semantic network type representation as part of the representation. A typical built-in principle of inference is *inheritance*. So, in Figure 14.10, the fact 'albatross flies' is inherited from the fact 'birds fly'. Similarly, through inheritance, we have 'Ross flies' and 'Kim walks'. Facts are inherited through the **isa** relation. In Prolog, we can state that the method of moving is inherited as:

```
moving_method( X, Method) :-
    isa( X, SuperX),                              % Climb isa hierarchy
    moving_method( SuperX, Method).
```

It is a little awkward to state a separate inheritance rule for each relation that can be inherited. Therefore, it is better to state a more general rule about facts, either explicitly stated in the network or inherited:

```
fact( Fact) :-                   % Fact not a variable; Fact = Rel( Arg1, Arg2)
    Fact, !.                     % Fact explicit in network – do not inherit

fact( Fact) :-
    Fact =.. [ Rel, Arg1, Arg2],
    isa( Arg1, SuperArg),                         % Climb isa hierarchy
    SuperFact =.. [ Rel, SuperArg, Arg2],
```

Our semantic network can now be asked some questions:

    ?- fact(moving_method(kim, Method)).

    Method = walk

This was inherited from the explicitly given fact that kiwis walk. On the other hand:

    ?- fact(moving_method(albert, Method)).

    Method = fly

This was inherited from the class **bird**. Note that in climbing up the **isa** hierarchy, the inherited fact is the one encountered first.

14.8.2 Frames

In frame representation, facts are clustered around objects. 'Object' here means either a concrete physical object or a more abstract concept, such as a class of objects, or even a situation. Good candidates for representation by frames are, for example, the typical meeting situation or game conflict situation. Such situations have, in general, some common stereotype structure that can be filled with details of a particular situation.

A *frame* is a data structure whose components are called *slots*. Slots have names and accommodate information of various kinds. So, in slots, we can find simple values, references to other frames or even procedures that can compute the slot value from other information. A slot may also be left unfilled. Unfilled slots can be filled through inference. As in semantic networks, the most common principle of inference is inheritance. When a frame represents a class of objects (such as albatross) and another frame represents a superclass of this class (such as bird), then the class frame can inherit values from the superclass frame.

Some knowledge about birds can be put into frames as follows:

    FRAME: bird
    a_kind_of: animal
    moving_method: fly
    active_at: daylight

This frame stands for the class of all birds. Its three slots say that birds are a kind of animal (animal is a superclass of bird), that a typical bird flies and that a bird is active during daylight. Here are the frames for two subclasses of bird – albatross and kiwi:

> FRAME: albatross
> a_kind_of: bird
> colour: black_and_white
> size: 115

> FRAME: kiwi
> a_kind_of: bird
> moving_method: walk
> active_at: night
> colour: brown
> size: 40

Albatross is a very typical bird and it inherits the flying ability and day-light activity from the frame bird. Therefore, nothing is stated about **moving_method** and **active_at** in the albatross frame. On the other hand, kiwi is a rather untypical bird, and the usual **moving_method** and **active_at** values for birds have to be overruled in the case of the kiwi. We can also have a particular *instance* of a class; for example, an albatross called Albert:

> FRAME: Albert
> instance_of: albatross
> size: 120

Notice the difference between the two relations **a_kind_of** and **instance_of**. The former is the relation between a class and a superclass, while the latter is the relation between a member of a class and the class.

The information in our example frames can be represented in Prolog as a set of facts, one fact for each slot value. This can be done in various ways. We will choose the following format for these facts:

> **Frame_name(Slot, Value)**

The advantage of this format is that now all the facts about a particular frame are collected together under the relation whose name is the name of the frame itself. Figure 14.11 gives some frames in this format.

To use such a set of frames, we need a procedure for retrieving facts about slot values. Let us implement such a fact retriever as a Prolog procedure

> **value(Frame, Slot, Value)**

where **Value** is the value of slot **Slot** in frame **Frame**. If the slot is filled – that is, its value is explicitly stated in the frame – then this is the value; otherwise the value is obtained through inference – for example, inheritance. To find a

% A frame is represented as a set of Prolog facts:
%   frame_name(Slot, Value)
% where Value is either a simple value or a procedure

% Frame bird: the prototypical bird

bird(a_kind_of, animal).
bird(moving_method, fly).
bird(active_at, daylight).

% Frame albatross: albatross is a typical bird with some
% extra facts: it is black and white, and it is 115 cm long

albatross(a_kind_of, bird).
albatross(colour, black_and_white).
albatross(size, 115).

% Frame kiwi: kiwi is a rather untypical bird in that it
% walks instead of flies, and it is active at night

kiwi(a_kind_of, bird).
kiwi(moving_method, walk).
kiwi(active_at, night).
kiwi(size, 40).
kiwi(colour, brown).

% Frame albert: an instance of a big albatross

albert(instance_of, albatross).
albert(size, 120).

% Frame ross: an instance of a baby albatross

ross(instance_of, albatross).
ross(size, 40).

% Frame animal: slot relative_size obtains its value by
% executing procedure relative_size

animal(relative_size, execute(relative_size(Object, Value), Object, Value)).

Figure 14.11   Some frames.

value by inheritance, we have to move from the current frame to a more general frame according to the **a_kind_of** relation or **instance_of** relation between frames. Such a move leads to a 'parent frame' and the value may be found in this frame explicitly, or through further inheritance. This direct retrieval or retrieval by inheritance can be stated in Prolog as:

```
value( Frame, Slot, Value) :-
  Query =.. [ Frame, Slot, Value],
  call( Query), !.                    % Value directly retrieved

value( Frame, Slot, Value) :-
  parent( Frame, ParentFrame),        % A more general frame
  value( ParentFrame, Slot, Value).

parent( Frame, ParentFrame) :-
  ( Query =.. [ Frame, a_kind_of, ParentFrame];
    Query =.. [ Frame, instance_of, ParentFrame] ),
  call( Query).
```

This is sufficient to find values from frames in Figure 14.11, as in the questions:

```
?- value( albert, active_at, AlbertTime).
```

AlbertTime = daylight

```
?- value( kiwi, active_at, KiwiTime).
```

KiwiTime = night

Let us now consider a more complicated case of inference when a procedure for *computing* the value is given in the slot instead of the value itself. For example, one slot for all animals could be their relative size with respect to the typical size of a grown-up instance of their species. Stated in percentages, for the two albatrosses in Figure 14.11, the relative sizes are: Albert 104%, Ross 35%. These figures are obtained as the ratio (in percentage) between the size of the particular individual and the typical size of the individual's class. For Ross, this is:

$$40/115 * 100\% = 34.78\%$$

Thus, the value for the slot relative_size is obtained by executing a procedure. This procedure is universal for all the animals, so it is rational to define the slot relative_size in the frame animal and fill this slot by the corresponding procedure. The frame interpreter value should now be able to answer the question:

```
?- value( ross, relative_size, R).
```

R = 34.78

The way this result is obtained should be something like the following. We start at the frame ross and, seeing no value for relative_size, climb up the chain of relations **instance_of** (to get to frame **albatross**), **a_kind_of** (to get to frame **bird**) and **a_kind_of** again, to get finally to frame **animal**. Here we find the procedure for computing relative size. This procedure needs the values in slot **size** of frame **ross** and frame **albatross**. These values can be obtained through inheritance by our existing **value** procedure. It remains to extend the procedure **value** to handle the cases where a procedure in a slot is to be executed. Before we do that, we need to consider how such a procedure can be (indirectly) represented as the content of a slot. Let the procedure for computing the relative size be implemented as a Prolog predicate:

```
relative_size( Object, RelativeSize) :-
    value( Object, size, ObjSize),
    value( Object, instance_of, ObjClass),
    value( ObjClass, size, ClassSize),
    RelativeSize is ObjSize/ClassSize * 100.     % Percentage of class size
```

We can now fill the slot **relative_size** in frame **animal** with the call of this procedure. In order to prevent the arguments **Object** and **RelativeSize** getting lost in communication between frames, we also have to state them as part of the **relative_size** slot information. The contents of this slot can be put all together as one Prolog term; for example, as:

```
execute( relative_size( Object, RelSize), Object, RelSize)
```

The **relative_size** slot of frame **animal** is then specified by:

```
animal( relative_size, execute( relative_size( Obj, Val), Obj, Val) ).
```

Now we are ready to modify the procedure **value** to handle procedural slots. First, we have to realize that the information found in a slot can be a procedure call; therefore, it has to be further processed by carrying out this call. This call may need, as arguments, slot values of the original frame in question. Our old procedure **value** forgets about this frame while climbing up to more general frames. Therefore, we have to introduce the original frame as an additional argument. The following piece of program does this:

```
value( Frame, Slot, Value) :-
    value( Frame, Frame, Slot, Value).
```

% Directly retrieving information in slot of (super)frame

```
value( Frame, SuperFrame, Slot, Value) :-
    Query =.. [ SuperFrame, Slot, Information],
    call( Query),                                 % Value directly retrieved
    process( Information, Frame, Value), !.        % Information is either a value
                                                   % or a procedure call
```

% Inferring value through inheritance

value(Frame, SuperFrame, Slot, Value) :-
  parent(SuperFrame, ParentSuperFrame),
  value(Frame, ParentSuperFrame, Slot, Value).

% process(Information, Frame, Value)

process(execute(Goal, Frame, Value), Frame, Value) :- !,
  call(Goal).

process(Value, _, Value).   % A value, not procedure call

In this extension of our frame interpreter we have come close to another programming paradigm called *object-oriented programming*. Although the terminology in that paradigm is usually different, the computation is essentially based on triggering the execution of procedures that belong to various frames. An interpreter for object-oriented programming is sketched in Chapter 20.

Of the many subtleties of inference among frames, we have not addressed the question of *multiple inheritance*. This problem arises when a frame has more than one 'parent' frame (according to the relation instance_of or a_kind_of). Then, an inherited slot value may potentially come from more than one parent frame and the question of which one to adopt arises. Our procedure value, as it stands, simply takes the first value encountered, found by the depth-first search among the frames that potentially can supply the value. However, other strategies or tie-breaking rules may be more appropriate.

EXERCISE

14.2 Trace the execution of the query

   ?- value(ross, relative_size, Value).

to make sure you understand clearly how information is passed throughout the frame network in our frame interpreter.

SUMMARY

- Typical functions required of an expert system are: solving problems in a given domain, explaining the problem-solving process, and handling uncertain and incomplete information.

- It is convenient to view an expert system as consisting of two modules: a shell and a knowledge base. A shell, in turn, consists of an inference mechanism and a user interface.

- Building an expert system shell involves decisions regarding the knowledge representation formalism, the inference mechanism, the user interaction facility and the treatment of uncertainty.

- If-then rules, or production rules, are the most common form of representing knowledge in expert systems.

- Two basic ways of reasoning in rule-based systems are: backward and forward chaining.

- Two usual types of explanation are associated with user's questions 'How?' and 'Why?'. A proof tree can be used as a 'how' explanation.

- Reasoning with uncertainty can be incorporated into the basic rule representation, and forward or backward chaining schemes. However, there are fundamental and still unsettled questions about how best to handle uncertainty.

- Other popular knowledge representation schemes, suitable for representing large sets of facts in a structured way, are semantic networks and frames. Here facts can be directly retrieved or inferred through built-in mechanisms such as inheritance.

- In this chapter, stylized Prolog implementations were developed for backward and forward chaining, generating proof trees, interpreting rules with uncertainty, inheritance in semantic networks and frames.

- Concepts discussed in this chapter are:

  expert systems
  knowledge base, expert system shell, inference engine
  if-then rules, production systems
  backward chaining, forward chaining
  'how' explanation, 'why' explanation
  categorical knowledge, uncertain knowledge
  semantic networks
  frames
  inheritance

References

An early collection of papers that deal with various aspects of expert systems and knowledge engineering is Michie (1979). Jackson (1986) is one of a number of introductory texts on expert systems that includes a description of some well-known systems. An early and influential expert system, MYCIN, is described by Shortliffe (1976). Buchanan and Shortliffe (1984) is a good collection of papers related to the MYCIN experiments. Pearl (1989) is an authoritative book on uncertainty and probabilistic reasoning in expert systems. Kanal and Lemmer (1986) is a collection of important papers on uncertainty. Brachman and Levesque (1985) is a frequently referenced collection of papers on knowledge representation. Minsky (1975) is the classical paper on frame-type representation.

Winston (1984) teaches how frame-like representation can be used to represent common-sense knowledge. Luger and Stubblefield (1989) review many knowledge representation schemes. Touretzky (1986) investigates problems of inheritance. Some of the examples in this chapter are taken from Bratko (1982), Reiter (1980) and Shortliffe (1976).

Brachman, R.J. and Levesque, H.J. (1985, eds.) *Readings in Knowledge Representation*. Los Altos, California: Morgan Kaufmann.

Bratko, I. (1982) Knowledge-based problem-solving in AL3. In: *Machine Intelligence 10* (J.E. Hayes, D. Michie, Y.H. Pao, eds.). Ellis Horwood.

Buchanan, B.G. and Shortliffe, E.H. (1984, eds.) *Rule-based Expert Systems: The MYCIN Experiments of the Stanford Heuristic Programming Project*. Addison-Wesley.

Jackson, P. (1986) *Introduction to Expert Systems*. Addison-Wesley.

Kanal, L.N. and Lemmer, J.F. (1986, eds.) *Uncertainty in Artificial Intelligence*. Amsterdam: North-Holland.

Luger, G.F. and Stubblefield, W.A. (1989) *Artificial Intelligence and the Design of Expert Systems*. Benjamin/Cummings.

Michie, D. (1979, ed.) *Expert Systems in the Microelectronic Age*. Edinburgh University Press.

Minsky, M. (1975) A framework for representing knowledge. In: *The Psychology of Computer Vision* (P. Winston, ed.). McGraw-Hill.

Pearl, J. (1989) *Probabilistic Reasoning in Intelligent Systems: Networks of Plausible Inference*. San Mateo, California: Morgan Kaufmann.

Reiter, J. (1980) *AL/X: An Expert System Using Plausible Inference*. Oxford: Intelligent Terminals Ltd.

Shortliffe, E. (1976) *Computer-based Medical Consultations: MYCIN*. Elsevier.

Touretzky, D.S. (1986) *The Mathematics of Inheritance Systems*. Los Altos, California: Morgan Kaufmann.

Winston, P.H. (1984) *Artificial Intelligence* (second edition). Addison-Wesley.

15 An Expert System Shell

15.1 Knowledge representation format
15.2 Designing the inference engine
15.3 Implementation
15.4 Dealing with uncertainty
15.5 Concluding remarks

In this chapter we develop a complete rule-based expert system shell using the backward chaining approach introduced in Chapter 14. It incorporates proof construction along the lines introduced in Chapter 14 and some other features not covered there. First, we will allow variables in if-then rules and introduce a feature known as 'query the user', which prompts the user for information only as and when it is needed during the reasoning process. After developing a 'categorical' shell in all details, we will see how it can be enhanced to handle uncertainty.

15.1 Knowledge representation format

Our work plan for developing the shell will be as follows:

(1)   Select and define details of the formalism for representing knowledge in the shell.

(2)   Design details of an inference mechanism that suits this formalism.

(3)   Add user-interaction facilities.

(4)   Add a facility for handling uncertainty.

Let us start with item 1 – knowledge representation formalism. We will use if-then rules with a syntax similar to that in Chapter 14. However, we need some extra information in rules. For example, rules will have names. These extra details are given in Figure 15.1 which shows a knowledge base in the format accepted by our intended shell. This knowledge base consists of simple rules that help to identify animals from their basic characteristics, assuming that the identification problem is limited just to a small number of animals.

Rules in this knowledge base are of the form:

RuleName : if Condition then Conclusion.

where **Condition** is a set of simple assertions combined by the logical operators **and** and **or**, and **Conclusion** is a simple assertion that must not contain logical operators. We will also allow for the operator **not** to be used in the condition part of rules, although with some reservations. By an appropriate Prolog definition of operators (as in Figure 15.1) these rules are syntactically legal Prolog clauses. The operator **and** binds stronger than **or**, which is the normal convention.

Notice that assertions in rules can be terms that contain variables. Our next example shows why variables are useful and enormously enhance the power of the knowledge representation language. This example knowledge base helps to locate failures in a simple electric network that consists of some electric devices and fuses. Such a network is shown in Figure 15.2. One rule can be:

    if
        light1 is on *and*
        light1 is not working *and*
        fuse1 is proved intact
    then
        light1 is proved broken.

Figure 15.1 A simple knowledge base for identifying animals. Adapted from Winston (1984). The relation 'askable' defines those things that can be asked of the user. The operators :, **if**, **then**, **and**, **or** are declared as in Figure 15.6.

% A small knowledge base for identifying animals

:- op(100, xfx, [has, gives, 'does not', eats, lays, isa]).
:- op(100, xf, [swims, flies]).

rule1 : if
        Animal has hair
        or
        Animal gives milk
    then
        Animal isa mammal.

rule2 : if
        Animal has feathers
        or
        Animal flies and
        Animal lays eggs
    then
        Animal isa bird.

rule3 : if
        Animal isa mammal and
        (Animal eats meat
          or
          Animal has 'pointed teeth' and
          Animal has claws and
          Animal has 'forward pointing eyes')
    then
        Animal isa carnivore.

rule4 : if
        Animal isa carnivore and
        Animal has 'tawny colour' and
        Animal has 'dark spots'
    then
        Animal isa cheetah.

rule5 : if
        Animal isa carnivore and
        Animal has 'tawny colour' and
        Animal has 'black stripes'
    then
        Animal isa tiger.

(continues)

Figure 15.1 (cont.)

rule6 : if

      Animal isa bird and
      Animal 'does not' fly and
      Animal swims

   then

      Animal isa penguin.

rule7 : if

      Animal isa bird and
      Animal isa 'good flyer'

   then

      Animal isa albatross.

fact : X isa animal :-
  member(X, [cheetah, tiger, penguin, albatross]).

askable(_ gives _, 'Animal' gives 'What').
askable(_ flies, 'Animal' flies).
askable(_ lays eggs, 'Animal' lays eggs).
askable(_ eats _, 'Animal' eats 'What').
askable(_ has _, 'Animal' has 'Something').
askable(_ 'does not' _, 'Animal' 'does not' 'DoSomething').
askable(_ swims, 'Animal' swims).
askable(_ isa 'good flier', 'Animal' isa 'good flier').

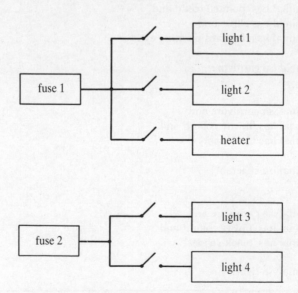

Figure 15.2 Connections between fuses and devices in a simple electric network.

Another rule can be:

> *if*
>> heater is working
>
> *then*
>> fuse1 is proved intact.

These two rules already rely on the facts (about our *particular* network) that *light1* is connected to *fuse1*, and that *light1* and *heater* share the same fuse. For another network we would need another set of rules. Therefore it is better to state rules more generally, using Prolog variables, so that they can be used for any network, and then add some extra information about a particular network. Thus one useful rule may be: if a device is on and not working and its fuse is intact then the device is broken. This translates into our rule formalism as:

> **broken_rule : if**   **Device is on and**
>> **not (Device is working) and**
>> **Device is connected to Fuse and**
>> **Fuse is proved intact**
>
>> **then**
>>> **Device is proved broken.**

A knowledge base of this sort is shown in Figure 15.3.

Figure 15.3   A knowledge base for locating a fault in a network such as the one in Figure 15.2.

% A small knowledge base for locating faults in an electric network

% If a device is on and not working and its fuse is intact
% then the device is broken

```
broken_rule :
            if
                on( Device) and
                device( Device) and
                not working( Device) and
                connected( Device, Fuse) and
                proved( intact( Fuse) )
            then
                proved( broken( Device) ).
```

(continues)

Figure 15.3 (cont.)

% If a unit is working then its fuse is OK

fuse_ok_rule :
      if
            connected(Device, Fuse) and
            working(Device)
      then
            proved(intact(Fuse)).

% If two different devices are connected to a fuse and
% are both on and not working then the fuse has failed
% NOTE: This assumes that at most one device is broken!

fused_rule :
      if
            connected(Device1, Fuse) and
            on(Device1) and
            not working(Device1) and
            samefuse(Device2, Device1) and
            on(Device2) and
            not working(Device2)
      then
            proved(failed(Fuse)).

same_fuse_rule :
      if
            connected(Device1, Fuse) and
            connected(Device2, Fuse) and
            different(Device1, Device2)
      then
            samefuse(Device1, Device2).

fact : different(X, Y) :- not (X = Y).

fact : device(heater).
fact : device(light1).
fact : device(light2).
fact : device(light3).
fact : device(light4).

fact : connected(light1, fuse1).
fact : connected(light2, fuse1).
fact : connected(heater, fuse1).
fact : connected(light3, fuse2).
fact : connected(light4, fuse2).

askable(on(D), on('Device')).
askable(working(D), working('Device')).

15.2   Designing the inference engine

15.2.1   Target behaviour

As discussed in Chapter 14, if-then rules like those in Figures 15.1 and 15.3 can be rewritten as Prolog rules and Prolog's own interpreter could be directly used as an expert system shell. However, the resulting behaviour is not quite satisfactory from the expert system point of view for at least two reasons:

(1)   We cannot conveniently ask for explanation; for example, *how* was the answer derived?

(2)   A complete set of data has to be input into the system (as Prolog facts) before any question can be asked. Much of this data may not be needed in the shell's inferencing about the case in hand. Thus, the user may do unnecessary work inputting irrelevant information. Worse still, the user may easily forget to provide all the relevant information, in which case the system will produce wrong answers.

To rectify these two drawbacks we need a better interaction between the user and the system during and after the reasoning process. Let us set as our goal that the system be capable of interacting with the user as the following example conversation illustrates (user's responses are in boldface and Prolog's output is in italics):

> *Question, please:*
> **peter isa tiger.**
>
> *Is it true: peter has hair?*
> **yes.**
>
> *Is it true: peter eats meat?*
> **no.**
>
> *Is it true: peter has pointed teeth?*
> **yes.**
>
> *Is it true: peter has claws?*
> **why.**
>
> *To investigate, by rule3, peter isa carnivore*
> *To investigate, by rule5, peter isa tiger*
> *This was your question*
>
> *Is it true: peter has claws?*
> **yes.**
>
> *Is it true: peter has forward pointing eyes?*
> **yes.**

Is it true: peter has tawny colour?
yes.

Is it true: peter has black stripes?
yes.

(peter isa tiger) is true

Would you like to see how?
yes.

peter isa tiger
 was derived by rule5 from
  peter isa carnivore
   was derived by rule3 from
    peter isa mammal
     was derived by rule1 from
      peter has hair
       was told
     and
     peter has pointed teeth
      was told
     and
     peter has claws
      was told
     and
     peter has forward pointing eyes
      was told
   and
   peter has tawny colour
    was told
   and
   peter has black stripes
    was told

As this conversation shows, the system asks questions of the user about 'primitive' information, such as:

Is it true: peter eats meat?

Such information cannot be found in the knowledge base or derived from other information. The user can respond to such queries in two ways:

(1) by supplying the relevant information as an answer to the query, or
(2) by asking the system *why* this information is needed.

The latter option is useful in order to enable the user to get insight into the system's current intentions. The user will ask 'why' if the system's query appears irrelevant, or if answering the query would require additional work on the part of the user. From the system's explanation the user will judge whether the information the system is asking for is worth the extra effort of obtaining that information. Suppose, for example, the system is asking 'Does the animal eat meat?' Then the user, not yet knowing the answer and not seeing the animal eating anything may decide that it is not worth waiting to actually catch the animal at eating meat.

We might use Prolog's trace facility in order to obtain some insight into the system's reasoning process. But such a trace facility would normally prove to be too rigid for our purpose. So, instead of using Prolog's own interpreting mechanism, which falls short of this type of user interaction, we will build a special interpreter facility on top of Prolog. This new interpreter will include a user-interaction facility.

15.2.2 Outline of the reasoning process

An answer to a given question can be found in several ways, according to the following principles:

To find an answer *Answ* to a question *Q* use one of the following:

- if *Q* is found as a fact in the knowledge base then *Answ* is '*Q* is true'.

- if there is a rule in the knowledge base of the form

   'if *Condition* then *Q*'

   then explore *Condition* and use the result to construct answer *Answ* to question *Q*.

- if *Q* is an 'askable' question then ask the user about *Q*.

- if *Q* is of the form *Q1 and Q2* then explore *Q1* and now:

   if *Q1* is false then *Answ* is '*Q* is false', else explore *Q2* and appropriately combine answers to both *Q1* and *Q2* into *Answ*.

- if *Q* is of the form *Q1 or Q2* then explore *Q1* and now:

   if *Q1* is true then *Answ* is '*Q* is true', or alternatively explore *Q2* and appropriately combine answers to both *Q1* and *Q2* into *Answ*.

Questions of the form

   not Q

are more problematic and will be discussed later.

15.2.3 Answering 'why' questions

A 'why' question occurs when the system asks the user for some information and the user wants to know *why* this information is needed. Suppose that the system has asked:

> *Is a true?*   .

The user may reply:

> **Why?**

An appropriate explanation can be along the following line:

> Because:
> I can use a to investigate b by rule R_a, and
> I can use b to investigate c by rule R_b, and
> . . .
> I can use y to investigate z by rule R_y, and
> z was your original question.

The explanation consists of showing the purpose of the information asked of the user. The purpose is shown in terms of a chain of rules and goals that connect this piece of information with the user's original question. We will call such a chain a *trace*. We can visualize a trace as a chain of rules that

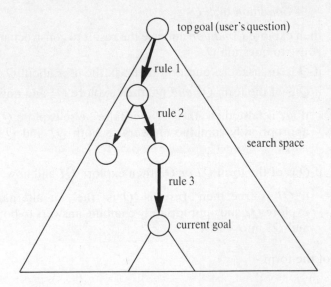

Figure 15.4 The 'why' explanation. The question 'Why are you interested in the current goal' is explained by the chain of rules and goals between the current goal and the user's original question at the top. The chain is called a trace.

connects the currently explored goal and the top goal in an AND/OR tree of questions. Figure 15.4 illustrates. So, the answering of 'why' queries is accomplished by moving from the current goal upwards in the search tree toward the top goal. To be able to do that we have to maintain the trace explicitly during the backward chaining process.

15.2.4 Answering 'how' questions

Once the system has come up with an answer to the user's question, the user may like to see *how* this conclusion was reached. A proper way of answering such a 'how' question is to display the evidence: that is, rules and subgoals from which the conclusion was reached. For our rule language, such evidence consists of a proof tree. The generation of proof trees was programmed in a stylized form in Chapter 14. We will use the same principle in a more elaborate way. An effective way of presenting proof trees as 'how' explanations is to use text indentation to convey the tree structure. For example:

> *peter isa carnivore*
>   *was derived by rule3 from*
>   *peter isa mammal*
>   *was derived by rule1 from*
>   *peter has hair*
>   *was told*
>   *and*
>   *peter eats meat*
>   *was told*

15.3 Implementation

We will now implement our shell along the ideas developed in the previous section. Figure 15.5 illustrates the main objects manipulated by the shell. **Goal** is a question to be investigated; **Trace** is a chain of ancestor goals and rules between **Goal** and the top-level question; **Answer** is a proof tree for **Goal**.

The main procedures of the shell will be:

    explore(Goal, Trace, Answer)

which finds an answer **Answer** to a question **Goal**;

    useranswer(Goal, Trace, Answer)

generates solutions for an 'askable' **Goal** by asking the user about **Goal** and answers 'why' questions;

    present(Answer)

Figure 15.5 The relation **explore(Goal, Trace, Answer)**. **Answer** is a proof tree for **Goal**.

displays the result and answers 'how' questions. These procedures are properly put into execution by the 'driver' procedure **expert**. These four main procedures are explained in the following sections and coded in Prolog in Figures 15.6 to 15.9. The programs in these figures are to be put together to form the complete shell program.

15.3.1 Procedure *explore*

The heart of the shell is the procedure

> explore(Goal, Trace, Answer)

which will find, in the backward chaining style, an answer **Answer** to a given question **Goal** by using the principles outlined in Section 15.2.2: either find **Goal** as a fact in the knowledge base, or apply a rule in the knowledge base, or ask the user, or treat **Goal** as an AND or OR combination of subgoals.

The meaning and the structure of the arguments are as follows:

Goal   is a question to be investigated, represented as an AND/OR combination of simple assertions. For example:

> **(X has feathers) or (X flies) and (X lays eggs)**

Trace   is a chain of ancestor goals and rules between **Goal** and the original, top goal, represented as a list of items of the form:

> **Goal by Rule**

This means that Goal is being investigated by means of rule Rule. For example, let the top goal be 'peter isa tiger', and the currently investigated goal be 'peter eats meat'. The corresponding trace, according to the knowledge base of Figure 15.1, is:

[(peter isa carnivore) by rule3, (peter isa tiger) by rule5]

This means the following:

I can use 'peter eats meat' in order
to investigate, by rule3, 'peter isa carnivore'.
Further, I can use 'peter isa carnivore' in order
to investigate, by rule5, 'peter isa tiger'.

Answer is a proof tree (that is, an AND/OR solution tree) for the question Goal. The general form for Answer is:

Conclusion was Found

where Found represents a justification for Conclusion. The following three example answers illustrate different possibilities:

(1) (connected(heater, fuse1) is true) was 'found as a fact'
(2) (peter eats meat) is false was told
(3) (peter isa carnivore) is true was ('derived by' rule3 from
        (peter isa mammal) is true was ('derived by' rule1 from
          (peter has hair) is true was told) and
        (peter eats meat) is true was told)

Figure 15.6 shows the Prolog code for explore. This code implements the principles of Section 15.2.2, using the data structures specified above.

15.3.2   Procedure *useranswer*

Procedure useranswer is an implementation of the 'query the user' facility. It queries the user for information when needed, and also explains to the user *why* it is needed. Before developing useranswer let us consider a useful auxiliary procedure:

getreply(Reply)

During conversation, the user is often expected to reply with 'yes', 'no' or 'why'. The purpose of getreply is to extract such an answer from the user and also to understand it properly if the user abbreviates ('y' or 'n') or makes a

Figure 15.6 The core procedure of an expert system shell.

```
% Procedure
%
% explore( Goal, Trace, Answer)
%
% finds Answer to a given Goal. Trace is a chain of ancestor
% goals and rules. 'explore' tends to find a positive answer
% to a question. Answer is 'false' only when all the
% possibilities have been investigated and they all resulted
% in 'false'.

:- op( 900, xfx, :).
:- op( 800, xfx, was).
:- op( 870, fx, if).
:- op( 880, xfx, then).
:- op( 550, xfy, or).
:- op( 540, xfy, and).
:- op( 300, fx, 'derived by').
:- op( 600, xfx, from).
:- op( 600, xfx, by).

% Program assumes: op( 700, xfx, is), op( 500, fx, not)

explore( Goal, Trace, Goal is true was 'found as a fact') :-
    fact : Goal.

% Assume only one rule about each type of goal

explore( Goal, Trace,
         Goal is TruthValue was 'derived by' Rule from Answer) :-
    Rule : if Condition then Goal,                    % Rule relevant to Goal
    explore( Condition, [Goal by Rule | Trace], Answer),
    truth( Answer, TruthValue).

explore( Goal1 and Goal2, Trace, Answer) :- !,
    explore( Goal1, Trace, Answer1),
    continue( Answer1, Goal1 and Goal2, Trace, Answer).

explore( Goal1 or Goal2, Trace, Answer) :-
    exploreyes( Goal1, Trace, Answer)                 % Positive answer to Goal1
    ;
    exploreyes( Goal2, Trace, Answer).                % Positive answer to Goal2

explore( Goal1 or Goal2, Trace, Answer1 and Answer2) :- !,
    not exploreyes( Goal1, Trace, _),
    not exploreyes( Goal2, Trace, _),                 % No positive answer
    explore( Goal1, Trace, Answer1),                  % Answer1 must be negative
    explore( Goal2, Trace, Answer2).                  % Answer2 must be negative

explore( Goal, Trace, Goal is Answer was told) :-
    useranswer( Goal, Trace, Answer).                 % User-supplied answer
```

Figure 15.6 (cont.)

```
exploreyes( Goal, Trace, Answer) :-
   explore( Goal, Trace, Answer),
   positive( Answer).

continue( Answer1, Goal1 and Goal2, Trace, Answer) :-
   positive( Answer1),
   explore( Goal2, Trace, Answer2),
   ( positive( Answer2),
     Answer = Answer1 and Answer2
     ;
     negative( Answer2),
     Answer = Answer2
   ).

continue( Answer1, Goal1 and Goal2, _, Answer1) :-
   negative( Answer1).

truth( Question is TruthValue was Found, TruthValue) :- !.

truth( Answer1 and Answer2, TruthValue) :-
   truth( Answer1, true),
   truth( Answer2, true), !,
   TruthValue = true
   ;
   TruthValue = false.

positive( Answer) :-
   truth( Answer, true).

negative( Answer) :-
   truth( Answer, false).
```

typing error. If the user's reply is unintelligible then **getreply** will request another reply from the user.

```
getreply( Reply) :-
   read( Answer),
   means( Answer, Reply), !          % Answer means something?
   ;
   nl, write( 'Answer unknown, try again please'), nl,   % No
   getreply( Reply).                 % Try again

means( yes, yes).
means( y, yes).
means( no, no).
means( n, no).
means( why, why).
means( w, why).
```

Note that **getreply** should be used with care because it involves interaction with the user accomplished through **read** and **write**, and can therefore only be understood procedurally, and not declaratively. For example, if we call **getreply** with:

        getreply(yes)

and the user types 'no', our procedure will respond with: 'Answer unknown, try again please.' Therefore, **getreply** should be called with its argument uninstantiated; for example, as:

        getreply(Reply),
        (Reply = yes, interpretyes(...)
        ;
        Reply = no, interpretno(...)
        ;
        ...)

The procedure

        useranswer(Goal, Trace, Answer)

asks the user about **Goal**. **Answer** is the result of this inquiry. **Trace** is used for explanation in the case that the user asks 'why'. **useranswer** should first check whether **Goal** is the kind of information that can be asked of the user. In our shell, such kinds of goal will be called 'askable'. Suppose, to begin with, that we define what is askable by a relation:

        askable(Goal)

This will be refined later. If **Goal** is 'askable' then **Goal** is displayed and the user will specify whether it is true or false. In the case that the user asks 'why', **Trace** will be displayed. If **Goal** is true then the user will also specify the values of variables in **Goal** (if there are any). This can be programmed as a first attempt as follows:

```
useranswer( Goal, Trace, Answer) :-
    askable( Goal),                          % Can Goal be asked of the user?
    ask( Goal, Trace, Answer).               % Ask user about Goal

ask( Goal, Trace, Answer) :-
    introduce( Goal),                        % Show question to user
    getreply( Reply),                        % Read user's reply
    process( Reply, Goal, Trace, Answer).    % Process the reply

process( why, Goal, Trace, Answer) :-        % User is asking 'why'
    showtrace( Trace),                       % Show why
    ask( Goal, Trace, Answer).               % Ask again
```

```
process( yes, Goal, Trace, Answer) :-        % User says Goal is true
   Answer = true,
   askvars( Goal)                            % Ask about variables
   ;
   ask( Goal, Trace, Answer).                % Ask for more solutions

process( no, Goal, Trace, false).            % User says Goal is false

introduce( Goal) :-
   nl, write( 'Is it true: '),
   write( Goal), write( ?), nl.
```

The call askvars(Goal) will ask the user to specify the value of each variable in
Goal:

```
askvars( Term) :-
   var( Term), !,                            % A variable?
   nl, write( Term), write( ' = '),
   read( Term).                              % Read variable's value

askvars( Term) :-
   Term = .. [Functor | Args],               % Get arguments of a structure
   askarglist( Args).                        % Ask about variables in arguments

askarglist( [ ] ).

askarglist( [Term | Terms] ) :-
   askvars( Term),
   askarglist( Terms).
```

Let us make a few experiments with this useranswer procedure. For
example, let the binary relation eats be declared as 'askable':

```
askable( X eats Y).
```

(In the following dialogue between Prolog and the user, the user-typed text is
in boldface and Prolog's output is in italics.)

```
?- useranswer( peter eats meat, [ ], Answer).
```

Is it true: peter eats meat?   % Question to user
yes.   % User's reply

Answer = true

A more interesting example that involves variables may look like this:

```
?- useranswer( Who eats What, [ ], Answer).
```

Is it true: _17 eats _18?   % Prolog gives internal names to variables
yes.   % Asking about variables
_17 = peter.
_18 = meat.

Answer = true
Who = peter
What = meat;   % Backtrack for more solutions

Is it true: _17 eats _18?
yes.
_17 = **susan.**
_18 = **bananas.**

Answer = true
Who = susan
What = bananas;

Is it true: _17 eats _18?
no.

Answer = false

15.3.3   Refining *useranswer*

One drawback of our **useranswer** procedure that shows in the foregoing conversation is the awkward appearance of Prolog-generated variable names in Prolog's output. Symbols like _17 should be replaced by some meaningful words when displayed to the user.

Another, more serious, defect of this version of **useranswer** is the following. If we subsequently use **useranswer** on the same goal, the user will have to repeat all the solutions. If our expert system would, during its reasoning process, come to explore the same 'askable' goal twice it would bore the user with exactly the same conversation again, instead of using the information previously supplied by the user.

Let us now rectify these two defects. First, an improvement of the external appearance of queries to the user can be based on introducing some standard format for each 'askable' goal. To this end, a second argument can be added to the relation **askable** to specify this format, as shown by the following example:

    askable(X eats Y, 'Animal' eats 'Something').

In querying the user, each variable in the question should then be replaced by keywords in the question format. For example:

    ?- useranswer(X eats Y, [ ], Answer).

Is it true: Animal eats Something?
yes.
Animal = **peter.**
Something = **meat.**

Answer = true
X = peter
Y = meat

In an improved version of **useranswer**, shown in Figure 15.7, this formatting of queries is done by the procedure:

> **format(Goal, ExternFormat, Question, Vars0, Variables)**

Figure 15.7 Expert system shell: querying the user and answering 'why' questions.

```
% Procedure
%
% useranswer( Goal, Trace, Answer)
%
% generates, through backtracking, user-supplied solutions to Goal.
% Trace is a chain of ancestor goals and rules used for 'why' explanation.

useranswer( Goal, Trace, Answer)  :-
    askable( Goal, _),                          % May be asked of the user
    freshcopy( Goal, Copy),                     % Variables in Goal renamed
    useranswer( Goal, Copy, Trace, Answer, 1).

% Do not ask again about an instantiated goal

useranswer( Goal, _, _, _, N)  :-
    N > 1,                                      % Repeated question?
    instantiated( Goal), !,                     % No variables in Goal
    fail.                                       % Do not ask again

% Is Goal implied true or false for all instantiations?

useranswer( Goal, Copy, _, Answer, _)  :-
    wastold( Copy, Answer, _),
    instance_of( Copy, Goal), !.                % Answer to Goal implied

% Retrieve known solutions, indexed from N on, for Goal

useranswer( Goal, _, _, true, N)  :-
    wastold( Goal, true, M),
    M >= N.

% Has everything already been said about Goal?

useranswer( Goal, Copy, _, Answer, _)  :-
    end_answers( Copy),
    instance_of( Copy, Goal), !,                % Everything was already said about Goal
    fail.

% Ask the user for (more) solutions

useranswer( Goal, _, Trace, Answer, N)  :-
    askuser( Goal, Trace, Answer, N).
```

(continues)

Figure 15.7 (cont.)

```
askuser( Goal, Trace, Answer, N) :-
  askable( Goal, ExternFormat),
  format( Goal, ExternFormat, Question, [ ], Variables),          % Get question format
  ask( Goal, Question, Variables, Trace, Answer, N).

ask( Goal, Question, Variables, Trace, Answer, N) :-
  nl,
  ( Variables = [ ], !,
    write( 'Is it true: ')                                        % Introduce question
    ;
    write( 'Any (more) solution to: ')                            % Introduce question
  ),
  write( Question), write( '? '),
  getreply( Reply), !,                                            % Reply = yes/no/why
  process( Reply, Goal, Question, Variables, Trace, Answer, N).

process( why, Goal, Question, Variables, Trace, Answer, N) :-
  showtrace( Trace),
  ask( Goal, Question, Variables, Trace, Answer, N).

process( yes, Goal, _, Variables, Trace, true, N) :-
  nextindex( Next),                                               % Get new free index for 'wastold'
  Next1 is Next + 1,
  ( askvars( Variables),
    assertz( wastold( Goal, true, Next) )                         % Record solution
    ;
    freshcopy( Goal, Copy),                                       % Copy of Goal
    useranswer( Goal, Copy, Trace, Answer, Next1)                 % More answers?
  ).

process( no, Goal, _, _, _, false, N) :-
  freshcopy( Goal, Copy),
  wastold( Copy, true, _), !,                                     % 'no' means: no more solutions
  assertz( end_answers( Goal) ),                                  % Mark end of answers
  fail
  ;
  nextindex( Next),                                               % Next free index for 'wastold'
  assertz( wastold( Goal, false, Next) ).                         % 'no' means: no solution

format( Var, Name, Name, Vars, [Var/Name | Vars] ) :-
  var( Var), !.

format( Atom, Name, Atom, Vars, Vars) :-
  atomic( Atom), !,
  atomic( Name).
```

Figure 15.7 (cont.)

```
format( Goal, Form, Question, Vars0, Vars) :-
   Goal = .. [Functor | Args1],
   Form = .. [Functor | Forms],
   formatall( Args1, Forms, Args2, Vars0, Vars),
   Question = .. [Functor | Args2].

formatall( [ ], [ ], [ ], Vars, Vars).

formatall( [X | XL], [F | FL], [Q | QL], Vars0, Vars) :-
   formatall( XL, FL, QL, Vars0, Vars1),
   format( X, F, Q, Vars1, Vars).

askvars( [ ] ).

askvars( [Variable/Name | Variables] ) :-
   nl, write( Name), write( ' = '),
   read( Variable),
   askvars( Variables).

showtrace( [ ] ) :-
   nl, write( 'This was your question'), nl.

showtrace( [Goal by Rule | Trace] ) :-
   nl, write( 'To investigate, by '),
   write( Rule), write( ', '),
   write( Goal),
   showtrace( Trace).

instantiated( Term) :-
   numbervars( Term, 0, 0).              % No variables in Term
```

```
% instance_of( T1, T2): instance of T1 is T2; that is,
% term T1 is more general than T2 or equally general as T2
```

```
instance_of( Term, Term1) :-            % Instance of Term is Term1
   freshcopy( Term1, Term2),            % Copy of Term1 with fresh set of variables
   numbervars( Term2, 0, _), !,
   Term = Term2.                        % This succeeds if Term1 is instance of Term

freshcopy( Term, FreshTerm) :-          % Make a copy of Term with variables renamed
   asserta( copy( Term) ),
   retract( copy( FreshTerm) ), !.

lastindex( 0).                          % Index for 'wastold' at start

nextindex( Next) :-                     % Next free index for 'wastold'
   retract( lastindex( Last) ), !,
   Next is Last + 1,
   assert( lastindex( Next) ).
```

Goal is a goal to be formatted. **ExternFormat** specifies the external format for **Goal**, defined by:

    askable(Goal, ExternFormat)

Question is **Goal** formatted according to **ExternFormat**. **Variables** is a list of variables that appear in **Goal** accompanied by their corresponding keywords (as specified in **ExternFormat**), added on a list **Vars0**. For example:

    ?- format(X gives documents to Y,
           'Who' gives 'What' to 'Whom',
           Question, [ ], Variables).

    Question = 'Who' gives documents to 'Whom',
    Variables = [X/'Who', Y/'Whom'].

The other refinement, to avoid repeated questions to the user, will be more difficult. First, all user's answers should be remembered so that they can be retrieved at some later point. This can be accomplished by asserting user's answers as elements of a relation. For example:

    assert(wastold(mary gives documents to friends, true)).

In a situation where there are several user-supplied solutions to the same goal there will be several facts asserted about that goal. Here a complication arises. Suppose that variants of a goal (the goal with variables renamed) appear at several places. For example:

    (X has Y) and   % First occurrence – Goal1
    ...
    (X1 has Y1) and   % Second occurrence – Goal2
    ...

Further suppose that the user will be asked (through backtracking) for several solutions to **Goal1**. After that the reasoning process will advance to **Goal2**. As we already have some solutions for **Goal1** we want the system to apply them automatically to **Goal2** as well (since they obviously satisfy **Goal2**). Now suppose that the system tries these solutions for **Goal2**, but none of them satisfies some further goal. So the system will backtrack to **Goal2** and should ask the user for more solutions. If the user does supply more solutions then these will have to be remembered as well. In the case that the system later backtracks to **Goal1** these new solutions will also have to be automatically applied to **Goal1**.

In order to properly use the information supplied by the user at different places we will index this information. So the asserted facts will have the form

    wastold(Goal, TruthValue, Index)

where Index is a counter of user-supplied answers. The procedure

>   useranswer(Goal, Trace, Answer)

will have to keep track of the number of solutions already produced through backtracking. This can be accomplished by means of another procedure, useranswer with four arguments,

>   useranswer(Goal, Trace, Answer, N)

where N is an integer. This call has to produce solutions to Goal indexed N or higher. A call

>   useranswer(Goal, Trace, Answer)

is meant to produce *all* solutions to Goal. Solutions will be indexed from 1 on, so we have the following relation:

>   useranswer(Goal, Trace, Answer) :-
>   useranswer(Goal, Trace, Answer, 1).

An outline of

>   useranswer(Goal, Trace, Answer, N)

is: generate solutions to Goal by first retrieving known solutions indexed from N onwards. When these are exhausted then start querying the user about Goal and assert the thus obtained new solutions properly indexed by consecutive numbers. When the user says there are no more solutions, assert:

>   end_answers(Goal)

If the user says in the first place that there are no solutions at all then assert:

>   wastold(Goal, false, Index)

When retrieving solutions, useranswer will have to properly interpret such information.

However, there is a further complication. The user may also specify general solutions, leaving some variables uninstantiated. If a positive solution is retrieved which is more general than or as general as Goal, then there is of course no point in further asking about Goal since we already have the most general solution. If

>   wastold(Goal, false, _)

then an analogous decision is to be made.

The **useranswer** program in Figure 15.7 takes all this into account. Another argument, **Copy** (a copy of **Goal**), is added and used in several matchings in place of **Goal** so that the variables of **Goal** are not destroyed. The program also uses two auxiliary relations. One is

> **instantiated(Term)**

which is true if **Term** contains no variables. The other is

> **instance_of(Term, Term1)**

where **Term1** is an instance of **Term**; that is, **Term** is at least as general as **Term1**. For example:

> **instance_of(X gives information to Y, mary gives information to Z)**

These two procedures both rely on another procedure:

> **numbervars(Term, N, M)**

This procedure 'numbers' the variables in **Term** by replacing each variable in **Term** by some newly generated term so that these 'numbering' terms correspond to integers between N and M − 1. For example, let these terms be of the form:

> **var/0, var/1, var/2, ...**

Then

> ?- **Term = f(X, t(a, Y, X)), numbervars(Term, 5, M).**

will result in:

```
Term = f( var/5, t( a, var/6, var/5) )
X = var/5
Y = var/6
M = 7
```

Such a **numbervars** procedure is often supplied as a built-in predicate in a Prolog system. If not, it can be programmed as follows:

```
numbervars( Term, N, Nplus1) :-
    var( Term), !,                      % Variable?
    Term = var/N,
    Nplus1 is N + 1.

numbervars( Term, N, M) :-
    Term =.. [Functor | Args],          % Structure or atomic
    numberargs( Args, N, M).            % Number variables in arguments
```

```
numberargs( [ ], N, N) :- !.

numberargs( [X | L], N, M) :-
    numbervars( X, N, N1),
    numberargs( L, N1, M).
```

15.3.4   Procedure *present*

The procedure

```
present( Answer)
```

in Figure 15.8 displays the final result of a consultation session and generates the 'how' explanation. Answer includes both an answer to the user's question, and a proof tree showing *how* this conclusion was reached. Procedure present first presents the conclusion. If the user then wants to see *how* the conclusion was reached, then the proof tree is displayed in a suitable form which constitutes a 'how' explanation. This form was illustrated by an example in Sections 15.2.1 and 15.2.4.

15.3.5   Top-level driver

For a convenient access to the shell from the Prolog interpreter we need a 'driver' procedure which may look like the procedure expert in Figure 15.9. expert starts the execution and coordinates the three main modules of the shell shown in Figures 15.6 to 15.8. For example:

```
?- expert.
```

Question, please: % Prompt the user
X isa animal and goliath isa X.   % User's question

Is it true: goliath has hair?
. . .

15.3.6   A comment on the shell program

Our shell program at some places appears to lack the declarative clarity that is typical of Prolog programs. The reason for this is that in such a shell we have to impose rather strict control over the execution because an expert system is expected not only to find an answer, but also to find it in a way that appears sensible to the user who keeps interacting with the system. Therefore, we have to implement a particular problem-solving *behaviour* and not just an input-output relation. Thus a resulting program is in fact more procedurally biased than usual. This is one example when we cannot rely on Prolog's own procedural engine, but have to specify the procedural behaviour in detail.

% Displaying the conclusion of a consultation and 'how' explanation

```
present( Answer) :-
  nl, showconclusion( Answer),
  nl, write( 'Would you like to see how? '),
  getreply( Reply),
  ( Reply = yes, !,
    show( Answer)                          % Show solution tree
    ;
    true
  ).

showconclusion( Answer1 and Answer2) :- !,
  showconclusion( Answer1), write( 'and '),
  showconclusion( Answer2).

showconclusion( Conclusion was Found) :-
  write( Conclusion).


% 'show' displays a complete solution tree

show( Solution) :-
  nl, show( Solution, 0), !.               % Indent by 0

show( Answer1 and Answer2, H) :- !,        % Indent by H
  show( Answer1, H),
  tab( H), write( and), nl,
  show( Answer2, H).

show( Answer was Found, H) :-              % Indent by H
  tab( H), writeans( Answer),              % Show conclusion
  nl, tab( H),
  write( 'was '),
  show1( Found, H).                        % Show evidence

show1( Derived from Answer, H) :- !,
  write( Derived), write( 'from'),         % Show rule name
  nl, H1 is H + 4,
  show( Answer, H1).                       % Show antecedent

show1( Found, _) :-                        % Found = 'told' or 'found as fact'
  write( Found), nl.

writeans( Goal is true) :- !,
  write( Goal).                            % Omit 'is true' on output

writeans( Answer) :-                       % This is negative answer
  write( Answer).
```

Figure 15.8 Expert system shell: displaying final result and 'how' explanation.

```
% Top-level driving procedure
expert :-
   getquestion( Question),                      % Input user's question
   ( answeryes( Question)                        % Try to find positive answer
   ;
     answerno( Question)                         % If no positive answer then find negative
   ).

answeryes( Question) :-                          % Look for positive answers to Question
   markstatus( negative),                        % No positive answer yet
   explore( Question, [ ], Answer),              % Trace is empty
   positive( Answer),                            % Look for positive answers
   markstatus( positive),                        % Positive answer found
   present( Answer), nl,
   write( 'More solutions? '),
   getreply( Reply),                             % Read user's reply
   Reply = no.                                   % Otherwise backtrack to 'explore'

answerno( Question) :-                           % Look for negative answer to question
   retract( no_positive_answer_yet), !,          % Has there been no positive answer?
   explore( Question, [ ], Answer),
   negative( Answer),
   present( Answer), nl,
   write( 'More negative solutions? '),
   getreply( Reply),
   Reply = no.                                   % Otherwise backtrack to 'explore'

markstatus( negative) :-
   assert( no_positive_answer_yet).

markstatus( positive) :-
   retract( no_positive_answer_yet), !
   ;
   true.

getquestion( Question) :-
   nl, write( 'Question, please'), nl,
   read( Question).
```

Figure 15.9 Expert system shell: a 'driver'. The shell is called from Prolog through the procedure expert.

15.3.7 Negated goals

It seems natural to allow for negation in the left-hand sides of rules and hence also in questions that are investigated by **explore**. A straightforward attempt to deal with negated questions is as follows:

```
        explore( not Goal, Trace, Answer) :- !,
           explore( Goal, Trace, Answer1),
           invert( Answer1, Answer).              % Invert truth value
```

> **invert(Goal is true was Found, (not Goal) is false was Found).**
>
> **invert(Goal is false was Found, (not Goal) is true was Found).**

This is fine if **Goal** is instantiated. If it is not, problems arise. Consider, for example:

> **?- expert.**
>
> *Question, please:*
> **not (X eats meat).**
>
> *Any (more) solution to: Animal eats meat?*
> **yes.**
> *Animal =* **tiger.**

Now the system will come up with the answer:

> *not (tiger eats meat) is false*

This is not satisfying. The problem stems from what we mean by a question such as:

> **not (X eats meat)**

We in fact want to ask: Is there an X such that X does not eat meat? But the way this question is interpreted by **explore** (as defined) is as follows:

(1)   Is there an X such that X eats meat?
(2)   Yes, tiger eats meat.

Thus

(3)   not (tiger eats meat) is false.

In short, the interpretation is: Is it true that no X eats meat? So we will get a positive answer only in the case that *nobody* eats meat. Said another way, **explore** will answer the question as if X was *universally* quantified:

> for *all* X: not (X eats meat)?

and not as if it was *existentially* quantified, which was our intention:

> for *some* X: not (X eats meat)?

If the question explored is instantiated then this problem disappears.

Otherwise, proper treatment is more complicated. Some decisions can be as follows:

To explore *not Goal*, explore *Goal* and now:

- if *Goal* is false then (*not Goal*) is true;
- if *Goal'* is a solution of *Goal*
  and *Goal'* is as general as *Goal*
  then (*not Goal*) is false;
- if *Goal'* is a solution of *Goal* and
  Goal' is more specific than *Goal*
  then we cannot say anything definite about *not Goal*.

We can avoid these complications by only allowing instantiated negated goals. This can often be achieved by proper statement of rules in the knowledge base. In Figure 15.3 we achieved this in 'broken_rule':

```
broken_rule : if
                on( Device) and
                device( Device) and              % Instantiate Device
                not working( Device) and
                connected( Device, Fuse) and
                proved( intact( Fuse))
            then
                proved( broken( Device)).
```

The condition

```
device( Device)
```

will 'protect' the subsequent condition

```
not working( Device)
```

from being evaluated uninstantiated.

EXERCISE

15.1 A knowledge base can in principle contain cycles. For example:

```
rule1: if bottle_empty then john_drunk.
rule2: if john_drunk then bottle_empty.
```

Using such a knowledge base, our **explore** procedure may start cycling between same goals. Modify **explore** to prevent such cycling. **Trace** can be used for this. However, some care is necessary: if the current goal *matches* a previous goal, this should not be considered a cycle if the current goal is more general than the previous one.

15.4 Dealing with uncertainty

Our expert system shell so far can only deal with categorical domains. In Chapter 14, a simple way of introducing uncertainty into a rule-based system was shown. Here we will consider a more sophisticated scheme, introduced by one of the early and best-known expert systems, Prospector. It should be noted that the Prospector model is not perfect, both from the theoretical and practical point of view. However, it has been used in many applications, in particular in mineral exploration and fault diagnosis.

15.4.1 The Prospector model

The likelihood of events is modelled by real numbers between 0 and 1. For simplicity we will be referring to these numbers as 'probabilities', although 'subjective certainties' would be more appropriate, because the Prospector model does not rigorously follow the probability theory. Relations between events can be represented diagrammatically as an 'inference network'. Figure 15.10 shows an example. Boxes represent events and arcs represent relations between events. Circles represent logical combinations of events (AND, OR, NOT).

Relations between events, pictured as arcs, mean a sort of 'soft implication'. Let there be two events, E and H, and let the knowledge of E affect our belief in H. If this effect was that of 'categorical implication' then we would simply write:

if E then H

In the case of 'soft implication' this relation can be less than certain, so some 'strength' can be associated with it:

if E then H with strength *Strength*

The strength with which the likelihood of E influences the belief in H is in Prospector modelled by two parameters:

N = 'necessity factor'
S = 'sufficiency factor'

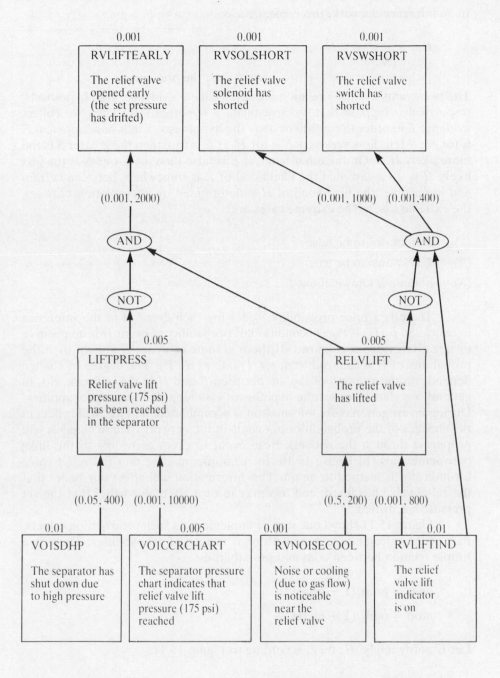

Figure 15.10 An AL/X inference network adapted from Reiter (1980). Numbers attached to boxes are prior probabilities of events; numbers attached to arcs indicate the strength of relations between events.

In an inference network, this is pictured as:

$$E \text{-------------} > H$$
$$(N,S)$$

The two events in such a relation are often called 'evidence' and 'hypothesis' respectively. Suppose that we investigate a hypothesis H. Then we collect evidence E in order to confirm or deny the hypothesis. S tells how *sufficient* E is for H; N tells how *necessary* E is for H. If E is true then the greater S is the more likely H is. On the other hand, if E is false then the lower N is the less likely H is. In a case that the likelihood of E is somewhere between certain and impossible, the likelihood of H is determined by interpolation between the extreme cases. The extreme cases are:

(1) E is known to be false

(2) E is known to be true

(3)   nothing is known about E

There is a prior probability $p_0(H)$ for each event H in the inference network. So $p_0(H)$ is the (unconditional) probability of event H if no positive or negative evidence is known. If there is some evidence E known then the probability of H is changed from $p_0(H)$ into $p(H \mid E)$. The degree of change depends on the strength of the arc between E and H in the network. So, in general, we start investigating hypotheses assuming their prior probabilities. During investigation more information is accumulated, and this will reflect in the changes of the probabilities of events in the network. These changes will propagate through the network from event to event according to the links between events. In Figure 15.10, for example, assume that the relief-valve lift-indicator is learned to be on. This information will affect our belief that the relief valve has lifted, and this may in turn affect our belief that the set pressure has drifted.

Figure 15.11 shows one way of implementing such propagation effects. Part of the calculation is done with *odds* instead of probabilities. There is a simple relation between odds and probabilities:

$$odds = prob/(1 - prob)$$
$$prob = odds/(1 + odds)$$

Let E 'softly imply' H; then, according to Figure 15.11,

$$odds(H) = M * odds_0(H)$$

where the multiplier M is determined by the prior and posterior probabilities

(a)

$$odds(H) = M * odds_0(H)$$

Interpolation rule
for multiplier M

(b)

Figure 15.11   Probability propagation rules in Prospector and AL/X: (a) 'soft implica-tion' with strength (N,S); (b) logical relations.

of E, and by the strength (N,S) of the link between E and H. Prospector's
rules (in Figure 15.11) that combine probabilities of logically combined events
(*min* and *max*) are supposed appropriately to model the human judgement
regarding the combinations of subjective certaintities.

15.4.2 Outline of an implementation

Let us first extend the rule language in order to handle uncertainty. Each rule can be added a 'strength modifier' defined by two non-negative real numbers S and N. A suitable format is:

> RuleName : if
>> Condition
>> then
>> Conclusion
>> with
>> strength(S, N).

Example rules from Figure 15.10 can be expressed in this form as follows:

> rule1 : if
>> not liftpress and
>> relvlift
>> then
>> rvliftearly
>> with
>> strength(0.001, 2000).

> rule4 : if
>> v01sdhp
>> then
>> liftpress
>> with
>> strength(0.05, 400).

To extend our expert system shell of Section 15.3 to deal with uncertainty, changes are needed in most procedures. Let us concentrate just on the procedure:

> explore(Goal, Trace, Answer)

We will assume here that **Goal** contains no variables (as in the cases of Prospector and AL/X). This greatly simplifies matters (especially in procedure **useranswer**). So **Goal** can be a logical combination of simple propositions. For example:

> not liftpress and relvlift

The chain of antecedent goals and rules, **Trace**, can be represented in the same way as in Section 15.3. The form of **Answer**, however, needs modification in order to introduce probabilities. We can combine a goal and its probability into a term of the form:

> **Goal : Probability**

So an example of **Answer** is:

> **rvliftind : 1 was told**

This means that the user has told the system that the event **rvliftind** certainly happened.

Another modification in the representation of **Answer** is necessary because several independent links can bear on the same event. Then the probability of this event can be multiplicatively affected by the odds multipliers, as in Figure 15.11, from all the links. In such a case, **Answer** will contain the list of all relevant derivation branches. An example of such an answer from the network of Figure 15.10 can be (arranged for better readability):

> **liftpress : 1 was 'derived by'**
> **[rule4 from v01sdhp : 1 was told,**
> **rule5 from v01ccrchart : 1 was told]**

Procedure **explore**, which produces answers in this form, is programmed in Figure 15.12. **explore** calls the predicate

> **implies(P0, P, Strength, Prob0, Prob)**

which is the 'soft implication' relation (see Figure 15.11). P0 is the prior probability of the evidence, E, and P is its posterior probability. **Strength** is the strength of the implication, represented as:

> **strength(N, S)**

Figure 15.12 Finding the likelihood of a hypothesis by certainty propagation in an inference network of the Prospector-AL/X type.

```
% Procedure
%
% explore( Goal, Trace, Answer)
%
% finds the likelihood that Goal is true. Answer
% contains this likelihood. Trace is the chain of ancestor
% goals and rules, and can be used for 'why' explanations.

explore( Goal, Trace, ( Goal : Prob) was 'derived by' RulesAnswers) :-
    bagof( Rule : if Condition then Goal with Strength,
        Rule : if Condition then Goal with Strength,
        Rules),                                              % All rules about Goal
    prior( Goal, Prob0),                                     % Prior probability of Goal
    modify( Prob0, Rules, Trace, Prob, RulesAnswers).        % Modify prior probability
```

(continues)

Figure 15.12 (cont.)

```
explore( Goal1 and Goal2, Trace,
        ( Goal1 and Goal2 : P) was 'derived from' ( Answer1 and Answer2) ) :-
  !,
  explore( Goal1, Trace, Answer1),
  explore( Goal2, Trace, Answer2),
  probability( Answer1, P1),
  probability( Answer2, P2),
  min( P1, P2, P).

explore( Goal1 or Goal2, Trace,
        ( Goal1 or Goal2 : P) was 'derived from' ( Answer1 and Answer2) ) :-
  !,
  explore( Goal1, Trace, Answer1),
  explore( Goal2, Trace, Answer2),
  probability( Answer1, P1),
  probability( Answer2, P2),
  max( P1, P2, P).

explore( not Goal, Trace, ( not Goal : Prob) was 'derived from' Answer) ) :-
  !,
  explore( Goal, Trace, Answer),
  probability( Answer, P),
  invert( P, Prob).

explore( Goal, Trace, ( Goal : Prob) was told) :-
  useranswer( Goal, Trace, Prob).                        % User-supplied answer


% modify( Prob0, Rules, Trace, Prob, RulesAnswers):
%
% There is a goal Goal whose prior probability is Prob0; Rules
% bear on Goal; the cumulative effect of these rules (through
% their condition parts) modifies Prob0 into Goal's posterior
% probability Prob; Trace is the list of Goal's ancestor goals
% and rules; RulesAnswers are the results of analysis of the
% condition parts of Rules.

modify( Prob0, [ ], Trace, Prob0, [ ] ).                 % No rule – no effect

modify( Prob0,
        [Rule : if Cond then Goal with Strength | Rules],
        Trace, Prob, [Rule from Answer | RulesAnswers] )
  :-
  explore( Cond, [Goal by Rule | Trace], Answer),        % Condition of first rule
  prior( Cond, P0),
  probability( Answer, P),
  implies( P0, P, Strength, Prob0, Prob1),               % A 'soft implication' rule
  modify( Prob1, Rules, Trace, Prob, RulesAnswers).
```

Prob0 and **Prob** are the prior and the posterior probability respectively of the hypothesis, H.

It should be noted that this is a very simple implementation that only caters for the probability propagation in an inference network, and may behave unintelligently. It pays no attention to what lines of analysis are currently most important. In a more elaborate version, the exploration process should be guided toward the most critical pieces of evidence. It should also aim at asking the user as few questions as possible.

Finally, a few comments about a new **useranswer** procedure. It would be simpler than that in Figure 15.7 since now we have no variables in queries to the user. This time the user will answer by a probability (instead of 'yes' or 'no'). In the case that the user knows nothing about the event asked, he or she will leave the prior probability of that event unchanged. The user may also answer 'why' and be shown **Trace** as a 'why' explanation. In addition the user should be allowed to ask: What is currently the probability of my hypothesis? The user may then, if tired of supplying information (or pressed by time), conclude the consultation session with a system's answer that is based on partial information only.

15.5   Concluding remarks

Our expert system shell can be elaborated in a number of ways. Several critical comments and suggestions for elaboration can be made at this point.

Our programs are a straightforward implementation of basic ideas, and do not pay much attention to the issue of efficiency. A more efficient implementation would require more sophisticated data structures, indexing or hierarchy of rules, etc.

Our **explore** procedure is susceptible to cycling if the rules in the knowledge base 'cyclicly' mention the same goal. This can be easily rectified by adding a cycle check in **explore**: test whether the current goal is an instance of another goal that is already on **Trace**.

Our 'how' explanation outputs a whole proof tree. In the case of a large proof tree it would be better to output just the top part of the tree and then let the user 'walk' through the rest of the tree as he or she wishes. The user would then inspect the proof tree selectively by using commands such as 'Move down branch 1', 'Move down branch 2', ..., 'Move up', 'Enough'.

In the 'how' and 'why' explanations, our shell just mentions rules by their names, and does not show the rules explicitly. The user should be offered the option to request rules to be displayed explicitly during a consultation session.

Querying the user so that the dialogue looks natural proved to be complicated. Our solution works to some extent, but further problems may appear in several ways, for example:

> *Is it true: susan flies?*
> **no.**
> *Is it true: susan isa good flyer?*

Of course not, if Susan cannot fly at all! Another example is:

> *Any (more) solution to: Somebody flies?*
> **yes.**
> *Somebody* = **bird.**
> *Is it true: albatross flies?*

To cope with such defects, additional relations between concepts dealt with by the expert system would have to be added. Typically, these new relations would specify hierarchical relations between objects and how properties are inherited. This can be done using semantic network or frame representations, as introduced in Chapter 14.

Another refinement of the user-querying procedure would involve the planning of an optimal querying strategy. The optimization objective would be to minimize the number of questions asked of the user before a conclusion is reached. There would be, of course, alternative strategies and which of them would eventually be the shortest would depend on user's answers. A decision of what alternative strategy to pursue can be based on some a *priori* probabilities to assess probabilistically the 'cost' of each alternative. This assessment might have to be updated after each user's answer.

There is another measure that can be optimized: the length of the derivation of a conclusion. This would tend to produce simple 'how' explanations. We can reduce the complexity of explanations also by selectively treating individual rules. Thus some rules would not be put into Trace and Answer in the explore procedure. In this case the knowledge base would have to specify which rules are 'traceable', and should therefore appear in explanations, and which should not.

An intelligent expert system should be probabilistically guided so that it concentrates on the currently most likely hypothesis among the competing ones. It should query the user about the information that discriminates best among the top hypotheses.

Our example expert systems were of classification, or 'analysis', type as opposed to the 'synthesis' type where the task is to *construct* something. The result can in the latter case be a plan of actions to accomplish some task – for example, a plan for a robot, a computer configuration that satisfies a given specification, or a forced combination in chess. Our fault diagnosis example can be naturally extended to involve actions; for example, if nothing can be inferred because devices are switched off the system may suggest 'Switch on light 3'. This would entail the problem of optimal plans: minimize the number of actions necessary to reach a conclusion.

Projects

Complete our shell that deals with uncertainties (add a corresponding **useranswer** and other procedures).

Consider critical comments and possible extensions to our expert system shell, as discussed, and design and implement corresponding improvements.

SUMMARY

- The shell, developed and programmed in this chapter,

  interprets if-then rules,
  provides 'how' and 'why' explanations, and
  queries the user about the information needed.

- The inference engine of our shell was extended to handle uncertainty according to the Prospector uncertainty scheme.

References

The design of our expert system shell is to some degree similar to that described by Hammond (1984). The scheme for handling uncertainty is from the influential Prospector system (Duda *et. al.* 1979). Some of the examples used in the text are adapted from Winston (1984) and Reiter (1980).

Duda, R., Gaschnig, J. and Hart, P. (1979) Model design in the Prospector consultant system for mineral exploration. In: *Expert Systems in the Microelectronic Age* (D. Michie, ed.). Edinburgh University Press.

Hammond, P. (1984) Micro-PROLOG for Expert Systems. In: *Micro-PROLOG: Programming in Logic* (K.L. Clark, F.G. McCabe, eds.). Prentice-Hall.

Reiter, J. (1980) AL/X: An Expert System Using Plausible Inference. Oxford: Intelligent Terminals Ltd.

Winston, P.H. (1984) *Artificial Intelligence* (second edition). Addison-Wesley.

16 Planning

Planning is a topic of traditional interest in Artificial Intelligence. It involves reasoning about the effects of actions and the sequencing of available actions to achieve a given cumulative effect. In this chapter we develop several simple planners that illustrate the principles of planning.

16.1 Representing actions

Figure 16.1 shows an example of a planning task. It is a kind of search problem in a corresponding state space, as discussed in Chapter 11. However, here the problem will be represented in a way that makes it possible to reason explicitly about the effects of actions among which the planner can choose.

Actions change the current state of the planning world, thereby causing the transition to a new state. However, an action does not normally change everything in the current state, just some component(s) of the state. A good representation should therefore take into account this 'locality' of the effects of actions. To facilitate the reasoning about such local effects of actions, a state will be represented as a list of relationships that are currently true. Of course, we choose to mention only those relationships that pertain to the planning problem. For planning in the blocks world, such relationships are

on(Block, Object)

and

clear(Object)

The latter expression says that there is nothing on the top of **Object**. In planning in the blocks world, such a relationship is important because a block to be moved must be clear, and a block or place to which the block is moved must also be clear. **Object** can be a block or a place. In our example, *a*, *b* and *c* are blocks, and 1, 2, 3 and 4 are places. The initial state of the world in Figure 16.1 can then be represented by the list of relationships:

[clear(2), clear(4), clear(b), clear(c), on(a, 1), on(b, 3), on(c, a)]

Notice that we distinguish between a relation and a relationship. For example, on(c, a) is a relationship; that is, a *particular instance* of the relation **on**. Relation **on** is, on the other hand, the set of all **on** relationships.

Each available action is defined in terms of its precondition and its effects. More precisely, each action is specified by three things:

(1) *precondition*: a condition that has to be satisfied in a situation for the action to be possible;

(2) *add-list*: a list of relationships that the action establishes in the situation – these conditions become true after the action is executed;

(3) *delete-list*: a list of relationships that the action destroys.

Preconditions will be defined by the procedure

can(Action, Cond)

Figure 16.1   A planning problem in the blocks world: find a sequence of actions that achieve the goals: *a* on *b*, and *b* on *c*. These actions transform the initial state (on the left) into a final state (on the right).

which says: **Action** can only be executed in a situation in which condition **Cond** holds.

The effects of an action will be defined by two procedures:

> add(Action, AddRels)
> del(Action, DelRels)

Here **AddRels** is a list of relationships that **Action** establishes. After **Action** is executed in a state, **AddRels** is added to the state to obtain the new state. **DelRels** is a list of relationships that **Action** destroys. These relationships are removed from the state to which **Action** is applied.

For our blocks world the only kind of action will be

> move(Block, From, To)

where **Block** is the block to be moved, **From** is the block's current position and **To** is its new position. A complete definition of this action is given in Figure 16.2. A definition of possible actions for a planning problem implicitly defines the space of all possible plans; therefore, such a definition will also be referred to as a *planning space*.

Planning in the blocks world is a traditional planning exercise, usually associated with robot programming when a robot is supposed to build structures from blocks. However, we can easily find many examples of planning in our everyday life. Figure 16.3 gives the definition of a planning space for manipulating a camera. This planning problem is concerned with getting a camera ready; that is, loading new film and replacing the battery if necessary. A plan to load a new film in this planning space is as follows: open the case to get the camera out, rewind old film, open the film slot, remove old film, insert new film, close the film slot. A state in which the camera is ready for taking pictures is:

> [slot_closed(battery), slot_closed(film), in(battery),
>   ok(battery), in(film), film_at_start, film_unused]

Figure 16.2 A definition of the planning space for the blocks world.

% Definition of action move(Block, From, To) in blocks world

% can(Action, Condition): Action possible if Condition true

```
can( move( Block, From, To), [ clear( Block), clear( To), on( Block, From)] )  :-
    block( Block),
    object( To),
    To \== Block,                                % Block cannot be moved to itself
    object( From),
    From \== To,                                 % Move to new position
    Block \== From.                              % Block not moved from itself
```

% add(Action, Relationships): Action establishes Relationships

```
add( move( Block, From, To), [ on( Block, To), clear( From)] ).
```

% del(Action, Relationships): Action destroys Relationships

```
del( move( Block, From, To), [ on( Block, From), clear( To)] ).

object( X) :-
    place( X)
    ;
    block( X).
```

% A blocks world

```
block( a).
block( b).
block( c).

place( 1).
place( 2).
place( 3).
place( 4).
```

% A state in blocks world
%
%   c
%   a   b
%   ====
%place 1 2 3 4

```
state1( [ clear( 2), clear( 4), clear( b), clear( c), on( a, 1), on( b, 3), on( c, a) ] ).
```

Figure 16.3   A definition of planning space for manipulating camera.

% Planning space for getting camera ready

% Opening the case

```
can( open_case, [ camera_in_case] ).
add( open_case, [ camera_outside_case] ).
del( open_case, [ camera_in_case] ).
```

% Closing the case

```
can( close_case, [ camera_outside_case, slot_closed( film), slot_closed( battery)] ).
add( close_case, [ camera_in_case] ).
del( close_case, [ camera_outside_case] ).
```

% Opening a slot (either film slot or battery slot)

```
can( open_slot( X), [ camera_outside_case, slot_closed( X)] ).
add( open_slot( X), [ slot_open( X)] ).
del( open_slot( X), [ slot_closed( X)] ).
```

% Closing a slot

```
can( close_slot( X), [ camera_outside_case, slot_open( X)] ).
add( close_slot( X), [ slot_closed( X)] ).
del( close_slot( X), [ slot_open( X)] ).
```

% Rewinding film

```
can( rewind, [ camera_outside_case, in( film), film_at_end] ).
add( rewind, [ film_at_start] ).
del( rewind, [ film_at_end] ).
```

% Removing battery or film

```
can( remove( battery), [ slot_open( battery), in( battery)] ).
can( remove( film), [ slot_open( film), in( film), film_at_start] ).
add( remove( X), [ slot_empty( X)] ).
del( remove( X), [ in( X)] ).
```

% Inserting new battery or film

```
can( insert_new( X), [ slot_open( X), slot_empty( X)] ).
add( insert_new( battery), [ in( battery), ok( battery)] ).
add( insert_new( film), [ in( film), film_at_start, film_unused] ).
del( insert_new( X), [ slot_empty( X)] ).
```

(continues)

Figure 16.3 (cont.)

% Taking pictures

can(take_pictures, [in(film), film_at_start, film_unused, in(battery), ok(battery),
                     slot_closed(film), slot_closed(battery)]).
add(take_pictures, [film_at_end]).
del(take_pictures, [film_at_start, film_unused]).

% A state with film used and battery weak (note: battery is
% assumed weak because ok(battery) is not included in the state)

state1([camera_in_case, slot_closed(film), slot_closed(battery), in(film),
       film_at_end, in(battery)]).

The goal of a plan is stated in terms of relationships that are to be established. For the blocks world task in Figure 16.1, the goal can be stated as the list of relationships:

> [on(a, b), on(b, c)]

For the camera problem, a goal list that ensures the camera is ready is:

> [in(film), film_at_start, film_unused, in(battery),
>   ok(battery), slot_closed(film), slot_closed(battery)]

In the next section we will show how such a representation can be used in a process known as 'means-ends analysis' by which a plan can be derived.

EXERCISES

16.1 Extend the blocks world definition of Figure 16.2 to include other types of objects, such as pyramids, balls and boxes. Add the corresponding extra condition 'safe-to-stack' in the **can** relation. For example, it is not safe to stack a block on a pyramid; a ball can be safely put into a box, but not on a block (it might roll off).

16.2 Define the planning space for the monkey and banana problem introduced in Chapter 2 where the actions are 'walk', 'push', 'climb' and 'grasp'.

16.2   Deriving plans by means-ends analysis

Consider the initial state of the planning problem in Figure 16.1. Let the goal be: on(a, b). The planner's problem is then to find a plan – that is, a sequence of actions – that achieves this goal. A typical planner would reason as follows:

(1)   Find an action that achieves on(a, b). By looking at the add relation, it is found that such an action has the form

   move(a, From, b)

for any From. Such an action will certainly have to be part of the plan, but we cannot execute it immediately in our initial state.

(2)   Now enable the action move(a, From, b). Look at the can relation to find the action's precondition. This is:

   [clear(a), clear(b), on(a, From)]

In the initial state we already have clear(b) and on(a, From) (where From = 1), but not clear(a). Now the planner concentrates on clear(a) as the new goal to be achieved.

(3)   Look at the add relation again to find an action that achieves clear(a). This is any action of the form

   move(Block, a, To)

The precondition for this action is:

   [clear(Block), clear(To), on(Block, a)]

This is satisfied in our initial situation if:

   Block = c   and   To = 2

So move(c, a, 2) can be executed in the initial state, resulting in a new state. This new state is obtained from the initial state by:

●   removing from the initial state all the relationships that the action move(c, a, 2) deletes;
●   adding to the resulting list all the relationships that the action adds.

This produces the list:

   [clear(a), clear(b), clear(c), clear(4), on(a, 1), on(b, 3), on(c, 2)]

Now the action move(a, 1, b) can be executed, which achieves the final goal on(a, b). The plan found can be written as the list:

   [move(c, a, 2), move(a, 1, b)]

This style of reasoning is called *means-ends analysis*. Notice that in the foregoing example a correct plan was found immediately, without any

Figure 16.4 The principle of means-ends planning.

backtracking. The example thus illustrates how the reasoning about goals and effects of actions directs the planning process in a proper direction. Unfortunately, it is not true that backtracking can always be avoided in this way. On the contrary, combinatorial complexity and search are typical of planning.

The principle of planning by means-ends analysis is illustrated in Figure 16.4. It can be stated as follows:

> To solve a list of goals **Goals** in state **State**, leading to state **FinalState**, do:
>
> If all the **Goals** are true in **State** then **FinalState** = **State**. Otherwise do the following steps:
>
> (1)   Select a still unsolved goal **Goal** in **Goals**.
>
> (2)   Find an action **Action** that adds **Goal** to the current state.
>
> (3)   Enable **Action** by solving the precondition **Condition** of **Action**, giving **MidState1**.
>
> (4)   Apply **Action** to **MidState1**, giving **MidState2** (in **MidState2**, **Goal** is true).
>
> (5)   Solve **Goals** in **MidState2**, leading to **FinalState**.

This is programmed in Prolog in Figure 16.5 as the procedure:

plan(State, Goals, Plan, FinalState)

Figure 16.5   A simple means-ends planner.

% A simple means-ends planner

% plan(InitialState, Goals, Plan, FinalState)

plan(State, Goals, [ ], State) :-
   satisfied(State, Goals).   % Goals true in State

Figure 16.5 (cont.)

```
% The way plan is decomposed into stages by conc, the precondition plan ( PrePlan)
% is found in breadth-first fashion. However, the length of the rest of plan is not restricted
% and goals are achieved in depth-first style.

plan( State, Goals, Plan, FinalState) :-
    conc( PrePlan, [Action | PostPlan], Plan),        % Divide plan
    select( State, Goals, Goal),                      % Select a goal
    achieves( Action, Goal),
    can( Action, Condition),
    plan( State, Condition, PrePlan, MidState1),
    apply( MidState1, Action, MidState2),
    plan( MidState2, Goals, PostPlan, FinalState).

% satisfied( State, Goals): Goals are true in State

satisfied( State, [ ]).

satisfied( State, [Goal | Goals]) :-
    member( Goal, State),                             % Usual list membership
    satisfied( State, Goals).

select( State, Goals, Goal) :-
    member( Goal, Goals),
    not member( Goal, State).                         % Goal not satisfied

% achieves( Action, Goal): Goal is in the add-list of Action

achieves( Action, Goal) :-
    add( Action, Goals),
    member( Goal, Goals).

% apply( State, Action, NewState):
%     Action executed in State produces NewState

apply( State, Action, NewState) :-
    del( Action, DelList),
    delete( State, DelList, State1), !,
    add( Action, AddList),
    conc( AddList, State1, NewState).

% delete( L1, L2, Diff): Diff is set-difference of lists L1 and L2

delete( [], _, [ ]).

delete( [X | L1], L2, Diff) :-
    member( X, L2), !,
    delete( L1, L2, Diff).

delete( [X | L1], L2, [X | Diff]) :-
    delete( L1, L2, Diff).
```

State and **FinalState** are the initial and final states of the plan respectively. **Goals** is the list of goals to be achieved and **Plan** is a list of actions that achieve the goals. It should be noted that this planning program assumes a definition of the planning space in which all the actions and goals are fully instantiated; that is, they do not contain any variables. Variables would require more complicated treatment.

The planner can now be used to find a plan for placing block *a* on *b*, starting in the initial state of Figure 16.1, as follows:

```
?- Start = [ clear( 2), clear( 4), clear( b), clear( c), on( a, 1), on( b, 3), on( c, a)],
   plan( Start, [ on( a, b)], Plan, FinState).

Plan = [ move( c, a, 2), move( a, 1, b)]
FinState = [ on( a, b), clear( 1), on( c, 2), clear( a), clear( 4), clear( c), on( b, 3)]
```

For the camera world, imagine an initial state with the battery weak and the film in the camera already used. Here are queries to find: a plan **FixBattery** to fix the battery; a plan **FixCamera** to get the camera ready for taking pictures:

```
?- Start = [ camera_in_case, slot_closed( film), slot_closed( battery), in( film),
            film_at_end, in( battery)],
   plan( Start, [ ok( battery)], FixBattery, _).

FixBattery = [ open_case, open_slot( battery), remove( battery),
              insert_new( battery)]


?- Start = [ camera_in_case, slot_closed( film), slot_closed( battery), in( film),
            film_at_end, in( battery)],
   can( take_pictures, CameraReady),      % Condition for taking pictures
   plan( Start, CameraReady, FixCamera, FinState).

CameraReady = [ in( film), film_at_start, film_unused, in( battery),
               ok( battery), slot_closed( film), slot_closed( battery)]

FixCamera = [ open_case, rewind, open_slot( film), remove( film),
             insert_new( film), open_slot( battery), remove( battery),
             insert_new( battery), close_slot( film), close_slot( battery)]

FinState = [ slot_closed( battery), slot_closed( film), in( battery), ok( battery),
            in( film), film_at_start, film_unused, camera_outside_case]
```

All this appears very smooth: the shortest plans are found in all cases. However, further experiments with our planner would reveal some difficulties. We will analyze the defects and introduce improvements in the next section.

16.3   Trace by hand the means-ends planning process for achieving on(a, 3) from the initial situation of Figure 16.1.

16.3   Protecting goals

If we try our planner on the blocks and camera worlds, it turns out that the blocks world is much more complex. This may appear surprising because the definition of the blocks world looks simpler than that of the camera world. The real reason for the greater difficulty of the blocks world lies in its higher combinatorial complexity. In the blocks world, the planner usually has more choice between several actions that all make sense with respect to the means-ends principle. More choice leads to higher combinatorial complexity. Experimenting with our planner on the blocks domain is thus more critical and can reveal several defects of the planner.

Let us try the task in Figure 16.1. Suppose that Start is a description of the initial state in Figure 16.1. Then the task of Figure 16.1 can be stated as the goal:

plan(Start, [on(a, b), on(b, c)], Plan, _)

The plan found by the planner is:

Plan = [move(b, 3, c),
         move(b, c, 3),
         move(c, a, 2),
         move(a, 1, b),
         move(a, b, 1),
         move(b, 3, c),
         move(a, 1, b)]

This plan containing seven steps is not exactly the most elegant! The shortest possible plan for this task only needs three steps. Let us analyze why our planner needs so many. The reason is that it pursues different goals at different stages of planning, as follows:

move(b, 3, c)	to achieve goal on(b, c)
move(b, c, 3)	to achieve clear(c) to enable next move
move(c, a, 2)	to achieve clear(a) to enable move(a, 1, b)
move(a, 1, b)	to achieve goal on(a, b)
move(a, b, 1)	to achieve clear(b) to enable move(b, 3, c)
move(b, 3, c)	to achieve goal on(b, c) (again)
move(a, 1, b)	to achieve goal on(a, b) (again)

The defect revealed here is that the planner sometimes destroys goals that have already been achieved. The planner easily achieved one of the two given goals, on(b, c), but then destroyed it immediately when it started to work on the other goal on(a, b). Then it attempted the goal on(b, c) again. This was re-achieved in two moves, but on(a, b) was destroyed in the meantime. Luckily, on(a, b) was then re-achieved without destroying on(b, c) again. This rather disorganized behaviour leads, even more drastically, to total failure in the next example:

    plan(Start, [clear(2), clear(3)], Plan, _)

The planner now indefinitely keeps extending the following sequence of moves:

    move(b, 3, 2)   to achieve clear(3)
    move(b, 2, 3)   to achieve clear(2)
    move(b, 3, 2)   to achieve clear(3)
    move(b, 2, 3)   to achieve clear(2)
    ...

Each move achieves one of the goals and at the same time destroys the other one. The planning space is unfortunately defined so that the places 2 and 3 are always considered first in moving *b* from its current position to a new position.

One idea that is obvious from the foregoing examples is that the planner should try to preserve the goals that have already been achieved. This can be done by maintaining the list of already achieved goals and, in the sequel, avoiding those actions that destroy goals in this list. Thus, we introduce a new argument into our **plan** relation:

    plan(State, Goals, ProtectedGoals, Plan, FinalState)

Here **ProtectedGoals** is a list of goals that **Plan** 'protects'. That is, no action in **Plan** may delete any of the goals in **ProtectedGoals**. Once a new goal is achieved, it is added to the list of protected goals. The program in Figure 16.6 is a modification of the planner of Figure 16.5 with goal protection introduced. The task of clearing 2 and 3 is now solved by a two-step plan:

    move(b, 3, 2)   achieving clear(3)
    move(b, 2, 4)   achieving clear(2) while protecting clear(3)

This is now clearly better than before, although still not optimal because only one move is really necessary: move(b, 3, 4).

Unnecessarily long plans result from the search strategy that our planner uses. To optimize the length of plans, the search behaviour of the planner should be studied. This will be done in the next section.

% A means-ends planner with goal protection

```
plan( InitialState, Goals, Plan, FinalState) :-
   plan( InitialState, Goals, [ ], Plan, FinalState).
```

% plan(InitialState, Goals, ProtectedGoals, Plan, FinalState):
%   Goals true in FinalState, ProtectedGoals never destroyed by Plan

```
plan( State, Goals, _, [ ], State) :-
   satisfied( State, Goals).                        % Goals true in State

plan( State, Goals, Protected, Plan, FinalState) :-
   conc( PrePlan, [Action | PostPlan], Plan),       % Divide plan
   select( State, Goals, Goal),                      % Select an unsatisfied goal
   achieves( Action, Goal),
   can( Action, Condition),
   preserves( Action, Protected),                    % Do not destroy protected goals
   plan( State, Condition, Protected, PrePlan, MidState1),
   apply( MidState1, Action, MidState2),
   plan( MidState2, Goals, [Goal | Protected], PostPlan, FinalState).
```

% preserves(Action, Goals):
%   Action does not destroy any one of Goals

```
preserves( Action, Goals) :-
   del( Action, Relations),
   not ( member( Goal, Relations),
         member( Goal, Goals) ).
```

Figure 16.6   A means-ends planner with goal protection. Predicates **satisfied**, **select**, **achieves** and **apply** are defined as in Figure 16.5.

16.4   Procedural aspects and breadth-first regime

The planners in Figures 16.5 and 16.6 use essentially depth-first search strategies, although not entirely. To get a clear insight into what is going on, we have to find in what order candidate plans are generated by the planner. The goal

conc(PrePlan, [Action | PostPlan], Plan)

in procedure **plan** is important in this respect. **Plan** is not yet instantiated at this point and **conc** generates, through backtracking, alternative candidates for **PrePlan** in the following order:

```
PrePlan = [ ];
PrePlan = [ _ ];
PrePlan = [ _, _ ];
PrePlan = [ _, _, _ ];
...
```

Short candidates for **PrePlan** come first. **PrePlan** establishes a precondition for **Action**. This entails the finding of an action whose precondition can be achieved by as short a plan as possible (in simulated breadth-first fashion). On the other hand, the candidate list for **PostPlan** is completely uninstantiated, and thus its length is unlimited. Therefore, the resulting search behaviour is 'globally' depth first and 'locally' breadth first. It is depth-first search with respect to the forward chaining of actions that are appended to the emerging plan. Each action is enabled by a 'preplan'. This preplan is, on the other hand, found in the breadth-first fashion.

One way of minimizing the length of plans is to force the planner into the breadth-first regime so that *all* alternative short plans are considered before any longer one. We can impose this strategy by embedding our planner into a procedure that generates candidate plans in the order of increasing length; for example:

```
breadth_first_plan( State, Goals, Plan, FinalState) :-
    candidate( Plan),                          % Generate short candidates first
    plan( State, Goals, Plan, FinalState).

candidate( [ ]).

candidate( [First | Rest]) :-
    candidate( Rest).
```

More elegantly, the same effect can be programmed by inserting a corresponding candidate plan generator directly into our **plan** procedure. Such a suitable generator is simply

```
conc( Plan, _, _ )
```

which through backtracking generates lists of increasing length. Our planner of Figure 16.5 then becomes modified as follows:

```
plan( State, Goals, Plan, FinState) :-
    conc( Plan, _, _ ),                        % Generate short candidates first
    conc( PrePlan, [Action | PostPlan], Plan),
    ...
```

Similar modification also brings the goal-protecting planner of Figure 16.6 into the breadth-first regime.

Let us try our modified planners, working now in the breadth-first regime, on our two example tasks. Assuming that Start is the initial situation of Figure 16.1, the goal

plan(Start, [clear(2), clear(3)], Plan, _)

produces:

Plan = [move(b, 3, 4)]

This is now optimal. But the task of Figure 16.1 will still be somewhat problematical. The goal

plan(Start, [on(a, b), on(b, c)], Plan, _)

produces the plan:

move(c, a, 2)
move(b, 3, a)
move(b, a, c)
move(a, 1, b)

We get this result with both of the planners, with or without protection, working in the breadth-first regime. The second move above is superfluous and apparently makes no sense. Let us investigate how it came to be included in the plan at all and why even the breadth-first search resulted in a plan longer than optimal.

We have to answer two questions. First, what reasoning led the planner to construct the funny plan above? Second, why did the planner not find the optimal plan in which the mysterious move(b, 3, a) is not included. Let us start with the first question. The last move, move(a, 1, b), achieves the goal on(a, b). The first three moves achieve the precondition for move(a, 1, b), in particular the condition clear(a). The third move clears *a*, and part of the precondition for the third move is on(b, a). This is achieved by the second move, move(b, 3, a). The first move clears *a* to enable the second move. This explains the reasoning behind our awkward plan and also illustrates what sort of exotic ideas may appear during means-ends planning.

The second question is: Why after move(c, a, 2) did the planner not immediately consider move(b, 3, c), which leads to the optimal plan? The reason is that the planner was working on the goal on(a, b) all the time. The action move(b, 3, c) is completely superfluous to this goal and hence not tried. Our four-step plan achieves on(a, b) and, by chance, also on(b, c). So on(b, c) is a result of pure luck and not of any conscious effort by the planner. Blindly pursuing just the goal on(a, b) and relevant preconditions, the planner saw no reason for move(b, 3, c) before move(b, 3, a).

It follows from the above example that the means-ends mechanism of planning as implemented in our planners is *incomplete*. It does not suggest all relevant actions to the planning process. The reason for this lies in its locality. The planner only considers those actions that pertain to the current goal and disregards other goals until the current goal is achieved. Therefore, it does not (unless by accident) produce plans in which actions that pertain to different goals are interleaved. The key question to completeness, thereby ensuring that optimal plans are within the planning scheme, is to enable interaction between different goals. This will be done in the next section through the mechanism of *goal regression*.

Before concluding this section, a note is needed regarding the efficiency of the depth-first and breadth-first planners discussed here. Although the breadth-first regime produced a much shorter plan for our example problem (although still suboptimal!), the computation time needed for this shorter plan is much longer than the time needed by the depth-first planner to find the longer seven-step plan. So the depth-first planner should not be considered *a priori* inferior to the breadth-first planner, even if it is inferior with respect to the length of plans. It should also be noted that the breadth-first effect was in our planners achieved through the technique of iterative deepening, discussed in Chapter 11.

EXERCISE

16.4 The natural places where domain-specific planning knowledge can be introduced into our planner are the predicates **select** and **achieves**. They select the next goal to be attempted (determining the order in which goals are achieved) and the action to be tried. Redefine these two predicates for the blocks world, so that the goals and actions are more intelligently selected. For this purpose, it is useful to add the current state **State** as an extra argument to the predicate **achieves**.

16.5   Goal regression

Suppose we are interested in a list of goals **Goals** being true in some state S. Let the state just before S be S0 and the action in S0 be A. Now let us ask the question: What goals **Goals0** have to be true in S0 to make **Goals** true in S?

$$\text{state S0: } \textbf{Goals0} \quad \xrightarrow{\quad A \quad} \quad \text{state S: } \textbf{Goals}$$

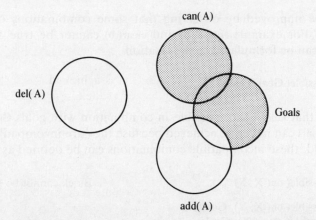

Figure 16.7   Relations between various sets of conditions in goal regression through action A. The shaded area represents the resulting regressed goals **Goals0**. Notice that the intersection between **Goals** and the delete-list of A must be empty.

Goals0 must have the following properties:

(1)   Action A must be possible in S0, therefore **Goals0** must imply the precondition for A.

(2)   For each goal G in **Goals** either

- action A adds G, or
- G is in **Goals0** and A does not delete G.

Determining **Goals0** from given **Goals** and action A will be called *regressing* **Goals** *through* action A. Of course, we are only interested in those actions that add some goal G in **Goals**. The relations between various sets of goals and conditions are illustrated in Figure 16.7.

The mechanism of goal regression can be used for planning in the following way:

> To achieve a list of goals **Goals** from some initial situation **StartState**, do:
>
> If **Goals** are true in **StartState** then the empty plan suffices;
>
> Otherwise select a goal G in **Goals** and an action A that adds G; then regress **Goals** through A obtaining **NewGoals** and find a plan for achieving **NewGoals** from **StartState**.

This can be improved by observing that some combinations of goals are impossible. For example, on(a, b) and clear(b) cannot be true at the same time. This can be formulated as the relation

impossible(Goal, Goals)

which says that Goal is not possible in combination with goals Goals; that is, Goal *and* Goals can never be achieved because they are incompatible. For our blocks world, these incompatible combinations can be defined as follows:

impossible(on(X, X), _).   % Block cannot be on itself

impossible(on(X, Y), Goals) :-
  member(clear(Y), Goals)
  ;
  member(on(X, Y1), Goals), Y1 \== Y   % Block cannot be in two places
  ;
  member(on(X1, Y), Goals), X1 \== X.   % Two blocks cannot be in same
                                          % place

impossible(clear(X), Goals) :-
  member(on(_, X), Goals).

A planner based on goal regression as outlined here is programmed in Figure 16.8. This program considers candidate plans in the breadth-first style when shorter plans are tried first. This is ensured by the goal

conc(PrePlan, [Action], Plan)

in the procedure plan. This planner finds the optimal, three-step plan for the problem of Figure 16.1.

EXERCISE

16.5 Trace the planning process, based on goal regression, for achieving on(a, b) from the initial situation of Figure 16.1. Suppose the plan is:

[move(c, a, 2), move(a, 1, b)]

If the goal-list after the second action of the plan is [on(a, b)], what are the regressed goal-lists before the second move and before the first move?

Figure 16.8   A planner based on goal regression. This planner searches in breadth-first style.

```
% A means-ends planner with goal regression

% plan( InitialState, Goals, Plan)

plan( State, Goals, [ ]) :-
    satisfied( State, Goals).                              % Goals true in State

plan( State, Goals, Plan) :-
    conc( PrePlan, [Action], Plan),                       % Divide plan achieving breadth-first effect
    select( State, Goals, Goal),                          % Select a goal
    achieves( Action, Goal),
    can( Action, Condition),                              % Ensure Action contains no variables
    preserves( Action, Goals),                            % Protect Goals
    regress( Goals, Action, RegressedGoals),              % Regress Goals through Action
    plan( State, RegressedGoals, PrePlan).

satisfied( State, Goals) :-
    delete( Goals, State, [ ]).                           % All Goals in State

select( State, Goals, Goal) :-                            % Select Goal from Goals
    member( Goal, Goals).                                 % A simple selection principle

achieves( Action, Goal) :-
    add( Action, Goals),
    member( Goal, Goals).

preserves( Action, Goals) :-                              % Action does not destroy Goals
    del( Action, Relations),
    not ( member( Goal, Relations),
        member( Goal, Goals) ).

regress( Goals, Action, RegressedGoals) :-               % Regress Goals through Action
    add( Action, NewRelations),
    delete( Goals, NewRelations, RestGoals),
    can( Action, Condition),
    addnew( Condition, RestGoals, RegressedGoals).        % Add precondition, check imposs.

% addnew( NewGoals, OldGoals, AllGoals):
%     AllGoals is the union of NewGoals and OldGoals,
%     NewGoals and OldGoals must be compatible

addnew( [ ], L, L).

addnew( [Goal | _], Goals, _) :-
    impossible( Goal, Goals),                             % Goal incompatible with Goals
    !,
    fail.                                                 % Cannot be added

addnew( [X | L1], L2, L3) :-
    member( X, L2), !,                                    % Ignore duplicate
    addnew( L1, L2, L3).
```

(continues)

Figure 16.8 (cont.)

```
addnew( [X | L1], L2, [X | L3]) :-
  addnew( L1, L2, L3).

% delete( L1, L2, Diff): Diff is set-difference of lists L1 and L2

delete( [ ], _, [ ]).

delete( [X | L1], L2, Diff) :-
  member( X, L2), !,
  delete( L1, L2, Diff).

delete( [X | L1], L2, [X | Diff]) :-
  delete( L1, L2, Diff).
```

16.6 Combining means-ends planning with best-first heuristic

The planners developed thus far only use very basic search strategies: depth-first or breadth-first search or a combination of these two. These strategies are completely uninformed in the sense that they do not use any domain-specific knowledge in choosing among alternatives. Consequently, they are in principle very inefficient, except in some special cases. There are several ways of introducing heuristic guidance, based on domain knowledge, into our planners. Some obvious places where domain-specific planning knowledge can be introduced into the planners are as follows:

- relation select(State, Goals, Goal) which decides in what order the goals are attempted. For example, a piece of useful knowledge about building block structures is that, at any time, everything has to be properly supported, and therefore structures have to be built in the bottom-up order. A heuristic selection rule based on this would say: the 'top-most' **on** relations should be achieved last (that is, they should be selected first by the goal regression planner as it builds plans backwards). Another heuristic would suggest that the selection of those goals that are already true in the initial situation should be deferred.

- relation achieves(Action, Goal) which decides which alternative action will be tried to achieve the given goal. (In fact, our planners also generate alternatives when executing the **can** predicate, when actions become instantiated.) Some actions seem better, for example, because they achieve several goals simultaneously; alternatively, through experience, we may be able to tell that some action's precondition will be easier to satisfy than others.

- decision about which of the alternative regressed goal sets to consider next: continue working on the one that looks easiest, because that one will be probably accomplished by the shortest plan.

This last possibility shows how we can impose the best-first search regime on our planner. This involves heuristically estimating the difficulty of alternative goal sets and then continuing to expand the most promising alternative goal set.

To use our best-first search program of Chapter 12, we have to specify the corresponding state space and a heuristic function; that is, we have to define the following:

(1)   A successor relation between the nodes in the state space
        s(Node1, Node2, Cost).

(2)   The goal nodes of the search by relation goal(Node).

(3)   A heuristic function by relation h(Node, HeuristicEstimate).

(4)   The start node of the search.

One way of formulating the state space is for goal sets to correspond to nodes in the state space. Then, in the state space there will be a link between two goal sets Goals1 and Goals2 if there is an action A such that

(1)   A adds some goal in Goals1,

(2)   A does not destroy any goal in Goals1, and

(3)   Goals2 is a result of regressing Goals1 through action A, as already defined by relation regress in Figure 16.8:

    regress(Goals1, A, Goals2)

For simplicity we will assume that all the actions have the same cost, and will accordingly assign cost 1 to all the links in the state space. Thus the successor relation will look something like this:

```
s( Goals1, Goals2, 1) :-
    member( Goal, Goals1),          % Select a goal
    achieves( Action, Goal),        % A relevant action
    can( Action, Condition),
    preserves( Action, Goals1),
    regress( Goals1, Action, Goals2).
```

Any goal set that is true in the initial situation of the plan is a goal node of the state-space search. The start node for search is the list of goals to be achieved by the plan.

Although the representation above contains all the essential information, it has a small deficiency. This is due to the fact that our best-first search program finds a solution path as a sequence of states and does not include actions between states. For example, the sequence of states (goal-lists) for achieving on(a, b) in the initial situation in Figure 16.1 is:

[[clear(c), clear(2), on(c, a), clear(b), on(a, 1)],	% True in initial situation
[clear(a), clear(b), on(a, 1)],	% True after move(c, a, 2)
[on(a, b)]]	% True after move(a, 1, b)

Notice that the best-first program returns the solution path in the inverse order. In our case this is in fact an advantage because plans are built in the backward direction, so the inverse sequence returned by the search program corresponds to the actual order in the plan. It is, however, awkward that the actions are not explicitly mentioned in the plan, although they could be reconstructed from the differences in the given goal-lists. But we can easily get actions explicitly into the solution path. We only have to add, to each state, the action that follows the state. So nodes of the state space become pairs of the form:

Goals −> Action

The state-space implementation in Figure 16.9 contains this representational detail. This implementation uses a very crude heuristic function. This is simply the number of yet unsatisfied goals in the goal-list.

% State-space representation of means-ends planning with goal regression

```
:- op( 300, xfy, −>).

s( Goals −> NextAction, NewGoals −> Action, 1) :-        % All costs are 1
    member( Goal, Goals),
    achieves( Action, Goal),
    can( Action, Condition),
    preserves( Action, Goals),
    regress( Goals, Action, NewGoals).

goal( Goals −> Action)  :-
    start( State),                                       % User-defined initial situation
    satisfied( State, Goals).                            % Goals true in initial situation

h( Goals −> Action, H)  :-                               % Heuristic estimate
    start( State),
    delete( Goals, State, Unsatisfied),                  % Unsatisfied goals
    length( Unsatisfied, H).                             % Number of unsatisfied goals
```

Figure 16.9 A state-space definition for means-ends planning based on goal regression. Relations **satisfied**, **achieves**, **preserves**, **regress**, **addnew** and **delete** are as defined in Figure 16.8.

The state-space definition in Figure 16.9 can now be used by the best-first program of Chapter 12 as follows. We have to consult the planning problem definition in terms of relations **add**, **del** and **can** (Figure 16.2 for the blocks world). We also have to supply the relation **impossible** and the relation **start**, which describes the initial situation of the plan. For the situation in Figure 16.1, this is:

> start([on(a, 1), on(b, 3), on(c, a), clear(b), clear(c), clear(2), clear(4)].

To solve the task of Figure 16.1 by our means-ends best-first planner, we can now call the best-first procedure by:

> ?- bestfirst([on(a, b), on(b, c)] −> stop, Plan).

The null action **stop** is added here because in our representation each goal-list must be followed, at least syntactically, by an action. But [on(a, b), on(b, c)] is the final goal-list of the plan which is not actually followed by any action. The solution is presented by the following list of goal-lists and actions between them:

> Plan = [
> [clear(2), on(c, a), clear(c), on(b, 3), clear(b), on(a, 1)] −> move(c, a, 2),
> [clear(c), on(b, 3), clear(a), clear(b), on(a, 1)] −> move(b, 3, c),
> [clear(a), clear(b), on(a, 1), on(b, c)] −> move(a, 1, b),
> [on(a, b), on(b, c)] −> stop]

Although this best-first planner uses the simple-minded heuristic estimates, it is fast compared with our other planners. On the other hand, in general it requires more memory than the others because it has to maintain the possibly large set of current competing alternatives.

EXERCISES

16.6 Consider the simple-minded heuristic function for the blocks world of Figure 16.9. Does this function satisfy the condition of the admissibility theorem for best-first search? (See Chapter 12 for the admissibility theorem.)

16.7 The example heuristic function for the blocks world developed in this chapter simply counts the goals to be achieved. This is very crude as some goals are clearly more difficult than others. For example, it is trivial to achieve on(a, b) if blocks *a* and *b* are already clear, whereas it is difficult if *a* and *b* are buried under high stacks of other blocks.

Therefore, a better heuristic function would try to estimate the difficulty of individual goals – for example, take into account the number of blocks to be removed before the block of interest could be moved. Propose such better heuristic functions and experiment with them.

16.8 Modify the planning state-space definition of Figure 16.9 to introduce the cost of actions:

   s(State1, State2, Cost)

The cost can, for example, depend on the weight of the object moved and the distance by which it is moved. Use this definition to find minimal cost plans in the blocks world.

16.7 Further refinements: uninstantiated actions and non-linear planning

The planners developed in this chapter are implemented in programs made as simple as possible to illustrate the principles. No thought has been given to their efficiency. By choosing better representations and corresponding data structures, significant improvements in efficiency are possible. Our planners can also be enhanced by two other essential mechanisms: allowing uninstantiated variables in goals and actions, and non-linear planning. They are briefly discussed in this section.

16.7.1 Uninstantiated actions and goals

All our algorithms were greatly simplified by the requirement that all the goals for the planner should always be completely instantiated. This requirement was attained by a proper definition of the planning space (relations **add**, **del** and **can**). In Figure 16.2, for example, the complete instantiation of variables is forced by the **can** relation, defined as:

   can(move(Block, From, To), [clear(Block), clear(To), on(Block, From)]) :-
       block(Block),
       object(To),
       ...

Goals like **block(Block)** above force the instantiation of variables. This may lead to the generation of numerous irrelevant alternative moves that are considered by the planner. For example, consider the situation in Figure 16.1 when the planner is asked to achieve the goal **clear(a)**. The relation **achieves** proposes this general move to achieve **clear(a)**:

>   move(Something, a, Somewhere)

Then the precondition is found by:

>   can(move(Something, a, Somewhere), Condition)

This forces, through backtracking, various alternative instantiations of **Something** and **Somewhere**. So all the following moves are considered before the one that works is found:

>   move(b, a, 1)
>   move(b, a, 2)
>   move(b, a, 3)
>   move(b, a, 4)
>   move(b, a, c)
>   move(c, a, 1)
>   move(c, a, 2)

A more powerful representation that avoids this inefficiency would allow uninstantiated variables in goals. For the blocks world, for example, one attempt to define such an alternative relation **can** would be simply:

>   can(move(Block, From, To), [clear(Block), clear(To), on(Block, From)]).

Now consider the situation in Figure 16.1 and the goal **clear(a)** again. Relation **achieves** again proposes the action:

>   move(Something, a, Somewhere)

This time, when **can** is evaluated, the variables remain uninstantiated, and the precondition list is:

>   [clear(Something), clear(Somewhere), on(Something, a)]

Notice that this goal-list, which the planner now has to attempt, contains variables. The goal-list is satisfied immediately in the initial situation if:

>   Something = c
>   Somewhere = 2

The key to this improvement in efficiency, where the right move was found virtually without search, is that uninstantiated moves and goals stand for *sets* of alternative moves and goals. Their instantiation is deferred until later, when it becomes clear what their values should be. On the other hand, the specification in Figure 16.2 forces immediate instantiation of actions and thereby also goals in action preconditions.

The foregoing example demonstrates the power of representation with variables. However, this method is not without complications. First, the foregoing attempt to define **can** is inadequate because it allows, in the situation of Figure 16.1, the move:

move(c, a, c)

As a result we get a situation where block *c* is on itself! Thus, a better definition of **can** would not allow a block to be moved to itself, as well as other similar restrictions. Here is such a definition:

```
can( move( Block, From, To),
    [ clear( Block), clear( To), on( Block, From), different( Block, To),
        different( From, To), different( Block, From)] ).
```

Here **different(X, Y)** means that X and Y do not denote the same object. A condition like **different(X, Y)** does not depend on the state of the world. So it cannot be made true by an action, but it has to be checked by evaluating the corresponding predicate. One way to handle such quasi goals is to add the following extra clause to the procedure **satisfied** in our planners:

```
satisfied( State, [Goal | Goals]) :-
    holds( Goal),                      % Goal independent of State
    satisfied( State, Goals).
```

Accordingly, predicates like **different(X, Y)** would have to be defined by the procedure **holds**:

```
holds( different( X, Y))
```

This definition could be along the following lines:

- If X and Y do not match then **different(X, Y)** holds.
- If X and Y are literally the same (X == Y) then this condition is false, and it will always be false regardless of further actions in the plan. Such conditions could then be handled in a similar way as goals declared in the relation **impossible**.
- Otherwise (X and Y match, but are not literally the same), we cannot tell at the moment. The decision whether they denote the same object or not should be postponed until X and Y become further instantiated.

As illustrated by this example, the evaluation of conditions like **different(X, Y)** that are independent of the state sometimes has to be deferred. Therefore, it would be practical to maintain such conditions as an extra argument of the procedure **plan** and handle them separately from those goals that are achieved by actions.

This is not the only complication introduced by variables. For example, consider the move:

move(a, 1, X)

Does this move delete the relation clear(b)? Yes, if X = b, and not, if different(X, b). This means that we have two possibilities, and the corresponding two alternatives are associated with the value of X: in one alternative, X is equal b; in the other, an extra condition different(X, Y) is added.

16.7.2   Non-linear planning

One deficiency of our planners is that they consider all possible orderings of actions even when the actions are completely independent. As an example, consider the planning task of Figure 16.10 where the goal is to build two stacks of blocks from two disjoint sets of blocks that are already well separated. The two stacks can be built independently of each other by two plans, one for each stack:

Plan1 = [move(b, a, c), move(a, 1, b)]
Plan2 = [move(e, d, f), move(d, 8, e)]

The important point is that these two plans do not interact with each other. Therefore, only the order of actions *within* each plan is important; it does not matter in which order they are executed – first P1 and then P2, or first P2 and then P1, or it is even possible to switch between them and execute a bit of one and then a bit of the other. For example, this is an admissible execution sequence:

[move(b, a, c), move(e, d, f), move(d, 8, e), move(a, 1, b)]

In spite of this, our planners would, in the planning process, potentially consider all 24 permutations of the four actions, although there are essentially

Figure 16.10   A planning task consisting of two independent subtasks.

only four alternatives – two permutations for each of the two constituent plans. This problem arises from the fact that our planners strictly insist on *complete* ordering of actions in a plan. An improvement then would be to allow, in the cases that the order does not matter, the precedence between actions to remain unspecified. Thus our plans would be *partially ordered sets* of actions, instead of totally ordered sequences. Planners that allow partial ordering are called *non-linear planners*.

Let us look at the main idea of non-linear planning by considering the example of Figure 16.1 again. The following is a sketch of how a non-linear planner may solve this problem. Analyzing the goals on(a, b) and on(b, c), the planner concludes that the following two actions will necessarily have to be included into the plan:

> M1 = move(a, X, b)
> M2 = move(b, Y, c)

There is no other way of achieving the two goals. But the order in which these two actions are to be executed is not yet specified. Now consider the preconditions of the two actions. The precondition for move(a, X, b) contains clear(a). This is not satisfied in the initial situation; therefore, we need an action of the form:

> M3 = move(U, a, V)

This has to precede the move M1, so we now have a constraint on the order of the actions:

> before(M3, M1)

Now we see if M2 and M3 can be the same move that achieves the objectives of both. This is not the case, so the plan will have to include three different moves. Now the planner has to answer the question: Is there a permutation of the three moves [M1, M2, M3] such that M3 precedes M1, the permutation is executable in the initial situation and the overall goals are satisfied in the resulting state. Due to the precedence constraint, only three out of altogether six permutations are taken into account:

> [M3, M1, M2]
> [M3, M2, M1]
> [M2, M3, M1]

The second of these satisfies the execution constraint by the instantiation: $U = c$, $V = 2$, $X = 1$, $Y = 3$. As can be seen from this example, the combinatorial complexity cannot be completely avoided by non-linear planning, but it can be alleviated.

Figure 16.11   A planning task in another blocks world:
Achieve on(a, c), on(b, c), on(c, d).

Projects

Develop a program, using the techniques of this chapter, for planning in a more interesting variation of the simple blocks world used throughout this chapter. Figure 16.11 shows an example task in this new world. The new world contains blocks of different sizes and the stability of structures has to be taken into account. To make the problem easier, assume that blocks can only be placed at whole-numbered positions, and they always have to be properly supported, so that they are safely stable. Also assume that they are never rotated by the robot and the move trajectories are simple: straight up until the block is above any other block, then horizontally, and then straight down. Design specialized heuristics to be used by this planner.

A robot world, more realistic and interesting than the one defined in Figure 16.2, would also comprise perception actions by a camera or touch sensor. For example, the action look(Position, Object) would recognize the object seen by the camera at Position (that is, instantiate variable Object). In such a world it is realistic to assume that the scene is not completely known to the robot, so it will possibly include, in its plan, actions whose only purpose is to acquire information. This can be further complicated by the fact that some measurements of this kind cannot be done immediately, as some objects cannot be seen (bottom objects cannot be seen by a top-view camera). Introduce other relevant goal relations and modify our planners if necessary.

Modify the goal regression planner of Figure 16.8 so that it will correctly handle variables in goals and actions, according to the discussion in Section 16.7.1.

Write a non-linear planner according to the outline in Section 16.7.2.

SUMMARY

- In planning, available actions are represented in a way that enables explicit reasoning about their effects and their preconditions. This can be done by stating, for each action, its precondition, its add-list (relationships the action establishes) and delete-list (relationships the action destroys).

- Means-ends derivation of plans is based on finding actions that achieve given goals and enabling the preconditions for such actions.

- *Goal protection* is a mechanism that prevents a planner destroying goals already achieved.

- Means-ends planning involves search through the space of relevant actions. The usual search techniques therefore apply to planning as well: depth-first, breadth-first and best-first search.

- To reduce search complexity, domain-specific knowledge can be used at several stages of means-ends planning, such as: which goal in the given goal-list should be attempted next; which action among the alternative actions should be tried first; heuristically estimating the difficulty of a goal-list in best-first search.

- Goal regression is a process that determines what goals have to be true before an action, to ensure that given goals are true after the action. Planning with goal regression typically involves backward chaining of actions.

- Allowing uninstantiated variables in goals and actions can make planning more efficient; however, on the other hand, it significantly complicates the planner.

- Non-linear planning recognizes the fact that actions in plans need not be always totally ordered. Leaving the order unspecified whenever possible allows economical treatment of sets of equivalent permutations of actions.

- Concepts discussed in this chapter are:

  action precondition, add-list, delete-list
  means-ends principle of planning
  goal protection
  goal regression
  non-linear planning

References

The early studies of basic ideas of means-ends problem solving and planning in Artificial Intelligence were done by Newell, Shaw and Simon (1960). These ideas were implemented in the celebrated program GPS (General Problem Solver) whose behaviour is studied in detail in Ernst and Newell (1969). Another well-known planning program is STRIPS (Fikes and Nilsson 1971) which can be viewed as an implementation of GPS. STRIPS introduced the representation of the planning space in the style of the relations **add**, **del** and **can**, which is also used in this chapter. The mechanisms of STRIPS, and various related ideas and refinements, are described in Nilsson (1980), where the elegant formulations of planning in logic by Green and Kowalski are also presented. Warren's (1974) program WARPLAN is an early interesting planner written in Prolog. It can be viewed as another implementation of STRIPS, refined in a certain respect. The WARPLAN program appeared in other places in the literature – for example, in Coelho and Cotta (1988). Waldinger (1977) studied phenomena of interaction among conjunctive goals, among them also the principle of goal regression. Difficulties that a planner with goal protection may have with the problem of Figure 16.1 are known in the literature as the Sussman anomaly (see, for example, Waldinger 1977). Early developments of non-linear planning are Sacerdoti (1977) and Tate (1977). Chapman (1987) is an attempt to provide a uniform theoretical framework for describing and investigating various mechanisms in non-linear planning proposed by different authors. Guaranteed completeness of a planner is theoretically desirable, but its price in terms of combinatorial complexity seems to be too high. Therefore, a practically more promising approach is one by Clark (1985) who studied various ways of introducing domain-specific knowledge into a planner to reduce combinatorial complexity.

Chapman, D. (1987) Planning for conjunctive goals. *Artificial Intelligence* **32**: 333–377.

Clark, P. (1985) *Towards an Improved Domain Representation for Planning*. Edinburgh University: Department of Artificial Intelligence, M.Sc. Thesis.

Coelho, H. and Cotta, J.C. (1988) *Prolog by Example*. Springer-Verlag.

Ernst, G.W. and Newell, A. (1969) *GPS: A Case Study in Generality and Problem Solving*. New York: Academic Press.

Fikes, R.E. and Nilsson, N.J. (1971) STRIPS: a new approach to the application of theorem proving to problem solving. *Artificial Intelligence* **2**: 189–208.

Newell, A., Shaw, J.C. and Simon, H.A. (1960) Report on a general problem-solving program for a computer. *Information Processing: Proc. Int. Conf. on Information Processing*. Paris: UNESCO.

Nilsson, N.J. (1980) *Principles of Artificial Intelligence*. Palo Alto: Tioga; also Springer-Verlag.

Sacerdoti, E.D. (1977) *A Structure for Plans and Behavior*. New York: Elsevier.

Tate, A. (1977) Generating project networks. *Proc. IJCAI 77*. Cambridge, Massachusetts.

Waldinger, R.J. (1977) Achieving several goals simultaneously. In: *Machine Intelligence* **8** (E.W. Elcock, D. Michie, eds.). Chichester: Ellis Horwood. Distributed by Wiley.

Warren, D.H.D. (1974) *WARPLAN: A System for Generating Plans*. University of Edinburgh: Department of Computational Logic, Memo 76.

17 Language Processing with Grammar Rules

17.1 Grammar rules in Prolog

17.2 Handling meaning

17.3 Defining the meaning of natural language

Many Prolog implementations provide a notational extension called DCG (definite clause grammars). This makes it very easy to implement formal grammars in Prolog. A grammar stated in DCG is directly executable by Prolog as a syntax analyzer. DCG also facilitates the handling of the semantics of a language so that the meaning of a sentence can be interleaved with the syntax. This chapter shows how DCG enables elegant definitions of the syntax and meaning of non-trivial natural language sentences, such as: 'Every woman that admires a man that paints likes Monet'.

17.1 Grammar rules in Prolog

Grammar is a formal device for defining sets of sequences of symbols. Such a sequence of symbols can be abstract, without any practical meaning, or, more interestingly, it can be a statement in a programming language, or a whole program; it can be a sentence in a natural language such as English.

One popular grammar notation is BNF (Backus-Naur form) which is commonly used in the definition of programming languages. We will start our discussion by considering BNF. A grammar comprises *production rules*. Here is a simple BNF grammar of two rules:

$$\langle s \rangle ::= a\ b$$
$$\langle s \rangle ::= a\ \langle s \rangle\ b$$

The first rule says: whenever the symbol *s* appears in a string, it can be rewritten with the sequence *ab*. The second rule says that *s* can be rewritten with the sequence *a*, followed by *s*, followed by *b*. In this grammar, *s* is always enclosed by brackets '⟨ ⟩'. This indicates that *s* is a *non-terminal* symbol of the grammar. On the other hand, *a* and *b* are *terminal* symbols. Terminal symbols can never be rewritten. In BNF, the two production rules above are normally written together as one rule:

$$\langle s \rangle ::= a\ b \mid a\ \langle s \rangle\ b$$

But for the purpose of this chapter we will be using the expanded, longer form.

A grammar can be used to *generate* a string of symbols, called a *sentence*. The generation process always starts with some starting non-terminal symbol, *s* in our example. Then symbols in the current sequence are replaced by other strings according to the grammar rules. The generation process terminates when the current sequence does not contain any non-terminal symbol. In our example grammar, the generation process can proceed as follows. Start with:

s

Now by the second rule, *s* is replaced by:

a s b

The second rule can be used again giving:

a a s b b

Applying the first rule, a sentence is finally produced:

$a\,a\,a\,b\,b\,b$

Obviously, our grammar can generate other sentences – for example, *ab*, *aabb*, etc. In general, this grammar generates strings of the form $a^n b^n$ for $n = 1, 2, 3, \ldots,$. The set of sentences, generated by a grammar, is called the *language* defined by the grammar.

Our example grammar is simple and very abstract. However, we can use grammars to define much more interesting languages. Formal grammars are used for defining programming languages and also subsets of natural languages.

Our next grammar is still very simple, but slightly less abstract. Suppose a robot arm can be sent sequences of commands:

up: move one step upwards, and
down: move one step downwards

Here are two examples of command sequences that such a robot would accept:

up
up up down up down

Such a sequence triggers the corresponding sequence of steps performed by the robot. We will call a sequence of steps a 'move'. A move, then, consists of one step, or a step followed by a move. This is captured by the following grammar:

$\langle move \rangle ::= \langle step \rangle$
$\langle move \rangle ::= \langle step \rangle \, \langle move \rangle$
$\langle step \rangle ::= up$
$\langle step \rangle ::= down$

We will use this grammar later to illustrate how the meaning can be handled within Prolog's grammar notation.

As shown earlier, a grammar generates sentences. In the opposite direction, a grammar can be used to *recognize* a given sentence. A recognizer decides whether a given sentence belongs to some language; that is, it recognizes whether the sentence can be generated by the corresponding grammar. The recognition process is essentially the inverse of generation. In recognition, the process starts with the given string of symbols, to which grammar rules are applied in the opposite direction to generation: if the current string contains a substring, equal to the right-hand side of some rule in the grammar, then this substring is rewritten with the left-hand side of this rule. The recognition process terminates successfully when the complete given sentence has been reduced to the starting non-terminal symbol of the grammar. If there is no way of reducing the given sentence to the starting non-terminal symbol, then the recognizer rejects the sentence.

In such a recognition process, the given sentence is effectively disassembled into its constituents; therefore, this process is often also called *parsing*. To implement a grammar, normally means to write a parsing program for the grammar. We will see that in Prolog such parsing programs can be written very easily. What makes this particularly elegant in Prolog is a special grammar rule notation, called DCG (definite clause grammar). Many Prolog implementations support this special notation for grammars. A grammar written in DCG is already a parsing program for this grammar. To transform a BNF grammar into DCG we only have to change some notational conventions. Our example BNF grammars can be written in DCG as follows:

```
s --> [ a], [ b].
s --> [ a], s, [ b].

move --> step.
move --> step, move.

step --> [ up].
step --> [ down].
```

Notice the differences between the BNF and DCG notations. ‘::=’ is replaced by ‘-->’. Non-terminals are not in brackets any more, but terminals are in square brackets, thereby making them Prolog lists. In addition, symbols are now separated by commas and each rule is terminated by a full stop as every Prolog clause.

In Prolog implementations that accept the DCG notation, our transformed grammars can be immediately used as recognizers of sentences. Such a recognizer expects sentences to be essentially represented as difference lists of terminal symbols. (Difference-list representation was introduced in Chapter 8.) So each sentence is represented by two lists: the sentence represented is the difference between both lists. The two lists are not unique, for example:

> *aabb* can be represented by lists [a, a, b, b] and [ ]
> or by lists [a, a, b, b, c] and [c]
> or by lists [a, a, b, b, 1, 0, 1] and [1, 0, 1]
> . . .

Taking into account this representation of sentences, our example DCG can be asked to recognize some sentences by questions:

```
?- s( [ a, a, b, b], [ ]).              % Recognize string aabb

yes
```

```
?- s( [ a, a, b], [ ]).
no

?- move( [ up, up, down], [ ]).
yes

?- move( [ up, up, left], [ ]).
no

?- move( [ up, X, up], [ ]).
X = up;
X = down;

no
```

Let us now explain *how* Prolog uses the given DCG to answer such questions. When Prolog consults grammar rules, it automatically converts them into normal Prolog clauses. In this way, Prolog converts the given grammar rules into a program for recognizing sentences generated by the grammar. The following example illustrates this conversion. Our four DCG rules about robot moves are converted into four clauses:

```
move( List, Rest) :-
    step( List, Rest).
move( List1, Rest) :-
    step( List1, List2),
    move( List2, Rest).
step( [up | Rest], Rest).
step( [down | Rest], Rest).
```

prolog

What is actually achieved by this conversion? Let us look at the **move** procedure. The relation **move** has two arguments – two lists:

```
move( List, Rest)
```

is true if the difference of the lists **List** and **Rest** is an acceptable move. Example relationships are

```
move( [ up, down, up], [ ]).
```

or

```
move( [ up, down, up, a, b, c], [ a, b, c])
```

or:

```
move( [ up, down, up], [ down, up])
```

Move → step, move

move → step, move.

Move → step

Figure 17.1 Relations between sequences of symbols.

Figure 17.1 illustrates what is meant by the clause:

        move(List1, Rest) :-
            step(List1, List2),
            move(List2, Rest).

The clause can be read as:

>   The difference of lists **List1** and **Rest** is a move if
>   the difference between **List1** and **List2** is a step and
>   the difference between **List2** and **Rest** is a move.

This also explains why difference-list representation is used: the pair
(**List1**, **Rest**) represents the concatenation of the lists represented by the pairs
(**List1**, **List2**) and (**List2**, **Rest**). As shown in Chapter 8, concatenating lists in
this way is much more efficient than with **conc**.

Now we are ready to formulate more generally the translation between
DCG and standard Prolog. Each DCG rule is translated into a Prolog clause
according to the following basic scheme: let the DCG rule be:

        n --> n1, n2, ..., nn.

If all **n1**, **n2**, ..., **nn** are non-terminals then the rule is translated into the
clause:

        n(List1, Rest) :-
            n1(List1, List2),
            n2(List2, List3),
            ...
            nn(Listn, Rest).

If some of **n1**, **n2**, ..., **nn** are terminals (in square brackets in the DCG rule) then it is handled differently. It does not appear as a goal in the clause, but is directly inserted into the corresponding list. As an example, consider the DCG rule:

> n --> n1, [t2], n3, [t4].

where **n1** and **n3** are non-terminals, and **t2** and **t4** are terminals. This is translated into the clause:

> n(List1, Rest) :-
>   n1(List1, [t2 | List3]),
>   n3(List3, [t4 | Rest]).

More interesting examples of grammars come from programming languages and natural languages. In both cases they can be elegantly implemented using DCG. Here is an example grammar for a simple subset of English:

> sentence --> noun_phrase, verb_phrase.
>
> verb_phrase --> verb, noun_phrase.
>
> noun_phrase --> determiner, noun.
>
> determiner --> [a].
> determiner --> [the].
>
> noun --> [cat].
> noun --> [mouse].
>
> verb --> [scares].
> verb --> [hates].

Example sentences generated by this grammar are:

> [the, cat, scares, a, mouse]
> [the, mouse, hates, the, cat]
> [the, mouse, scares, the, mouse]

Let us add nouns and verbs in plural to enable the generation of sentences like [the, mice, hate, the, cats]:

> noun --> [cats].
> noun --> [mice].
>
> verb --> [scare].
> verb --> [hate].

The grammar thus extended will generate the intended sentence. However, in addition, it will unfortunately also generate some unintended, incorrect English sentences, such as:

> [the, mouse, hate, the cat]

The problem lies in the rule:

> sentence --> noun_phrase, verb_phrase.

This states that *any* noun phrase and verb phrase can be put together to form a sentence. But in English and many other languages, the noun phrase and verb phrase in a sentence are not independent: they have to agree in number. Both have to be either singular or plural. This phenomenon is called *context dependence*. A phrase depends on the context in which it occurs. Context dependencies cannot be directly handled by BNF grammars, but they can be easily handled by DCG grammars, using an extension that DCG provides with respect to BNF – namely, *arguments* that can be added to non-terminal symbols of the grammar. For example, we may add 'number' as an argument of noun phrase and verb phrase:

> noun_phrase(Number)
>
> verb_phrase(Number)

With this argument added we can easily modify our example grammar to force number agreement between the noun phrase and verb phrase:

> sentence(Number) --> noun_phrase(Number), verb_phrase(Number).
>
> verb_phrase(Number) --> verb(Number), noun_phrase(Number1).
>
> noun_phrase(Number) --> determiner(Number), noun(Number).
>
> noun(singular) --> [mouse].
>
> noun(plural) --> [mice].
>
> ...

When DCG rules are read by Prolog and converted into Prolog clauses, the arguments of non-terminals are simply added to the usual two list arguments, with the convention that the two lists come last. Thus:

> sentence(Number) --> noun_phrase(Number), verb_phrase(Number).

is converted into:

> sentence(Number, List1, Rest) :-
>   noun_phrase(Number, List1, List2),
>   verb_phrase(Number, List2, Rest).

Questions to Prolog now have to be modified accordingly so that the extra arguments are included:

    ?- sentence(plural, [the, mice, hate, the, cats], [ ]).
    yes

    ?- sentence(plural, [the, mice, hates, the, cats], [ ]).
    no

    ?- sentence(plural, [the, mouse, hates, the, cat], [ ]).
    no

    ?- sentence(Number, [the, mouse, hates, the, cat], [ ]).
    Number = singular

    ?- sentence(singular, [the, What, hates, the, cat], [ ]).
    What = cat;
    What = mouse;
    no

EXERCISES

17.1 Translate into standard Prolog the DCG rule:

    s --> [a], s, [b].

17.2 Write a Prolog procedure

    translate(DCGrule, PrologClause)

that translates a given DCG rule into the corresponding Prolog clause.

17.3 One DCG rule in our grammar about robot moves is:

    move --> step, move.

If this rule is replaced by

    move --> move, step.

the language, defined by the so-modified grammar, is the same. However, the corresponding recognition procedure in Prolog is different. Analyze the difference. What is the advantage of the original grammar? How would the two grammars handle the question:

    ?- move([up, left], [ ]).

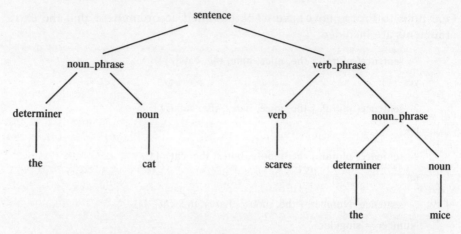

Figure 17.2 The parse tree of the sentence 'The cat scares the mice'.

17.2 Handling meaning

17.2.1 Constructing parse trees

Let us first illustrate by an example the concept of a *parse tree*. According to our example grammar, the sentence

[the, cat, scares, the, mice]

is parsed as shown by the parse tree of Figure 17.2. Some parts of the sentence are called *phrases* – those parts that correspond to non-terminals in the parse tree. In our example, [the, mice] is a phrase corresponding to the non-terminal **noun_phrase**; [scares, the, mice] is a phrase corresponding to **verb_phrase**. Figure 17.2 shows how the parse tree of a sentence contains, as subtrees, parse trees of phrases.

Here now is a definition of parse tree. The parse tree of a phrase is a tree with the following properties:

(1) All the leaves of the tree are labelled by terminal symbols of the grammar.

(2) All the internal nodes of the tree are labelled by non-terminal symbols; the root of the tree is labelled by the non-terminal that corresponds to the phrase.

(3) The parent-children relation in the tree is as specified by the rules of the grammar. For example, if the grammar contains the rule

s --> p, q, r.

then the tree may contain the node s whose children are p, q and r:

Sometimes it is useful to have the parse tree explicitly represented in the program to perform some computation on it – for example, to extract the meaning of a sentence. The parse tree can be easily constructed using arguments of non-terminals in the DCG notation. We can conveniently represent a parse tree by a Prolog term whose functor is the root of the tree and whose arguments are the subtrees of the tree. For example, the parse tree for the noun phrase 'the cat' would be represented as:

```
noun_phrase( determiner( the), noun( cat))
```

To generate a parse tree, a DCG grammar can be modified by adding to each non-terminal its parse tree as an argument. For example, the parse tree of a noun phrase in our grammar has the form:

```
noun_phrase( DetTree, NounTree)
```

Here **DetTree** and **NounTree** are the parse trees of a determiner and a noun respectively. Adding these parse trees as arguments into our noun phrase grammar rule results in the modified rule:

```
noun_phrase( noun_phrase( DetTree, NounTree)) -->
    determiner( DetTree), noun( NounTree).
```

This rule can be read as:

> A noun phrase whose parse tree is **noun_phrase(DetTree, NounTree)** consists of:
>
> - a determiner whose parse tree is **DetTree**, and
> - a noun whose parse tree is **NounTree**.

We can now modify our whole grammar accordingly. To ensure number agreement, we can retain the number as the first argument and add the parse tree as the second argument. Here is part of the modified grammar:

```
sentence( Number, sentence( NP, VP)) -->
    noun_phrase( Number, NP),
    verb_phrase( Number, VP).
```

```
verb_phrase( Number, verb_phrase( Verb, NP)) -->
    verb( Number, Verb),
    noun_phrase( Number1, NP).

noun_phrase( Number, noun_phrase( Det, Noun)) -->
    determiner( Det),
    noun( Number, Noun).

determiner( determiner( the)) --> [ the].

noun( singular, noun( cat)) --> [ cat].

noun( plural, noun( cats)) --> [ cats].
```

When this grammar is read by Prolog it is automatically translated into a standard Prolog program. The first grammar rule above is translated into the clause:

```
sentence( Number, sentence( NP, VP), List, Rest) :-
    noun_phrase( Number, NP, List, Rest0),
    verb_phrase( Number, VP, Rest0, Rest).
```

Accordingly, a question to Prolog to parse a sentence has to be stated in this format; for example:

```
?- sentence( Number, ParseTree, [ the, mice, hate, the, cat], [ ]).

Number = plural
ParseTree = sentence( noun_phrase( determiner( the), noun( mice)),
            verb_phrase( verb( hate), noun_phrase( determiner( the),
            noun( cat))))
```

17.2.2 From the parse tree to the meaning

Prolog grammars are particularly well suited for the treatment of the meaning of a language, in particular in natural languages. Arguments that are attached to non-terminal symbols of a grammar can be used to handle the meaning of sentences. One approach to extract the meaning involves two stages:

(1) Generate the parse tree of the given sentence.
(2) Process the parse tree to compute the meaning.

Of course this is only practical if the syntactic structure, represented by the parse tree, also reflects the semantic structure; that is, both the syntactic and semantic decomposition have similar structures. In such a case, the meaning of a sentence can be composed from the meanings of the syntactic phrases into which the sentence has been parsed.

A simple example will illustrate this two-stage method. For simplicity we will consider robot moves again. A grammar about robot moves that

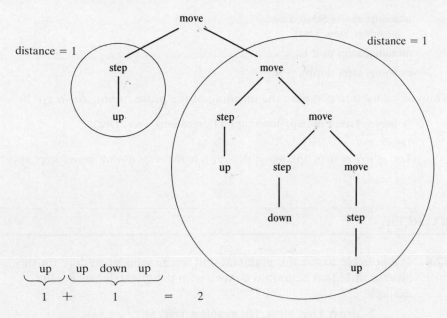

Figure 17.3   Extracting the meaning of a move as its distance.

generates the parse tree is:

```
move( move( Step)) --> step( Step).
move( move( Step, Move)) --> step( Step), move( Move).

step( step( up)) --> [ up].
step( step( down)) --> [ down].
```

Let us define the meaning of a move as the distance between the robot's position before the move and after it. Let each step be 1 mm in either the positive or negative direction. So the meaning of the move '*up up down up*' is $1 + 1 - 1 + 1 = 2$. The distance of a move can be computed from the move's parse tree as illustrated in Figure 17.3. The corresponding arithmetic is:

distance('*up up down up*') =
distance('*up*') + distance('*up down up*') = $1 + 1 = 2$

The following procedure computes the meaning of a move (as the corresponding distance) from the move's parse tree:

```
% meaning( ParseTree, Value)

meaning( move( Step, Move), Dist) :-
   meaning( Step, D1),
   meaning( Move, D2),
   Dist is D1 + D2.
```

```
meaning( move( Step), Dist :-
    meaning( Step, Dist).

meaning( step( up), 1).

meaning( step( down), -1).
```

This can be used to compute the meaning of the move '*up up down up*' by:

```
?- move( Tree, [ up, up, down, up], [ ]), meaning( Tree, Dist).

Dist = 2
Tree = move( step( up), move( step( up), move( step( down), move( step( up)))))
```

EXERCISE

17.4 Is it possible to use this grammar and the **meaning** procedure for the inverse task; that is, to find a move with the given distance – for example:

```
?- move( Tree, Move, [ ]), meaning( Tree, 5).
```

Discuss this application.

17.2.3 Interleaving syntax and semantics in DCG

The DCG notation actually makes it possible to incorporate the meaning directly into a grammar, thereby avoiding the intermediate construction of the parse tree. There is another notational extension, provided by DCG, that is useful in this respect. This extension allows us to insert normal Prolog goals into grammar rules. Such goals have to be enclosed in curly brackets to make them distinguishable from other symbols of the grammar. Thus everything enclosed in curly brackets is, when encountered, executed as normal Prolog goals. This execution may, for example, involve arithmetic computation.

This feature can be used to rewrite our robot move grammar so that the meaning extraction is interleaved directly with the syntax. To do that, we have to add the meaning; that is, the move's distance as an argument of the non-terminals **move** and **step**. For example

```
move( Dist)
```

now denotes a **move** phrase whose meaning is **Dist**. A corresponding grammar is:

```
move( D) --> step( D).
move( D) --> step( D1), move( D2), {D is D1 + D2}.

step( 1) --> [ up].
step( -1) --> [ down].
```

The second rule here exemplifies the curly bracket notation. This rule can be read as follows:

A move whose meaning is **D** consists of:

- a step whose meaning is **D1**, and
- a move whose meaning is **D2**, where the relation **D is D1 + D2** must also be satisfied.

In fact, handling semantics by incorporating the meaning formation rules directly into a DCG grammar is so convenient that the intermediate stage of constructing the parse tree is often avoided altogether. Avoiding such an intermediate stage results in a 'collapsed' program. The usual advantages of this are a shorter and more efficient program, but there are also disadvantages: the collapsed program may be less transparent, less flexible and harder to modify.

As a further illustration of this technique of interleaving the syntax and meaning, let us make our robot example a little more interesting. Suppose that the robot can be in one of two gears: *g1* or *g2*. When a step command is received in gear *g1*, the robot will move by 1 mm up or down; in gear *g2* it will move by 2 mm. Let the whole program for the robot consist of the gear commands (to switch to gear *g1* or *g2*) and step commands, finally ending with *stop*. Example programs are:

> *stop*
> *g1 up up stop*
> *g1 up up g2 down up stop*
> *g1 g1 g2 up up g1 up down up g2 stop*

The meaning (that is, the distance) of the last program is:

$$\text{Dist} = 2 * (1 + 1) + 1 * (1 - 1 + 1) = 5$$

To handle such robot programs, our existing robot move grammar has to be extended with the following rules:

```
prog( 0) --> [ stop].
prog( Dist) --> gear( _ ), prog( Dist).
prog( Dist) --> gear( G), move( D), prog( Dist1), {Dist is G * D + Dist1}.

gear( 1) --> [ g1].
gear( 2) --> [ g2].
```

·17.3 Defining the meaning of natural language

17.3.1 Meaning of simple sentences in logic

Defining the meaning of natural language is an extremely difficult problem
that is the subject of on-going research. An ultimate solution to the problem
of formalizing the complete syntax and meaning of a language like English
seems to be as far away as ever. But (relatively) simple subsets of natural
languages have been successfully formalized and consequently implemented
as working programs.

In defining the meaning of a language, the first question is: How will
the meaning be represented? There are of course many alternatives and good
choice will depend on the particular application. The important question
therefore is: What will the meaning extracted from natural language text be
used for? A typical application is natural language access to a database. This
involves answering natural language questions regarding information in the
database and updating the database by new information extracted from
natural language input. In such a case, the target representation of the
meaning extraction process would be a language for querying and updating
the database.

Logic has been accepted as a good candidate for representing the
meaning of natural language sentences. In comparison with database formalisms, logic is in general more powerful and, while essentially subsuming
database formalisms, also allows more subtle semantic issues to be dealt with.
In this section we will show how interpretations of simple natural language
sentences in logic can be constructed using the DCG notation. The logical
interpretations will be encoded as Prolog terms. We will only look at some
interesting ideas, so many details necessary for a more general coverage will be
omitted. A more complete treatment would be far beyond the scope of this
book.

To start with, it is best to look at some natural language sentences and
phrases and try to express in logic what they mean. Let us consider first the
sentence 'John paints'. The natural way to express the meaning of this
sentence in logic, as a Prolog term, is:

    paints(john)

Notice that 'paints' here is an intransitive verb and therefore the corresponding predicate **paints** only has one argument.

Our next example sentence is 'John likes Annie'. The formalized
meaning of this can be:

    likes(john, annie)

The verb 'likes' is transitive and accordingly the predicate **likes** has two
arguments.

Let us now try to define, by DCG rules, the meaning of such simple sentences. We will start with the bare syntax and then gradually incorporate the meaning into these rules. Here is a grammar that comfortably covers the syntax of our example sentences:

```
sentence --> noun_phrase, verb_phrase.

noun_phrase --> proper_noun.

verb_phrase --> intrans_verb.          % Intransitive verb
verb_phrase --> trans_verb, noun_phrase.   % Transitive verb

intrans_verb --> [ paints].
trans_verb --> [ likes].

proper_noun --> [ john].
proper_noun --> [ annie].
```

Now let us incorporate meaning into these rules. We will start with the simpler categories – noun and verb – and then proceed to the more complicated ones. Our foregoing examples suggest the following definitions. The meaning of proper noun john is simply john:

```
proper_noun( john) --> [ john].
```

The meaning of an intransitive verb like 'paints' is slightly more complicated. It can be stated as

```
paints( X)
```

where X is a variable whose value only becomes known from the context; that is, from the noun phrase. Correspondingly, the DCG rule for paints is:

```
intrans_verb( paints( X)) --> [ paints].
```

Let us now look at the question: How can we construct from the two meanings, john and paints(X), the intended meaning of the whole sentence: paints(john)? We have to force the argument X of paints to become equal to john.

It may be helpful at this point to consider Figure 17.4. This shows how the meanings of phrases accumulate into the meaning of the whole sentence. To achieve the effects of the propagation of the meanings of phrases, we can first simply define that noun_phrase and verb_phrase receive their meanings from proper_noun and intrans_verb respectively:

```
noun_phrase( NP) --> proper_noun( NP).

verb_phrase( VP) --> intrans_verb( VP).
```

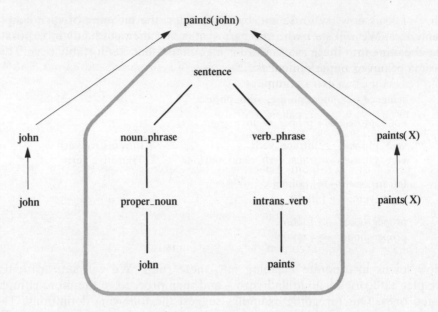

Figure 17.4 The parse tree of the sentence 'John paints' with meaning attached to the nodes. The logical meaning of each phrase is attached to the corresponding nonterminal in the tree. The arrows indicate how the meanings of phrases accumulate.

It remains to define the meaning of the whole sentence. Here is a first attempt:

> sentence(S) --> noun_phrase(NP), verb_phrase(VP), {compose(NP, VP, S)}.

The goal **compose(NP, VP, S)** has to assemble the meanings of the noun phrase **john** and the verb phrase **paints(X)**. Let us say that X is the *actor* in **paints(X)**. Let us define the relation

> actor(VP, Actor)

so that **Actor** is the **actor** in the meaning **VP** of a verb phrase. One clause of the procedure **actor** then is:

> actor(paints(X), X).

Once the **actor** relation is available, the composition of the noun phrase's and verb phrase's meanings can be defined as:

> compose(NP, VP, VP) :-   % Meaning of sentence is VP where
>   actor(VP, NP).   % actor in VP is NP

This works, but there is a shorter method. We can avoid the extra predicates **compose** and **actor** if we make the argument X in term **paints(X)** 'visible' from the outside of the term, so that it becomes accessible for instantiation. This can be achieved by redefining the meaning of **verb_phrase** and **intrans_verb** so that X becomes an extra argument:

> intrans_verb(Actor, paints(Actor)) --> [paints].
>
> verb_phrase(Actor, VP) --> intrans_verb(Actor, VP).

This makes the argument **Actor** easily accessible and facilitates a simpler definition of the meaning of a sentence:

> sentence(VP) --> noun_phrase(Actor), verb_phrase(Actor, VP).

This forces the 'actor' argument of the verb's meaning to become equal to the meaning of the noun phrase.

This technique of making parts of meanings visible is a rather common trick in incorporating meaning into DCG rules. The technique essentially works as follows. The meaning of a phrase is defined in a 'skeleton' form – for example, **paints(SomeActor)**. This defines the general form of the meaning, but leaves some of it uninstantiated (here, variable **SomeActor**). Such an uninstantiated variable serves as a slot that can be filled later depending on the meaning of other phrases in the context. This filling of slots can be accomplished by Prolog matching. To facilitate this, however, slots are made visible by being added as extra arguments to non-terminals. We will adopt the following convention regarding the order of these arguments: first will come the 'visible slots' of the phrase's meaning, followed by the meaning itself – for example, **verb_phrase(Actor, VPMeaning)**.

This technique can be applied to transitive verbs as follows. The meaning of the verb 'likes' is **likes(Somebody, Something)** (somebody likes something) where **Somebody** and **Something** are slots that should be visible from outside. Thus:

> trans_verb(Somebody, Something, likes(Somebody, Something)) --> [likes].

A verb phrase with a transitive verb contains a noun phrase that provides the value for **Something**. Therefore:

> verb_phrase(Somebody, VP) -->
>   trans_verb(Somebody, Something, VP), noun_phrase(Something).

The foregoing discussion has introduced some basic ideas; the DCG rules given handle but the simplest sentences. When noun phrases contain determiners like 'a' and 'every', the meaning expressions become more complicated. We will look at this in the next section.

17.3.2   Meaning of determiners 'a' and 'every'

Sentences that contain determiners such as 'a' are much more difficult to handle than those in the previous section. Let us consider an example sentence: 'A man paints'. It would now be a gross mistake to think that the meaning of this sentence is paints(man). The sentence really says: There exists some man that paints. In logic this is phrased as:

> There exists an X such that
> X is a man and X paints.

In logic, the variable X here is said to be *existentially* quantified ('there exists'). We will choose to represent this by the Prolog term:

> exists(X, man(X) and paints(X))

The first argument in this term is a variable, X – the variable that is meant to be existentially quantified. and is assumed to be declared as an infix operator:

> :- op(100, xfy, and).

The syntactic entity that dictates this logic interpretation is, possibly surprisingly, the determiner 'a'. So 'a' in a way dominates the whole sentence. To better understand how the meaning is constructed, let us look at the noun phrase 'a man'. Its meaning is:

> There exists some X such that
> X is a man.

However, in sentences where the phrase 'a man' appears, such as 'a man paints', we always want to say something else about this man (not only that he exists, but also that he paints). So a suitable form for the meaning of the noun phrase 'a man' is:

> exists(X, man(X) and Assertion)

where Assertion is some statement about X. This statement about X depends on the context; that is, on the verb phrase that follows the noun phrase 'a man'. The variable Assertion will only be instantiated when the context in which it appears becomes known.

A similar line of thought leads us to find a proper formulation of the meaning of the determiner 'a'. This determiner indicates that:

> There exists some X such that
> X has some property (for example, man(X)) and
> some further assertion about X holds (for example, paints(X)).

As a Prolog term this can be represented as:

> exists(X, **Property** and **Assertion**)

Both variables **Property** and **Assertion** are slots for meanings from the context to be plugged in. To facilitate the importation of the meanings from other phrases in context, we can, as explained in the previous section, make parts of the meaning of determiner 'a' visible. A suitable DCG rule for determiner 'a' is:

> determiner(X, **Prop**, **Assn**, exists(X, **Prop** and **Assn**)) --> [a].

The logical meaning of the tiny determiner 'a' may seem surprisingly complicated.

Another determiner, 'every', can be handled in a similar way. Consider the sentence: 'Every woman dances'. The logic interpretation of this is:

> For all X,
> if X is a woman then X dances.

We will represent this by the following Prolog term:

> all(X, woman(X) => dances(X))

where '=>' is an infix operator denoting logical implication. Determiner 'every' thus indicates a meaning whose skeleton structure is:

> all(X, **Property** => **Assertion**)

A DCG rule that defines the meaning of determiner 'every' and makes the slots in the skeleton visible is:

> determiner(X, **Prop**, **Assn**, all(X, **Prop** => **Assn**)) --> [every].

Having defined the meaning of determiners, we shall now concentrate on how their meaning integrates with the meanings of other phrases in the context, leading finally to the meaning of the whole sentence. We can get a first idea by looking again at the sentence 'A man paints' whose meaning is:

> exists(X, man(X) and paints(X))

We have already defined the meaning of 'a' as:

> exists(X, **Prop** and **Assn**)

Comparing these two meanings it is immediately obvious that the main structure of the meaning of the sentence is dictated by the determiner. The

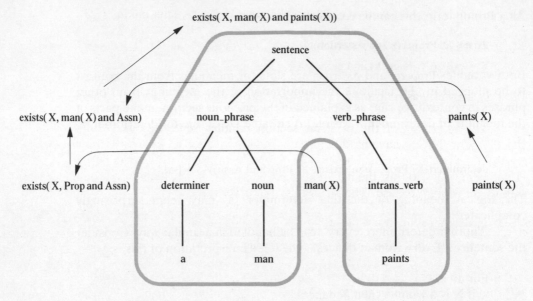

Figure 17.5 Accumulation of meaning for the sentence 'A man paints'. Determiner 'a' dictates the overall form of the meaning of the sentence. Arrows indicate the importation of meaning between phrases.

meaning of the sentence can be assembled as illustrated by Figure 17.5: start with the skeleton meaning enforced by 'a':

exists(X, Prop and Assn)

Prop then becomes instantiated by the noun and **Assn** by the verb phrase. The main structure of the meaning of the sentence is received from the noun phrase. Notice that this is different from the simpler grammar in the previous section where it was the verb phrase that provided the sentence's meaning structure. Again, applying the technique of making some parts of the meaning visible, the relations between meanings indicated in Figure 17.5 can be stated by the following DCG rules:

sentence(S) --> noun_phrase(X, Assn, S), verb_phrase(X, Assn).

noun_phrase(X, Assn, S) --> determiner(X, Prop, Assn, S), noun(X, Prop).

verb_phrase(X, Assn) --> intrans_verb(X, Assn).

intrans_verb(X, paints(X)) --> [paints].

determiner(X, Prop, Assn, exists(X, Prop and Assn)) --> [a].

noun(X, man(X)) --> [man].

This grammar can be asked to construct the meaning of 'A man paints':

> ?- sentence(S, [a, man, paints], [ ]).
>
> S = exists(X, man(X) and paints(X))

Prolog's answer was polished by replacing a Prolog-generated variable name like _123 with X.

The grammar of the previous section handles sentences like 'John paints'. Now that we have modified our grammar we need to ensure that this new grammar that can handle 'A man paints' can also handle the simpler 'John paints'. To do this, the meaning of proper nouns has to be incorporated into the new noun phrase. The following rules accomplish this:

> proper_noun(john) --> [john].
>
> noun_phrase(X, Assn, Assn) --> proper_noun(X).

This last rule simply says that the whole meaning of this kind of noun phrase is the same as the value in the second 'visible slot' – that is, Assn. This slot's value is obtained from the context (from the verb phrase) as in the question:

> ?- sentence(S, [john, paints], [ ]).
>
> S = paints(john)

EXERCISE

17.5 Study how our modified grammar constructs the meaning of 'John paints'. Essentially the following should happen: the meaning received from the verb phrase becomes the noun phrase's meaning, which eventually becomes the sentence's meaning.

17.3.3 Handling relative clauses

Nouns can be qualified by relative clauses – for example, 'Every man that paints admires Monet'. The phrase 'every man that paints' is a noun phrase in which 'that paints' is a relative clause. To cover this syntactically, our grammar rules about noun phrase can be redefined as follows:

> noun_phrase --> determiner, noun, rel_clause.
>
> rel_clause --> [that], verb_phrase.
> rel_clause --> [ ].   % Empty relative clause

Let us now consider the meaning of such noun phrases. The sentence 'Every man that paints admires Monet' logically means:

> For all X,
>   if X is a man and X paints
>   then X admires Monet.

This can be represented as the Prolog term:

> all(X, man(X) and paints(X) => admires(X, monet))

where it is assumed that the operator 'and' binds stronger than '=>'. Thus a suitable form for the logical meaning of the noun phrase 'every man that paints' is:

> all(X, man(X) and paints(X) => Assn)

In general, this form is:

> all(X, Prop1 and Prop2 => Assn)

Prop1 is determined by the noun, Prop2 by the verb phrase of the relative clause and Assn by the verb phrase of the sentence. DCG rules for the noun phrase that ensure this are:

> rel_clause(X, Prop1, Prop1 and Prop2) --> [that], verb_phrase(X, Prop2).

> noun_phrase(X, Assn, S) -->
>   determiner(X, Prop12, Assn, S), noun(X, Prop1),
>   rel_clause(X, Prop1, Prop12).

To cover the case of the empty relative clause we have to add:

> rel_clause(X, Prop1, Prop1) --> [ ].

Figure 17.6 gives a complete DCG with the features developed in this section, including determiners 'a' and 'every', and relative clauses. This grammar is capable of extracting the logical meaning of sentences, such as:

> John paints.
> Every man that paints admires Monet.
> Annie admires every man that paints.
> Every woman that admires a man that paints likes Monet.

```
:-  op( 100, xfy, and).
:-  op( 150, xfy, =>).

sentence( S) -->
    noun_phrase( X, Assn, S), verb_phrase( X, Assn).

noun_phrase( X, Assn, S) -->
    determiner( X, Prop12, Assn, S), noun( X, Prop1), rel_clause( X, Prop1, Prop12).

noun_phrase( X, Assn, Assn) -->
    proper_noun( X).

verb_phrase( X, Assn) -->
    trans_verb( X, Y, Assn1), noun_phrase( Y, Assn1, Assn).

verb_phrase( X, Assn) -->
    intrans_verb( X, Assn).

rel_clause( X, Prop1, Prop1 and Prop2) -->
    [ that], verb_phrase( X, Prop2).

rel_clause( X, Prop1, Prop1) --> [].

determiner( X, Prop, Assn, all( X, Prop => Assn)) --> [ every].

determiner( X, Prop, Assn, exists( X, Prop and Assn)) --> [ a].

noun( X, man( X)) --> [ man].

noun( X, woman( X)) --> [ woman].

proper_noun( john) --> [ john].

proper_noun( annie) --> [ annie].

proper_noun( monet) --> [ monet].

trans_verb( X, Y, likes( X, Y)) --> [ likes].

trans_verb( X, Y, admires( X, Y)) --> [ admires].

intrans_verb( X, paints( X)) --> [ paints].

% Some tests

test1( Meaning) :-
    sentence( Meaning, [ john, paints], [ ]).

test2( Meaning) :-
    sentence( Meaning, [ a, man, paints], [ ]).

test3( Meaning) :-
    sentence( Meaning, [ every, man, that, paints, admires, monet], [ ]).

test4( Meaning) :-
    sentence( Meaning, [ annie, admires, every, man, that, paints], [ ]).

test5( Meaning) :-
    sentence( Meaning, [ every, woman, that, admires, a, man, that, paints, likes, monet], [ ]).
```

Figure 17.6   A DCG handling the syntax and meaning of a small subset of natural language.

For example, these sentences can be submitted to our grammar as the questions:

?- sentence(Meaning1, [every, man, that, paints, admires, monet], [ ]).

Meaning1 = all(X, man(X) and paints(X) => admires(X, monet))

?- sentence(Meaning2, [annie, admires, every, man, that, paints], [ ]).

Meaning2 = all(X, man(X) and paints(X) => admires(annie, X))

?- sentence(Meaning3, [every, woman, that, admires, a, man, that, paints, likes, monet], [ ]).

Meaning3 = all(X, woman(X) and exists(Y, (man(Y) and paints(Y)) and admires(X, Y)) => likes(X, monet))

A further interesting problem concerns the use of the meanings extracted from natural language input to answer questions. For example, how can we modify our program so that, after it has processed the given sentences, it can answer questions like: 'Does Annie admire anybody who admires Monet?' The answer to this logically follows from the sentences above, and we just have to make our program do some necessary reasoning. In general, we need a theorem prover to deduce answers from the meanings represented in logic. Of course, it is most practical to simply use Prolog itself as such a theorem prover. To do that we would have to translate the logical meanings into equivalent Prolog clauses. This exercise in general requires some work, but in some cases such a translation is trivial. Here are some easily translatable meanings written as Prolog clauses:

```
paints( john).

admires( X, monet) :-
  man( X),
  paints( X).

admires( annie, X) :-
  man( X),
  paints( X).
```

The example query 'Does Annie admire anybody who admires Monet?' would have to be translated into the Prolog query:

?- admires(annie, X), admires(X, monet).

X = john

EXERCISE

17.6 Extend the grammar of Figure 17.6 to handle composite sentences
with connectives 'if', 'then', 'and', 'or', 'neither', 'nor', etc. For
example: John paints and Annie sings. If Annie sings then every
teacher listens.

Project

Modify the grammar of Figure 17.6 to represent the meaning of sentences as
directly executable Prolog clauses. Write a program that reads natural language sentences in normal format (not as lists; see a relevant program in
Chapter 6) and asserts their meaning as Prolog clauses. Extend the grammar
to handle simple questions in natural language which would result in a
complete conversation system for a small subset of natural language. You
may also consider use of the grammar to generate sentences with the given
meaning as natural language answers to the user.

SUMMARY

- Standard grammar notations, such as BNF, can be trivially translated
  into the DCG notation (definite clause grammars). A grammar in DCG
  can be read and executed directly by Prolog as a recognizer for the
  language defined by the grammar.
- The DCG notation allows non-terminal symbols of the grammar to have
  arguments. This enables the treatment of context dependencies in a
  grammar and direct incorporation of the semantics of a language into its
  grammar.
- Interesting DCG grammars have been written that cover the syntax and
  meaning of non-trivial subsets of natural language.

References

Pereira and Warren (1980) is a classical paper on how DCG rules can be used to define the
syntax and meaning of natural language sentences. The coverage of this theme in this
chapter follows their treatment. In their excellent book, Pereira and Shieber (1987) give
many further developments of this, including an elegant connection between the corresponding mathematical basis for defining meaning and its implementation in Prolog. Many
aspects of natural language processing in Prolog are discussed in a thorough and useful
book by Gazdar and Mellish (1989). Markus (1986) gives a DCG grammar to interpret

natural language queries to databases. Szpakowicz (1987) gives an example of applying DCG in programming language translation. Exercise 17.6 is borrowed from Kononenko and Lavrac (1988) who also give a solution.

Gazdar, G. and Mellish, C. (1989) *Natural Language Processing in Prolog*. Addison-Wesley.

Kononenko, I. and Lavrac, N. (1988) *Prolog through Examples: A Practical Programming Guide*. Wilmslow, England: Sigma Press.

Markus, C. (1986) *Prolog Programming*. Addison-Wesley.

Pereira, F.C.N. and Shieber, S.M. (1987) *Prolog and Natural-Language Analysis*. Menlo Park, CA: CSLI – Center for the Study of Language and Information.

Pereira, F.C.N. and Warren, D.H.D. (1980) Definite clause grammars for language analysis – a survey of the formalism and comparison with augmented transition networks. *Artificial Intelligence* **13**: 231–278.

Szpakowicz, S. (1987) Logic grammars. *BYTE* (August 1987): 185–195.

18 Machine Learning

18.1 Introduction
18.2 The problem of learning concepts from examples
18.3 Learning concepts by induction: a detailed example
18.4 A program that learns relational descriptions
18.5 Learning simple attributional descriptions
18.6 Induction of decision trees
18.7 Learning from noisy data and tree pruning
18.8 Success of learning

Of the forms of learning, learning concepts from examples is the most common and best understood. Learning algorithms depend on the language in which the learned concepts are represented. In this chapter we develop programs that learn concepts represented by relational descriptions, if-then rules and decision trees. We also look at the pruning of decision trees as a method for learning from noisy data – when examples possibly contain errors.

18.1 Introduction

There are several forms of learning, ranging from 'learning by being told' to 'learning by discovery'. In the former case, the learner is explicitly told what is to be learned. In this sense, programming is a kind of learning by being told. The main burden in this type of learning is on the teacher although the learner's task can also be difficult as it may not be easy to understand what the teacher had in mind. So learning by being told may require intelligent communication including a learner's model of the teacher. At the other extreme, in learning by discovery, the learner autonomously discovers new concepts merely from unstructured observations or by planning and performing experiments in the environment. There is no teacher involved here and all the burden is on the learner. The learner's environment plays the role of an oracle.

Between these two extremes lies another form of learning: learning from examples. Here the initiative is distributed between the teacher and the learner. The teacher provides examples for learning and the learner is supposed to make generalizations about the examples – that is, find a kind of theory, underlying the given examples. The teacher can help the learner by selecting good training instances and by describing the examples in a language that permits formulating elegant general rules. In a sense, learning from examples exploits the known empirical observation that experts (that is 'teachers') find it easier to produce good examples than to provide explicit and complete general theories. On the other hand, the task of the learner to generalize from examples can be difficult.

Learning from examples is also called *inductive learning*. Inductive learning is the most researched kind of learning in Artificial Intelligence and this research has produced many solid results. From examples, several types of task can be learned: one can learn to diagnose a patient or a plant disease, to predict weather, to predict the behaviour of a new chemical compound, to predict mechanical properties of steel on the basis of some of its chemical characteristics, to improve efficiency in solving symbolic integration problems or to control a dynamic system. Machine learning techniques have been applied to all these particular tasks and many others. All these tasks can be formulated as learning concepts from examples. Practical methods exist that can be readily used in complex applications, in particular in the development of expert systems. The most obvious kind of application is in association with knowledge acquisition for expert systems, thus helping to alleviate the knowledge-acquisition bottleneck. Accordingly, in this chapter we will be mostly concerned with learning concepts from examples.

We will first define the problem of learning concepts from examples more formally. To illustrate key ideas we will then follow a detailed example of learning concepts represented by semantic networks. Then we will look at induction of rules and decision trees from examples described in terms of attributes.

18.2 The problem of learning concepts from examples

18.2.1 Concepts as sets

The problem of learning concepts from examples can be formalized as follows. Let U be the universal set of objects – that is, all of the objects that the learner may encounter. There is in principle no limitation on the size of U. A concept C can be formalized as a subset of objects in U. To learn concept C means to learn to recognize objects in C. In other words, once C is learned, the system is able, for any object X in U, to recognize whether X is in C.

This definition of concept is sufficiently general to enable the formalization of such diverse concepts as an arch, arithmetic multiplication or a certain disease, as shown in the following:

- The concept of an arch in the blocks world: The universal set U is the set of all structures made of blocks in a blocks world. Arch is the subset of U containing all the arch-like structures and nothing else.

- The concept of multiplication: The universal set U is the set of tuples of numbers. *Mult* is the set of all triples of numbers (a, b, c) such that $a * b = c$. More formally:

  $$Mult = \{(a, b, c) \mid a * b = c\}$$

- The concept of a certain disease: U is the set of all possible patient descriptions in terms of some chosen repertoire of features. D is the set of all those descriptions of patients that suffer from the disease in question.

18.2.2 Description languages for objects and concepts

For any kind of learning we need a language for describing objects and a language for describing concepts. In general we distinguish between two kinds of description:

- *relational descriptions* and
- *attribute descriptions*.

In a relational description (also called structural description) an object is described in terms of its components and the relations between them. A relational description of an arch may say the following: the arch is a structure consisting of three components (two posts and a lintel); each component is a block; both posts support the lintel; the posts do not touch. Such a description is relational because it talks about relations between components. On the other hand, in an attribute description we describe an object in terms of its global features. Such a description is a vector of attribute values. An attribute description may, for example, mention the attributes length, height and colour. So an attribute description of a particular arch may be: length = 9 m, height = 7 m, colour = yellow.

Description languages that can be used in learning programs are of course similar to those that can be used for representing knowledge in general. Some formalisms often used in machine learning are:

- attribute vectors to represent objects;
- if-then rules to represent concepts;
- decision trees to represent concepts;
- semantic networks;
- predicate logic of various types (for example, Prolog).

Some of these representations will be explained and used later in this chapter.

Once we have an object and a concept definition, we need a decision rule to establish whether the object belongs to the concept. Such a rule will determine whether the object satisfies the concept description. In the usual terminology of machine learning we say that the object matches the concept description. The word 'match' is used here rather generally; it should not, of course, be confused with the more specific matching of terms in Prolog. Matching between objects and concept descriptions can be formalized as a matching predicate or a matching function of two arguments:

> match(Object, Concept_description)

The definition of matching depends on the particular learning system. In the case that **match** is a predicate it will just say that **Object** does or does not satisfy **Concept_description**. If **match** is a function it may say to what degree **Object** satisfies **Concept_description**. Alternatively, in the case that **Object** does not satisfy **Concept_description**, **match** may produce a symbolic description of the differences or reasons why not. Such differences can be used in updating the concept description.

18.2.3 The problem of learning from examples

The target of learning is a concept description, and the source of information for learning is examples. An example for learning a concept C is a pair

> (Object, Class)

where **Object** is an object description and **Class** is either '+' or '−'. If **Object** belongs to C then **Class** = '+', otherwise **Class** = '−'. We say that **Object** is either a positive example or a negative example of the concept to be learned.

The problem of learning concept C from examples can now be stated as follows: Given a set S of examples (called learning or training set), find a formula F expressed in the concept description language, such that:

For all objects X:
(1)   if X is a positive example in the training set S then X matches F;
(2)   if X is a negative example in S then X does not match F.

As the result of learning, F is the 'system's understanding' of the concept C as learned from examples. According to this definition, F and C 'agree' on all the given example objects in S. There is, however, no *a priori* guarantee that F will correspond to C on other objects as well. The major aim of learning is to learn to classify unseen objects (that is, those contained in U but not contained in the training set S) with respect to C. Therefore, one important criterion of success of learning is the classification accuracy of F on unseen objects. Consequently, the learned concept description F should be more general than the positive training examples themselves. Such generalization of learning examples is the essence of inductive learning. There are other criteria of success, which will be discussed in Section 18.8.

18.3   Learning concepts by induction: a detailed example

Learning about structures in the blocks world, and about arches in particular, was introduced as a study domain by Winston (1975) and became a classical illustration of the mechanisms involved in learning. We will also use this domain as an illustration, and our treatment will basically, although not entirely, follow Winston's program called ARCHES.

The program ARCHES can be made to learn the concept of an arch from teacher-supplied examples and counter-examples as shown in Figure 18.1. The given examples are processed sequentially and the learner gradually updates the 'current hypothesis' – that is, the current definition of the concept being learned. In the case of Figure 18.1, after all four examples have been processed by the learner, the hypothesis (that is, the learner's final under-standing of an arch) may informally look like this:

(1)   An arch consists of three parts; let us call them post1, post2 and lintel.

(2)   post1 and post2 are rectangles; lintel can be a more general figure, a kind of polygon, for example (this may be concluded from examples 1 and 4 in Figure 18.1).

(3)   post1 and post2 must not touch (this can be concluded from the negative example 2).

(4)   post1 and post2 must suport lintel (this can be concluded from the negative example 3).

Figure 18.1 A sequence of examples and counter-examples for learning the concept of arch.

In general, when a concept is learned by sequentially processing the learning examples, the learning process proceeds through a sequence of hypotheses, H_1, H_2, etc., about the concept that is being learned. Each hypothesis in this sequence represents an approximation to the target concept and is the result of the examples seen so far. After the next example is processed, the current hypothesis is updated resulting in the next hypothesis. This process can be stated as the following algorithm:

To learn a concept C from a given sequence of examples E_1, E_2, ..., E_n, (where E_1 must be a positive example of C) do:

(1)   Adopt E_1 as the initial hypothesis H_1 about C.

(2)   Process all the remaining examples: for each E_i ($i = 2, 3, ...$) do:

    2.1   Match the current hypothesis H_{i-1} with E_i; let the result of matching be some description D of the differences between H_{i-1} and E_i.

    2.2   Act on H_{i-1} according to D and according to whether E_i is a positive or a negative example of C. The result of this is a refined hypothesis H_i about C.

The final result of this procedure is H_n which represents the system's understanding of the concept C as learned from the given examples. In an actual implementation, steps 2.1 and 2.2 need some refinements. These are complicated and vary between different learning systems. To illustrate some ideas and difficulties, let us consider in more detail the case of learning about the arch from examples in Figure 18.1.

First, we have to become more specific about the representation. The ARCHES program uses semantic networks to represent both learning examples and concept descriptions. Figure 18.2 shows examples of semantic networks. These are essentially graphs in which nodes correspond to entities and links indicate relations between entities.

The first example, represented by a semantic network, becomes the current hypothesis of what an arch is (see H_1 in Figure 18.2).

The second example (E_2 in Figure 18.2) is a negative example of an arch. It is easy to match E_2 to H_1. As both networks are very similar it is easy to establish the correspondence between nodes and links in H_1 and E_2. The result of matching shows the difference D between H_1 and E_2; that is, there is an extra relation, **touch**, in E_2. Since this is the only difference, the system concludes that this must be the reason why E_2 is not an arch. The system now updates the current hypothesis H_1 by applying the following general heuristic principle of learning:

if
>example is negative and
>example contains a relation R which is not in the current
>hypothesis H

then
>forbid R in H (add **must_not_R** in H)

This learning heuristic is stated as a condition-action rule. The result of applying this rule on H_1 will be a new hypothesis H_2 (see Figure 18.2). Notice that the new hypothesis has an extra link **must_not_touch** which imposes an additional constraint on a structure should it be an arch. Therefore we say that this new hypothesis H_2 is *more specific* than H_1.

The next negative example in Figure 18.1 is represented by the semantic network E_3 in Figure 18.2. Matching this to the current hypothesis H_2 reveals two differences: two **support** links, present in H_2, are not present in E_3. Now the learner has to make a guess between three possible explanations:

(1) E_3 is not an arch because the left **support** link is missing, or

(2) E_3 is not an arch because the right **support** link is missing, or

(3) E_3 is not an arch because both **support** links are missing.

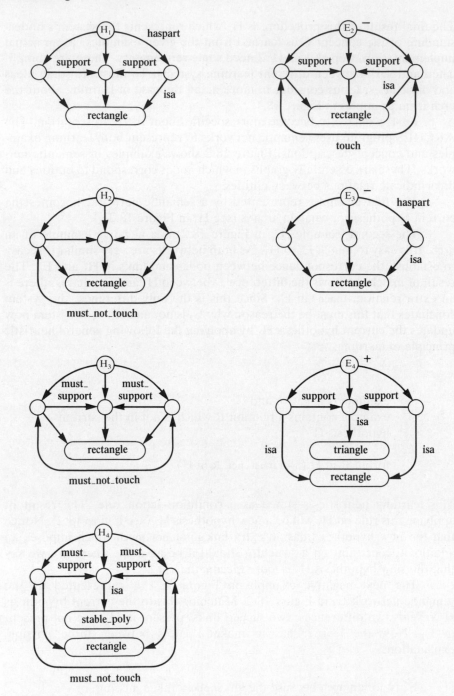

Figure 18.2 Evolving hypotheses about the arch. At each stage the current hypothesis H_i is compared with the next example E_{i+1} and the next, refined hypothesis H_{i+1} is produced.

Accordingly, the learner has to choose between the three possible ways of updating the current hypothesis. Let us assume that the learner's mentality is more towards radical changes and therefore acts according to explanation 3. The learner will thus assume that both **support** links are necessary and will therefore convert both **support** links in H_2 into **must_support** links in the new hypothesis H_3 (see Figure 18.2). The situation of missing links can be handled by the following condition-action rule which is another general heuristic about learning:

> *if*
>> example is negative and
>> example does not contain a relation R which is present in the current hypothesis H
>
> *then*
>> require R in the new hypothesis (add **must_R** in H)

Notice again that, as a result of processing a negative example, the current hypothesis has become still more specific since further necessary conditions are introduced: two **must_support** links. Notice also that the learner could have chosen a more conservative action; namely, to introduce just one **must_support** link instead of two. Obviously, then, the learning style can be modelled through the set of condition-action rules the learner uses to update the current hypothesis. By varying these rules the learning style can be varied between conservative and cautious to radical and reckless.

The last example, E_4, in our training sequence is again positive. Matching the corresponding semantic networks E_4 to H_3 shows the difference: the top part is a triangle in E_4 and a rectangle in H_3. The learner may now redirect the corresponding **isa** link in the hypothesis from rectangle to a new object class: **rectangle_or_triangle**. Alternative (and more common) reaction in a learning program is based on a predefined hierarchy of concepts. Suppose that the learner has, as the domain-specific background knowledge, a taxonomy of concepts, as in Figure 18.3. Having found that, according to this taxonomy, rectangle and triangle are both a kind of **stable_poly**, the learner may update the current hypothesis to obtain H_4 (see Figure 18.2).

Notice that this time a positive example has been processed which resulted in a more general new hypothesis (stable polygon instead of rectangle). We say that the current hypothesis was *generalized*. The new hypothesis now allows the top part to be a trapezium although no example of an arch with a trapezium was ever shown to the learner. If the system was now shown the arch in Figure 18.4 and asked to classify it, it would declare it as an arch since its semantic network representation completely satisfies the system's understanding of an arch – that is, the hypothesis H_4.

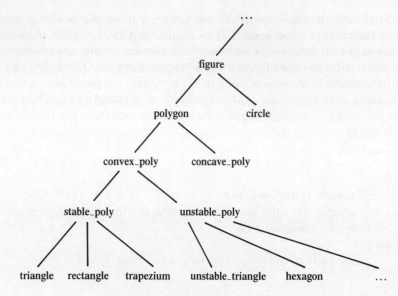

Figure 18.3 A hierarchy of concepts.

Here are some important points illustrated by the foregoing example:

- The procedure for matching an object to a concept description depends on the learning system. Matching is often complicated and can be computationally complex due to combinatorial processes. For example, in the case of semantic networks used as a description language, we may have to try all possible candidate correspondences between the nodes in the two networks that are being matched to establish the best fit.

- Given two concept descriptions, one of them may be more general than the other, or more specific than the other; or they can be incomparable with respect to their generality or specificity.

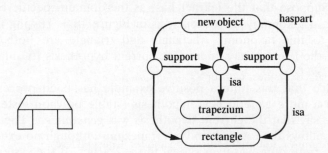

Figure 18.4 Left: a new object; right: its representation. This object matches the concept definition H_4 of the arch in Figure 18.2, using the concept hierarchy of Figure 18.3.

- Modifications of a concept description during the learning process enhance either: the generality of the description in order to make the description match a given positive example; or the specificity of the description in order to prevent the description from matching a negative example.

- Concept modification principles for a given learning system can be represented as condition-action rules. By means of such rules, the 'mentality' of the learning system can be modelled, ranging from conservative to reckless.

18.4   A program that learns relational descriptions

Let us now program in Prolog the learning of relational descriptions, as discussed in the previous section, around the arches example. As usual, we are interested in a concise and transparent program; we will not be particularly concerned with efficiency. Figure 18.5 shows such a program. The top-level task is to induce a concept description from a list of examples:

   learn(ListOfExamples, ConceptDescription)

Figure 18.5   An implementation of a simplified and modified version of Winston's learning procedure called ARCHES.

```
% An ARCHES-like learning program

% Representation:
% Object = object( ListOfParts, ListOfRelations)
% Concept = concept( ListOfParts, MustRelations, Relations, MustNotRels)
% Positive example = + Object
% Negative example = − Object
% Parts in an object are denoted by variables, parts in a concept description
% are denoted by constants

% learn( ListOfExamples, ConceptDescription):
%    induces a concept description from a list of examples

learn( [FirstExample | Examples], ConceptDesc) :-
    initialize( FirstExample, InitialHypothesis),
    process_examples( InitialHypothesis, Examples, ConceptDesc).

process_examples( ConceptDesc, [ ], ConceptDesc).
```

(continues)

Figure 18.5 (cont.)

```
process_examples( CurDesc, [Example | Examples], FinDesc) :-
  object_type( Example, Object, Type),
  match( Object, CurDesc, Difference),
  update( Type, Difference, CurDesc, NewDesc),
  process_examples( NewDesc, Examples, FinDesc).

initialize( + object( Parts, Rels), concept( Parts, [], Rels, [])) :-
  namevars( Parts, [ part1, part2, part3, part4, part5, part6]).
% Turn variables in the object into constants, assume 6 parts at the most


% Actions to specialize or generalize the current hypothesis:
% update( TypeOfExample, Difference, CurDesc, NewDesc)

% The forbid-relation rule: an extra relation in a negative example
% must be forbidden in the concept description

update( negative, _ + [ ExtraRelation],
        concept( Parts, Musts, Rels, MustNots),
        concept( Parts, Musts, Rels, [ExtraRelation | MustNots])).


% The require-relation rule: missing relations in a negative example
% must be required in the concept description

update( negative, Missing + _,
        concept( Parts, Musts, Rels, MustNots),
        concept( Parts, NewMusts, NewRels, MustNots))  :-
  Missing = [_ | _],                                    % Missing non-empty
  conc( Missing, Musts, NewMusts),                      % Add Missing to Musts
  list_diff( Rels, Missing, _ + NewRels).               % Remove Missing from Rels


% One missing and one extra relation in a negative example can
% also be handled by both forbid extra and require missing

update( negative, [ MissR] + [ ExtraR], CurDesc, NewDesc) :-
  update( negative, [] + [ ExtraR], CurDesc, InterDesc),   % Forbid
  update( negative, [ MissR] + [], InterDesc, NewDesc).     % and require


% The climb-taxonomy rule: generalize an isa relation by climbing a-kind-of taxonomy

update( positive, [ isa( Object, Class1)] + [ isa( Object, Class2)],
        concept( Parts, Musts, Rels, MustNots),
        concept( Parts, Musts, NewRels, MustNots)) :-
  % Find Class, the most specific superclass of Class1 and Class2
  climb( Class1, Class),
  climb( Class2, Class), !,
  replace( isa( Object, Class1), Rels, isa( Object, Class), NewRels).
```

Figure 18.5 (cont.)

```
% match( Object, ConceptDescription, Difference)

match( object( OParts, ORels),
       concept( CParts, Musts, Rels, MustNots), Missing + Extras) :-
   list_diff( ORels, Musts, [ ] + RestRels),            % Match musts
   short_lists( Missing + Extras),                      % Generate short lists
   list_diff( OParts, CParts, [ ] + [ ]),               % Match parts
   list_diff( RestRels, Rels, Missing + Extras),        % Match other relations
   list_diff( Extras, MustNots, MustNots + _ ).         % All MustNots missing

% list_diff( List1, List2, List2LessList1 + List1LessList2)

list_diff( List1, [ ], [ ] + List1).

list_diff( List1, [X | List2], Miss + Extras) :-
   delete( List1, List11, X, Miss11, Miss),
   list_diff( List11, List2, Miss11 + Extras).

% delete( List, ListPossiblyLessX, X, DelList, DelListPossiblyPlusX)
% If X is deleted from List then DelListPossiblyPlusX = DelList,
% if not then ListPossiblyLessX = List and DelListPossiblyPlusX = [X | DelList]
% (If X is not deleted then it is missing in List)

delete( [ ], [ ], X, Dels, [X | Dels]).

delete( [Y | L], L, X, Dels, Dels) :-
   X == Y, !                                            % Literally equal: necessarily delete
   ;
   X = Y.                                               % X, Y match: possibly delete

delete( [Y | L], [Y | L1], X, Dels, Dels1) :-
   delete( L, L1, X, Dels, Dels1).

object_type( + Object, Object, positive).               % Positive example

object_type( - Object, Object, negative).               % Negative example

% replace( Item, List, NewItem, NewList):
%    remove Item from List and add NewItem producing NewList

replace( Item, List, NewItem, [NewItem | List1]) :-
   delete( List, List1, Item, _, _ ).

% climb( Class1, Class2):
%    climb a-kind-of relation from Class1 to Class2

climb( Class, Class).

climb( Class, SuperClass) :-
   ako( Class1, Class),                                 % Class a kind of Class1
   climb( Class1, SuperClass).
```

(continues)

Figure 18.5 (cont.)

```
% namevars( List, NameList)
%    instantiates variables in a list of variables to names in NameList
namevars( List, NameList) :-
  conc( List, _, NameList).

conc( [ ], L, L).

conc( [X | L1], L2, [X | L3]) :-
  conc( L1, L2, L3).
```

```
% Generator of difference templates List1 + List2: short lists are generated
% first to force finding good match;
% order of generation: []+[], []+[_], [_]+[], []+[_,_], [_]+[_], ...
short_lists( L1 + L2) :-
  conc( L, _, [_,_,_]),                              % Up to 3 elements in both lists
  conc( L1, L2, L).
```

```
% ------------------------------------------------------------------------------------
% Examples for learning about the arch
example(
  + object( [ A, B, C],
      [ support( A, C), support( B, C),
        isa( A, rectangle), isa( B, rectangle), isa( C, rectangle)])).


example(
  − object( [ A, B, C],
      [ support( A, C), support( B, C), touch( A, B),
        isa( A, rectangle), isa( B, rectangle), isa( C, rectangle)])).
example(
  − object( [ A, B, C],
      [ isa( A, rectangle), isa( B, rectangle), isa( C, rectangle)])).
example(
  + object( [ A, B, C],
      [ support( A, C), support( B, C),
        isa( A, rectangle), isa( B, rectangle), isa( C, triangle)])).
```

```
% Taxonomy
ako( figure, polygon).
ako( figure, circle).
ako( polygon, convex_poly).
ako( polygon, concave_poly).
ako( convex_poly, stable_poly).
ako( convex_poly, unstable_poly).
ako( stable_poly, triangle).
ako( stable_poly, rectangle).
ako( stable_poly, trapezium).
ako( unstable_poly, unstable_triangle).
ako( unstable_poly, hexagon).
```

The first example, which must always be positive, is used to construct an initial hypothesis about the concept to be learned, and the final concept description is elicited by processing the rest of the examples:

```
learn( [FirstExample | Examples], ConceptDesc)  :-
   initialize( FirstExample, InitialHypo),
   process_examples( InitialHypo, Examples, ConceptDesc).
```

The examples are processed one by one. Each example is matched against the current concept description. The current concept description is then updated according to the differences between the current description and the example object, depending also on the type of the example (positive or negative). This can be captured by the following clause:

```
process_examples( CurDesc, [Example | Examples], FinDesc)  :-
   object_type( Example, Object, Type),              % Type is + or −
   match( Object, CurDesc, Difference),
   update( Type, Difference, CurDesc, NewDesc),
   process_examples( NewDesc, Examples, FinDesc).
```

Let us now consider the representation in Prolog for examples, objects and concept descriptions. The program of Figure 18.5 uses the following representation:

```
Object = object( ListOfParts, ListOfRelations)
Example = + Object      (positive example)
Example = − Object      (negative example)
```

Concept description is more complex. Again, we have parts and relations, but the relations are classified into three categories:

(1)   must relations (those that have to be present);
(2)   desirable relations; and
(3)   must-not relations (those that must not be present).

The representation in the program of Figure 18.5 is:

```
ConceptDesc = concept( Parts, Musts, Relations, MustNots)
```

where Musts is a list of must relations, Relations is a list of desirable relations and MustNots is a list of must-not relations. The most complicated predicate in the program is:

```
match( Object, Concept, Difference)
```

This is defined to be true in our program if:

(1)   All must relations in **Concept** appear in **Object**.

(2)   No must-not relation in **Concept** appears in **Object**.

(3)   **Object** and **Concept** have equal numbers of parts in their lists of parts.

(4)   **Difference** contains two things: first, the missing relations (those desirable relations that are not in **Object**) and, second, the extra relations – those relations in **Object** that do not appear as desirable in **Concept**. **Difference** is therefore a pair of lists:

> **Difference = Missing + Extras**

The **match** procedure should attempt to minimize these differences. The number of differences depends on how the parts in **Object** are chosen to correspond to the parts in **Concept**. Therefore, it is important to find a good correspondence. The procedure **match** in Figure 18.5 does this in a simple-minded way. To minimize the differences represented by a pair of lists

> **Missing + Extras**

the procedure looks for a correspondence between the parts in the object and the concept description that makes the lists **Missing** and **Extras** as short as possible. This search for minimal differences is essentially done in a simple breadth-first manner where consecutive attempts at matching are made with limited lengths of the lists **Missing** and **Extras**. These length limits are gradually increased until **match** succeeds. To this end, the procedure

> **short_lists(List1 + List2).**

generates, through backtracking, list templates of increasing length.

Both objects and concepts are represented by semantic networks – that is, a kind of graph. The matching process has to establish the correspondence between nodes in the two graphs; in particular, it has to find what part of the object corresponds to what part of the concept. In our chosen representation we have a list of parts for both the object and the concept description. The matching procedure has to assign to each element in one list one element in the other list. Such an assignment is easy to implement in Prolog through instantiation of variables. Hence, one list contains variables only while the other list contains constants only. For example, let the two lists of parts be:

> L1 = [part1, part2, part3]
> L2 = [A, B, C]

The possible pairings correspond to the permutations of the list L1 of parts, and may thus be realized by the following instantiations:

> A = part1,   B = part2,   C = part3
> A = part1,   B = part3,   C = part2
> A = part2,   B = part1,   C = part3
> ...

In principle, it does not matter which one of the two lists contains variables and which one constants. In our case one list belongs to a concept description and the other to a concrete object. As a concept description is a general definition of a concept, it would be more natural to have variables in the concept description and constants in the object description. The alternative, and less natural choice, is constants in the concept description and variables in the object description. In matching, this choice amounts to the same effect. As it turns out, this second, less natural alternative is more practical for the following reason. After matching, the concept description is updated, producing a new concept description. If the concept description contained variables, these would turn into constants during matching, and the constants would have to be turned into variables again when the new concept description is constructed. It is therefore more practical to have variables in object descriptions and not in concept descriptions.

The foregoing considerations determine the details of our representation, illustrated by the following examples. The first learning example in Figure 18.1 is represented as:

```
+ object(
  [ A, B, C],                                              % Parts
  [ support( A, C), support( B, C),                        % Relations
    isa( A, rectangle), isa( B, rectangle), isa( C, rectangle)] )
```

Here A and B are the two posts and C is the lintel. The final induced description of the arch concept (H_4 in Figure 18.2) is:

```
concept(
  [ part1, part2, part3],                                  % Parts
  [ support( part1, part3), support( part2, part3)],       % Musts
  [ isa( part1, rectangle), isa( part2, rectangle),        % Desirables
    isa( part3, stable_poly)],
  [ touch( part1, part2)] )                                % Must-nots
```

The concept has three parts. When looking for a best match between a concept and an object, the **match** procedure in effect considers all the permutations of the parts. This is accomplished by the **list_diff** procedure.

Rules for updating the current concept description according to differences are implemented as the relation:

> **update(ExampleType, Difference, CurrentDesc, NewDesc)**

where **Difference** = **MissingRelations** + **ExtraRelations**. For example, one heuristic update rule is:

> If a negative example contains an extra relation
> then this relation must be forbidden in the concept
> (that is, this relation is included among the must-nots).

This rule is programmed as:

```
update( negative, _ + [ Relation],                    % One extra relation
        concept( Parts, Musts, Rels, MustNots),
        concept( Parts, Musts, Rels, [Relation | MustNots]).
```

The program in Figure 18.5 also contains a set of examples for learning about the arch and a corresponding taxonomy (the **ako** relation, 'a kind of'). To learn a description of the arch concept from these examples, the following question can be posed to Prolog:

```
?- bagof( E, example( E), Examples),
   learn( Examples, ArchDesc).

ArchDesc = concept( [ part1, part2, part3],
                    [ support( part1, part3), support( part2, part3)],
                    [ isa( part3, stable_poly), isa( part1, rectangle),
                      isa( part2, rectangle)],
                    [ touch( part1, part2)])
Examples = ...
```

EXERCISES

18.1 Design a sequence of examples and corresponding **ako** relations to teach the learning system the concept of house (as a triangle or trapezium on a rectangle).

18.2 Analyze how the **match** procedure in Figure 18.5 could be further refined. One way is to associate costs with various kinds of differences between an object and a concept description. The 'total cost' of the differences between an object and a concept description would then be the sum of individual differences, and the matching problem would be to minimize this total cost. Formulate the matching procedure as the best-first search to minimize this cost.

Project

The program in Figure 18.5 insists on equal numbers of parts in a concept and in objects that belong to the concept. Thus, this program cannot learn concepts that contain a variable number of parts, such as arches of variable height in which the two posts consist of any number of rectangles. Extend the program so that it could learn such concepts. Such concepts are often best defined recursively. For example, the column concept can be defined as a rectangle supported by another column.

18.5   Learning simple attributional descriptions

18.5.1   Describing objects and concepts by attributes

In this section we look at a kind of learning where examples and concepts are described in terms of a set of attributes. In principle, attributes can be of various types, depending on their possible values. So an attribute can be numerical or non-numerical. Further, if the attribute is non-numerical, its set of values can be ordered or unordered. We will limit ourselves to non-numerical attributes with unordered value sets. Such a set is typically small, containing a few values only.

An object is described in terms of attributes by specifying concrete values of the attributes in the object. Such a description is then a vector of attribute values.

Figure 18.6 shows some objects that will be used as an illustration in this section. The objects in Figure 18.6 belong to five classes: nut, screw, key, pen, scissors. Suppose that these objects have been shown to a vision system. Their silhouettes have been captured by camera and further processed by a vision program. This program can then extract some attribute values of each object from the camera image. In our case, the attributes are: the size, the shape and the number of holes in an object. Let the possible values of these attributes be:

      size: small, large
      shape: long, compact, other
      holes: none, 1, 2, 3, many

Assume that the vision system has extracted the three attribute values for each object. Figure 18.7 shows the attribute definitions and gives these examples represented as a set of Prolog clauses of the form:

      example(Class, [Attribute1 = Val1, Attribute2 = Val2, ...]).

Figure 18.6 Camera image of some objects.

---

attribute(size, [small, large]).
attribute(shape, [long, compact, other]).
attribute(holes, [none, 1, 2, 3, many]).

example(nut, [size = small, shape = compact, holes = 1]).
example(screw, [size = small, shape = long, holes = none]).
example(key, [size = small, shape = long, holes = 1]).
example(nut, [size = small, shape = compact, holes = 1]).
example(key, [size = large, shape = long, holes = 1]).
example(screw, [size = small, shape = compact, holes = none]).
example(nut, [size = small, shape = compact, holes = 1]).
example(pen, [size = large, shape = long, holes = none]).
example(scissors, [size = large, shape = long, holes = 2]).
example(pen, [size = large, shape = long, holes = none]).
example(scissors, [size = large, shape = other, holes = 2]).
example(key, [size = small, shape = other, holes = 2]).

Figure 18.7 Attribute definitions and examples for learning to recognize objects from their silhouettes (from Figure 18.6).

Now assume that these clauses are communicated to a learning program that is supposed to learn about the classes from the example objects. The result of the learning will be a description of classes in the form of rules that can be used for classifying new objects. The format of rules is exemplified by the following possible rules for the classes **nut** and **key**:

> nut <= = [[size = small, holes = 1]]
>
> key <= = [[shape = long, holes = 1], [shape = other, holes = 2]]

The meaning of these rules is:

> An object is a nut if
> its size is small and
> it has 1 hole.

> An object is a key if
> its shape is long and
> it has 1 hole
> or
> its shape is other and
> it has 2 holes.

The general form of such rules is:

> Class <= = [Conj1, Conj2, ...]

where Conj1, Conj2, etc., are lists of attribute values of the form:

> [Att1 = Val1, Att2 = Val2, ...]

A class description [Conj1, Conj2, ...] is interpreted as follows:

(1)   an object matches the description if the object satisfies at least one of Conj1, Conj2, etc.;

(2)   an object satisfies a list of attribute values Conj if all the attribute values in Conj are as in the object.

For example, an object described by

> [size = small, shape = long, holes = 1]

matches the rule for **key** by satisfying the first attribute-value list in the rule. Thus attribute values in Conj are related conjunctively: none of them may be contradicted by the object. On the other hand, the lists Conj1, Conj2, etc., are related disjunctively: at least one of them has to be satisfied.

The matching between an object and a concept description can be stated in Prolog as:

```
match( Object, Description) :-
    member( Conjunction, Description),
    satisfy( Object, Conjunction).

satisfy( Object, Conjunction) :-
    not (
        member( Att = Val, Conjunction),      % Value in concept
        member( Att = ValX, Object),          % and value in object
        ValX \== Val).                        % are different
```

Notice that this definition allows for partially specified objects when some attribute value may be unspecified – that is, not included in the attribute-value list. In such a case this definition assumes that the unspecified value satisfies the requirement in Conjunction.

18.5.2 Construction of class descriptions

Now we will consider how a class description can be constructed from a set of examples. As opposed to the previous section (learning relational descriptions), the class description will not be constructed by processing the examples sequentially. Instead, all the examples will be processed 'in one shot'.

The main requirement here is that the constructed description of a class exactly matches the examples belonging to the class; that is, the description matches all the example objects of this class and no other example object. When an object matches a description, we also say that the description *covers* the object. Thus we have to construct a description for the given class that covers all the examples of this class and no other example. Such a description

---

Figure 18.8 A program that induces attribute-based rules.

```
% Learning of simple attributional descriptions

:- op( 300, xfx, <==).

% learn( Class): collect learning examples into a list, construct and
% output a description for Class, and assert the corresponding rule about Class

learn( Class) :-
    bagof( example( ClassX, Obj), example( ClassX, Obj), Examples),   % Collect examples
    learn( Examples, Class, Description),                              % Induce rule
    nl, write( Class), write( ' <=='), nl,                            % Output rule
    writelist( Description),
    assert( Class <== Description).                                   % Assert rule
```

Figure 18.8 (cont.)

```
% learn( Examples, Class, Description):
%    Description covers exactly the examples of class Class in list Examples

learn( Examples, Class, [ ]) :-
    not member( example( Class, _ ), Examples).          % No example to cover

learn( Examples, Class, [Conj | Conjs]) :-
    learn_conj( Examples, Class, Conj),
    remove( Examples, Conj, RestExamples),               % Remove examples that match Conj
    learn( RestExamples, Class, Conjs).                  % Cover remaining examples


% learn_conj( Examples, Class, Conj):
%    Conj is a list of attribute values satisfied by some examples of class Class and
%    no other class

learn_conj( Examples, Class, [ ]) :-
    not ( member( example( ClassX, _ ), Examples),       % There is no example
        ClassX \== Class), !.                            % of different class

learn_conj( Examples, Class, [Cond | Conds]) :-
    choose_cond( Examples, Class, Cond),                 % Choose attribute value
    filter( Examples, [ Cond], Examples1),
    learn_conj( Examples1, Class, Conds).

choose_cond( Examples, Class, AttVal) :-
    findall( AV/Score, score( Examples, Class, AV, Score), AVs),
    best( AVs, AttVal).                                  % Best score attribute value

best( [ AttVal/_], AttVal).

best( [ AV0/S0, AV1/S1 | AVSlist], AttVal) :-
    S1 > S0, !,                                          % AV1 better than AV0
    best( [AV1/S1 | AVSlist], AttVal)
    ;
    best( [AV0/S0 | AVSlist], AttVal).


% filter( Examples, Condition, Examples1):
%    Examples1 contains elements of Examples that satisfy Condition

filter( Examples, Cond, Examples1) :-
    findall( example( Class, Obj),
            ( member( example( Class, Obj), Examples), satisfy( Obj, Cond)),
            Examples1).


% remove( Examples, Conj, Examples1):
%    removing from Examples those examples that match Conj gives Examples1

remove( [ ], _, [ ]).
```

(continues)

Figure 18.8 (cont.)

```
remove( [example( Class, Obj) | Es], Conj, Es1) :-      % First example matches Conj
    satisfy( Obj, Conj), !,                              % Remove it
    remove( Es, Conj, Es1).

remove( [E | Es], Conj, [E | Es1]) :-                   % Retain first example
    remove( Es, Conj, Es1).

satisfy( Object, Conj) :-
    not ( member( Att = Val, Conj),
        member( Att = ValX, Object),
        ValX \== Val).

match( Object, Description) :-
    member( Conj, Description),
    satisfy( Object, Conj).

score( Examples, Class, AttVal, Score) :-
    candidate( Examples, Class, AttVal),                % A suitable attribute value
    filter( Examples, [ AttVal], Examples1),            % Examples1 satisfy condition Att = Val
    length( Examples1, N1),                             % Length of list
    count_pos( Examples1, Class, NPos1),                % Number of positive examples
    NPos1 > 0,                                          % At least one positive example matches AttVal
    Score is 2 * NPos1 − N1.

candidate( Examples, Class, Att = Val) :-
    attribute( Att, Values),                            % An attribute
    member( Val, Values),                               % A value
    suitable( Att = Val, Examples, Class).

suitable( AttVal, Examples, Class) :-
    % At least one negative example must not match AttVal
    member( example( ClassX, ObjX), Examples),
    ClassX \== Class,                                   % Negative example
    not satisfy( ObjX, [ AttVal]), !.                   % that does not match

% count_pos( Examples, Class, N):
%     N is the number of positive examples of Class

count_pos( [], _, 0).

count_pos( [example( ClassX,_ ) | Examples], Class, N) :-
    count_pos( Examples, Class, N1),
    ( ClassX = Class, !, N is N1 + 1; N = N1).

member( X, [X | _]).

member( X, [_ | L]) :-
    member( X, L).

writelist( [ ]).

writelist( [X | L]) :-
    tab( 2), write( X), nl,
    writelist( L).
```

is said to be 'complete and correct': complete because it covers all the positive examples and correct because it covers no negative example. The procedure

    learn(Examples, Class, Description)

in the program of Figure 18.8 constructs such descriptions. It works roughly as follows:

> To cover all the examples of class **Class** in **Examples** do:
>
> > if no example in **Examples** belongs to **Class** then **Description** = [ ],
> > otherwise **Description** = [Conj | Conjs] where **Conj** and **Conjs** are obtained as follows:
> >
> > (1)   construct a list **Conj** of attribute values that covers at least one positive example of **Class** and no example of any other class;
> >
> > (2)   remove from **Examples** all the objects covered by **Conj** and cover the remaining, uncovered objects by description **Conjs**.

Each attribute-value list is constructed by the procedure:

    learn_conj(Examples, Class, Conjunction)

The attribute-value list **Conjunction** emerges gradually, starting with the empty list and adding to this list conditions of the form:

    Attribute = Value

Notice that, in this way, the attribute-value list becomes more and more specific (it covers less objects). The attribute-value list is acceptable when it becomes so specific that it only covers positive examples of **Class**.

The process of constructing such a conjunction is highly combinatorial. Each time a new attribute-value condition is added, there are almost as many alternative candidates to be added as there are attribute-value pairs. It is not immediately clear which of them is the best. In general, we would like to cover all the positive examples with as few attribute-value lists as possible, and with as short lists as possible. Thus learning can be viewed as a search among possible descriptions with the objective of minimizing the length of the concept description. Because of the high combinatorial complexity of this search, we normally have to resort to some heuristic. The program in Figure 18.8 relies on a heuristic scoring function that is used locally. At each point, only the best-estimated attribute value is added to the list, immediately disregarding all other candidates. The search is thus reduced to a deterministic procedure without any backtracking; however, there is the risk of overlooking the shortest concept description. The heuristic estimate is simple and based on the following intuition: a useful attribute-value condition should discriminate well between positive and negative examples. Thus, it should cover as many positive examples as possible and as few negative examples as possible. Figure 18.9 shows the construction of such a heuristic scoring function implemented in our program as the procedure:

score(Examples, Class, AttributeValue, Score)

The program in Figure 18.8 can be run to construct some class descriptions for the examples in Figure 18.7 with the query:

?- learn(nut), learn(key), learn(scissors).

nut <= =
  [shape = compact, holes = 1]

key <= =
  [shape = other, size = small]
  [holes = 1, shape = long]

scissors <= =
  [holes = 2, size = large]

The procedure learn also asserts rules about the corresponding classes in the program. These rules can be used to classify new objects. A corresponding

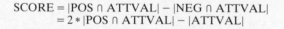

$$SCORE = |POS \cap ATTVAL| - |NEG \cap ATTVAL|$$
$$= 2 * |POS \cap ATTVAL| - |ATTVAL|$$

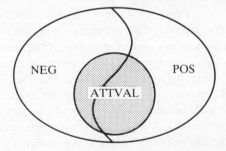

Figure 18.9 Heuristic scoring of an attribute value. POS is the set of positive examples of the class to be learned; NEG is the set of negative examples of this class. The shaded area, ATTVAL, represents the set of objects that satisfy the attribute-value condition. The heuristic score of the attribute value is the number of positive examples in ATTVAL minus the number of negative examples in ATTVAL.

recognition procedure that uses the learned descriptions is:

```
classify( Object, Class)  :-
    Class <= = Description,         % Learned rule about Class
    match( Object, Description).
```

18.6   Induction of decision trees

Induction of decision trees is a popular method for learning attribute-type descriptions. Concept descriptions are in this case represented by decision trees. Induction of trees is relatively efficient and easy to program.

Figure 18.10 shows a decision tree induced from the examples of Figure 18.7 (that is, the objects in Figure 18.6). Internal nodes in the tree are labelled with attributes. The leaves of the tree are labelled with classes or the symbol 'null'. 'null' indicates that no learning example corresponds to that leaf. Branches in the tree are labelled with attribute values. In classifying an object, a path is traversed in the tree starting at the root node and ending at a leaf. At each internal node, we follow the branch labelled by the attribute value in the object. For example, an object described by

[size = small, shape = compact, holes = 1]

would be, according to this tree, classified as a nut (following the path: holes = 1, shape = compact). Notice that, in this case, the attribute value size = small is not needed to correctly classify the object.

In comparison with if-then rules to describe classes, discussed in the previous section, trees are a more constrained representation, which has both

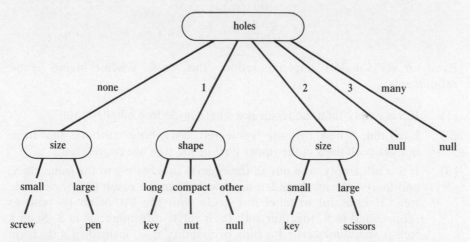

Figure 18.10 A decision tree induced from examples of Figure 18.7 (shown graphically in Figure 18.6).

advantages and disadvantages. Some concepts are more awkward to represent with trees than with rules: although every rule-based description can be translated into a corresponding decision tree, the resulting tree may have to be much lengthier than the rule-based description. This is an obvious disadvantage of trees. On the other hand, the fact that trees are more constrained reduces the combinatorial complexity of the learning process. This may lead to substantial improvement in the efficiency of learning. Decision tree learning is one of the most efficient forms of learning. It should be noted, however, that computational efficiency of learning is only one criterion of success in learning, as will be discussed later in this chapter.

The basic tree induction algorithm is as follows:

> To construct a decision tree T for a learning set S do:
>
> > if all the examples in S belong to the same class, C,
> > then the result is a single node tree labelled C
> > otherwise
> > > select the most 'informative' attribute, A, whose values
> > > are $v_1, \ldots, v_n$;
> > > partition S into $S_1, \ldots, S_n$ according to the value of A;
> > > construct (recursively) subtrees $T_1, \ldots, T_n$ for $S_1, \ldots, S_n$;
> > > final result is the tree whose root is A and whose subtrees
> > > are $T_1, \ldots, T_n$, and the links between A and the subtrees are labelled by $v_1, \ldots, v_n$; thus the decision tree looks like this:
>
>

Even in its simplest implementation, this basic scheme needs some refinements:

(1)   If S is empty then the result is a single-node tree labelled 'null'.

(2)   Each time a new attribute is selected, only those attributes that have not yet been used in the upper part of the tree are considered.

(3)   If S is not empty, and not all the objects in S belong to the same class, and there is no attribute left to choose, then the result is a single-node tree. It is useful to label this node with the list of all the classes represented in S, together with their relative frequencies in S. Such a tree is sometimes called a class probability tree, instead of a decision tree. We say that in such a case the set of available attributes is incomplete: the available attributes are not sufficient to distinguish

between class values of some objects (objects that belong to different classes have exactly the same attribute values).

(4)   We have to specify the criterion for selecting the 'most informative' attribute. Often, this criterion is based on concepts from information theory. Such a criterion can be developed as follows. To classify an object, a certain amount of information is needed. After we have learned the value of some attribute in the object, we only need some remaining amount of information to classify the object. This remaining amount is normally smaller than the initial amount, and will be called the 'residual information'. The 'most informative' attribute is the one that minimizes the residual information. The computation of the amount of information needed is based on the *entropy* measure. So for a domain exemplified by the learning set S, the average amount of information *I* per object is given by the entropy measure:

$$I = -\sum_{c} p(c) \log_2 p(c)$$

where c stands for classes and $p(c)$ is the probability that an object in S is of class c. After applying an attribute A, the set S is partitioned into subsets according to the values of A. The residual information *Ires* is then equal to the weighted sum of the amounts of information for the subsets:

$$Ires(A) = -\sum_{v} p(v) \sum_{c} \frac{p(v, c)}{p(v)} \log_2 \left(\frac{p(v, c)}{p(v)} \right)$$

where v stands for the values of A, $p(v)$ is the probability of value v in set S, and $p(v, c)$ is the probability of value v and class c occurring in the same object in S; probabilities $p(v)$ and $p(v, c)$ are usually approximated by statistics on set S.

The intuition behind using the information content criterion is as follows. We are interested in small trees; therefore, we need powerful attributes to discriminate between classes. Ideally, such a powerful attribute should divide the objects in S into subsets so that only one class is represented in each set. Such a totally uniform set (uniform with respect to the class) is said to be 'pure'. In a non-ideal situation, the set is not completely pure, but we want it to be 'as pure as possible'. Thus, we prefer attributes that minimize the 'impurity' of resulting subsets. The entropy measure is in fact a measure of impurity. Further refinements can be made to the information-theoretic criterion given above. Also, there exist other sensible measures of impurity, like the Gini index, defined by:

$$Gini = \sum_{i \neq j} p(i) p(j)$$

where *i* and *j* are classes. After applying attribute A, the resulting Gini index is

$$Gini(A) = \sum_v p(v) \sum_{i \neq j} p(i \mid v)\, p(j \mid v)$$

where *v* stands for values of A and $p(i \mid v)$ denotes the conditional probability of class *i* given attribute A has value *v*.

It should be noted that impurity measures as used here assess the effect of a single attribute. Therefore, the criterion 'most informative' is local in the sense that it does not reliably predict the combined effect of several attributes applied jointly. The basic tree induction algorithm is based on this local minimization of impurity. Global optimization would be computationally much more expensive.

Let us now sketch a procedure to induce decision trees:

> **induce_tree(Attributes, Examples, Tree)**

where **Tree** is a decision tree induced from **Examples** using attributes in list **Attributes**. If the examples and attributes are represented as in Figure 18.7, we can collect all the examples and available attributes into lists, used as arguments for our induction procedure:

```
induce_tree( Tree) :-
    findall( example( Class, Obj), example( Class, Obj), Examples),
    findall( Att, attribute( Att, _ ), Attributes),
    induce_tree( Attributes, Examples, Tree).
```

The tree has a different form depending on the following three main cases:

(1)　**Tree = null** if the example set is empty.

(2)　**Tree = leaf(Class)** if all of the examples are of the same class **Class**.

(3)　**Tree = tree(Attribute, [Val1 : SubTree1, Val2 : Subtree2, ...])** if examples belong to more than one class, **Attribute** is the root of the tree, **Val1**, **Val2**, ... are its values, and **SubTree1**, **SubTree2**, ... are the corresponding decision subtrees.

These three cases are handled by the following three clauses:

```
% induce_tree( Attributes, Examples, Tree)

induce_tree( _, [ ], null) :- !.

induce_tree( _, [example( Class,_ ) | Examples], leaf( Class)) :-
    not ( member( example( ClassX, _ ), Examples),      % No other example
        ClassX \== Class), !.                           % of different class
```

```
induce_tree( Attributes, Examples, tree( Attribute, SubTrees)) :-
    choose_attribute( Attributes, Examples, Attribute),
    delete( Attribute, Attributes, RestAtts),            % Delete Attribute
    attribute( Attribute, Values),
    induce_trees( Attribute, Values, RestAtts, Examples, SubTrees).
```

induce_trees induces decision SubTrees for subsets of Examples according to Values of Attribute:

```
% induce_trees( Att, Vals, RestAtts, Examples, SubTrees)

induce_trees( _, [], _, _, [] ).

induce_trees( Att, [Val1 | Vals], RestAtts, Exs, [Val1 : Tree1 | Trees]) :-
    attval_subset( Att = Val1, Exs, ExampleSubset),
    induce_tree( RestAtts, ExampleSubset, Tree1),
    induce_trees( Att, Vals, RestAtts, Exs, Trees).
```

attval_subset(Attribute = Value, Examples, Subset) is true if Subset is the subset of examples in Examples that satisfy the condition Attribute = Value:

```
attval_subset( AttributeValue, Examples, ExampleSubset) :-
    findall( example( Class, Obj),
            ( member( example( Class, Obj), Examples),
              satisfy( Obj, [ AttributeValue])),
            ExampleSubset).
```

The predicate choose_attribute selects the attribute that discriminates well among the classes. This involves the impurity criterion. The following clause minimizes the chosen impurity measure using setof. setof will order the available attributes according to increasing impurity:

```
choose_attribute( Atts, Examples, BestAtt) :-
    setof( Impurity/Att,
            ( member( Att, Atts), impurity1( Examples, Att, Impurity)),
            [ MinImpurity/BestAtt | _] ).
```

Procedure

```
impurity1( Examples, Attribute, Impurity)
```

implements a chosen impurity measure. Impurity is the combined impurity of the subsets of examples after dividing the list Examples according to the values of Attribute.

EXERCISES

18.3 Implement a chosen impurity measure by writing the **impurity1** predicate. This measure can be, for example, the residual information content or Gini index as discussed previously in this section. For the examples in Figure 18.7 and attribute 'size', use of the Gini index as impurity measure gives:

> ?- **Examples** = ...   % Examples from Figure 18.7
>   **impurity1(Examples, size, Impurity).**
>
> **Impurity = 0.647619**

Approximating probabilities by relative frequencies, **Impurity** is calculated as follows:

$$
\begin{aligned}
\text{Impurity} &= \textit{Gini}(\text{ size}) \\
&= p(\text{small}) * (p(\text{nut} \mid \text{small}) * p(\text{screw} \mid \text{small}) + \ldots) \\
&\quad + p(\text{large}) * (\ldots) \\
&= 7/12 * (3/7 * 2/7 + \ldots) + 5/12 * (\ldots) \\
&= 7/12 * 0.653061 + 5/12 * 0.64 \\
&= 0.647619
\end{aligned}
$$

18.4 Complete the tree induction program of this section and test it on some learning problem – for example, the one in Figure 18.7. Note that the procedure **choose_attribute**, using **setof**, is very inefficient and can be improved. Also add a procedure

> **show(DecisionTree)**

for displaying decision trees in a readable form. For the tree in Figure 18.10, a suitable form is:

```
holes
  none
    size
      small -> screw
      large -> pen
  1
    shape
      long -> key
      compact -> nut
      other -> null
  2
    size
      small -> key
      large -> scissors
  3 -> null
  many -> null
```

18.7 Learning from noisy data and tree pruning

In many applications the data for learning is imperfect. One common problem is errors in attribute values and class values. In such cases we say that the data is *noisy*. Noise of course makes the learning task more difficult and requires special mechanisms. In the case of noise, we usually abandon the requirement that learned concept descriptions match all the positive examples and no negative ones. Thus, we allow the learned description to misclassify some of the learning objects. This concession is sensible because of possible errors in the data. We hope the misclassified learning objects are those that contain errors and misclassifying such objects only indicates that erroneous data has in fact been successfully ignored.

Inducing decision trees from noisy data with the basic tree induction algorithm gives rise to two problems: first, induced trees unreliably classify new objects and, second, induced trees tend to be large and thus hard to understand. It can be shown that some of this tree complexity is the result of noise in the learning data. The learning algorithm, in addition to discovering genuine regularities of the problem domain, also traces noise in the data. As an example, consider a situation in which we are to construct a subtree of a decision tree and the current subset of objects for learning is S. Let there be 100 objects in S, 99 of them belonging to class C1 and one of them to class C2. Knowing that there is noise in the learning data and that all these objects agree in the values of the attributes already selected up to this point in the decision tree, it seems plausible that the class C2 object is in S only as a result of an error in the data. If so, it is best to ignore this object and simply return a leaf of the decision tree labelled with class C1. Since the basic tree induction algorithm would in this situation further expand the decision tree, we have, by stopping at this point, in effect pruned a subtree of the complete decision tree. Tree pruning is the key to coping with noise in tree induction programs. A program may effectively prune decision trees by using some criterion that indicates whether to stop expanding the tree or not. The stopping criterion would typically take into account the number of examples in the node, the prevalence of the majority class at the node, to what extent an additional attribute selected at this node would reduce the impurity of the example set, etc. This kind of pruning, accomplished through stopping the tree expansion, is called *forward pruning* as opposed to another kind of pruning, called *post-pruning*. Working in the post-pruning regime, a learning program first constructs the complete tree and then estimates its subtrees with respect to their reliability, and then prunes those that seem unreliable. We will now look at one method of post-pruning in more detail.

The key decision in post-pruning is whether to prune a subtree or not. This decision can be based on classification error estimates of decision subtrees. Suppose we are at a node in the tree and we have to decide whether to prune the subtrees of this node or not. One way to decide is as follows. Let there be the set S of examples that fall into this node, and k classes altogether in the learning problem. There are altogether N examples in S and the majority class in S is C. n out of N examples in S belong to C and other examples in S belong to other classes. Now assume that we choose to prune the subtrees of this node. Accordingly, this node becomes a leaf and is labelled with class C. What will be the expected classification error at this leaf? This error can be estimated probabilistically, but in such an estimate we have to assume some prior distribution of the probabilities of classes. If there is no reason to assume some classes *a priori* more likely than others, then one reasonable assumption is that the prior distribution of these probabilities is uniform and equal for all the classes. Then the expected probability of the classification error $E(S)$ for set S is:

$$E(S) = \frac{N - n + k - 1}{N + k}$$

Such an error estimator can be directly applied to estimate the classification error at each leaf of a decision tree. So if Node is a leaf of a decision tree with set S of examples falling into Node, then:

$$\text{Error(Node)} = E(S)$$

This error estimator can be easily generalized to estimate classification errors of non-leaf nodes in a decision tree. Let Node be a non-leaf node of a decision tree and let Node's successors be Node_1, Node_2, etc. Let the probabilities of branches from Node to Node_i be P_i. Then we define:

$$\text{BackedUpError(Node)} = \sum_i P_i * \text{Error(Node}_i)$$

The probabilities P_i can be approximated by relative frequencies of attribute values in sets of examples that fall into nodes Node_i. Note that the backed-up error estimate is obtained from the node's subtrees. We can now compare the node's 'static' error with its backed-up error. In the case that the static error is lower then we prune the node's subtree. Thus, for an internal node Node, the error estimate is:

$$\text{Error(Node)} = \min(E(\text{Node}), \text{BackedUpError(Node)})$$

This formula suggests the following pruning algorithm to optimize the estimated classification error. Given a complete (unpruned) decision tree, the algorithm starts at the bottom of the tree and progresses toward the root of the tree, backing up the error estimates and pruning inferior subtrees. This algorithm guarantees that all of the subtrees are pruned optimally with respect to the classification error estimates. As a result, it will minimize the expected error at the root of the tree; that is, the expected error of the whole tree. Of course, a pruned tree thus obtained is only optimal with respect to error estimates.

Figure 18.11 shows the pruning of a decision tree by the procedure described above. In this figure, the left-most leaf of the unpruned tree has class frequences [3, 2], meaning that there are three objects of class C1 and two objects of class C2 falling into this leaf. The static error estimate for these

Before pruning:

After pruning:

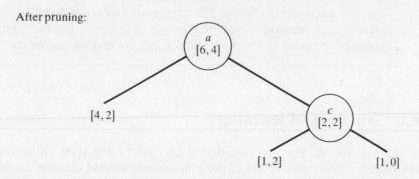

Figure 18.11 Pruning of decision trees to minimize error estimates. Pairs of numbers in square brackets are the numbers of class C1 and class C2 examples that fall into the corresponding nodes. The other numbers attached to the nodes are error estimates. For internal nodes, the first number is a static error estimate and the second number is a backed-up estimate. The lower of the two numbers (in bold face) is propagated upwards.

class frequences is:

$$E = \frac{N - n + k - 1}{N + k} = \frac{5 - 3 + 2 - 1}{5 + 2} = 0.429$$

For the right-hand child of node b, the error estimate is 0.333. For node b, the static error estimate is:

$$E(b) = 0.375$$

The backed-up error estimate for b is:

$$BackedUpError(b) = \frac{5}{6} * 0.429 + \frac{1}{6} * 0.333 = 0.413$$

Because the backed-up estimate is greater than the static estimate, the subtrees of b are pruned and the static estimate is therefore adapted:

$$Error(b) = 0.375$$

EXERCISE

18.5 Write a procedure

> **prunetree(Tree, PrunedTree)**

that prunes a decision tree **Tree** according to the classification error estimates discussed in the text. The leaves of **Tree** contain class frequency information represented as lists of integers. Let the number of classes be stored in the program as a fact: **number_of_classes(K).**

18.8 Success of learning

We started this chapter by considering the ARCHES style of learning. ARCHES is a good illustration of the main principles and ideas in learning. Also, its sequential style of processing examples is perhaps closer to human learning than the one-shot learning in the other two approaches discussed in this chapter. On the other hand, learning of attributional descriptions, either in the form of rules or trees, is simpler than learning relational descriptions, and better understood. Therefore, these simpler approaches have until now enjoyed much more attention and success in practical applications.

It has been shown that learning is inherently a combinatorial process. It involves search among possible concept descriptions. This search can be heuristically guided. It can also be significantly constrained by the 'linguistic bias'; that is, the effect of the concept description language only allowing certain forms of concept descriptions to be constructed. Both our algorithms for learning attributional descriptions were very strongly heuristically guided – for example, by the impurity criterion. Therefore, these algorithms are efficient, although in our Prolog implementation (Figure 18.8) the evaluation of such a heuristic is itself rather inefficient. These heuristics require the computation of certain statistics for which Prolog is not the most suitable.

In general, the success of learning is measured by several criteria. In the following sections we will look at some usual criteria, and discuss the benefits of tree pruning in the view of these criteria.

18.8.1   Criteria for success of learning

Here are some usual criteria for measuring the success of a learning system:

- Classification accuracy: This is usually defined as the percentage of objects correctly classified by the learned concept description F. We distinguish between two types of classification accuracy:

    Accuracy on unseen objects; that is, those not contained in the training set S.

    Accuracy on the objects in S. (Of course, this is only interesting when exact agreement between F and the target concept C on S is not required in the learning algorithm.)

- Transparency of the induced concept description F: It is often important for the generated description to be comprehensible in order to tell the user something interesting about the application domain. Such a description can also be used by humans directly, without machine help, as an enhancement to humans' own knowledge. In this sense, machine learning is one approach to computer-aided synthesis of new knowledge, an idea propounded by Michie (1986). This criterion is also very important when the induced descriptions are used in an expert system whose behaviour has to be transparent.

- Computational complexity: What are the required computer resources in terms of time and space? Usually, we distinguish between two types of complexity:

    Generation complexity (resources needed to induce a concept description from examples).

    Execution complexity (complexity of classifying an object using the induced description).

18.8.2 How pruning affects accuracy and transparency of decision trees

Pruning of decision trees is of fundamental importance because of its beneficial effects when dealing with noisy data. Pruning affects two measures of success of learning: first, the classification accuracy of a decision tree on new objects and, second, the transparency of a decision tree. Let us consider both of these effects of pruning.

The comprehensibility of a description depends on its structure and size. A well-structured decision tree is easier to understand than a completely unstructured tree. On the other hand, if a decision tree is small (consisting of just 10 or so nodes) then it is easy to understand regardless of its structure. Since pruning reduces the size of a tree, it contributes to the transparency of a decision tree. As has been shown experimentally in many noisy domains, such as medical diagnosis, the reduction of tree size can be dramatic. The number of nodes is reduced to, say, 10% of their original number, while retaining at least the same range of the classification accuracy.

Tree pruning can also improve the classification accuracy of a tree. This effect of pruning may appear counter-intuitive since, by pruning, we throw away some information, and it would seem that as a result some accuracy should be lost. However, in the case of learning from noisy data, a correct amount of pruning normally improves the accuracy. This phenomenon can be explained in statistical terms: statistically, pruning works as a sort of noise suppression mechanism. By pruning, we eliminate errors in learning data that are due to noise, rather than throw away healthy information.

SUMMARY

- Forms of learning include: learning by being told, learning from examples, learning by discovery. Learning concepts from examples is also called inductive learning.

- Learning from examples involves:

  objects and concepts
  positive and negative examples of concept to be learned
  matching between objects and concept descriptions

- Matching can be complicated and combinatorially complex.

- The goal of learning from examples is to construct a formula in the concept description language that matches all the given positive examples and no negative example.

- The inductive learning process involves search among possible concept descriptions, and is inherently combinatorial. To reduce computational complexity it can be heuristically guided.

- During its construction, a concept description may be generalized or specialized. Normally, the final concept description is a generalization of the positive learning examples.
- Programs developed in this chapter are:

  An ARCHES-like program that learns relational descriptions from examples defined by semantic networks.

  A program that learns if-then rules from examples defined by attribute vectors.

  A program that learns decision trees from examples defined by attribute vectors.

- Pruning decision trees is a powerful method for learning from noisy data.
- Criteria for assessing the success of a method of learning from examples include:

  accuracy of learned concept descriptions
  transparency of learned concept descriptions
  computational efficiency in both constructing a concept description and in classifying new objects

- Concepts discussed in this chapter are:

  machine learning
  learning concepts from examples, inductive learning
  concept description language
  relational descriptions
  attribute-based descriptions
  matching of objects and concept descriptions
  generality and specificity of concept descriptions
  generalization and specialization of descriptions
  ARCHES-type learning of relational descriptions
  AQ-type learning of rules
  TDIDT – top-down induction of decision trees (or ID3-type learning)
  learning from noisy data
  tree pruning, post-pruning

References

Our treatment of learning relational descriptions (Section 18.3) follows the ideas of Winston's ARCHES program (Winston 1975). The program in Section 18.5 that constructs attribute-based descriptions is a simple version of the AQ-type learning. The AQ family of learning programs was developed by Michalski and his co-workers (for example, Michalski 1983).

Induction of decision trees is one of the most widely used approaches to learning, also known under the name TDIDT (top-down induction of decision trees, coined by Quinlan,

1986). TDIDT learning was much influenced by Quinlan's early program ID3, Iterative Dichotomizer 3, (Quinlan 1979) and tree induction is therefore often simply referred to as ID3. Tree induction was also studied outside AI by Breiman and his co-workers (1984) who independently discovered several pertinent mechanisms, including pruning of decision trees. The technique of tree pruning based on the classification of error estimates (in Section 18.7) is from Niblett and Bratko (1986). Several other refinements of the basic tree induction algorithm are necessary to make it a practical knowledge acquisition tool in complex applications with real-life data. Such refinements and their exhaustive experimental verification in which machine-learned knowledge outperforms human experts are presented in Bratko and Kononenko (1987), Cestnik *et al.* (1987) and Quinlan *et al.* (1987). Structuring decision trees to improve their transparency was studied by Shapiro (1987).

Let us mention some of the many interesting developments in machine learning that could not be covered in this chapter.

An early attempt at machine learning is Samuel's learning program that played the game of checkers (1959). This program improved its position-evaluation function through the experience it obtained in the games it played.

Mitchell (1979) developed the idea of 'version space' as an attempt to handle economically the search among alternative concept descriptions.

Logic formalisms are used as a concept description language in several learning programs. First-order predicate logic is, for example, used in MARVIN (Sammut and Banerji 1986), CIGOL (Muggleton and Buntine 1988) and FOIL (Quinlan 1989).

An interesting approach to learning is explanation-based learning; see, for example, Mitchell *et al.* (1986). Here the learning system uses background knowledge to reason about a given example to 'explain' the example by a deductive process. Examples are so used to guide the learning system toward proper generalizations in forming a general rule from an example. One approach to explanation-based generalization is programmed in Chapter 20 of this book as a kind of meta-programming exercise.

Some learning programs learn by autonomous discovery. They discover new concepts through exploration, making their own experiments. A celebrated example of this kind of program is AM, Automatic Mathematician (Lenat 1982). AM, for example, starting with the concepts of set and 'bag', discovered the concepts of number, addition, multiplication, prime number, etc.

Current research in machine learning is published in the AI literature, most notably in the journals *Machine Learning* (Boston: Kluwer) and *Artificial Intelligence* (Amsterdam: North-Holland). Many important papers on learning are collected in Michalski, Carbonell and Mitchell (1983, 1986). Kodratoff (1988) discusses various approaches to learning.

Bratko, I. and Kononenko, I. (1987) Learning diagnostic rules from incomplete and noisy data. In: *Interactions in AI and Statistics* (B. Phelps, ed.). London: Gower Technical Press.

Breiman, L., Friedman, J.H., Olshen, R.A. and Stone, C.J. (1984) *Classification and Regression Trees*. Belmont, California: Wadsworth Int. Group.

Cestnik, B., Kononenko, I. and Bratko, I. (1987) ASISTANT 86: a knowledge elicitation tool for sophisticated users. In: *Progress in Machine Learning* (I. Bratko, N. Lavrac, eds.). Wilmslow, England: Sigma Press; distributed by Wiley.

Kodratoff, Y. (1988) *Introduction to Machine Learning*. London: Pitman.

Lenat, D.B. (1982) AM: discovery in mathematics as heuristic search. In: *Knowledge-Based Systems in Artificial Intelligence* (R. Davis, D.B. Lenat, eds.). McGraw-Hill.

Michalski, R.S. (1983) A theory and methodology of inductive learning. In: *Machine Learning: An Artificial Intelligence Approach* (R.S Michalski, J.G. Carbonell, T.M. Mitchell, eds.). Tioga Publishing Company.

Michalski, R.S., Carbonell, J.G. and Mitchell, T.M. (1983, eds.) *Machine Learning: An Artificial Intelligence Approach*. Palo Alto, CA: Tioga Publishing Company.

Michalski, R.S., Carbonell, J.G. and Mitchell, T.M. (1986, eds.) *Machine Learning: An Artificial Intelligence Approach,* Volume II. Los Altos, CA: Morgan Kaufmann.

Michie, D. (1986) The superarticulacy phenomenon in the context of software manufacture. In: *Proc. of the Royal Society*, London, A 405, pp. 189–212. Also reprinted in *Expert Systems: Automating Knowledge Acquisition* (D. Michie and I. Bratko). Addison-Wesley.

Mitchell, T.M. (1977) Version spaces: a candidate elimination approach to rule learning. In: *Proc. Fifth IJCAI*, Cambridge, MA.

Mitchell, T.M., Keller, R.M. and Kedar-Cabelli, S.T. (1986) Explanation-based generalisation: a unifying view. *Machine Learning* **1**: 47–80.

Muggleton, S. and Buntine, W. (1988) Machine invention of first-order predicates by inverting resolution. In: *Proc. Fifth Machine Learning Workshop*, Ann Arbor, MI.

Niblett, T. and Bratko, I. (1986) Learning decision rules in noisy domains. In: *Research and Development in Expert Systems III* (M.A. Bramer, ed.). Cambridge University Press.

Quinlan, J.R. (1979) Discovering rules by induction from large collections of examples. In: *Expert Systems in the Microelectronic Age* (D. Michie, ed.). Edinburgh University Press.

Quinlan, J.R. (1986) Induction of decision trees. *Machine Learning* **1**: 81–106.

Quinlan, J.R. (1989) Learning relations: comparison of symbolic and connectionist approach. In: *Proc. ISSEK Workshop 89*, Udine, Italy.

Quinlan, J.R., Compton, P., Horn, K.A. and Lazarus, L. (1987) Inductive knowledge acquisition: a case study. In: *Applications of Expert Systems* (J.R. Quinlan, ed.). Addison-Wesley.

Sammut, C. and Banerji, R.B. (1986) Learning concepts by asking questions. In: *Machine Learning: An Artificial Intelligence Approach, Volume II* (R.S. Michalski, J.G. Carbonell, T.M. Mitchell, eds.). Los Altos, CA: Morgan Kaufmann.

Samuel, A.L. (1959) Some studies in machine learning using the game of checkers. *IBM Journal of Research and Development* **3**: 211–229. Also in *Computers and Thought* (E.A. Feigenbaum, I. Feldman, eds.). McGraw-Hill, 1963.

Shapiro, A. (1987) *Structured Induction in Expert Systems*. Glasgow: Turing Institute Press, in association with Addison-Wesley.

Winston, P.H. (1975) Learning structural descriptions from examples. In: *The Psychology of Computer Vision* (P.H. Winston, ed.). McGraw-Hill.

19 Game Playing

In this chapter we will consider techniques for playing two-person, perfect-information games, such as chess. For interesting games, trees of possible continuations are far too complex to be searched exhaustively, so other approaches are necessary. One method is based on the minimax principle, efficiently implemented as the alpha-beta algorithm. In addition to this standard technique, we will develop in this chapter a program based on the Advice Language approach for introducing pattern knowledge into a chess-playing program. This rather detailed example further illustrates how well Prolog is suited for the implementation of knowledge-based systems.

19.1 Two-person, perfect-information games

The kind of games that we are going to discuss in this chapter are called two-person, perfect-information games. Examples of games of this kind are chess, checkers and go. In such games there are two players that make moves alternatively, and both players have the complete information of the current situation in the game. Thus this definition excludes most card games. The game is over when a position is reached that qualifies as 'terminal' by the rules of the game – for example, mate in chess. The rules also determine what is the outcome of the game that has ended in this terminal position.

Such a game can be represented by a *game tree*. The nodes in such a tree correspond to situations, and the arcs correspond to moves. The initial situation of the game is the root node; leaves of the tree correspond to terminal positions.

In most games of this type the outcome of the game can be *win*, *loss* or *draw*. We will now consider games with just two outcomes: *win* and *loss*. Games where a draw is a possible outcome can be reduced to two outcomes: *win*, *not-win*. The two players will be called 'us' and 'them'. 'Us' can win in a non-terminal 'us-to-move' position if there is a legal move that leads to a won position. On the other hand, a non-terminal 'them-to-move' position is won for 'us' if *all* the legal moves from this position lead to won positions. These rules correspond to AND/OR tree representation of problems discussed in Chapter 13. The concepts from AND/OR trees and games correspond as follows:

game positions	problems
terminal won position	goal node, trivially solved problem
terminal lost position	unsolvable problem
won position	solved problem
us-to-move position	OR node
them-to-move position	AND node

Clearly, many concepts from searching AND/OR trees can be adapted for searching game trees.

A simple program that finds whether an us-to-move position is won can be defined as follows:

```
won( Pos) :-
    terminalwon( Pos).           % A terminal won position

won( Pos) :-
    not terminallost( Pos),
    move( Pos, Pos1),            % A legal move to Pos1
    not ( move( Pos1, Pos2),     % No opponent's move leads to a
        not won( Pos2) ).        % not-won position
```

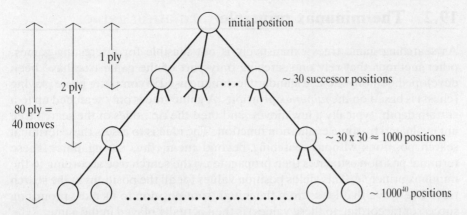

Figure 19.1   The complexity of game trees in chess. The estimates here are based on an approximation that there are about 30 legal moves from each chess position, and that terminal positions occur at a depth of 40 moves. One move is 2 plies (1 half-move by each side).

The rules of the game are built into the predicates **move(Pos, Pos1)** to generate legal moves, and **terminalwon(Pos)** and **terminallost(Pos)** to recognize terminal positions that are won or lost by the rules of the game. The last rule above says, through the double use of **not**: there is no them-move that leads to a not-won position. In other words: *all* them-moves lead to a won position.

As with analogous programs for searching AND/OR graphs, the above program uses the depth-first strategy. In addition, this program does not prevent cycling between positions. This may cause problems as the rules of some games allow repetition of positions. However, this repetition is often only superficial. By rules of chess, for example, after a three-fold repetition the game can be claimed a draw.

The foregoing program shows the basic principle. However, much more powerful techniques are necessary for practically dealing with complicated games like chess or go. The combinatorial complexity of these games makes our naive search algorithm, which only stops at terminal positions of the game, completely infeasible. Figure 19.1 illustrates this point with respect to chess. The search space of astronomical proportions includes some 10^{120} positions. It can be argued that equal positions in the tree of Figure 19.1 occur at different places. Still, it has been shown that the number of different positions is far beyond anything manageable by forseeable computers.

Project

Write a program to play some simple game (like *nim*) using the straightforward AND/OR search approach.

19.2   The minimax principle

As searching game trees exhaustively is not feasible for interesting games, other methods that rely on searching only part of the game tree have been developed. Among these, a standard technique used in computer game playing (chess) is based on the *minimax* principle. A game tree is only searched up to a certain depth, typically a few moves, and then the tip nodes of the search tree are evaluated by some evaluation function. The idea is to assess these terminal search positions without searching beyond them, thus saving time. These terminal position estimates then propagate up the search tree according to the minimax principle. This yields position values for all the positions in the search tree. The move that leads from the initial, root position to its most promising successor (according to these values) is then actually played in the game.

Notice that we distinguish between a 'game tree' and a 'search tree'. A search tree is normally a part of the game tree (upper part) – that is, the part that is explicitly generated by the search process. Thus, terminal search positions do not have to be terminal positions of the game.

Much depends on the evaluation function which, in most games of interest, has to be a heuristic estimator that estimates the winning chances from the point of view of one of the players. The higher the value the higher the player's chances are to win, and the lower the value the higher the opponent's chances are to win. As one of the players will tend to achieve a high position value, and the other a low value, the two players will be called MAX and MIN respectively. Whenever MAX is to move, he or she will choose a move that maximizes the value; on the contrary, MIN will choose a move that minimizes the value. Given the values of the bottom-level positions in a search tree, this principle (called *minimax*) will determine the values of all the other positions in the search tree. Figure 19.2 illustrates. In the figure, levels of positions with MAX to move alternate with those with MIN to move. The bottom-level position values are determined by the evaluation function. The values of the internal nodes can be computed in a bottom-up fashion, level by level, until the root node is reached. The resulting root value in Figure 19.2 is 4, and accordingly the best move for MAX in position *a* is *a-b*. The best MIN's reply is *b-d*, etc. This sequence of play is also called the *main variation*. The main variation defines the 'minimax-optimal' play for both sides. Notice that the value of the positions along the main variation does not vary. Accordingly, correct moves are those that preserve the value of the game.

We distinguish between the bottom-level values and the backed-up values. The former values are called 'static' since they are obtained by a 'static' evaluation function, as opposed to backed-up values that are obtained 'dynamically' by propagation of static values up the tree.

The value propagation rules can be formalized as follows. Let us denote the static value of a position P by

$v(P)$

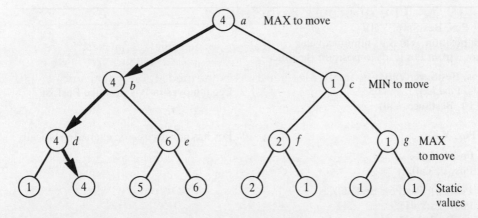

Figure 19.2 Static values (bottom level) and minimax backed-up values in a search tree. The indicated moves constitute the *main variation* – that is, the minimax optimal play for both sides.

and the backed-up value by:

$$V(P)$$

Let $P_1, \ldots, P_n$ be legal successor positions of P. Then the relation between static values and backed-up values can be defined as:

$$V(P) = v(P) \qquad \text{if } P \text{ is a terminal position in a search tree } (n = 0)$$
$$V(P) = \max_i V(P_i) \quad \text{if } P \text{ is a MAX-to-move position}$$
$$V(P) = \min_i V(P_i) \quad \text{if } P \text{ is a MIN-to-move position}$$

A Prolog program that computes the minimax backed-up value for a given position is shown in Figure 19.3. The main relation in this program is

minimax(Pos, BestSucc, Val)

where **Val** is the minimax value of a position **Pos**, and **BestSucc** is the best successor position of **Pos** (the move to be played to achieve **Val**). The relation

moves(Pos, PosList)

corresponds to the legal-move rules of the game: **PosList** is the list of legal successor positions of **Pos**. The predicate **moves** is assumed to fail if **Pos** is a terminal search position (a leaf of the search tree). The relation

best(PosList, BestPos, BestVal)

```
% minimax( Pos, BestSucc, Val):
%    Pos is a position, Val is its minimax value;
%    best move from Pos leads to position BestSucc

minimax( Pos, BestSucc, Val) :-
    moves( Pos, PosList), !,                          % Legal moves in Pos produce PosList
    best( PosList, BestSucc, Val)
    ;
    staticval( Pos, Val).                             % Pos has no successors: evaluate statically

best( [ Pos], Pos, Val) :-
    minimax( Pos, _, Val), !.

best( [Pos1 | PosList], BestPos, BestVal) :-
    minimax( Pos1, _, Val1),
    best( PosList, Pos2, Val2),
    betterof( Pos1, Val1, Pos2, Val2, BestPos, BestVal).

betterof( Pos0, Val0, Pos1, Val1, Pos0, Val0) :-      % Pos0 better than Pos1
    min_to_move( Pos0),                               % MIN to move in Pos0
    Val0 > Val1, !                                    % MAX prefers the greater value
    ;
    max_to_move( Pos0),                               % MAX to move in Pos0
    Val0 < Val1, !.                                   % MIN prefers the lesser value

betterof( Pos0, Val0, Pos1, Val1, Pos1, Val1).        % Otherwise Pos1 better than Pos0
```

Figure 19.3 A straightforward implementation of the minimax principle.

selects the 'best' position **BestPos** from a list of candidate positions **PosList**. **BestVal** is the value of **BestPos**, and hence also of **Pos**. 'Best' is here either maximum or minimum, depending on the side to move.

19.3 The alpha-beta algorithm: an efficient implementation of minimax

The program in Figure 19.3 systematically visits *all* the positions in the search tree, up to its terminal positions in a depth-first fashion, and statically evaluates *all* the terminal positions of this tree. Usually not all this work is necessary in order to correctly compute the minimax value of the root position. Accordingly, the search algorithm can be economized. The improvement can be based on the following idea: Suppose that there are two alternative moves; once one of them has been shown to be clearly inferior to the other, it is not necessary to know *exactly* how much inferior it is for making the correct decision. For example, we can use this principle to reduce the search in the tree of Figure 19.2. The search process here proceeds as follows:

(1) Start with position *a*.

(2)   Move down to b.

(3)   Move down to d.

(4)   Take the maximum of d's successors yielding $V(d) = 4$.

(5)   Backtrack to b and move down to e.

(6)   Consider the first successor of e whose value is 5. At this point MAX (who is to move in e) is guaranteed at least the value of 5 in position e regardless of other (possibly better) alternatives from e. This is sufficient for MIN to realize that, at node b, the alternative e is inferior to d, even without knowing the exact value of e.

On these grounds we can neglect the second successor of e and simply assign to e an *approximate* value 5. This approximation will, however, have no effect on the computed value of b and, hence, of a.

The celebrated *alpha-beta algorithm* for efficient minimaxing is based on this idea. Figure 19.4 illustrates the action of the alpha-beta algorithm on our example tree of Figure 19.2. As Figure 19.4 shows, some of the backed-up values are approximate. However, these approximations are sufficient to determine the root value precisely. In the example of Figure 19.4, the alpha-beta principle reduces the search complexity from eight static evaluations (as originally in Figure 19.2) to five static evaluations.

As said before, the key idea of the alpha-beta pruning is to find a 'good enough' move, not necessarily the best, that is sufficiently good to make the correct decision. This idea can be formalized by introducing two bounds, usually denoted *Alpha* and *Beta*, on the backed-up value of a position. The meaning of these bounds is: *Alpha* is the minimal value that MAX is already

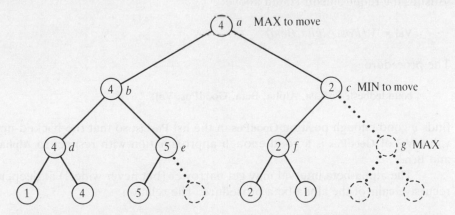

Figure 19.4 The tree of Figure 19.2 searched by the alpha-beta algorithm. The alpha-beta search prunes the nodes shown by dotted lines, thus economizing the search. As a result, some of the backed-up values are inexact (nodes c, e, f; compare with Figure 19.2). However, these approximations suffice for determining the root value and the main variation correctly.

guaranteed to achieve, and *Beta* is the maximal value that MAX can hope to achieve. From MIN's point of view, *Beta* is the worst value for MIN that MIN is guaranteed to achieve. Thus, the actual value (that is to be found) lies between *Alpha* and *Beta*. If a position has been shown that its value lies outside the *Alpha-Beta* interval then this is sufficient to know that this position is not in the main variation, without knowing the exact value of this position. We only have to know the exact value of this position if this value is between *Alpha* and *Beta*. Formally, we can define a 'good enough' backed-up value *V(P,Alpha,Beta)* of a position *P*, with respect to *Alpha* and *Beta*, as any value that satisfies the following requirements:

$$V(P,Alpha,Beta) < Alpha \qquad if \qquad V(P) < Alpha$$
$$V(P,Alpha,Beta) = V(P) \qquad if \qquad Alpha \leq V(P) \leq Beta$$
$$V(P,Alpha,Beta) > Beta \qquad if \qquad V(P) > Beta$$

Obviously we can always compute the exact value of a root position *P* by setting the bounds as follows:

$$V(P, - infinity, + infinity) = V(P)$$

Figure 19.5 shows a Prolog implementation of the alpha-beta algorithm. The main relation is

alphabeta(Pos, Alpha, Beta, GoodPos, Val)

where **GoodPos** is a 'good enough' successor of **Pos**, so that its value **Val** satisfies the requirements stated above:

Val = *V(Pos,Alpha,Beta)*

The procedure

boundedbest(PosList, Alpha, Beta, GoodPos, Val)

finds a good enough position **GoodPos** in the list **PosList** so that the backed-up value **Val** of **GoodPos** is a good enough approximation with respect to **Alpha** and **Beta**.

The alpha-beta interval may get narrower (but never wider!) at deeper recursive calls of the alpha-beta procedure. The relation

newbounds(Alpha, Beta, Pos, Val, NewAlpha, NewBeta)

defines the new interval (**NewAlpha**, **NewBeta**). This is always narrower than or equal to the old interval (**Alpha**, **Beta**). So at deeper levels in the search tree, the *Alpha-Beta* bounds tend to shrink, and positions at deeper levels are

% The alpha-beta algorithm

```
alphabeta( Pos, Alpha, Beta, GoodPos, Val) :-
   moves( Pos, PosList), !,
   boundedbest( Poslist, Alpha, Beta, GoodPos, Val);
   staticval( Pos, Val).                                    % Static value of Pos

boundedbest( [Pos | PosList], Alpha, Beta, GoodPos, GoodVal) :-
   alphabeta( Pos, Alpha, Beta, _, Val),
   goodenough( PosList, Alpha, Beta, Pos, Val, GoodPos, GoodVal).

goodenough( [ ], _, _, Pos, Val, Pos, Val) :- !.           % No other candidate

goodenough( _, Alpha, Beta, Pos, Val, Pos, Val) :-
   min_to_move( Pos), Val > Beta, !;                        % Maximizer attained upper bound
   max_to_move( Pos), Val < Alpha, !.                       % Minimizer attained lower bound

goodenough( PosList, Alpha, Beta, Pos, Val, GoodPos, GoodVal) :-
   newbounds( Alpha, Beta, Pos, Val, NewAlpha, NewBeta),    % Refine bounds
   boundedbest( PosList, NewAlpha, NewBeta, Pos1, Val1),
   betterof( Pos, Val, Pos1, Val1, GoodPos, GoodVal).

newbounds( Alpha, Beta, Pos, Val, Val, Beta) :-
   min_to_move( Pos), Val > Alpha, !.                       % Maximizer increased lower bound

newbounds( Alpha, Beta, Pos, Val, Alpha, Val) :-
   max_to_move( Pos), Val < Beta, !.                        % Minimizer decreased upper bound

newbounds( Alpha, Beta, _, _, Alpha, Beta).                % Otherwise bounds unchanged

betterof( Pos, Val, Pos1, Val1, Pos, Val) :-               % Pos better than Pos1
   min_to_move( Pos), Val > Val1, !;
   max_to_move( Pos), Val < Val1, !.

betterof( _, _, Pos1, Val1, Pos1, Val1).                   % Otherwise Pos1 better
```

Figure 19.5 An implementation of the alpha-beta algorithm.

evaluated with tighter bounds. Narrower intervals allow for grosser approximations, and thus more tree pruning. An interesting question is now: How much effort the alpha-beta algorithm saves compared with the exhaustive minimax search program of Figure 19.3?

The efficiency of the alpha-beta search depends on the order in which positions are searched. It is advantageous to consider strong moves for each side first. It is easy to demonstrate by examples that if the order is unfortunate then the alpha-beta procedure will have to visit *all* the positions visited by the exhaustive minimax search. That means that in the worst case alpha-beta will have no advantage over the exhaustive minimax search. If the order is favourable, however, savings can be significant. Let N be the number of terminal search positions statically evaluated by the exhaustive minimax algorithm. It has been proved that in the best case, when the strongest move is always considered first, the alpha-beta algorithm will only have to statically evaluate $\sqrt{N}$ positions.

On a similar note, this same result is relevant in a practical aspect in tournament play. In a tournament, a chess-playing program is usually given a certain amount of time for computing the next move in the game, and the depth to which the program can search will depend on this amount of time. The alpha-beta algorithm will be able, in the best case, to search *twice as deep* as the exhaustive minimax search. Experience shows that the same evaluation function applied at a greater depth in the tree will usually produce stronger play.

The economization effect of the alpha-beta algorithm can also be expressed in terms of the effective branching factor (number of branches stemming from each internal node) of the search tree. Assume that the game tree has a uniform branching factor b. Due to the pruning effect, alpha-beta will only search some of the branches, thus effectively reducing the branching factor. The reduction is, in the best case, from b to $\sqrt{b}$. In chess-playing programs the effective branching factor due to the alpha-beta pruning becomes about 6 compared to the total of about 30 legal moves. A less optimistic view on this result is that in chess, even with alpha-beta, deepening the search by 1 ply (one halph-move) increases the number of terminal search positions by a factor of about 6.

Project

Consider a two-person game (for example, some non-trivial version of tic-tac-toe). Write game-definition relations (legal moves and terminal game positions) and propose a static evaluation function to be used for playing the game with the alpha-beta procedure.

19.4 Minimax-based programs: refinements and limitations

The minimax principle, together with the alpha-beta algorithm, is the basis of many successful game-playing programs, most notably chess programs. The general scheme of such a program is: perform the alpha-beta search on the current position in the game, up to some fixed depth limit (dictated by the time constraints imposed by tournament rules), using a game-specific evaluation function for evaluating the terminal positions of the search. Then execute the best move (according to alpha-beta) on the play board, accept the opponent's reply, and start the same cycle again.

The two basic ingredients, then, are the alpha-beta algorithm and a heuristic evaluation function. To build a good program for a complicated game like chess many refinements to this basic scheme are needed. We will briefly review some standard techniques.

Much depends on the evaluation function. If we had a perfect evaluation function we would only have to consider the immediate successors of the current position, thus practically eliminating search. But for games like chess, any evaluation function of practically acceptable computational complexity will necessarily be just a heuristic estimate. This estimate is based on 'static' features of the position (for example, the number of pieces on the board) and will therefore be more reliable in some positions than in others. Consider for example such a material-based evaluation function for chess and imagine a position in which White is a knight up. This function will, of course, assess the position in White's favour. This is fine if the position is quiescent, Black having no violent threat at his disposal. On the other hand, if Black can capture the White's queen on the next move, such an evaluation can result in a disastrous blunder, as it will not be able to perceive the position *dynamically*. Clearly, we can better trust the static evaluation in quiescent positions than in turbulent positions in which each side has direct threats of capturing the opponent's pieces. Obviously, we should use the static evaluation only in quiescent positions. Therefore a standard trick is to extend the search in turbulent positions beyond the depth limit until a quiescent position is reached. In particular, this extension includes sequences of piece captures in chess.

Another refinement is *heuristic pruning*. This aims at achieving a greater depth limit by disregarding some less promising continuations. This technique will prune branches in addition to those that are pruned by the alpha-beta technique itself. Therefore this entails the risk of overlooking some good continuation and incorrectly computing the minimax value.

Yet another technique is *progressive deepening*. The program repeatedly executes the alpha-beta search, first to some shallow depth, and then increases the depth limit on each iteration. The process stops when the time limit has been reached. The best move according to the deepest search is then played. This technique has the following advantages:

- enables the time control; when the time limit is reached there will always be some best move found so far;
- the minimax values of the previous iteration can be used for preliminary ordering of positions on the next iteration, thus helping the alpha-beta algorithm to search strong moves first.

Progressive deepening entails some overhead (researching upper parts of the game tree), but this is relatively small compared with the total effort.

A known problem with programs that belong to this general scheme is the 'horizon effect'. Imagine a chess position in which the program's side inevitably loses a knight. But the loss of the knight can be delayed at the cost of a lesser sacrifice, a pawn say. This intermediate sacrifice may push the actual loss of the knight beyond the search limit (beyond the program's 'horizon'). Not seeing the eventual loss of the knight, the program will then prefer this variation to the quick death of the knight. So the program will eventually lose *both* the pawn (unnecessarily) and the knight. The extension of search up to a quiescent position can alleviate the horizon effect.

There is, however, a more fundamental limitation of the minimax-based programs which lies in the limited form of the domain-specific knowledge they use. This becomes very conspicuous when we compare the best chess programs with human chess masters. Strong programs often search millions (and more) of positions before deciding on the move to play. It is known from psychological studies that human masters typically search just a few tens of positions, at most a few hundred. Despite this apparent inferiority, chess masters usually beat programs. The masters' advantage lies in their knowledge, which far exceeds that contained in the programs. Games between machines and strong human players show that the enormous advantage in the calculating power cannot completely compensate the lack of knowledge.

Knowledge in minimax-based programs takes three main forms:

- evaluation function,
- tree-pruning heuristics,
- quiescence heuristics.

The evaluation function reduces many aspects of a game situation into a single number, and this reduction can have a detrimental effect. A good player's understanding of a game position, on the contrary, spans over many dimensions. Let us consider an example from chess: an evaluation function will evaluate a position as equal simply by stating that its value is 0. A master's assessment of the same position can be much more informative and indicative of a further course of the game. For example, Black is a pawn up, but White has a good attacking initiative that compensates the material, so chances are equal.

In chess, minimax-based programs often play well in sharp tactical struggles when precise calculation of forced variations is decisive. Their weakness shows in quiet positions where their play falls short of long-range plans that prevail in such slow, strategic games. Lack of a plan makes an impression that the program keeps wandering during the game from one idea to another. This is particularly evident in chess endgames.

In the rest of this chapter we will consider another approach to game playing, based on introducing pattern knowledge into a program by means of 'advice'.

19.5 Pattern knowledge and the mechanism of 'advice'

19.5.1 Goals and move-constraints

The method of representing game-specific knowledge that we consider in this section belongs to the family of Advice Languages. In Advice Languages the user specifies, in a declarative way, what ideas should be tried in certain types of situations. Ideas are formulated in terms of goals and means of achieving the goals. An Advice Language interpreter then finds out, through search, which idea actually works in a given situation.

The fundamental concept in Advice Languages is a 'piece-of-advice'. A piece-of-advice suggests what to do (or to *try* to do) next in a certain type of position. Generally speaking, advice is expressed in terms of *goals* to be achieved, and *means* of achieving these goals. The two sides are called 'us' and 'them'; advice always refers to the 'us' point of view. Each piece-of advice has four ingredients:

- *better-goal*: a goal to be achieved;
- *holding-goal*: a goal to be maintained during play toward the better-goal;
- *us-move-constraints*: a predicate on moves that selects a subset of all legal us-moves (moves that should be considered of interest with respect to the goals specified);
- *them-move-constraints*: a predicate to select moves to be considered by 'them' (moves that may undermine the goals specified).

As a simple example from the chess endgame king and pawn vs. king, consider the straightforward idea of queening the pawn by simply pushing the pawn forward. This can be expressed in the form of advice as:

- *better-goal*: pawn queened;
- *holding-goal*: pawn is not lost;
- *us-move-constraints*: pawn move;
- *them-move-constraints*: approach the pawn with the king.

19.5.2   Satisfiability of advice

We say that a given piece-of-advice is *satisfiable* in a given position if 'us' can force the achievement of the better-goal specified in the advice under the conditions that:

(1)   the holding-goal is never violated,

(2)   all the moves played by 'us' satisfy us-move-constraints,

(3)   'them' is only allowed to make moves that satisfy them-move-constraints.

The concept of a *forcing-tree* is associated with the satisfiability of a piece-of-advice. A forcing-tree is a detailed strategy that guarantees the achievement of the better-goal under the constraints specified by the piece-of-advice. A forcing-tree thus specifies exactly what moves 'us' has to play on any 'them' reply. More precisely, a forcing-tree T for a given position P and a piece-of-advice A is a subtree of the game tree such that:

- the root node of T is P;
- all the positions in T satisfy the holding-goal;
- all the terminal nodes in T satisfy the better-goal, and no internal node in T satisfies the better-goal;
- there is exactly one us-move from each internal us-to-move position in T; and that move must satisfy the us-move-constraints
- T contains all them-moves (that satisfy the them-move-constraints) from each non-terminal them-to-move position in T.

Each piece-of-advice can be viewed as a definition of a small special game with the following rules. Each opponent is allowed to make moves that satisfy his or her move-constraints; a position that does not satisfy the holding-goal is won for 'them'; a position that satisfies the holding-goal and the better-goal is won for 'us'. A non-terminal position is won for 'us' if the piece-of-advice is satisfiable in this position. Then 'us' will win by executing a corresponding forcing-tree in the play.

19.5.3 Integrating pieces-of-advice into rules and advice-tables

In Advice Languages, individual pieces-of-advice are integrated in the complete knowledge representation schema through the following hierarchy. A piece-of-advice is part of an if-then rule. A collection of if-then rules is an *advice-table*. A set of advice-tables is structured into a hierarchical network. Each advice-table has the role of a specialized expert to deal with some specific subproblem of the whole domain. An example of such a specialized expert is an advice-table that knows how to mate in the king and rook vs. king ending in chess. This table is summoned when such an ending occurs in a game.

For simplicity, we will consider a simplified version of an Advice Language in which we will only allow for one advice-table. We shall call this version Advice Language 0, or AL0 for short. Here is the structure of AL0 already syntactically tailored toward an easy implementation in Prolog.

A program in AL0 is called an *advice-table*. An advice-table is an *ordered* collection of if-then rules. Each rule has the form:

RuleName : if Condition then AdviceList

Condition is a logical expression that consists of predicate names connected by logical connectives **and, or, not**. **AdviceList** is a list of names of pieces-of-advice.

An example of a rule called 'edge_rule', from the king and rook vs. king ending, can be:

> **edge_rule :**
>   **if their_king_on_edge and our_king_close**
>   **then [mate_in_2, squeeze, approach, keeproom, divide].**

This rule says: if in the current position their king is on the edge and our king is close to their king (or more precisely, kings are less than four squares apart), then try to satisfy, in the order of preference as stated, the pieces-of-advice: 'mate_in_2', 'squeeze', 'approach', 'keeproom', 'divide'. This advice-list specifies pieces-of-advice in the decreasing order of ambition: first try to mate in two moves, if that is not possible then try to 'squeeze' the opponent's king toward a corner, etc. Notice that with an appropriate definition of operators, the rule above is a syntactically correct Prolog clause.

Each piece-of-advice will be specified by a Prolog clause of another form:

> **advice(AdviceName,**
>   **BetterGoal :**
>   **HoldingGoal :**
>   **Us_Move_Constraints :**
>   **Them_Move_Constraints).**

The goals are expressions that consist of predicate names and logical connectives **and, or, not**. Move-constraints are, again, expressions that consist of predicate names and the connectives **and** and **then**: **and** has the usual logical meaning, **then** prescribes the ordering. For example, a move-constraint of the form

> **MC1 then MC2**

says: first consider those moves that satisfy **MC1**, and then those that satisfy **MC2**.

For example, a piece-of-advice to mate in 2 moves in the king and rook vs. king ending, written in this syntax, is:

> **advice(mate_in_2,**
>   **mate :**
>   **not rooklost :**
>   **(depth = 0) and legal then (depth = 2) and checkmove :**
>   **(depth = 1) and legal).**

Here the better-goal is **mate**, the holding-goal is **not rooklost** (rook is not lost). The us-move-constraints say: at depth 0 (the current board position) try any legal move, then at depth 2 (our second move) try checking moves only. The depth is measured in plies. Them-move-constraints are: any legal move at depth 1.

In playing, an advice-table is then used by repeating, until the end of the game, the following main cycle: build a forcing-tree, then play according to this tree until the play exits the tree; build another forcing-tree, etc. A forcing-tree is generated each time as follows: take the current board position Pos and scan the rules in the advice-table one by one; for each rule, match Pos with the precondition of the rule, and stop when a rule is found such that Pos satisfies its precondition. Now consider the advice-list of this rule: process pieces-of-advice in this list one by one until a piece-of-advice is found that is satisfiable in Pos. This results in a forcing-tree that is the detailed strategy to be executed across the board.

Notice the importance of the ordering of rules and pieces-of-advice. The rule used is the first rule whose precondition matches the current position. There must be for any possible position at least one rule in the advice-table whose precondition will match the position. Thus an advice-list is selected. The first satisfiable piece-of-advice in this list is applied.

An advice-table is thus largely a non-procedural program. An AL0 interpreter accepts a position and by executing an advice-table produces a forcing-tree which determines the play in that position.

19.6 A chess endgame program in Advice Language 0

Implementation of an AL0-based game-playing program can be conveniently divided into three modules:

(1)   an AL0 interpreter,
(2)   an advice-table in AL0,
(3)   a library of predicates (including rules of the game) used in the advice-table.

This structure corresponds to the usual structure of knowledge-based systems as follows:

- The AL0 interpreter is an inference engine.
- The advice-table and the predicate library constitute a knowledge base.

19.6.1   A miniature AL0 interpreter

A miniature, game-independent AL0 interpreter is implemented in Prolog in Figure 19.6. This program also performs the user interaction during play. The central function of the program is the use of knowledge in an AL0 advice-table; that is, interpreting an AL0 advice-program for the generation of forcing-trees and their execution in a game. The basic forcing-tree generation algorithm is similar to the depth-first search in AND/OR graphs of Chapter

13; a forcing-tree corresponds to an AND/OR solution tree. On the other hand, it also resembles the generation of a proof tree in an expert system shell (Chapters 14 and 15).

For simplicity, in the program of Figure 19.6 'us' is supposed to be White, and 'them' is Black. The program is started through the procedure

> playgame(Pos)

where **Pos** is a chosen initial position of a game to be played. If it is 'them' to move in **Pos** then the program reads a move from the user, otherwise the program consults the advice-table that is attached to the program, generates a forcing-tree and plays its move according to the tree. This continues until the end of the game is reached as specified by the predicate **end_of_game** (mate, for example).

A forcing-tree is a tree of moves, represented in the program by the following structure

> Move .. [Reply1 .. Ftree1, Reply2 .. Ftree2, ...]

where '..' is an infix operator; **Move** is the first move for 'us'; **Reply1**, **Reply2**, etc. are the possible 'them' replies; and **Ftree1**, **Ftree2**, etc. are forcing-subtrees that correspond to each of the 'them' replies respectively.

19.6.2   An advice-program for the king and rook vs. king ending

A broad strategy for winning with the king and rook against the sole opponent's king is to force the king to the edge, or into a corner if necessary, and then deliver mate in a few moves. An elaboration of this broad principle is:

While making sure that stalemate is never created or the rook left undefended under attack, repeat until mate:

(1) Look for a way to mate the opponent's king in two moves.

(2) If the above is not possible, then look for a way to constrain further the area on the chessboard to which the opponent's king is confined by our rook.

(3) If the above is not possible, then look for a way to move our king closer to the opponent's king.

(4) If none of the above pieces-of-advice 1, 2 or 3 works, then look for a way of maintaining the present achievements in the sense of 2 and 3 (that is, make a waiting move).

(5) If none of 1, 2, 3 or 4 is attainable, then look for a way of obtaining a position in which our rook divides the two kings either vertically or horizontally.

Figure 19.6   A miniature implementation of Advice Language 0.

```
% A miniature implementation of Advice Language 0
%
% This program plays a game from a given starting position using knowledge
% represented in Advice Language 0

:- op( 200, xfy, :).
:- op( 220, xfy, .. ).
:- op( 185, fx, if).
:- op( 190, xfx, then).
:- op( 180, xfy, or).
:- op( 160, xfy, and).
:- op( 140, fx, not).

playgame( Pos) :-                                      % Play a game starting in Pos
  playgame( Pos, nil).                                 % Start with empty forcing-tree

playgame( Pos, ForcingTree) :-
  show( Pos),
  ( end_of_game( Pos),                                 % End of game?
    write( 'End of game'), nl, !
  ;
    playmove( Pos, ForcingTree, Pos1, ForcingTree1), !,
    playgame( Pos1, ForcingTree1)
  ).


% Play 'us' move according to forcing-tree

playmove( Pos, Move .. FTree1, Pos1, FTree1) :-
  side( Pos, w),                                       % White = 'us'
  legalmove( Pos, Move, Pos1),
  showmove( Move).


% Read 'them' move

playmove( Pos, FTree, Pos1, FTree1) :-
  side( Pos, b),
  write( 'Your move: '),
  read( Move),
  ( legalmove( Pos, Move, Pos1),
    subtree( FTree, Move, FTree1), !                   % Move down forcing-tree
  ;
    write( 'Illegal move'), nl,
    playmove( Pos, FTree, Pos1, FTree1)
  ).
```

Figure 19.6 (cont.)

% If current forcing-tree is empty generate a new one

```
playmove( Pos, nil, Pos1, FTree1) :-
    side( Pos, w),
    resetdepth( Pos, Pos0),                    % Pos0 = Pos with depth 0
    strategy( Pos0, FTree), !,                 % Generate new forcing-tree
    playmove( Pos0, FTree, Pos1, FTree1).
```

% Select a forcing-subtree corresponding to Move

```
subtree( FTrees, Move, FTree) :-
    member( Move .. FTree, FTrees), !.

subtree( _, _, nil).

strategy( Pos, ForcingTree) :-                 % Find forcing-tree for Pos
    Rule : if Condition then AdviceList,       % Consult advice-table
    holds( Condition, Pos, _), !,              % Match Pos against precondition
    member( AdviceName, AdviceList),           % Try pieces-of-advice in turn
    nl, write( 'Trying'), write( AdviceName),
    satisfiable( AdviceName, Pos, ForcingTree), !.   % Satisfy AdviceName in Pos

satisfiable( AdviceName, Pos, FTree) :-
    advice( AdviceName, Advice),               % Retrieve piece-of-advice
    sat( Advice, Pos, Pos, FTree).             % 'sat' needs two positions
                                               % for comparison predicates

sat( Advice, Pos, RootPos, FTree) :-
    holdinggoal( Advice, HG),
    holds( HG, Pos, RootPos),                  % Holding-goal satisfied
    sat1( Advice, Pos, RootPos, FTree).

sat1( Advice, Pos, RootPos, nil) :-
    bettergoal( Advice, BG),
    holds( BG, Pos, RootPos), !.               % Better-goal satisfied

sat1( Advice, Pos, RootPos, Move .. FTrees) :-
    side( Pos, w), !,                          % White = 'us'
    usmoveconstr( Advice, UMC),
    move( UMC, Pos, Move, Pos1),               % A move satisfying move-constr.
    sat( Advice, Pos1, RootPos, FTrees).

sat1( Advice, Pos, RootPos, FTrees) :-
    side( Pos, b), !,                          % Black = 'them'
    themmoveconstr( Advice, TMC),
    bagof( Move .. Pos1, move( TMC, Pos, Move, Pos1), MPlist),
    satall( Advice, MPlist, RootPos, FTrees).  % Satisfiable in all successors

satall( _, [], _, [] ).
```

(continues)

Figure 19.6 (cont.)

```
satall( Advice, [Move .. Pos | MPlist], RootPos, [Move .. FT | MFTs] ) :-
  sat( Advice, Pos, RootPos, FT),
  satall( Advice, MPlist, RootPos, MFTs).
```

% Interpreting holding and better-goals:
% A goal is an AND/OR/NOT combination of predicate names

```
holds( Goal1 and Goal2, Pos, RootPos) :- !,
  holds( Goal1, Pos, RootPos),
  holds( Goal2, Pos, RootPos).

holds( Goal1 or Goal2, Pos, RootPos) :- !,
  ( holds( Goal1, Pos, RootPos)
  ;
    holds( Goal2, Pos, RootPos)
  ).

holds( not Goal, Pos, RootPos) :- !,
  not holds( Goal, Pos, RootPos).

holds( Pred, Pos, RootPos) :-
  ( Cond =.. [ Pred, Pos]              % Most predicates do not depend on RootPos
  ;
    Cond =.. [ Pred, Pos, RootPos] ),
  call( Cond).
```

% Interpreting move-constraints

```
move( MC1 and MC2, Pos, Move, Pos1) :- !,
  move( MC1, Pos, Move, Pos1),
  move( MC2, Pos, Move, Pos1).

move( MC1 then MC2, Pos, Move, Pos1) :- !,
  ( move( MC1, Pos, Move, Pos1)
  ;
    move( MC2, Pos, Move, Pos1)
  ).
```

% Selectors for components of piece-of-advice

```
bettergoal( BG : _, BG).

holdinggoal( BG : HG : _, HG).

usmoveconstr( BG : HG : UMC : _, UMC).

themmoveconstr( BG : HG : UMC : TMC, TMC).

member( X, [X | L] ).

member( X, [Y | L] ) :-
  member( X, L).
```

These principles are implemented in detail as an AL0 advice-table in Figure 19.7. This table can be run by the AL0 interpreter of Figure 19.6. Figure 19.8 illustrates the meaning of some of the predicates used in the table and the way the table works.

The predicates used in the table are:

Goal predicates

mate	their king mated
stalemate	their king stalemated
rooklost	their king can capture our rook
rookexposed	their king can attack our rook before our king can get to defend the rook
newroomsmaller	area to which their king is restricted by our rook has shrunk
rookdivides	rook divides both kings either vertically or horizontally
okapproachedcsquare	our king approached 'critical square', see Figure 19.9; here this means that the Manhattan distance has decreased
lpatt	'L-pattern' (Figure 19.9)
roomgt2	the 'room' for their king is greater than two squares

Move-constraints predicates

depth = N	move occurring at **depth = N** in the search tree
legal	any legal move
checkmove	checking move
rookmove	a rook move
nomove	fails for any move
kingdiagfirst	a king move, with preference for diagonal king moves

Figure 19.7   An AL0 advice-table for king and rook vs. king. The table consists of two rules and six pieces-of-advice.

% King and rook vs. king in Advice Language 0

% Rules

edge_rule : if   their_king_edge and kings_close
       then [mate_in_2, squeeze, approach, keeproom,
           divide_in_2, divide_in_3].

(continues)

Figure 19.7 (cont.)

else_rule : if   true
           then [squeeze, approach, keeproom, divide_in_2, divide_in_3].

% Pieces-of-advice

advice(mate_in_2,
        mate :
        not rooklost and their_king_edge :
        (depth = 0) and legal then (depth = 2) and checkmove :
        (depth = 1) and legal).

advice(squeeze,
        newroomsmaller and not rookexposed and
        rookdivides and not stalemate :
        not rooklost :
        (depth = 0) and rookmove :
        nomove).

advice(approach,
        okapproachedcsquare and not rookexposed and not stalemate and
        (rookdivides or lpatt) and (roomgt2 or not our_king_edge) :
        not rooklost :
        (depth = 0) and kingdiagfirst :
        nomove).

advice(keeproom,
        themtomove and not rookexposed and rookdivides and okorndle and
        (roomgt2 or not okedge) :
        not rooklost :
        (depth = 0) and kingdiagfirst :
        nomove).

advice(divide_in_2,
        themtomove and rookdivides and not rookexposed :
        not rooklost :
        (depth < 3) and legal :
        (depth < 2) and legal).

advice(divide_in_3,
        themtomove and rookdivides and not rookexposed :
        not rooklost :
        (depth < 5) and legal :
        (depth < 4) and legal).

Figure 19.8   A game fragment played by the advice-table of Figure 19.7, illustrating the method of squeezing their king toward a corner. Pieces-of-advice used in this sequence are **keeproom** (waiting move preserving 'room') and **squeeze** ('room' has shrunk). The area to which their king is confined by our rook ('room') is shadowed. After the last **squeeze**, 'room' shrinks from eight to six squares.

(a)

(b)

Figure 19.9   (a) Illustration of the 'critical square' (a crucial square in the squeezing manoeuvres, indicated by a cross); the White king approaches the critical square by moving as indicated. (b) The three pieces form an L-shaped pattern.

The arguments of these predicates are either positions (goal predicates) or moves (move-constraints predicates). Goal predicates can have one or two arguments. One argument is always the current search node; the second argument (if it exists) is the root node of the search tree. The second argument is needed in the so-called comparison predicates, which compare in some respect the root position and the current search position. An example is the predicate **newroomsmaller** which tests whether the 'room' for their king has shrunk (Figure 19.8). These predicates, together with chess rules for king and rook vs. king, and a board displaying procedure (**show(Pos)**), are programmed in Figure 19.10.

An example of how this advice-program plays is shown in Figure 19.8. The game would continue from the last position of Figure 19.8 as in the following variation (assuming 'them' moves as given in the variation). The algebraic chess notation is used where the files of the chessboard are numbered 'a', 'b', 'c', etc, and ranks are numbered 1, 2, 3, etc. For example, the move 'BK b7' means: move the Black king to the square in file 'b' and rank 7.

. . .	BK b7
WK d5	BK c7
WK c5	BK b7
WR c6	BK a7
WR b6	BK a8
WK b5	BK a7
WK c6	BK a8
WK c7	BK a7
WR c6	BK a8
WR a6	mate

Some questions can now be asked. First, is this advice-program *correct* in the sense that it mates against any defence if the game starts from any king and rook vs. king position? It is shown in Bratko (1978) by means of a formal proof that an advice-table, effectively the same as the one in Figure 19.7, is correct in this sense.

Another question can be: Is this advice program *optimal* in the sense that it always delivers mate in the smallest number of moves? It can easily be shown by examples that the program's play is not optimal in this sense. It is known that optimal variations (optimally played by both sides) in this ending are at most 16 moves long. Although our advice-table can be rather far from this optimum, it was shown that the number of moves needed by this advice-table is still very safely under 50. This is important because of the 50-moves rule in chess: in endgames such as king and rook vs. king the stronger side has to mate within 50 moves; if not, a draw can be claimed.

Figure 19.10   Predicate library for king and rook vs. king.

```
% Predicate library for king and rook vs. king

% Position is represented by: Side..Wx : Wy..Rx : Ry..Bx : By..Depth
% Side is side to move ('w' or 'b')
% Wx, Wy are X and Y-coordinates of White king
% Rx, Ry are X and Y-coordinates of White rook
% Bx, By are coordinates of Black king
% Depth is depth of position in search tree

% Selector relations
side( Side.._, Side).              % Side to move in position
wk( _..WK.._, WK).                 % White king coordinates
wr( _.._..WR.._, WR).              % White rook coordinates
bk( _.._.._.._..BK.._, BK).        % Black king coordinates
depth( _.._.._.._..Depth, Depth).  % Depth of position in search tree

resetdepth( S..W..R..B..D, S..W..R..B..0).    % Copy of position with depth 0

% Some relations between squares
n( N, N1) :-                       % Neighbour integers 'within board'
   ( N1 is N + 1;
     N1 is N − 1),
   in( N1).

in( N) :-
   N > 0, N < 9.

diagngb( X : Y, X1 : Y1) :-        % Diagonal neighbour squares
   n( X, X1), n( Y, Y1).
```

(continues)

Figure 19.10 (cont.)

```
verngb( X : Y, X : Y1) :-                          % Vertical neighbour squares
  n( Y, Y1).

horngb( X : Y, X1 : Y) :-                           % Horizontal neighbour squares
  n( X, X1).

ngb( S, S1) :-                                       % Neighbour squares, first diagonal
  diagngb( S, S1);
  horngb( S, S1);
  verngb( S, S1).

end_of_game( Pos) :-
  mate( Pos).

% Move-constraints predicates
% These are specialized move generators:
% move( MoveConstr, Pos, Move, NewPos)

move( depth < Max, Pos, Move, Pos1) :-
  depth( Pos, D),
  D < Max, !.

move( depth = D, Pos, Move, Pos1) :-
  depth( Pos, D), !.

move( kingdiagfirst, w..W..R..B..D, W-W1, b..W1..R..B..D1) :-
  D1 is D + 1,
  ngb( W, W1),                                       % 'ngb' generates diagonal moves first
  not ngb( W1, B),                                   % Must not move into check
  W1 \== R.                                          % Must not collide with rook

move( rookmove, w..W..Rx : Ry..B..D, Rx : Ry-R, b..W..R..B..D1) :-
  D1 is D + 1,
  coord( I),                                         % Integer between 1 and 8
  ( R = Rx : I; R = I : Ry),                         % Move vertically or horizontally
  R \== Rx : Ry,                                     % Must have moved
  not inway( Rx : Ry, W, R).                         % White king not in way

move( checkmove, Pos, R-Rx : Ry, Pos1) :-
  wr( Pos, R),
  bk( Pos, Bx : By),
  (Rx = Bx; Ry = By),                                % Rook and Black king in line
  move( rookmove, Pos, R-Rx : Ry, Pos1).

move( legal, w..P, M, P1) :-
  ( MC = kingdiagfirst; MC = rookmove),
  move( MC, w..P, M, P1).

move( legal, b..W..R..B..D, B-B1, w..W..R..B1..D1) :-
  D1 is D + 1,
  ngb( B, B1),
  not check( w..W..R..B1..D1).
```

Figure 19.10 (cont.)

```
legalmove( Pos, Move, Pos1) :-
  move( legal, Pos, Move, Pos1).

check( _ .. W .. Rx : Ry .. Bx : By .._ ) :-
  ngb( W, Bx : By);                               % King's too close
  ( Rx = Bx; Ry = By),
  Rx : Ry \ == Bx : By,                           % Not rook captured
  not inway( Rx : Ry, W, Bx : By).

inway( S, S1, S1) :- !.

inway( X1 : Y, X2 : Y, X3 : Y) :-
  ordered( X1, X2, X3), !.

inway( X : Y1, X : Y2, X : Y3) :-
  ordered( Y1, Y2, Y3).

ordered( N1, N2, N3) :-
  N1 < N2, N2 < N3;
  N3 < N2, N2 < N1.

coord(1). coord(2). coord(3). coord(4).
coord(5). coord(6). coord(7). coord(8).

% Goal predicates

true( Pos).

themtomove( b .._ ).                              % Black = 'them' to move

mate( Pos) :-
  side( Pos, b),
  check( Pos),
  not legalmove( Pos, _, _ ).

stalemate( Pos) :-
  side( Pos, b),
  not check( Pos),
  not legalmove( Pos, _, _ ).

newroomsmaller( Pos, RootPos) :-
  room( Pos, Room),
  room( RootPos, RootRoom),
  Room < RootRoom.

rookexposed( Side .. W .. R .. B .._ ) :-
  dist( W, R, D1),
  dist( B, R, D2),
  ( Side = w, !, D1 > D2 + 1
  ;
    Side = b, !, D1 > D2).
```

(continues)

Figure 19.10 (cont.)

```
okapproachedcsquare( Pos, RootPos) :-
  okcsquaremdist( Pos, D1),
  okcsquaremdist( RootPos, D2),
  D1 < D2.

okcsquaremdist( Pos, Mdist) :-          % Manhattan distance between WK and critical square
  wk( Pos, WK),
  cs( Pos, CS),                          % Critical square
  manhdist( WK, CS, Mdist).

rookdivides( _.. Wx : Wy.. Rx : Ry.. Bx : By.._ ) :-
  ordered( Wx, Rx, Bx), !;
  ordered( Wy, Ry, By).

lpatt( _.. W.. R.. B.._ ) :-             % L-pattern
  manhdist( W, B, 2),
  manhdist( R, B, 3).

okorndle( _.. W.. R.._, _.. W1.. R1.._ ) :-
  dist( W, R, D),
  dist( W1, R1, D1),
  D =< D1.

roomgt2( Pos) :-
  room( Pos, Room),
  Room > 2.

our_king_edge( _.. X : Y.._ ) :-         % White king on edge
  ( X = 1, !; X = 8, !; Y = 1, !; Y = 8).

their_king_edge( _.. W.. R.. X : Y.._ ) :-   % Black king on edge
  ( X = 1, !; X = 8, !; Y = 1, !; Y = 8).

kings_close( Pos) :-                      % Distance between kings < 4
  wk( Pos, WK), bk( Pos, BK),
  dist( WK, BK, D),
  D < 4.

rooklost( _.. W.. B.. B.._ ).            % Rook has been captured

rooklost( b.. W.. R.. B.._ ) :-
  ngb( B, R),                            % Black king attacks rook
  not ngb( W, R).                        % White king does not defend

dist( X : Y, X1 : Y1, D) :-              % Distance in king moves
  absdiff( X, X1, Dx),
  absdiff( Y, Y1, Dy),
  max( Dx, Dy, D).

absdiff( A, B, D) :-
  A > B, !, D is A-B;
  D is B-A.
```

Figure 19.10 (cont.)

```
max( A, B, M) :-
  A > = B, !, M = A;
  M = B.

manhdist( X : Y, X1 : Y1, D) :-                    % Manhattan distance
  absdiff( X, X1, Dx),
  absdiff( Y, Y1, Dy),
  D is Dx + Dy.

room( Pos, Room) :-                                % Area to which B. king is confined
  wr( Pos, Rx : Ry),
  bk( Pos, Bx : By),
  ( Bx < Rx, SideX is Rx − 1; Bx > Rx, SideX is 8 − Rx),
  ( By < Ry, SideY is Ry − 1; By > Ry, SideY is 8 − Ry),
  Room is SideX * SideY, !
  ;
  Room is 64.                                      % Rook in line with Black king

cs( _ .. W .. Rx : Ry .. Bx : By .. _, Cx : Cy) :-    % 'Critical square'
  ( Bx < Rx, !, Cx is Rx − 1; Cx is Rx + 1),
  ( By < Ry, !, Cy is Ry − 1; Cy is Ry + 1).

% Display procedures

show( Pos) :-
  nl,
  coord( Y), nl,
  coord( X),
  writepiece( X : Y, Pos),
  fail.

show( Pos) :-
  side( Pos, S), depth( Pos, D),
  nl, write( 'Side= '), write( S),
  write( 'Depth= '), write( D), nl.

writepiece( Square, Pos) :-
  wk( Pos, Square), !, write( 'W');
  wr( Pos, Square), !, write( 'R');
  bk( Pos, Square), !, write( 'B');
  write( '.').

showmove( Move) :-
  nl, write( Move), nl.
```

Project

Consider some other simple chess endgame, such as king and pawn vs. king, and write an AL0 program (together with the corresponding predicate definitions) to play this endgame.

SUMMARY

- Two-person games fit the formalism of AND/OR graphs. AND/OR search procedures can be therefore used to search game trees.

- The straightforward depth-first search of game trees is easy to program, but is too inefficient for playing interesting games. In such cases, the minimax principle, in association with an evaluation function and depth-limited search, offers a more feasible approach.

- The alpha-beta algorithm is an efficient implementation of the minimax principle. The efficiency of alpha-beta depends on the order in which alternatives are searched. In the best case, alpha-beta in effect reduces the branching factor of a game tree to its square root.

- Some refinements to the basic alpha-beta algorithm include: extending the search until a quiescent position is reached, progressive deepening and heuristic pruning.

- Numerical evaluation is a very restrictive form of applying game-specific knowledge. A more knowledge-intensive approach to game playing should provide for pattern-based knowledge. Advice Languages realize such an approach, where knowledge is represented in terms of goals and means of achieving goals.

- Programs written in this chapter are: an implementation of minimax and alpha-beta, an interpreter for Advice Language 0, and an advice-table for playing the king and rook vs. king chess endgame.

- Concepts introduced and discussed in this chapter are:

  two-person, perfect-information games
  game trees
  evaluation function, minimax principle
  static values, backed-up values
  alpha-beta algorithm
  progressive deepening, heuristic pruning, quiescence heuristics
  horizon effect
  Advice Languages
  goals, constraints, piece-of-advice, advice-table

References

The minimax principle, implemented as the alpha-beta algorithm, is the most popularly used approach to game-playing programs, in particular to chess programs. The minimax principle was introduced by Shannon (1950). The development of the alpha-beta technique had a rather complicated history when several researchers independently discovered or implemented the method or at least part of it. This interesting history is described by Knuth and Moore (1975) who also present a more compact formulation of the alpha-beta algorithm using the 'neg-max' principle instead of minimax, and give a mathematical analysis of its performance. The most comprehensive treatment of several minimax-based algorithms and their analyses is Pearl (1984). There is another interesting question regarding the minimax principle: knowing that the static evaluation is only reliable to some degree, will the minimax backed-up values be more reliable than the static values themselves? Pearl (1984) has also collected results of mathematical analyses that pertain to this question. Results on error propagation in minimax trees explain when and why the minimax look-ahead is beneficial.

The collection of papers Bramer (1983) covers in depth several aspects of computer game playing. Frey (1983) is a good collection of articles on computer chess. On-going research on chess is published in the Advances in Computer Chess series and in the ICCA journal.

The Advice Language approach to using pattern knowledge in chess was introduced by Michie, and further developed in Bratko and Michie (1980a, b), and Bratko (1982, 1984, 1985). The king and rook vs. king advice-program of this chapter is a slight modification of the advice-table that was mathematically proved correct in Bratko (1978). Van Emden (1982) has also programmed this advice-table in Prolog.

Other interesting experiments in knowledge-intensive approach to chess (as opposed to search-intensive approaches) include Berliner (1977), Pitrat (1977) and Wilkins (1980).

Advances in Computer Chess Series: Vols. 1–2 (M.R.B. Clarke, ed.) Edinburgh University Press; Vol. 3 (M.R.B. Clarke, ed.) Pergamon Press; Vol. 4 (D. Beal, ed.) Pergamon Press; Vol. 5 (D. Beal, ed.) North-Holland.

Berliner, H.J. (1977) A representation and some mechanisms for a problem solving chess program. In: *Advances in Computer Chess 1* (M.R.B. Clarke, ed.). Edinburgh University Press.

Bramer, M.A. (1983, ed.) *Computer Game Playing: Theory and Practice*. Ellis Horwood and John Wiley.

Bratko, I. (1978) Proving correctness of strategies in the AL1 assertional language. *Information Processing Letters* **7**: 223–230.

Bratko, I. (1982) Knowledge-based problem solving in AL3. In: *Machine Intelligence 10* (J. Hayes, D. Michie, J.H. Pao, eds.). Ellis Horwood (an abbreviated version also appears in Bramer 1983).

Bratko, I. (1984) Advice and planning in chess end-games. In: *Artificial and Human Intelligence* (S. Amarel, A. Elithorn, R. Banerji, eds.). North-Holland.

Bratko, I. (1985) Symbolic derivation of chess patterns. In: *Progress in Artificial Intelligence* (L. Steels, J.A. Campbell, eds.). Ellis Horwood and John Wiley.

Bratko, I. and Michie, D. (1980a) A representation of pattern-knowledge in chess endgames. In: *Advances in Computer Chess 2* (M.R.B. Clarke, ed.). Edinburgh University Press.

Bratko, I. and Michie, D. (1980b) An advice program for a complex chess programming task. *Computer Journal* **23**: 353–359.

Frey, P.W. (1983, ed.) *Chess Skill in Man and Machine* (second edition). Springer-Verlag.

Knuth, D.E. and Moore, R.W. (1975) An analysis of alpha-beta pruning. *Artificial Intelligence* **6**: 293–326.

Pearl, J. (1984) Heuristics: *Intelligent Search Strategies for Computer Problem Solving.* Addison-Wesley.

Pitrat, J. (1977) A chess combination program which uses plans. *Artificial Intelligence* **8**: 275–321.

Shannon, C.E. (1950) Programming a computer for playing chess. *Philosophical Magazine* **41**: 256–275.

van Emden, M. (1982) Chess end-game advice: a case study in computer utilisation of knowledge. In: *Machine Intelligence 10* (J. Hayes, D. Michie, J.H. Pao, eds.). Ellis Horwood.

Wilkins, D.E. (1980) Using patterns and plans in chess. *Artificial Intelligence* **14**: 165–203.

20 Meta-Programming

20.1 Meta-programs and meta-interpreters
20.2 Prolog meta-interpreters
20.3 Explanation-based generalization
20.4 Object-oriented programming
20.5 Pattern-directed programming
20.6 A simple theorem prover as a pattern-directed program

Due to its symbol-manipulation capabilities, Prolog is a powerful language for implementing other languages and programming paradigms. In this chapter we discuss the writing of Prolog meta-interpreters – that is, interpreters for Prolog in Prolog. We look at a special program-compilation technique, called explanation-based generalization, that was invented as an approach to machine learning. We also develop simple interpreters for two other approaches to programming: object-oriented programming and pattern-directed programming.

20.1 Meta-programs and meta-interpreters

A *meta-program* is a program that takes other programs as data. Interpreters and compilers are examples of meta-programs. *Meta-interpreter* is a particular kind of meta-program: an interpreter for a language written in that same language. So a Prolog meta-interpreter is an interpreter for Prolog, itself written in Prolog.

Due to its symbol-manipulation capabilities, Prolog is a powerful language for meta-programming. Therefore, it is often used as an implementation language for other languages. It has often been observed that Prolog is particularly suitable as a language for rapid prototyping where we are interested in implementing new ideas quickly. This is important when we want to develop a new language or a new programming paradigm or program architecture. New ideas are rapidly implemented and experimented with. In prototyping the emphasis is on bringing new ideas to life quickly and cheaply, so that they can be immediately tested. On the other hand, there is not much emphasis on efficiency of implementation. Once the ideas are developed, a prototype may have to be re-implemented, possibly in another, more efficient programming language. Even if this is necessary, the prototype is useful because it usually helps to speed up the creative development stage.

Several meta-programs can be found in previous chapters of this book; for example, if-then rule interpreters of Chapters 14 and 15. They process the language of if-then rules which is, in fact, a programming language, although programs written in it are usually called knowledge bases because of their specific contents. In this chapter we show some further examples to illustrate how easily meta-programs can be written in Prolog:

- writing Prolog meta-interpreters;
- explanation-based generalization;
- implementing other programming paradigms in Prolog, in particular object-oriented programming and pattern-directed programming.

20.2 Prolog meta-interpreters

20.2.1 Basic Prolog meta-interpreter

A Prolog meta-interpreter takes a Prolog program and a Prolog goal, and executes the goal with respect to the program; that is, the meta-interpreter attempts to prove that the goal logically follows from the program. However, to be of any practical interest, the meta-interpreter must not behave exactly as the original Prolog interpreter; it has to offer some additional functionality, such as generating a proof tree or tracing the execution of programs.

We will, for simplicity, assume that the program has already been consulted by the Prolog system that executes the meta-interpreter. So our meta-interpreter can be stated as a procedure prove with one argument, the goal to be satisfied:

> prove(Goal)

The simplest Prolog meta-interpreter is trivial:

> prove(Goal) :-
>   call(Goal).

Here all the work has been delegated (by call) to the original Prolog interpreter, and our meta-interpreter behaves exactly like the original Prolog interpreter. This is of course of no practical value because it does not provide any additional feature. To enable features such as the generation of proof trees, we first have to reduce the 'grain size' of the interpreter. This reduction in granularity of the meta-interpreter is made possible by a built-in predicate, provided in many Prolog implementations:

> clause(Head, Body)

This 'retrieves' a clause from the consulted program. Head is the head of the retrieved clause and Body is its body. For a unit clause (a fact), Body = true. In a non-unit clause (a rule), the body can contain one or several goals. If it contains one goal, then Body is this goal. If the body contains several goals then they are retrieved as a pair:

> Body = (FirstGoal , OtherGoals)

The comma in this term is a built-in infix operator. In the standard Prolog notation, this pair is equivalently written as:

> ,(FirstGoal, OtherGoals)

Here OtherGoals may again be a pair consisting of another goal and remaining goals. In a call clause(Head, Body), the first argument Head must not be a variable. Suppose the consulted program contains the usual member procedure. Then the clauses of member can be retrieved by:

> ?- clause(member(X, L), Body).
>
> X = _14
> L = [_14 | _15]
> Body = true;

```
% The basic Prolog meta-interpreter

prove( true).

prove( ( Goal1, Goal2)) :-
    prove( Goal1),
    prove( Goal2).

prove( Goal) :-
    clause( Goal, Body),
    prove( Body).
```

Figure 20.1 The basic Prolog meta-interpreter.

```
X = _14
Y = [_15 | _16]
Body = member( _14, _16)
```

Figure 20.1 shows a basic meta-interpreter for Prolog at the level of granularity that has proved to be useful for most purposes. It should be noted, however, that this is a meta-interpreter for pure Prolog only. It does not handle built-in predicates, in particular the cut. The usefulness of this basic meta-interpreter lies in the fact that it provides a scheme that can be easily modified to obtain interesting effects. One such well-known extension results in a trace facility for Prolog.

EXERCISE

20.1 What happens if we try to execute the meta-interpreter of Figure 20.1 with itself – for example, by:

> ?- prove(prove(member(X, [a, b, c]))).

There is a problem because our meta-interpreter cannot execute built-in predicates such as clause. How could the meta-interpreter be easily modified to be able to execute itself, as in the query above?

20.2.2   A tracing meta-interpreter

A first attempt to extend the basic meta-interpreter of Figure 20.1 to a tracing interpreter is:

> prove(true) :- !.

```
prove( ( Goal1, Goal2)) :- !,
   prove( Goal1),
   prove( Goal2).

prove( Goal) :-
   write( 'Call: '), write( Goal), nl,
   clause( Goal, Body),
   prove( Body),
   write( 'Exit: '), write( Goal), nl.
```

The cuts are needed here to prevent the display of 'true' and composite goals of the form (Goal1, Goal2). This tracer has several defects: there is no trace of failed goals and no indication of backtracking when the same goal is re-done. The tracer in Figure 20.2 is an improvement in these respects. To aid readability, it also indents the displayed goals proportionally to the depth of

---

```
% trace( Goal): execute Prolog goal Goal displaying trace information

trace( Goal) :-
   trace( Goal, 0).

trace( true, Depth) :- !.                        % Red cut

trace( ( Goal1, Goal2), Depth) :- !,             % Red cut
   trace( Goal1, Depth),
   trace( Goal2, Depth).

trace( Goal, Depth) :-
   display( 'Call: ', Goal, Depth),
   clause( Goal, Body),
   Depth1 is Depth + 1,
   trace( Body, Depth1),
   display( 'Exit: ', Goal, Depth),
   display_redo( Goal, Depth).

trace( Goal, Depth) :-                            % All alternatives exhausted
   display( 'Fail: ', Goal, Depth),
   fail.

display( Message, Goal, Depth) :-
   tab( Depth), write( Message),
   write( Goal), nl.

display_redo( Goal, Depth) :-
   true                                          % First succeed simply
   ;
   display( 'Redo: ', Goal, Depth),              % Then report backtracking
   fail.                                         % Force backtracking
```

Figure 20.2 A Prolog meta-interpreter for tracing programs in pure Prolog.

inference at which they are called. It is, however, still restricted to pure Prolog only. An example call of this tracer is:

```
?- trace( ( member( X, [ a, b]), member( X, [ b, c]))).

Call: member( _0085, [ a, b])
Exit: member( a, [ a, b])
Call: member( a, [ b, c])
  Call: member( a, [ c])
    Call: member( a, [ ])
    Fail: member( a, [ ])
  Fail: member( a, [ c])
Fail: member( a, [ b, c])
Redo: member( a, [ a, b])
  Call: member( _0085, [ b])
  Exit: member( b, [ b])
Exit: member( b, [ a, b])
Call: member( b, [ b, c])
Exit: member( b, [ b, c])
```

This tracer outputs the following information for each goal executed:

(1)   The goal to be executed (**Call: Goal**).

(2)   Trace of the subgoals (indented).

(3)   If the goal is satisfied then its final instantiation is displayed (**Exit: InstantiatedGoal**); if the goal is not satisfied then **Fail: Goal** is displayed.

(4)   In the case of backtracking to a previously satisfied goal, the message is: **Redo: InstantiatedGoal** (instantiation in the previous solution of this goal).

Of course, it is possible to further shape the tracing interpreter according to specific user's requirements.

20.2.3   Generating proof trees

Another well-known extension of the basic interpreter of Figure 20.1 is the generation of proof trees. So after a goal is satisfied, its proof tree is available for further processing. In Chapters 14 and 15, the generation of proof trees was implemented for rule-based expert systems. Although the syntax of rules there was different from Prolog, the principles of generating a proof tree are the same. These principles are easily introduced into the meta-interpreter of Figure 20.1. For example, we may choose to represent a proof tree depending on the case as follows:

(1)   For a goal **true**, the proof tree is **true**.

(2) For a pair of goals (Goal1, Goal2), the proof tree is the pair (Proof1, Proof2) of the proof trees of the two goals.

(3) For a goal Goal that matches the head of a clause whose body is Body, the proof tree is Goal $<==$ Proof where Proof is the proof tree of Body.

This can be incorporated into the basic meta-interpreter of Figure 20.1 as follows:

```
:- op( 500, xfy, <==).

prove( true, true).

prove( ( Goal1, Goal2), ( Proof1, Proof2)) :-
   prove( Goal1, Proof1),
   prove( Goal2, Proof2).

prove( Goal, Goal <== Proof) :-
   clause( Goal, Body),
   prove( Body, Proof).
```

Such a proof tree can be used in various ways. In Chapters 14 and 15 it was used as the basis for generating the 'how' explanation in an expert system. In the next section we will look at another interesting use of a proof tree, explanation-based generalization.

20.3 Explanation-based generalization

The idea of explanation-based generalization comes from machine learning where the objective is to generalize given examples into general descriptions of concepts. *Explanation-based generalization* (EBG) is a way of building such descriptions from typically one example only. The lack of examples is compensated by the system's 'background knowledge', usually called *domain theory*.

EBG rests on the following idea for building generalized descriptions: given an instance of the target concept, use the domain theory to *explain how* this instance in fact satisfies the concept. Then analyze the explanation and try to generalize it so that it applies not only to the given instance, but also to a set of 'similar' instances. This generalized explanation then becomes part of the concept description and can be subsequently used in recognizing instances of this concept. It is also required that the constructed concept description must be 'operational'; that is, it must be stated in terms of concepts declared by the user as operational. Intuitively, a concept description is operational if it is (relatively) easy to use. It is entirely up to the user to specify what is operational.

In an implementation of EBG, these abstract ideas have to be made more concrete. One way of realizing them in the logic of Prolog is:

- A concept is realized as a predicate.
- A concept description is a predicate definition.
- An explanation is a proof tree that demonstrates how the given instance satisfies the target concept.
- A domain theory is represented as a set of available predicates defined as a Prolog program.

The task of explanation-based generalization can then be stated as:

Given:

A domain theory: A set of predicates available to the explanation-based generalizer, including the target predicate whose operational definition is to be constructed.

Operationality criteria: These specify the predicates that may be used in the target predicate definition.

Training example: A set of facts describing a particular situation and an instance of the target concept, so that this instance can be derived from the given set of facts and the domain theory.

Find:

A generalization of the training instance and an operational definition of the target concept; this definition consists of a sufficient condition (in terms of the operational predicates) for this generalized instance to satisfy the target concept.

Thus stated, explanation-based generalization can be viewed as a kind of program compilation from one form into another. The original program defines the target concept in terms of domain theory predicates. The compiled program defines the same target concept (or subconcept) in terms of the 'target language' – that is, operational predicates only. The compilation mechanism provided by EBG is rather unusual. Execute the original program on the given example which results in a proof tree. Then generalize this proof tree so that the structure of the proof tree is retained, but the constants are replaced by variables whenever possible. In the generalized proof tree thus obtained, some nodes mention operational predicates. The tree is then reduced so that only these 'operational nodes' and the root are retained. The result constitutes an operational definition of the target concept.

All this is best understood by an example of EBG at work. Figure 20.3 defines two domains for EBG. The first domain theory is about giving a gift,

% A domain theory: about gifts

gives(Person1, Person2, Gift) :-
  likes(Person1, Person2),
  would_please(Gift, Person2).

gives(Person1, Person2, Gift) :-
  feels_sorry_for(Person1, Person2),
  would_comfort(Gift, Person2).

would_please(Gift, Person) :-
  needs(Person, Gift).

would_comfort(Gift, Person) :-
  likes(Person, Gift).

feels_sorry_for(Person1, Person2) :-
  likes(Person1, Person2),
  sad(Person2).

feels_sorry_for(Person, Person) :-
  sad(Person).

% Operational predicates

operational(likes(_, _)).
operational(needs(_, _)).
operational(sad(_)).

% An example situation

likes(john, annie).
likes(annie, john).
likes(john, chocolate).
needs(annie, tennis_racket).
sad(john).

% Another domain theory: about lift movement

% go(Level, GoalLevel, Moves) if
%   list of moves Moves brings lift from Level to GoalLevel

go(Level, GoalLevel, Moves) :-
  move_list(Moves, Distance),   % A move list and distance travelled
  Distance = : = GoalLevel − Level.

move_list([ ], 0).

move_list([Move1 | Moves], Distance + Distance1) :-
  move_list(Moves, Distance),
  move(Move1, Distance1).

move(up, 1).
move(down, −1).

operational(A = : = B).

Figure 20.3   Two problem definitions for explanation-based generalization.

while the second is about lift movements. Let us consider the first domain. Let the training instance be:

    gives(john, john, chocolate)

Our proof-generating meta-interpreter finds this proof:

    gives(john, john, chocolate) <= =
      (feels_sorry_for(john, john) <= = sad(john) ,
        would_comfort(chocolate, john) <= = likes(john, chocolate)
)

This proof can be generalized by replacing constants john and chocolate by variables:

    gives(Person, Person, Thing) <= =
      (feels_sorry_for(Person, Person) <= = sad(Person) ,
        would_comfort(Thing, Person) <= = likes(Person, Thing)
)

Predicates sad and likes are specified as operational in Figure 20.3. An operational definition of the predicate gives is now obtained by eliminating all the nodes from the proof tree, apart from the 'operational' ones and the root. This results in:

    gives(Person, Person, Thing) <= =
      (sad(Person) ,
        likes(Person, Thing)
)

Thus a sufficient condition Condition for gives(Person, Person, Thing) is:

    Condition = (sad(Person), likes(Person, Thing))

This new definition can now be added to our original program with:

    asserta((gives(Person, Person, Thing) :- Condition))

As a result, we have the following new clause about gives that only requires the evaluation of operational predicates:

    gives(Person, Person, Thing) :-
      sad(Person),
      likes(Person, Thing).

Through the generalization of the given instance

    gives(john, john, chocolate)

a definition (in operational terms) of giving as self-consolation was derived as one general case of **gives**. Another case of this concept would result from the example:

gives(john, annie, tennis_racket).

The explanation-based generalization would in this case produce the clause:

gives(Person1, Person2, Thing) :-
  likes(Person1, Person2),
  needs(Person2, Thing).

The lift domain in Figure 20.3 is slightly more complicated and we will experiment with it when we have EBG implemented in Prolog.

EBG can be programmed as a two-stage process: first, generate a proof tree for the given example, and, second, generalize this proof tree and extract the 'operational nodes' from it. Our proof-generating meta-interpreter could be used for this. The two stages are, however, not necessary. A more direct way is to modify the basic meta-interpreter of Figure 20.1 so that the generalization is inter-twined with the process of proving the given instance. The so-modified meta-interpreter, which carries out EBG, will be called **ebg** and will now have three arguments:

ebg(Goal, GenGoal, Condition)

where **Goal** is the given example to be proved, **GenGoal** is the generalized goal and **Condition** is the derived sufficient condition for **GenGoal**, stated in terms of operational predicates. Figure 20.4 shows such a generalizing meta-interpreter. For our gift domain of Figure 20.3, **ebg** can be called as:

?- ebg(gives(john, john, chocolate), gives(X, Y, Z), Condition).

X = Y
Condition = (sad(X), likes(X, Z))

Let us now try the lift domain. Let the goal to be solved and generalized be to find a move sequence **Moves** that brings the lift from level 3 to level 6:

go(3, 6, Moves)

We can invoke **ebg** and cash the resulting generalized goal and its condition by:

?- Goal = go(3, 6, Moves),
    GenGoal = go(Level1, Level2, GenMoves),
    ebg(Goal, GenGoal, Condition),
    asserta((GenGoal :- Condition)).

```
% ebg( Goal, GeneralizedGoal, SufficientCondition):
%     SufficientCondition in terms of operational predicates guarantees that
%     generalization of Goal, GeneralizedGoal, is true.
%     GeneralizedGoal must not be a variable

ebg( true, true, true).

ebg( Goal, GenGoal, GenGoal) :-
    operational( GenGoal),
    call( Goal).

ebg( ( Goal1, Goal2), ( Gen1, Gen2), Cond) :-
    ebg( Goal1, Gen1, Cond1),
    ebg( Goal2, Gen2, Cond2),
    and( Cond1, Cond2, Cond).                    % Cond = ( Cond1, Cond2) simplified

ebg( Goal, GenGoal, Cond) :-
    not operational( Goal),
    clause( GenGoal, GenBody),
    freshcopy( ( GenGoal, GenBody), ( Goal, Body)),
    ebg( Body, GenBody, Cond).

freshcopy( Term, Copy) :-
    asserta( term_to_copy( Term)),
    retract( term_to_copy( Copy)), !.            % Retract once only


% and( Cond1, Cond2, Cond):
%     Cond is (possibly simplified) conjunction of Cond1 and Cond2

and( true, Cond, Cond) :- !.                     % (true and Cond) <==> Cond

and( Cond, true, Cond) :- !.                     % (Cond and true) <==> Cond

and( Cond1, Cond2, ( Cond1, Cond2)).
```

Figure 20.4 Explanation-based generalization.

```
Goal = go( 3, 6, [ up, up, up])
GenGoal = go( Level1, Level2, [ up, up, up])
Condition = ( 0 + 1 + 1 + 1 =:= Level2 − Level1)
Moves = [ up, up, up]
.....
```

The resulting new clause about go is:

```
go( Level1, Level2, [ up, up, up]) :-
    0 + 1 + 1 + 1 =:= Level2 − Level1.
```

By means of EBG, the straight three-step upward movement has thus been generalized to any two levels at distance three. To solve the goal go(3, 6, Moves), the original program performs a search. Using the new derived clause, moving up between any two levels at distance three (for example, go(7, 10, Moves)) is solved immediately, without search.

The ebg meta-interpreter in Figure 20.4 is, again, a derivation of the basic meta-interpreter of Figure 20.1. This new meta-interpreter calls the procedure freshcopy. The call

freshcopy(Term, Copy)

constructs, for a given term Term, a copy Copy of this term with variables renamed. This is useful when we want to preserve a term as it is, while at the same time processing the term so that its variables may become instantiated. We can use the copy in this processing, so that the variables in the original term remain unaffected.

The last clause of the ebg procedure deserves special explanation. The call

clause(GenGoal, GenBody)

retrieves a clause that can be used to prove the generalized goal. This means that the meta-interpreter is actually trying to prove the generalized goal. The next line, however, imposes a constraint on this:

freshcopy((GenGoal, GenBody), (Goal, Body))

This requires that GenGoal and Goal match. The matching is done on the copy of GenGoal, so that variables in the general goal remain intact. The point of requiring this match is to limit the execution of the generalized goal to those alternative branches (clauses) that are applicable to the given example (Goal). In this way the example guides the execution of the generalized goal. This guidance is the essence of program compilation in the EBG style.

Once an example has been generalized and stated in terms of operational predicates, it can be added as a new clause to the program to answer future similar questions by evaluating operational predicates only. In this way the EBG compilation technique transforms a program into an 'operational' language. The translated program can be executed by an interpreter that only 'knows' the operational language. One possible advantage of this can be a more efficient program. The efficiency may be improved in two ways: first, operational predicates may be easier to evaluate than other predicates; second, the sequence of predicate evaluation indicated by the example may be more suitable than the one in the original program, so that failed branches do not appear in the compiled definition at all. When a program is compiled by the EBG technique, care is needed during compilation so that new clauses do not interfere in an uncontrolled way with the original clauses.

EXERCISE

20.2 It may appear that the same compilation effect achieved in EBG can be obtained without an example, simply by substituting goals in the original concept definition by their subgoals, taken from corresponding clauses of the domain theory, until all the goals are reduced to operational subgoals. Discuss this idea with respect to EBG and show that the guidance by an example in EBG is essential. Also show that, on the other hand, EBG-generated new concept definitions are only a generalization of given examples and are therefore not necessarily equivalent to the original program (new concept definitions may be incomplete).

20.4 Object-oriented programming

The paradigm of object-oriented programming is a kind of simulation. A program in this paradigm is stated in terms of *objects* that *send messages* to each other. Computation occurs as a result of objects responding to these messages. Each object has some private memory and some procedures called *methods*. An object can also *inherit* a method from another object. This is similar to the inheritance mechanism in frame-based representation discussed in Chapter 14. An object responds to a message by executing one of the object's methods. The message determines which method is to be executed. In fact, the act of sending a message to an object is a kind of procedure call. Implementing an object-oriented program amounts to simulating the sending of messages between objects and objects responding to the messages.

To translate this paradigm into Prolog terms, let us consider as a first example an object-oriented program about geometric figures. One object in such a program is a rectangle whose methods can be: a procedure to describe itself, and a procedure to compute its area. If a rectangle is sent the message area(A) it responds by calculating its area and the variable A becomes instantiated to the area. In our implementation, objects will be represented as the relation:

object(Object, Methods)

where Object is a term that names the object (and possibly specifies its parameters) and Methods is a list of Prolog terms specifying the methods. The terms in this list have the form of Prolog clauses – that is, Prolog facts and rules (except that they do not end with a period). In our Prolog implementation, an object definition will possibly specify a whole class of objects, such as the class of all rectangles referred to as rectangle(Length, Width). A particular rectangle with sides 4 and 3 is then referred to as **rectangle(4, 3)**. In general, then, the object **rectangle(Length, Width)** with two methods **area** and **describe** can be defined by:

```
object( rectangle( Length, Width),
  [ ( area( A) :-
        A is Length * Width),
    ( describe :-
        write( 'Rectangle of size '),
        write( Length * Width)) ] ).
```

In our implementation, the sending of a message to an object will be simulated by the procedure:

```
send( Object, Message)
```

We can make the rectangle with sides 4 and 3 decribe itself and compute its area by sending it the corresponding messages:

```
?-  Rec1 = rectangle( 4, 3),
    send( Rec1, describe),
    send( Rec1, area( Area)).

Rectangle of size 4 * 3
Area = 12
```

The procedure **send(Object, Message)** is easy to program. We first have to retrieve the methods of **Object**. These methods in fact specify a Prolog program that is local to **Object**. We have to execute **Message** as a goal with this program. The program, represented as a list, consists of items of the form **Head :- Body**, or just **Head** in the case of empty body. To execute **Message** we have to find some head that matches **Message** and then execute the corresponding body with Prolog's own interpreter.

Before we program this, we have to consider the other essential mechanism of object-oriented programming: *inheritance* of methods according to the 'is a' relation between objects. For example, a square is a rectangle. For calculating its area, a square can use the same formula as the rectangles. So a square does not need its own **area** method; it may inherit this method from the class of rectangles. To make this happen, we have to define the object **square** and also state that it is a rectangle.

```
object( square( Side),
  [ ( describe :-
        write( 'Square with side '),
        write( Side)) ] ).

isa( square( Side), rectangle( Side, Side)).
```

Figure 20.5 A simple interpreter for object-oriented programs.

% An interpreter for object-oriented programs

% send(Message, Object):
%   find Object's methods and execute the method that corresponds to Message

```
send( Object, Message) :-
   get_methods( Object, Methods),          % Find Object's methods
   process( Message, Methods).             % Execute corresponding method

get_methods( Object, Methods) :-
   object( Object, Methods).               % Private methods

get_methods( Object, Methods) :-
   isa( Object, SuperObject),
   get_methods( SuperObject, Methods).     % Inherited methods

process( Message, [Message | _ ]).         % Use a fact

process( Message, [ (Message :- Body) | _ ]) :-   % Use a rule
   call( Body).

process( Message, [ _ | Methods]) :-
   process( Message, Methods).
```

Now:

      ?- send(square(5), area(Area)).

      Area = 25

The message **area(Area)** is processed as follows: first, the object **square(5)** searches for **area(Area)** among its methods and cannot find it. Then through the **isa** relation it finds its 'super-object' **rectangle(5, 5)**. The super-object has the relevant method **area** which is executed.

    An interpreter for object-oriented programs along the lines discussed here is given in Figure 20.5. Figure 20.6 comprises a completed object-oriented program about geometric figures.

    Until now we have not mentioned the problem of *multiple inheritance*. This arises when the **isa** relation defines a *lattice* so that an object has more than one parent object, as is the case for **square** in Figure 20.6. So more than one parent object may potentially supply a method to be inherited by the object. In such a case the question is which one of the several potentially inherited methods should be used. The program of Figure 20.5 searches for an applicable method among the objects in the graph defined by the **isa** relation. The search strategy in Figure 20.5 is simply depth first although some other strategy may be more appropriate. Breadth first would, for example, ensure that the 'closest inheritable' method is used.

Figure 20.6   An object-oriented program about geometric figures.

```
/*                        polygon( [ Side1, Side2, ... ])
                          /                        \
         rectangle( Length, Width)        reg_polygon( Side, N)
                      \              /        \
                         square( Side)        pentagon( Side)
*/
```

```prolog
object( polygon( Sides),                    % Polygon with sides Sides
  [ ( perimeter( P) :-
      sum( Sides, P))]).                    % Perimeter is the sum of sides

object( reg_polygon( Side, N),              % Regular polygon with N sides
  [ ( perimeter( P) :-
      P is Side * N),
    ( describe :- write( 'Regular polygon'))]).

object( square( Side),
  [ ( describe :-
      write( 'Square with side '),
      write( Side))]).

object( rectangle( Length, Width),
  [ ( area( A) :-
      A is Length * Width),
    ( describe :-
      write( 'Rectangle of size '),
      write( Length * Width))]).

object( pentagon( Side),
      [ ( describe :- write( 'Pentagon'))]).

isa( square( Side), rectangle( Side, Side)).

isa( square( Side), reg_polygon( Side, 4)).

isa( rectangle( Length, Width), polygon( [ Length, Width, Length, Width])).

isa( pentagon( Side), reg_polygon( Side, 5)).

isa( reg_polygon( Side, N), polygon( L)) :-
  makelist( Side, N, L).

% makelist( Item, N, List):
%    List is the list in which Item appears N times

makelist( _, 0, [ ]).

makelist( Item, N, [Item | List]) :-
  N > 0, N1 is N − 1,
  makelist( Item, N1, List).
```

(continues)

Figure 20.6 (cont.)

% sum(ListOfNumbers, Sum):
%   Sum is the sum of numbers in ListOfNumbers

sum([ ], 0).

sum([Number | Numbers], Sum) :-
  sum(Numbers, Sum1),
  Sum is Sum1 + Number.

To further illustrate the style of object-oriented programming let us consider the situation in Figure 20.7. The figure shows a robot world: a number of blocks arranged in stacks on the table. There is a camera on the ceiling that can capture the top view of the objects on the table. For simplicity we assume that all of the blocks are cubes with side equal 1. The blocks have names a, b, ..., and the camera can recognize by name those blocks that are not obstructed from the top, and locate them with respect to the x and y coordinates. Suppose that we are interested in computing the locations of the objects – that is, their x, y and z coordinates. Each block has some local information, so it knows what block (if any) is immediately above it or underneath it. Thus the xy coordinates of a block B can be obtained in two ways:

(1)   If the block has a clear top then it can be seen by the camera, which will determine the xy coordinates of the block. This is accomplished by sending the message **look(B, X, Y)** to the camera.

 Camera

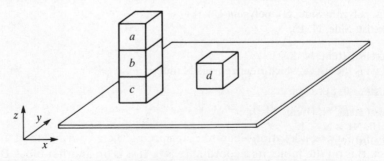

Figure 20.7   A robot world.

```
% A robot world: table, blocks and camera

object( camera,
   [ look( a, 1, 1),                          % Find xy coord. of a visible block
     look( d, 3, 2),
     xy_coord( 2, 2),                         % xy coordinates of camera
     z_coord( 20)]).                          % z coordinate of camera

object( block( Block),
   [ ( xy_coord( X, Y) :-
         send( camera, look( Block, X, Y))),
     ( xy_coord( X, Y) :-
         send( Block, under( Block1)),
         send( Block1, xy_coord( X, Y))),
     ( z_coord( 0) :-
         send( Block, on( table))),
     ( z_coord( Z) :-
         send( Block, on( Block1)),
         send( Block1, z_coord( Z1)),
         Z is Z1 + 1)]).

object( physical_object( Name),
   [ ( coord( X, Y, Z) :-
         send( Name, xy_coord( X, Y)),
         send( Name, z_coord( Z)))]).

object( a, [ on( b)]).
object( b, [ under( a), on( c)]).
object( c, [ under( b), on( table)]).
object( d, [ on( table)]).

isa( a, block( a)).
isa( b, block( b)).
isa( c, block( c)).
isa( d, block( d)).
isa( block( Name), physical_object( Name)).
isa( camera, physical_object( camera)).
```

Figure 20.8   An object-oriented program about a robot world.

(2)   If block B is underneath some block B1 then it is helpful to observe that all of the blocks in the same stack share the same *xy* coordinates. So to determine the *xy* coordinates of block B, send the message xy_coord(X, Y) to block B1.

Similar considerations lead to determining the *z* coordinate of a block. If block B is on the table, its *z* coordinate is 0. If B is on another block B1 then send the message z_coord(Z1) to B1 and add the height of B1 to Z1, thereby obtaining the *z* coordinate of B. This is programmed in Figure 20.8 where blocks *a*, *b*, etc., are defined as instances of the block class **block(BlockName)** from which they inherit the methods **xy_coord** and **z_coord**.

Let us conclude this section with a general comment regarding the benefits of object-oriented programming. Our example object-oriented programs can be implemented (in fact more compactly) in the usual Prolog style without reference to objects and messages. These examples illustrate the principles, but are too small to convincingly indicate the possible advantages of object-oriented programming. The object-oriented model is obviously advantageous in writing programs for simulation systems in which physical components in fact exchange a kind of message – for example, in a manufacturing process there are flows of material between machines. Another benefit of the object-oriented model is that it provides a new framework for organizing large programs. Both memory and procedures (methods) are clustered around objects, and the inheritance mechanism provides a way of structuring the program.

EXERCISES

20.3 Study what happens when the message-sending question

```
?- send( square( 6), perimeter( P)).
```

is interpreted by the programs in Figures 20.5 and 20.6. Are there alternatives for backtracking? How can the program of Figure 20.5 be modified to prevent undesired alternatives?

20.4 The interpreter in Figure 20.5 is inefficient because it spends much time looking for appropriate methods. Write a compiler for object-oriented programs that compiles object definitions (their methods in particular) into a more efficient Prolog program. Such a compiler would, for example, in compiling the program of Figure 20.6, generate clauses like:

```
area( square( Side), Area)  :-
    Area is Side * Side.

area( rectangle( Length, Width), Area)  :-
    Area is Length * Width.
```

Also, redefine the procedure **send(Object, Message)** so that it would use these new generated clauses.

20.5 Pattern-directed programming

20.5.1 Pattern-directed architecture

By *pattern-directed systems* we here refer to an architecture for program systems. This architecture is better suited for certain types of problems than conventional systems organization. Among problems that naturally fit into the pattern-directed architecture are many Artificial Intelligence applications – for example, expert systems. The main difference between conventional systems and pattern-directed systems is in the mechanisms of invocation of program modules. In conventional organization, modules of the system call each other according to a fixed, explicitly predefined scheme. Each program module decides which module will be executed next by *explicitly* calling other modules. The corresponding flow of execution is sequential and deterministic.

In contrast to this, in pattern-directed organization the modules of the system are not directly called by other modules. Instead, they are 'called' by *patterns* that occur in their 'data environment'. Therefore such modules are called *pattern-directed modules*. A *pattern-directed program* is a collection of pattern-directed modules. Each module is defined by:

(1) a precondition pattern, and
(2) an action to be executed if the data environment matches the pattern.

The execution of program modules is triggered by patterns that occur in the system's environment. The data environment is usually called the *database*. We can imagine such a system as shown in Figure 20.9.

There are some notable observations about Figure 20.9. There is no hierarchy among modules, and there is no explicit indication about which module can invoke which other module. Modules communicate with the database rather than with other modules directly. The structure itself, in principle, permits execution of several modules in parallel, since the state of the database may simultaneously satisfy several preconditions and thus, in principle, fire several modules at the same time. Consequently such an organization can also serve as a natural model of parallel computation in which each module would be physically implemented by its own processor.

Pattern-directed architecture has certain advantages. One major advantage is that the design of the system does not require all the connections between modules to be carefully planned and defined in advance. Consequently, each module can be designed and implemented relatively autonomously. This renders a high degree of modularity. The modularity is manifested, for example, in that the removal of some module from the system is not necessarily fatal. After the removal, the system would often still be able to solve problems, only *the way* of solving problems might change. The same is true for the addition of new modules and for modifications of the existing

Data environment

Figure 20.9   A pattern-directed system.

modules. If similar modifications are carried out in systems with conventional organization, at least the calls between modules have to be properly modified.

The high degree of modularity is especially desirable in systems with complex knowledge bases because it is difficult to predict in advance all the interactions between individual pieces of knowledge in the base. The pattern-directed architecture offers a natural solution to this: each piece of knowledge, represented by an if-then rule, can be regarded as a pattern-directed module.

Let us further elaborate the basic scheme of pattern-directed systems with the view on an implementation. Figure 20.9 suggests that the parallel implementation would be most natural. However, let us assume the system is to be implemented on a traditional sequential processor. Then in a case that the triggering patterns of several modules simultaneously occur in the database there is a conflict: which of all these potentially active modules will actually be executed? The set of potentially active modules is called a *conflict set*. In an actual implementation of the scheme of Figure 20.9 on a sequential processor, we need an additional program module, called the *control module*. The control module resolves the conflict by choosing and activating one of the modules in the conflict set. One simple rule of resolving conflicts can be based on a predefined, fixed ordering of modules.

The basic life cycle of pattern-directed systems, then, consists of three steps:

(1) *Pattern matching*: find in the database all the occurrences of the condition patterns of the program modules. This results in a conflict set.

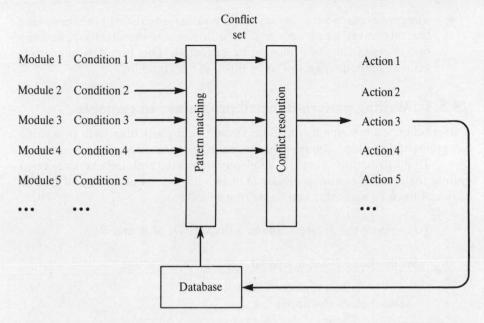

Figure 20.10 The basic life cycle of pattern-directed systems. In this example the database satisfies the condition pattern of modules 1, 3 and 4; module 3 is chosen for execution.

(2)   *Conflict resolution*: choose one of the modules in the conflict set.

(3)   *Execution*: execute the module that was chosen in step 2.

This implementational scheme is illustrated in Figure 20.10.

20.5.2   Prolog programs as pattern-directed systems

Prolog programs themselves can be viewed as pattern-directed systems. Without much elaboration, the correspondence between Prolog and pattern-directed systems is along the following lines:

- Each Prolog clause in the program can be viewed as a pattern-directed module. The module's condition part is the head of the clause, the action part is specified by the clause's body.

- The system's database is the current list of goals that Prolog is trying to satisfy.

- A clause is fired if its head matches the first goal in the database.

- To execute a module's action (body of a clause) means: replace the first goal in the database with the list of goals in the body of the clause (with the proper instantiation of variables).

- The process of module invocation is non-deterministic in the sense that several clauses' heads may match the first goal in the database, and any one of them can, in principle, be executed. This non-determinism is actually implemented in Prolog through backtracking.

20.5.3 Writing pattern-directed programs: an example

Pattern-directed systems can also be viewed as a particular style of writing programs and thinking about problems, called *pattern-directed programming*.

To illustrate this, consider an elementary programming exercise: computing the greatest common divisor D of two integer numbers A and B. The classical Euclid's algorithm can be written as follows:

To compute the greatest common divisor, D, of A and B:

While A and B are not equal, repeat the following:

if $A > B$ then replace A with $A - B$
else replace B with $B - A$.

When this loop is over, A and B are equal; now the greatest common divisor D is A (or B).

We can define the same process by two pattern-directed modules:

Module 1

Condition   There are two numbers X and Y in the database such that $X > Y$.

Action   Replace X in the database with the difference $X - Y$.

Module 2

Condition   There is a number X in the database.

Action   Output X and stop.

Whenever the condition of Module 1 is satisfied, so is the condition of Module 2 and we have a conflict. This will be in our case resolved by a simple control rule: Module 1 is always preferred to Module 2. Initially the database contains the two numbers A and B.

As a pleasant surprise, our pattern-directed program in fact solves a more general problem: computing the greatest common divisor of any number of integers. If several integers are stored in the database the system will output the greatest common divisor of all of them. Figure 20.11 shows a possible sequence of changes in the database before the result is obtained, when the initial database contains four numbers: 25, 10, 15, 30. Notice that a module's precondition can be satisfied at several places in the database.

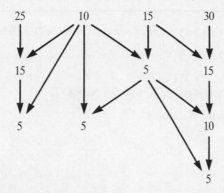

Figure 20.11 A possible execution of the pattern-directed program for computing the greatest common divisor of a set of numbers. In this example tha database initially contains the numbers 25, 10, 15 and 30. Vertical arrows connect numbers with their replacements. The final state of the database is: 5, 5, 5, 5.

We will in this chapter implement an interpreter for a simple language for specifying pattern-directed systems, and illustrate the flavour of pattern-directed programming by programming exercises.

20.5.4   A simple interpreter for pattern-directed programs

Let us choose the following syntax for specifying pattern-directed modules:

    ConditionPart ---> ActionPart

The condition part is a list of conditions

    [Cond1, Cond2, Cond3, ...]

where **Cond1**, **Cond2**, etc. are simply Prolog goals. The precondition is satisfied if all the goals in the list are satisfied. The action part is a list of actions:

    [Action1, Action2, ...]

Each action is, again, simply a Prolog goal. To execute an action list, all the actions in the list have to be executed. That is, all the corresponding goals have to be satisfied. Among available actions there will be actions that manipulate the database: *add*, *delete* or *replace* objects in the database. The action 'stop' stops further execution.

Figure 20.12 shows our pattern-directed program for computing the greatest common divisor written in this syntax.

% Production rules for finding greatest common divisor (Euclid algorithm)

:- op(300, fx, number).

[number X, number Y, X > Y]   --->
[NewX is X − Y, replace(number X, number NewX)].

[number X]   ---> [write(X), stop].

% An initial database

number 25.

number 10.

number 15.

number 30.

Figure 20.12   A pattern-directed program to find the greatest common divisor of a set of numbers.

The simplest way to implement this pattern-directed language is to use Prolog's own built-in database mechanism. Adding an object into the database and deleting an object can be accomplished simply by the built-in procedures:

    assert(Object)   retract(Object)

Replacing an object with another object is also easy:

    replace(Object1, Object2) :-
        retract(Object1), !,
        assert(Object2).

The cut in this clause is used to prevent **retract** from deleting (through backtracking) more than one object from the database.

A small interpreter for pattern-directed programs along these lines is shown in Figure 20.13. This interpreter is perhaps an oversimplification in some respects. In particular, the conflict resolution rule in the interpreter is extremely simple and rigid: always execute the *first* potentially active pattern-directed module (in the order as they are written). So the programmer's control is reduced just to the ordering of modules. The initial state of the database for this interpreter has to be asserted as Prolog facts, possibly by consulting a file. Then the execution is triggered by the goal:

    ?- **run**.

% A small interpreter for pattern-directed programs
% The system's database is manipulated through assert/retract

:- op(800, xfx, --->).

% run: execute pattern-directed modules until action 'stop' is triggered

```
run :-
    Condition ---> Action,          % A production rule
    test( Condition),               % Precondition satisfied?
    execute( Action).
```

% test([Condition1, Condition2, ...]) if all conditions true

```
test( [ ]).                         % Empty condition

test( [First | Rest]) :-            % Test conjunctive condition
    call( First),
    test( Rest).
```

% execute([Action1, Action2, ...]): execute list of actions

```
execute( [ stop]) :- !.             % Stop execution

execute( [ ]) :-                    % Empty action (execution cycle completed)
    run.                            % Continue with next execution cycle

execute( [First | Rest]) :-
    call( First),
    execute( Rest).

replace( A, B) :-                   % Replace A with B in database
    retract( A), !,                 % Retract once only
    assert( B).
```

Figure 20.13   A small interpreter for pattern-directed programs.

20.5.5   Possible improvements

Our simple interpeter for pattern-directed programs is sufficient for illustrating some ideas of pattern-directed programming. For more complex applications it should be elaborated in several respects. Here are some critical comments and indications for improvements.

The conflict resolution is in our interpreter reduced to a fixed, predefined order. Much more flexible schemas are often desired. To enable more sophisticated control, all the potentially active modules should be found and fed into a special user-programmable control module.

When the database is large and there are many pattern-directed modules in the program then pattern matching can become extremely inefficient. The efficiency in this respect can be improved by a more sophisticated organization of the database. This may involve the indexing of the information in the database, or partitioning of the information into sub-bases, or partitioning of the set of pattern-directed modules into subsets. The idea of partitioning is to make only a *subset* of the database or of the modules accessible at any given time, thus reducing the pattern matching to such a subset only. Of course, in such a case we would need a more sophisticated control mechanism that would control the transitions between these subsets in the sense of activating and de-activating a subset. A kind of meta-rules could be used for that.

Unfortunately our interpreter, as programmed, precludes any backtracking due to the way that the database is manipulated through assert and retract. So we cannot study alternative execution paths. This can be improved by using a different implementation of the database, avoiding Prolog's assert and retract. One way would be to represent the whole state of the database by a Prolog term passed as an argument to the run procedure. The simplest possibility is to organize this term as a list of objects in the database. The interpreter's top level could then look like this:

```
run( State)  :-
    Condition ---> Action,
    test( Condition, State),
    execute( Action, State).
```

The execute procedure would then compute a new state and call run with this new state.

Project

Implement an interpreter for pattern-directed programs that does not maintain its database as Prolog's own internal database (with assert and retract), but as a procedure argument according to the foregoing remark. Such a new interpreter would allow for automatic backtracking. Try to design a representation of the database that would facilitate efficient pattern matching.

20.6   A simple theorem prover as a pattern-directed program

Let us implement a simple theorem prover as a pattern-directed system. The prover will be based on the *resolution principle*, a popular method for mechanical theorem proving. We will limit our discussion to proving theorems in the simple *propositional logic* just to illustrate the principle, although our resolution mechanism will be easily extendable to handle the first-order predicate calculus (logic formulas that contain variables). Basic Prolog itself is a special case of a resolution-based theorem prover.

The theorem-proving task can be defined as: given a formula, show that the formula is a theorem; that is, the formula is always true regardless of the interpretation of the symbols that occur in the formula. For example, the formula

$$p \vee \sim p$$

read as '*p* or not *p*', is always true regardless of the meaning of *p*.

We will be using the following symbols as logic operators:

~	negation, read as 'not'
&	conjunction, read as 'and'
v	disjunction, read as 'or'
=>	implication, read as 'implies'

The precedence of these operators is such that 'not' binds strongest, then 'and', then 'or', and then 'implies'.

In the resolution method we negate the conjectured theorem and then try to show that this negated formula is a contradiction. If the negated formula is in fact a contradiction then the original formula must be a tautology. Thus the idea is: demonstrating that the negated formula is a contradiction is equivalent to proving that the original formula is a theorem (always holds). The process that aims at detecting the contradiction consists of a sequence of *resolution steps*.

Let us illustrate the principle with a simple example. Suppose we want to prove that the following propositional formula is a theorem:

$$(a => b) \, \& \, (b => c) => (a => c)$$

This formula is read as: if *b* follows from *a*, and *c* follows from *b*, then *c* follows from *a*.

Before the resolution process can start we have to get our negated, conjectured theorem into a form that suits the resolution process. The suitable form is the *conjunctive normal form*, which looks like this:

$$(p_1 \vee p_2 \vee \ldots) \, \& \, (q_1 \vee q_2 \vee \ldots) \, \& \, (r_1 \vee r_2 \vee \ldots) \, \& \, \ldots$$

Here all *p*'s, *q*'s and *r*'s are simple propositions or their negations. This form is also called the *clause form*. Each conjunct is called a *clause*. So $(p_1 \vee p_2 \vee \ldots)$ is a clause.

We can transform any propositional formula into this form. For our example theorem, this transformation can proceed as follows. The theorem is

$$(a => b) \, \& \, (b => c) => (a => c)$$

The negated theorem is:

$$\sim ((a => b) \, \& \, (b => c) => (a => c))$$

The following known equivalence rules will be useful when transforming this formula into the normal conjunctive form:

(1) $x => y$ is equivalent to $\sim x \text{ v } y$

(2) $\sim(x \text{ v } y)$ is equivalent to $\sim x \, \& \sim y$

(3) $\sim(x \, \& \, y)$ is equivalent to $\sim x \text{ v } \sim y$

(4) $\sim(\sim x)$ is equivalent to x

Applying rule 1 to our formula we get:

$$\sim (\sim ((a => b) \, \& \, (b => c)) \text{ v } (a => c))$$

By rules 2 and 4 we get:

$$(a => b) \, \& \, (b => c) \, \& \sim(a => c)$$

Using rule 1 at several places we get:

$$(\sim a \text{ v } b) \, \& \, (\sim b \text{ v } c) \, \& \sim(\sim a \text{ v } c)$$

By rule 2 we finally get the clause form we need:

$$(\sim a \text{ v } b) \, \& \, (\sim b \text{ v } c) \, \& \, a \, \& \sim c$$

This consists of four clauses: $(\sim a \text{ v } b)$, $(\sim b \text{ v } c)$, a, $\sim c$. Now the resolution process can start.

The basic resolution step can occur any time that there are two clauses such that some proposition p occurs in one of them, and $\sim p$ occurs in the other. Let two such clauses be:

$$p \text{ v } Y \quad \text{and} \quad \sim p \text{ v } Z$$

where p is a proposition, and Y and Z are propositional formulas. Then the resolution step on these two clauses produces a third clause:

$$Y \text{ v } Z$$

It can be shown that this clause logically follows from the two initial clauses. So by adding the expression $(Y \text{ v } Z)$ to our formula we do not alter the validity of the formula. The resolution process thus generates new clauses. If the 'empty clause' (usually denoted by 'nil') occurs then this will signal that a

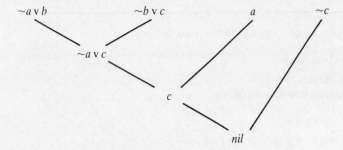

Figure 20.14   Proving the theorem $(a => b)$ & $(b => c) => (a => c)$ by the resolution method. The top line is the negated theorem in the clause form. The empty clause at the bottom signals that the negated theorem is a contradiction.

contradiction has been found. The empty clause *nil* is generated from two clauses of the forms:

> x and $\sim x$

which is obviously a contradiction.

Figure 20.14 shows the resolution process that starts with our negated conjectured theorem and ends with the empty clause.

Figure 20.15 shows how this resolution process can be formulated as a pattern-directed program. This program operates on clauses asserted into the database. The resolution principle can be formulated as a pattern-driven activity:

> *if*
> > there are two clauses *C1* and *C2*, such that *P* is a (disjunctive) sub-expression of *C1*, and $\sim P$ is a subexpression of *C2*
> *then*
> > remove *P* from *C1* (giving *CA*), remove $\sim P$ from *C2* (giving *CB*), and add into the database a new clause: *CA* v *CB*.

Written in our pattern-directed language this becomes:

```
[ clause( C1), delete( P, C1, CA),
  clause( C2), delete( ~P, C2, CB) ] --->
[ assert( clause( CA v CB) ) ].
```

This rule needs a little elaboration to prevent repeated actions on the same clauses, which would merely produce new copies of already existing clauses. The program in Figure 20.15 records into the database what has already been done by asserting:

```
done( C1, C2, P)
```

% Production rules for resolution theorem proving

% Contradicting clauses

```
[ clause( X), clause( ~X) ] --->
[ write('Contradiction found'), stop].
```

% Remove a true clause

```
[ clause( C), in( P, C), in( ~P, C) ] --->
[ retract( C) ].
```

% Simplify a clause

```
[ clause( C), delete( P, C, C1), in( P, C1) ] --->
[ replace( clause( C), clause( C1)) ].
```

% Resolution step, a special case

```
[ clause( P), clause( C), delete( ~P, C, C1), not done( P, C, P) ] --->
[ assert( clause( C1)), assert( done( P, C, P)) ].
```

% Resolution step, a special case

```
[ clause( ~P), clause( C), delete( P, C, C1), not done( ~P, C, P) ] --->
[ assert( clause( C1)), assert( done( ~P, C, P)) ].
```

% Resolution step, general case

```
[ clause( C1), delete( P, C1, CA),
  clause( C2), delete( ~P, C2, CB), not done( C1,C2,P) ] --->
[ assert( clause( CA v CB)), assert( done( C1, C2, P)) ].
```

% Last rule: resolution process stuck

```
[] ---> [ write('Not contradiction'), stop].
```

% delete(P, E, E1) if deleting a disjunctive subexpression P from E gives E1

```
delete( X, X v Y, Y).

delete( X, Y v X, Y).

delete( X, Y v Z, Y v Z1) :-
  delete( X, Z, Z1).

delete( X, Y v Z, Y1 v Z) :-
  delete( X, Y, Y1).
```

% in(P, E) if P is a disjunctive subexpression in E

```
in( X, X).

in( X, Y) :-
  delete( X, Y, _ ).
```

Figure 20.15   A pattern-directed program for simple resolution theorem proving.

```
% Translating a propositional formula into (asserted) clauses

:- op( 100, fy, ~).                              % Negation
:- op( 110, xfy, &).                             % Conjunction
:- op( 120, xfy, v).                             % Disjunction
:- op( 130, xfy, =>).                            % Implication


% translate( Formula): translate propositional Formula
%     into clauses and assert each resulting clause C as clause( C)

translate( F & G)  :-                            % Translate conjunctive formula
  !,                                             % Red cut
  translate( F),
  translate( G).

translate( Formula)  :-
  transform( Formula, NewFormula),               % Transformation step on Formula
  !,                                             % Red cut
  translate( NewFormula).

translate( Formula)  :-                          % No more transformation possible
  assert( clause( Formula)).


% Transformation rules for propositional formulas

% transform( Formula1, Formula2):
%     Formula2 is equivalent to Formula1, but closer to clause form

transform( ~( ~X), X).                           % Eliminate double negation

transform( X => Y, ~X v Y).                      % Eliminate implication

transform( ~ ( X & Y), ~X v ~Y).                 % De Morgan's law

transform( ~ ( X v Y), ~X & ~Y).                 % De Morgan's law

transform( X & Y v Z, ( X v Z) & ( Y v Z)).      % Distribution

transform( X v Y & Z, ( X v Y) & ( X v Z)).      % Distribution

transform( X v Y, X1 v Y)  :-
  transform( X, X1).                             % Transform subexpression

transform( X v Y, X v Y1)  :-
  transform( Y, Y1).                             % Transform subexpression

transform( ~ X, ~ X1)  :-
  transform( X, X1).                             % Transform subexpression
```

Figure 20.16 Translating a propositional calculus formula into a set of (asserted) clauses.

The condition parts of rules will then recognize and prevent such repeated actions.

The rules in Figure 20.15 also deal with some special cases that would otherwise require the explicit representation of the empty clause. Also, there are two rules that just simplify clauses when possible. One of these rules recognizes true clauses such as

$a \lor b \lor \sim a$

and removes them from the database since they are useless for detecting a contradiction. The other rule removes redundant subexpressions. For example, this rule would simplify the clause

$a \lor b \lor a$

into $a \lor b$.

A remaining question is how to translate a given propositional formula into the clause form. This is not difficult and the program of Figure 20.16 does it. The procedure

translate(Formula)

translates a formula into a set of clauses C1, C2, etc., and asserts these clauses into the database as:

clause(C1).
clause(C2).
...

Now the pattern-directed theorem prover can be triggered by the goal **run**. So, to prove a conjectured theorem using these programs, we translate the negated theorem into the clause form and start the resolution process. For our example theorem, this is done by the question:

?- **translate(~((a => b) & (b => c) => (a => c))), run.**

The program will respond with 'Contradiction found' meaning that the original formula is a theorem.

SUMMARY

- Meta-programs treat other programs as data. A Prolog meta-interpreter is an interpreter for Prolog in Prolog.

- It is easy to write Prolog meta-interpreters that generate execution traces, proof trees and offer other extra features.

- Explanation-based generalization is a special technique for program compilation. It can be viewed as symbolic execution of a program, guided by a specific example. Explanation-based generalization was invented as an approach to machine learning.

- An object-oriented program consists of objects that send messages between themselves. Objects respond to messages by executing their methods. Methods can also be inherited from other objects.

- A pattern-directed program is a collection of pattern-directed modules whose execution is triggered by patterns in the 'database'.

- Prolog programs themselves can be viewed as pattern-directed systems.

- The parallel implementation of pattern-directed systems would be most natural. The sequential implementation requires conflict resolution among the modules in the conflict set.

- A simple interpreter for pattern-directed programs was implemented in this chapter and applied to resolution-based theorem proving in propositional logic.

- Concepts discussed in this chapter are:

  meta-programs, meta-interpreters
  explanation-based generalization
  object-oriented programming
  objects, methods, messages
  inheritance of methods
  pattern-directed systems, pattern-directed architecture
  pattern-directed programming
  pattern-directed module
  conflict set, conflict resolution
  resolution-based theorem proving, resolution principle

References

Writing Prolog meta-interpreters is part of the general Prolog programming culture. Sterling and Shapiro (1986) give some other interesting examples of Prolog meta-interpreters. The idea of explanation-based generalization was developed in the area of machine learning. The formulation used in this chapter is as in the paper by Mitchell, Keller and Kedar-Cabelli (1986). Our EBG program is similar to that in Kedar-Cabelli and McCarty (1987). Our interpreter for object-oriented programs is similar to the one in Stabler (1986). Prolog++ (Logic Programming Associates 1989) is an efficient implementation of an object-oriented environment on top of Prolog. Waterman and Hayes-Roth (1978) is the classical book on pattern-directed systems. Several elaborations of the basic pattern-directed architecture can be found under the name *blackboard systems*. A useful collection of papers on blackboard systems is Engelmore and Morgan (1988). Fundamentals of mechanical theorem proving can be found in Nilsson (1980), including the algorithm for transforming the first-order predicate calculus formulas into the clausal form. Clocksin and Mellish (1981) give a Prolog program that does this transformation.

Clocksin, F.W. and Mellish, C.S. (1981) *Programming in Prolog*. Springer-Verlag.

Engelmore, R. and Morgan, T. (1988) *Blackboard Systems*. Addison-Wesley.

Kedar-Cabelli, S.T. and McCarty, L.T. (1987) Explanation-based generalization as resolution theorem proving. In: *Proc. 4th Int. Machine Learning Workshop*, Irvine, CA. Morgan Kaufmann.

Logic Programming Associates (1989) *Prolog++: an Object Oriented Extension to Prolog*. London.

Mitchell, T.M., Keller, R.M. and Kedar-Cabelli, S.T. (1986) Explanation-based generalization: a unifying view. *Machine Learning* **1**: 47–80.

Nilsson, N.J. (1980) *Principles of Artificial Intelligence*. Tioga; also Springer-Verlag.

Stabler, E.P. (1986) Object-oriented programming in Prolog. *AI Expert* (October 1986): 46–57.

Sterling, L. and Shapiro, E. (1986) *The Art of Prolog*. MIT Press.

Waterman, D.A. and Hayes-Roth, F. (1978, eds.) *Pattern-Directed Inference Systems*. Academic Press.

Solutions to Selected Exercises

Chapter 1

1.1 (a)   no

     (b)   X = pat

     (c)   X = bob

     (d)   X = bob, Y = pat

1.2 (a)   ?- parent(X, pat).

     (b)   ?- parent(liz, X).

     (c)   ?- parent(Y, pat), parent(X, Y).

1.3 (a)   happy(X) :-
         parent(X, Y).

     (b)   hastwochildren(X) :-
         parent(X, Y),
         sister(Z, Y).

1.4 grandchild(X, Z) :-
     parent(Y, X),
     parent(Z, Y).

1.5 aunt(X, Y) :-
     parent(Z, Y),
     sister(X, Z).

1.6 Yes it is.

1.7 (a)   no backtracking

     (b)   no backtracking

     (c)   no backtracking

     (d)   backtracking

Chapter 2

2.1 (a) variable

(b) atom

(c) atom

(d) variable

(e) atom

(f) structure

(g) number

(h) syntactically incorrect

(i) structure

(j) structure

2.3 (a) yes

(b) no

(c) no

(d) $D = 2, E = 2$

(e) P1 = point(-1,0)
P2 = point(1,0)
P3 = point(0,Y)
This can represent the family of triangles with two vertices on the *x*-axis at 1 and -1 respectively, and the third vertex anywhere on the *y*-axis.

2.4 seg(point(5,Y1), point(5,Y2))

2.5 regular(rectangle(point(X1,Y1), point(X2,Y1), point(X2,Y3), point(X1,Y3))).

% This assumes that the first point is the left bottom vertex

2.6 (a) A = two

(b) no

(c) C = one

(d) D = s(s(1));
D = s(s(s(s(s(1)))))

2.7 relatives(X, Y) :-
predecessor(X, Y)
;
predecessor(Y, X)
;
predecessor(Z, X),
predecessor(Z, Y)
;
predecessor(X, Z),
predecessor(Y, Z).

2.8   translate(1, one).
translate(2, two).
translate(3, three).

2.9   In the case of Figure 2.10 Prolog does slightly more work.

2.10   According to the definition of matching of Section 2.2, this succeeds. X becomes a sort of circular structure in which X itself occurs as one of the arguments.

Chapter 3

3.1   (a)   conc(L1, [_, _, _], L)

(b)   conc([_, _, _ | L2], [_, _, _], L)

3.2   (a)   last(Item, List) :-
conc(_, [Item], List).

(b)   last(Item, [Item]).

last(Item, [First | Rest]) :-
last(Item, Rest).

3.3   evenlength([ ]).

evenlength([First | Rest]) :-
oddlength(Rest).

oddlength([_]).

oddlength([First | Rest]) :-
evenlength(Rest).

3.4   reverse([ ], [ ]).

reverse([First | Rest], Reversed) :-
reverse(Rest, ReversedRest),
conc(ReversedRest, [First], Reversed).

3.5   % This is easy using reverse
palindrome(List) :-
reverse(List, List).

% Alternative solution, not using reverse
palindrome1([ ]).

palindrome1([_]).

palindrome1(List) :-
conc([First | Middle], [First], List),
palindrome1(Middle).

3.6   shift([First | Rest], Shifted) :-
conc(Rest, [First], Shifted).

3.7   translate([ ], [ ]).

        translate([Head | Tail], [Head1 | Tail1]) :-
          means(Head, Head1),
          translate(Tail, Tail1).

3.8   % The following assumes the order of elements in Subset as in Set
        subset([ ], [ ]).

        subset([First | Rest], [First | Sub]) :-   % Retain First in subset
          subset(Rest, Sub).

        subset([First | Rest], Sub) :-   % Remove First
          subset(Rest, Sub).

3.9   dividelist([ ], [ ], [ ]).   % Nothing to divide

        dividelist([X], [X], [ ]).   % Divide one-element list

        dividelist([X, Y | List], [X | List1], [Y | List2]) :-
          dividelist(List, List1, List2).

3.10   canget(state(_, _, _, has), [ ]).   % Nothing to do

        canget(State, [Action | Actions]) :-
          move(State, Action, NewState),   % First action
          canget(NewState, Actions).   % Remaining actions

3.11   flatten([Head | Tail], FlatList) :-   % Flatten non-empty list
          flatten(Head, FlatHead),
          flatten(Tail, FlatTail),
          conc(FlatHead, FlatTail, FlatList).

        flatten([ ], [ ]).   % Flatten empty list

        flatten(X, [X]).   % Flatten a non-list
        % Note: On backtracking this program produces rubbish

3.12   Term1 = plays(jimmy, and(football, squash))
        Term2 = plays(susan, and(tennis, and(basketball, volleyball)))

3.13   :- op(300, xfx, was).
        :- op(200, xfx, of).
        :- op(100, fx, the).

3.14   (a)   A = 1 + 0

        (b)   B = 1 + 1 + 0

        (c)   C = 1 + 1 + 1 + 1 + 0

        (d)   D = 1 + 1 + 0 + 1;
             D = 1 + 0 + 1 + 1;
             D = 0 + 1 + 1 + 1   % Further backtracking causes indefinite cycling

3.15 :- op(100, xfx, in).
      :- op(300, fx, concatenating).
      :- op(200, xfx, gives).
      :- op(100, xfx, and).
      :- op(300, fx, deleting).
      :- op(100, xfx, from).

% List membership
Item in [Item | List].

Item in [First | Rest] :-
    Item in Rest.

% List concatenation
concatenating [ ] and List gives List.

concatenating [X | L1] and L2 gives [X | L3] :-
    concatenating L1 and L2 gives L3.

% Deleting from a list
deleting Item from [Item | Rest] gives Rest.

deleting Item from [First | Rest] gives [First | NewRest] :-
    deleting Item from Rest gives NewRest.

3.16 max(X, Y, X) :-
    X > = Y.

    max(X, Y, Y) :-
    X < Y.

3.17 maxlist([X], X).   % Maximum of single-element list

    maxlist([X, Y | Rest], Max) :-   % At least two elements in list
        maxlist([Y | Rest], MaxRest),
        max(X, MaxRest, Max).   % Max is the greater of X and MaxRest

3.18 sumlist([ ], 0).

    sumlist([First | Rest], Sum) :-
        sumlist(Rest, SumRest),
        Sum is First + SumRest.

3.19 ordered([X]).   % Single-element list is ordered

    ordered([X, Y | Rest]) :-
        X = < Y,
        ordered([Y | Rest]).

3.20 subsum([ ], 0, [ ]).

    subsum([N | List], Sum, [N | Sub]) :-   % N is in subset
        Sum1 is Sum − N,
        subsum(List, Sum1, Sub).

    subsum([N | List], Sum, Sub) :-   % N is not in subset
        subsum(List, Sum, Sub).

3.21 between(N1, N2, N1) :-
    N1 =< N2

    between(N1, N2, X) :-
    N1 < N2,
    NewN1 is N1 + 1,
    between(NewN1, N2, X).

3.22 :- op(900, fx, if).
    :- op(800, xfx, then).
    :- op(700, xfx, else).
    :- op(600, xfx, :=).

    if Val1 > Val2 then Var := Val3 else Anything :-
    Val1 > Val2,
    Var = Val3.

    if Val1 > Val2 then Anything else Var := Val4 :-
    Val1 =< Val2,
    Var = Val4.

Chapter 4

4.1 (a) ?- family(person(_, Name, _, _), _, []).

    (b) ?- child(person(Name, SecondName, _, works(_, _))).

    (c) ?- family(person(_, Name, _, unemployed),
                 person(_, _, _, works(_, _)), _).

    (d) ?- family(Husband, Wife, Children),
             dateofbirth(Husband, date(_, _, Year1)),
             dateofbirth(Wife, date(_, _, Year2)),
             (Year1 − Year2 >= 15
               ;
               Year2 − Year1 >= 15
             ),
             member(Child, Children).

4.2 twins(Child1, Child2) :-
    family(_, _, Children),
    del(Child1, Children, OtherChildren),   % Delete Child1
    member(Child2, OtherChildren),
    dateofbirth(Child1, Date),
    dateofbirth(Child2, Date).

4.3 nth_member(1, [X | L], X).   % X is first element of list [X | L]

    nth_member(N, [Y | L], X) :-   % X is nth element of [Y | L]
    N1 is N − 1,
    nth_member(N1, L, X).

4.4   The input string shrinks on each non-silent cycle, and it cannot shrink indefinitely.

4.5   accepts(State, [ ], _) :-
 final(State).

accepts(State, [X | Rest], MaxMoves) :-
 MaxMoves > 0,
 trans(State, X, State1),
 NewMax is MaxMoves − 1,
 accepts(State1, Rest, NewMax).

accepts(State, String, MaxMoves) :-
 MaxMoves > 0,
 silent(State, State1),
 NewMax is MaxMoves − 1,
 accepts(State1, String, NewMax).

4.7 (a) jump(X/Y, X1/Y1) :-   % Knight jump from X/Y to X1/Y1
 (dxy(Dx, Dy)   % Knight distances in x and y directions
 ;
  dxy(Dy, Dx),   % or the other way round
 ),
 X1 is X + Dx,
 inboard(X1),   % X1 is within chessboard
 Y1 is Y + Dy,
 inboard(Y1).   % Y1 is within chessboard

dxy(2, 1).   % 2 squares to right, 1 forward
dxy(2, −1).   % 2 squares to right, 1 backward
dxy(−2, 1).   % 2 to left, 1 forward
dxy(−2, −1).   % 2 to left, 1 backward

inboard(Coord) :-   % Coordinate within chessboard
 0 < Coord,
 Coord < 9.

(b) knightpath([Square]).   % Knight sitting on Square

knightpath([S1, S2 | Rest]) :-
 jump(S1, S2),
 knightpath([S2 | Rest]).

(c) ?- knightpath([2/1,R,5/4,S,X/8]).

Chapter 5

5.1 (a) X = 1;
     X = 2;

(b)   X = 1
        Y = 1;

        X = 1
        Y = 2;

        X = 2
        Y = 1;

        X = 2
        Y = 2;

(c)   X = 1
        Y = 1;

        X = 1
        Y = 2;

5.2   class(Number, positive) :-
        Number > 0, !.

       class(0, zero) :- !.

       class(Number, negative).

5.3   split([ ], [ ], [ ]).

       split([X | L], [X | L1], L2) :-
        X >= 0, !,
        split(L, L1, L2).

       split([X | L], L1, [X | L2]) :-
        split(L, L1, L2).

5.4   member(Item, Candidates), not member(Item, RuledOut)

5.5   difference([ ], _, [ ]).

       difference([X | L1], L2, L) :-
        member(X, L2), !,
        difference(L1, L2, L).

       difference([X | L1], L2, [X | L]) :-
        difference(L1, L2, L).

5.6   unifiable([ ], _, [ ]).

       unifiable([First | Rest], Term, List) :-
        not(First = Term), !,
        unifiable(Rest, Term, List).

       unifiable([First | Rest], Term, [First | List]) :-
        unifiable(Rest, Term, List).

Chapter 6

6.1   findterm(Term) :-   % Assuming current input stream is file f
           read(Term), !,   % Current term in F matches Term?
           write(Term)   % If yes, display it
           ;
           findterm(Term).   % Otherwise process the rest of file

6.2   findallterms(Term) :-
           read(CurrentTerm),   % Assuming CurrentTerm not a variable
           process(CurrentTerm, Term).

           process(end_of_file, _) :- !.

           process(CurrentTerm, Term) :-
           (not(CurrentTerm = Term), !   % Terms do not match
             ;
             write(CurrentTerm), nl   % Otherwise output current term
           ),
           findallterms(Term).   % Do the rest of file

6.4   starts(Atom, Character) :-
           name(Character, [Code]),
           name(Atom, [Code | _]).

6.5   plural(Noun, Nouns) :-
           name(Noun, CodeList),
           name(s, CodeS),
           conc(CodeList, CodeS, NewCodeList),
           name(Nouns, NewCodeList).

Chapter 7

7.2   add(Item, List) :-
           var(List), !,   % List represents empty list
           List = [Item | Tail].

           add(Item, [_ | Tail]) :-
           add(Item, Tail).

           member(X, List) :-
           var(List), !,   % List represents empty list
           fail.   % so X cannot be a member

           member(X, [X | Tail]).

           member(X, [_ | Tail]) :-
           member(X, Tail).

7.6   (a)   ?- retract(product(X, Y, Z)), fail.

           (b)   ?- retract(product(X, Y, 0)), fail.

7.7   copy(Term, Copy) :-
        asserta(term_to_copy(Term)),
        retract(term_to_copy(Copy)).

7.9   copy(Term, Copy) :-
        bagof(X, X = Term, [Copy]).

Chapter 8

8.2   add_at_end(L1 − [Item | Z2], Item, L1 − Z2).

8.3   reverse(A − Z, L − L) :-   % Result is empty list if
        A = = Z, !.   % A − Z represents empty list

       reverse([X | L] − Z, RL − RZ) :-   % Non-empty list
        reverse(L − Z, RL − [X | RZ]).

Chapter 9

9.1   list([ ]).

       list([_ | Tail]) :-
        list(Tail).

9.2   mem(X, X then Anything).

       mem(X, Y then List) :-
        mem(X, List).

9.3   convert([ ], donothing).

       convert([First | Tail], First then Rest) :-
        convert(Tail, Rest).

9.4   convert([ ], EmptyList, _, EmptyList).   % Convert empty list

       convert([First | Tail], NewList, Functor, Empty) :-
        NewList =.. [Functor, First, NewTail],
        convert(Tail, NewTail, Functor, Empty).

9.8   msort([ ], [ ]).

       msort([X], [X]).

       msort(List, SortedList) :-
        divide(List, List1, List2),   % Divide into approx. equal lists
        msort(List1, Sorted1),
        msort(List2, Sorted2),
        merge(Sorted1, Sorted2, SortedList).   % Merge sorted lists

       divide([ ], [ ], [ ]).

       divide([X], [X], [ ]).

       divide([X, Y | L], [X | L1], [Y | L2]) :-   % Put X, Y into separate lists
        divide(L, L1, L2).

9.9 (a)   binarytree(nil).

binarytree(t(Left, Root, Right)) :-
   binarytree(Left),
   binarytree(Right).

9.10 height(nil, 0).

height(t(Left, Root, Right), H) :-
   height(Left, LH),
   height(Right, RH),
   max(LH, RH, MH),
   H is 1 + MH.

max(A, B, A) :-
   A > = B, !.

max(A, B, B).

9.11 linearize(nil, [ ]).

linearize(t(Left, Root, Right), List) :-
   linearize(Left, List1),
   linearize(Right, List2),
   conc(List1, [Root | List2], List).

9.12 maxelement(t(_, Root, nil), Root) :- !.   % Root is right-most element

maxelement(t(_, _, Right), Max) :-   % Right subtree non-empty
   maxelement(Right, Max).

9.13 in(Item, t(_, Item, _), [Item]).

in(Item, t(Left, Root, _), [Root | Path]) :-
   gt(Root, Item),
   in(Item, Left, Path).

in(Item, t(_, Root, Right), [Root | Path]) :-
   gt(Item, Root),
   in(Item, Right, Path).

9.14 % Display a binary tree from top to bottom
   % This program assumes that each node is just one character

show(Tree) :-
   dolevels(Tree, 0, more).   % Do all levels from top

dolevels(Tree, Level, alldone) :- !.   % No more nodes beyond Level

dolevels(Tree, Level, more) :-   % Do all levels from Level
   traverse(Tree, Level, 0, Continue), nl,   % Output nodes at Level
   NextLevel is Level + 1,
   dolevels(Tree, NextLevel, Continue).   % Do lower levels

```
        traverse( nil, _, _, _).

        traverse( t( Left, X, Right), Level, Xdepth, Continue) :-
          NextDepth is Xdepth + 1,
          traverse( Left, Level, NextDepth, Continue),       % Traverse left subtree
          ( Level = Xdepth, !,                                % Node X at Level?
            write( X), Continue = more                        % Output node, more to do
            ;
            write(' ')                                        % Otherwise leave space
          ),
          traverse( Right, Level, NextDepth, Continue).       % Traverse right subtree
```

Chapter 10

10.1
```
    in( Item, l( Item) ).                          % Item found in leaf

    in( Item, n2( T1, M, T2) ) :-                  % Node has two subtrees
      gt( M, Item), !,                             % Item not in second subtree
      in( Item, T1)                                % Search first subtree
      ;
      in( Item, T2).                               % Otherwise search the second

    in( Item, n3( T1, M2, T2, M3, T3) ) :-         % Node has three subtrees
      gt( M2, Item), !,                            % Item not in second or third
      in( Item, T1)                                % Search first subtree
      ;
      gt( M3, Item), !,                            % Item not in third subtree
      in( Item, T2)                                % Search second subtree
      ;
      in( Item, T3).                               % Search third subtree
```

10.3
```
    avl( Tree) :-
      avl( Tree, Height).                          % Tree is AVL-tree with height Height

    avl( nil, 0).                                  % Empty tree is AVL and has height 0

    avl( t( Left, Root, Right), H) :-
      avl( Left, HL),
      avl( Right, HR),
      ( HL is HR; HL is HR + 1; HL is HR − 1),     % Subtrees heights almost equal
      max1( HL, HR, H).

    max1( U, V, M) :-                              % M is 1 + max of U and V
      U > V, !, M is U + 1
      ;
      M is V + 1.
```

Chapter 11

11.1
```
    depthfirst1( [Node | Path], [Node | Path] ) :-
      goal( Node).
```

```
        depthfirst1( [Node | Path], Solution) :-
          s( Node, Node1),
          not member( Node1, Path),
          depthfirst1( [Node1, Node | Path], Solution).
```

11.6   solve(StartSet, Solution) :-   % StartSet is list of start nodes
         bagof([Node], member(Node, StartSet), CandidatePaths),
         breadthfirst(CandidatePaths, Solution).

11.7   % Let 'origs(Node1, Node2)' be the original state-space relation
         % Define new s relation:

         s(Node1, Node2) :-
           origs(Node2, Node1).

11.8   % States for bidirectional search are pairs of nodes StartNode-EndNode
         % of the original state space, denoting start and goal of search

         s(Start − End, NewStart − NewEnd) :-
           origs(Start, NewStart),   % A step forward
           origs(NewEnd, End).   % A step backward

         % goal(Start − End) for bidirectional search

         goal(Start − Start).   % Start equal end

         goal(Start − End) :-
           origs(Start, End).   % Single step to end

Chapter 16

16.6   No. The reason is that one action may achieve more than one goal
         simultaneously.

Chapter 17

17.1   s([a | List], Rest) :-
           s(List, [b | Rest]).

17.3   The modified definition is less efficient and may lead to indefinite cycling.

Chapter 18

18.5
         % prunetree(Tree, PrunedTree): PrunedTree is optimally pruned Tree
         %   with respect to estimated classification error
         %   Assume trees are binary:
         %   Tree = leaf(Node, ClassFrequencyList), or
         %   Tree = tree(Root, LeftSubtree, RightSubtree)

         prunetree(Tree, PrunedTree) :-
           prune(Tree, PrunedTree, Error, FrequencyList).
```
```

```
% prune( Tree, PrunedTree, Error, FrequencyList):
%     PrunedTree is optimally pruned Tree with classification Error,
%     FrequencyList is the list of frequencies of classes at root of Tree

prune( leaf( Node, FreqList), leaf( Node, FreqList), Error, FreqList) :-
    static_error( FreqList, Error).

prune( tree( Root, Left, Right), PrunedT, Error, FreqList) :-
    prune( Left, Left1, LeftError, LeftFreq),
    prune( Right, Right1, RightError, RightFreq),
    sumlists( LeftFreq, RightFreq, FreqList),      % Add corresponding elements
    static_error( FreqList, StaticErr),
    sum( LeftFreq, N1),
    sum( RightFreq, N2),
    BackedErr is ( N1 * LeftError + N2 * RightError) / ( N1 + N2),
    decide( StaticErr, BackedErr, Root, FreqList, Left1, Right1, Error, PrunedT).

% Decide to prune or not:

decide( StatErr, BackErr, Root, FreqL, _, _, StatErr, leaf( Root, FreqL)) :-
    StatErr =< BackErr, !.             % Static error smaller: prune subtrees

% Otherwise do not prune:

decide( _, BackErr, Root, _, Left, Right, BackErr, tree( Root, Left, Right)).

% static_error( ClassFrequencyList, Error): estimated class. error

static_error( FreqList, Error) :-
    max( FreqList, Max),                % Maximum number in FreqList
    sum( FreqList, All),                % Sum of numbers in FreqList
    number_of_classes( NumClasses),
    Error is ( All - Max + NumClasses - 1) / ( All + NumClasses).

sum( [ ], 0).

sum( [Number | Numbers], Sum) :-
    sum( Numbers, Sum1),
    Sum is Sum1 + Number.

max( [X], X).

max( [X,Y | List], Max) :-
    X > Y, !, max( [X | List], Max)
    ;
    max( [Y | List], Max).

sumlists( [ ], [ ], [ ]).

sumlists( [X1 | L1], [X2 | L2], [X3 | L3]) :-
    X3 is X1 + X2,
    sumlists( L1, L2, L3).
```

% A tree

tree1(tree(a,   % Root
          tree(b, leaf(e, [3,2]), leaf(f, [1,0])),   % Left subtree
          tree(c, tree(d, leaf(g, [1,1]), leaf(h, [0,1])), leaf(i, [1,0])))).

number_of_classes(2).

% Test query: ?- tree1(Tree), prunetree(Tree, PrunedTree).

Chapter 20

20.1 Add this clause to the meta-interpreter:

       prove(clause(Head, Body)) :-
         clause(Head, Body).

20.3 There are alternatives because **square(6)** inherits the **perimeter** method from several objects. This multiple inheritance can be prevented by a cut in the **send** procedure.

Index